THE CREATION OF AMERICA

This alternative history of the American Revolution portrays the colonists as conquerors and their revolution as a rebellion over control of conquests. In contrast to the usual views of the Revolution, here the colonists' rhetoric about liberty and virtue is seen as war propaganda to disguise disputes over political power. None of the Revolutionary leaders intended the nation to be democratic, and none was opposed to empire. Rather, their aim was to create their own empire independent of Britain. The author supports his claims with much documented detail, including information on the involuntary participation of Indians and blacks in addition to the usual players.

Francis Jennings holds a Ph.D. in American Civilization from the University of Pennsylvania. Before his retirement in 1981, he was director of the Center for the History of the American Indian, Newberry Library. He is the author of numerous books and articles, including *The Invasion of America* (1975), *The Ambiguous Iroquois Empire* (1985), *Empire of Fortune* (1990), *The Founders of America* (1993), and *Benjamin Franklin, Politician* (1996).

BOOKS BY FRANCIS JENNINGS

The Covenant Chain Trilogy:

The Invasion of America: Indians, Colonialism and the Cant of Conquest

The Ambiguous Iroquois Empire: The Covenant Chain Confederation of Indian Tribes with English Colonies

Empire of Fortune: Crowns, Colonies, and Tribes in the Seven Years War in America

The Founders of America: How Indians Discovered the Land, Pioneered in It, and Created Great Classical Civilizations; How They Were Plunged into a Dark Age by Invasion and Conquest; and How They Are Reviving

Benjamin Franklin, Politician: The Mask and the Man

Editor: The Newberry Library Center for the History of the American Indian Bibliographical Series

Editor, with William N. Fenton and Mary A. Druke:

The History and Culture of Iroquois Diplomacy

Iroquois Indians: A Documentary History

FRANCIS JENNINGS

THE CREATION
OF AMERICA

THROUGH REVOLUTION TO EMPIRE

CAMBRIDGE
UNIVERSITY PRESS

PUBLISHED BY THE PRESS SYNDICATE OF THE UNIVERSITY OF CAMBRIDGE
The Pitt Building, Trumpington Street, Cambridge, United Kingdom

CAMBRIDGE UNIVERSITY PRESS
The Edinburgh Building, Cambridge CB2 2RU, UK   http://www.cup.cam.ac.uk
40 West 20th Street, New York, NY 10011-4211, USA   http://www.cup.org
10 Stamford Road, Oakleigh, Melbourne 3166, Australia
Ruiz de Alarcón 13, 28014 Madrid, Spain

© Francis Jennings 2000

First published 2000

Printed in the United States of America

Typeface Ehrhardt 10½/12½ pt.   *System* QuarkXPress [BTS]

A catalog record for this book is available from the British Library.

Library of Congress Cataloging in Publication Data
Jennings, Francis, 1918–
The creation of America : through revolution to empire / Francis Jennings.
      p.   cm.
Includes bibliographical references (p.) and index.
ISBN 0-521-66255-9 (hardback) – ISBN 0-521-66481-0 (paperback)
   1. United States – Politics and government – 1775–1783.   2. United
States – History – Revolution, 1775–1783 – Causes.   I. Title.
            E210.J43   2000
            973.3 – dc21
                                                        99-054612

ISBN 0 521 66255 9   hardback
ISBN 0 521 66481 0   paperback

In memory of
Lawrence William (Bill) Towner
scholar, humanist, statesman, friend

CONTENTS

Part IV The Clone Establishes Its Form

Part V More Conquests

ACKNOWLEDGMENTS

In first rank of essential debts, I owe deep gratitude to the staffs of the James C. King Home, which is my own home. They literally saved my life with surgery and watchful care during recuperation, and they made possible the rest periods during which this book could be completed. Much gratitude is also owed to friends Richard H. Brown and Fred Hoxie for helping me through this extremely difficult time.

As to scholarship, I had the example of Gary B. Nash in *Red, White, and Black: The Peoples of Early America*, which made the first approach to the whole human population during the American Revolution and afterward. More recently, Alfred F. Young provided me with a conspectus of students and interpretations from his unrivaled store of knowledge on the subject. Neither is responsible for my decisions to blunder along my own path. Both have shown alternatives from which to choose.

Partly because of advancing years, and ill health, I have not journeyed abroad for this book, but it emerged from a background of much help during a substantial career. This began with an encouraging grant from the American Philosophical Society. Cedar Crest College's sabbatical year and pay sent me to Britain where hospitality from the University of London's Institute of United States Studies allowed concentrated study at the British Library and Public Record Office, as well as cordial collegiality with Esmond Wright and Howell Daniels. Two lovely months at the Rockefeller Foundation's Villa Serbelloni in Bellagio stimulated thinking and writing. The National Foundation for the Humanities provided funds to the Newberry Library to support my projects there, and the Newberry subsequently granted fellowships for my personal studies. Other fellowships gave access to unique manuscript collections at the Omohundro Institute of Early American History and Culture in Williamsburg, Virginia, the John Carter Brown Library in Providence, Rhode Island, and the Henry E. Huntington Library in San Marino, California. I must not overlook graduate school at the University of Pennsylvania and the great manuscript collections of the

Historical Society of Pennsylvania. Seminars of the Philadelphia Center for Early American Studies opened discussions with experts. Besides such institutional assistance, many academic professionals in anthropology as well as history have given guidance along the sinuous paths of interdisciplinary research; they are mentioned individually in my books' notes.

In short, I did not begin this book from scratch. As the names indicate, materials had been gathered and studied from a variety of specialized source collections, and I owe much gratitude to the staffs and funding agencies that made this possible. It is gratifying to acknowledge translations of two of my books: an Italian edition by Einaudi of *The Invasion of America*; and a translation by Editions Rocher of *The Founders of America* for French readers.

I am happy to repeat that my work, for whatever it may be worth, was made possible by traditions of dedicated scholarship and freedom of discussion that have evolved in my native country.

Part I

———— • ————

ENGLAND EXTENDS CONQUESTS
TO NORTH AMERICA

1

INTRODUCTION

A long time ago when, for my sins, I tried to teach American history in a rough high school for slum boys, I thought to brighten the usual routine with an "educational" film on the Revolution. Astonishingly, my students groaned. I had to wonder why.

There was no need to wonder long. As the "educational" film's actors strutted pompously about, they looked more like Martians than honest-to-goodness human beings. And as they declaimed about refusing to be slaves, my students' eyes glazed over. My students were black.

I began dimly to see the error of conceiving the American Revolution as an unqualified struggle for liberty. Undeniably something of that sort had been involved, but liberty for whom and for what?

Certain lower-caste persons in the shapes of African Americans and Amerindians were excluded at the start from Thomas Jefferson's declaration of the equality of all men. Liberty was variously distributed in the Revolution. This exceedingly ambiguous word was certainly not an unqualified goal for Virginia's gentlemen Revolutionaries nor South Carolina's. The *majority* of South Carolina's human population were plantation slaves.

At minimum, all writers agree that thirteen American mainland colonies seceded from the British empire between 1776 and 1783, but they did not break out abruptly; they had been accumulating resentments for a long time. Many scholars have devoted lifelong careers to understanding the Revolution, and their fully documented explanations differ widely from each other. I am grateful to them and I must take account of their work in this study, but I have no respect for the mythology that sets up pompous mannekins orating Profound Thoughts at each other in tales impossible to reconcile with empirical reality.

In 1902, the Philadelphia aristocrat Sydney George Fisher wrote that histories of the American Revolution were like stories "about something that had never happened, and that was contrary to the ordinary experience of human nature . . . like an occurrence in a fairy tale."[1] He was treated as a nonentity by New Englanders who claimed the Revolution as their own property and who continued the fairy tale more devoutly than ever.

My book – the one you now hold – is an effort to tell the Revolution for adults. It differs from the fairy tale in the ways that bills at Christmas differ from the gifts of Santa Claus. The Revolutionaries were real people acting as politicians. Is it necessary in the late twentieth century to elaborate on what *politicians* implies? Like those of modern times, the Revolutionaries served particular interests by whatever means promised to work best for themselves. In the long view, one must see human beings of mixed characters manning the crown as well as the colonies as they strove first to define their sides out of the chaos of multitudinous interests and then to gain institutional and personal power.

The climactic phenomenon of the American Revolution evolved quite naturally, perhaps inevitably, out of the inherent stresses between the center of an empire and its peripheries. A rickety structure, tacked together in fits and starts, the British empire grew without plan except for yearnings after power and wealth. The Revolution was an episode in the history of an empire that the seceding colonies *had helped to create* and with which they identified themselves. It seems necessary to understand the growth and evolution of the colonies' places and roles in the empire.

One thing is certain: They did not oppose empire as such. From their day of first arrival, every single colonial desired and worked to expand English rule over more territory and more people. When the colonists determined to secede, they wanted to rule those territories and peoples themselves instead of acting as agents for Great Britain. When the Revolutionaries won, they organized their newly independent polity in the form and functions of a new empire.

There is much revelation in the repeated rejoicings of Revolutionary leaders over their achievement of *empire*. They used that precise, explicit word again and again, and they meant it. Richard W. Van Alstyne introduced his study *The Rising American Empire* by saying, "The title of this book comes straight from George Washington. . . . The phrase describes precisely what he and his contemporaries had in mind, that is to say an *imperium* – a dominion, state or sovereignty that would expand in population and territory, and increase in strength and power."[2] Reaching for power has implication for policy and behavior. The present study examines the means by which Americans first helped to create the British empire, then

1 Sydney George Fisher, *The True History of the American Revolution* (Philadelphia, Pa.: J. B. Lippincott Co., 1902), 7–8. Mr. Fisher's blunt style is refreshingly free of the usual bombast.
2 Richard W. Van Alstyne, *The Rising American Empire* (1960; reprinted, Chicago: Quadrangle, 1965), 1.

seceded from it to make their own. Examined from that viewpoint, the American Revolution appears to be evolutionary rather than a break with tradition. True enough, the Revolution involved considerable violence. So did the tradition.

In plain terms, King George III and his bought-and-paid-for Parliament determined to force the colonists to surrender to orders and policies from London – but not only the colonists. George and his minions asserted repressive policies and heavy taxes over the people of England at the same time.

Perhaps because the colonists had a political cushion, so to speak, in their semiautonomous assemblies, they were a little slower than the English to raise strong protest. Tough merchants of the City of London, Whig aristocrats opposed to royal prerogative, indomitable printers of the metropolis, independent judges with life tenure, and politically oriented violent mobs fought the crown's repression while Americans still were gearing up for serious resistance.

In the upshot, of course, the Americans could secede, which was not an option for Englishmen, but detailed examination shows that certain civic liberties were won by the English resistance though it fell short of reforming Parliament's representation. Parliament was compelled to accept members chosen by a constituency's voters; Parliament's members were guaranteed immunity from royal punishment because of opposition; newspapers battled for freedom of the press and won; chattel slaves were emancipated; the independence of trial juries was strengthened. These were liberties of substance, and they were won by hard struggle.

On the Atlantic's western shore, victories were more ambiguous. Instead of slavery being ended, the institution was strengthened and protected against attack, with the result that owners of slaves thereafter dominated national policy making for three-quarters of a century. Conspicuously, the victorious. States immediately increased attacks upon tribal Indians and even against British Canada. Although modern historians call the new United States a triumph of liberty, and it was indeed that for a privileged portion of the people, it did not seem so to slaves or to Indians who tried vainly to keep their lands from being plundered.

In this book I have tried to include all the actors as human – every single two-legged creature without fur or feathers. I have tried to see, however dimly, the human persons who were American Indians defending their country and liberty against Revolutionary invaders; the human persons who were held in slavery and were at least as hopeful for liberty as their Revolutionary masters; the human persons who remained faithful to their liege lord and royal master with all the traditional associations he represented and who, in their own words, "passed through all the horrors of civil war and bore what was worse than death, the hatred of their fellow countrymen."[3] Also, indeed, some other persons condemned to the present day by fellow countrymen, the people of peace and tolerance, disfranchised and punished for wanting no part of humans killing other humans.

Without notice of all these people who were caught up in the Revolution, depiction of it becomes mere war propaganda in behalf of one part against the desires and interests of the whole. Two thousand years ago, Aristotle called such logic fallacious.

I have tried to reconceive as a whole process the making and rending of the British empire – to show the energy by which colonies were born and grew, and how they varied from each other yet still shared institutions and passions with each other and their parent peoples.

In a sense, this book is not so much revisionist as a choice of existing but neglected interpretations. It rejects what currently dominant writers like to call "mainstream" history – that is, theirs – and opts instead for studies done by specialists drudging through sources neglected by the mainstreamers. Such specialists have produced a large body of work generally omitted from standard preachments because of its irrefutable contradictions of orthodoxy. I have not indulged myself by simply dreaming up an eccentric fantasy. Rather, I have given attention to the implications of some of these alternative researches.

For the most part, my source materials are secondary studies rather than original manuscripts. At my age, regretfully, I can no longer anticipate enough years to plan feasibly the time required for examining primary sources. Happily, many new, though neglected, specialized studies have appeared in recent years that reduce reliably the burdens of scholarship, and my earlier books are grounded in discoveries opening useful insights. In a sense their bibliographies are supplemental to this one's.[4]

This book is an essay rather than a reference text, yet by its nature it discloses more subject material than standard texts, and its reasoning is supported by documented evidence. Its form is substantially chronological, though with some setbacks and forward looks for subordinate themes. This book is one alternative to current mythology. There will be more, and some will be better. I can boast of proven ability to make mistakes, and I feel quite certain that some will appear in these pages. All that having been said and allowed, the current state of history demonstrates beyond rational argument the need for conceiving it without assumptions of divine Election or Social Darwinism about inherent racial and national superiority and inferiority.

---

3 "For the Unity of Empire" inscription on monument in front of Hamilton-Wentworth Court House, Canada.

4 *The Invasion of America*, 1975; *The Ambiguous Iroquois Empire*, 1984; *Empire of Fortune*, 1988; *Founders of America*, 1993; *Benjamin Franklin, Politician*, 1996.

My job is to make an individual contribution to a movement happily under way.

Even at the very beginning of English attempts at colonization, established data suggest a need for new angles of interpretation. When Sir Walter Ralegh's abandoned colony at Roanoke picked itself up and emigrated to Chief Manteo's town of Croatoan in 1586, ethnocentrism has dictated that bloodlusting savages exterminated those *white* and *civilized* colonists. But it seems clear that the Roanoke people went voluntarily to Croatoan for refuge, and it is quite well established today that Indians all over North America were trying desperately to rebuild populations ravaged by epidemic disease. It would be perfectly rational for Manteo's people to adopt those Roanoke refugees who had been abandoned by their civilized countrymen, and it would have been equally rational for the adoptees to settle down where they were given "savage" hospitality. It is conceivable – it can be neither proved nor disproved – that Roanoke's people became part of the ancestry of today's tribe of Lumbee Indians. Would it not be wondrous if Virginia Dare, the first English child born on American soil, became one of those Lumbee ancestors?

I like this as a pleasanter notion than equally speculative and equally unprovable racist snarls about murderous savages. More evidence exists for subsequent events. Let us accept the door opened to them by the courtesy of Virginia Dare.

2

———— • ————

ORIGINS

The American Revolutionaries inherited a mixed tradition from England of conquests and uprisings. From ancient times the British Isles had been among the most fought-over regions of Europe. Hadrian's Wall still bears testimony to Roman conquest. Everyone knows how Angles and Saxons and Jutes eased in after Roman withdrawal. Family names (my own among them) give linguistic evidence of Scandinavians who raided and stayed. And, of course, the Tower of London shows that Normans battered their way in, whereupon the tide turned and "Englishmen" of scrambled ethnicity took arms to France, to Wales, to Ireland, and to Scotland with varied success.

Emerging from this bellicose history, one can see the gradual agglomeration of local powers in central institutions of church and state, and the gradual reduction of local customs under royal and canon laws. Because of primitive technology, the force of law diminished with distance from its source. Far off noblemen obeyed orders if and when they felt like it, and kings could do little about such independence because they depended on those same nobles for troops.

Thus it was in feudal times when land was the source of wealth and power. "Modern times" began with the growth of commerce and its management by money. With money, a king could hire armies to enforce his edicts. The centralized nation-state developed in tandem with the body of merchants and bankers whose money could be alienated by taxes for use as the king desired.

This was the situation at the beginning of England's colonization in North America. James I, who presided over the founding of Virginia, did so rather absentmindedly as he concentrated on pulling together his nearer realms. With the king's sanction, money started the colonizing, and it was not the king's money. Never afterward did colonists permit the crown to forget that *they* had financed the colonial enterprises and had put their own bodies among the risks. The assertion gave moral advantage in disputes with the crown. (No one cared to notice that some of the earliest funding came from piracy against Spaniards and profiteering in trade with Indians.)

In the background of such disputes was another facet of England's tradition – the resistances to royal authority that frequently broke out in uprisings. The English people were a saucy lot, and their Celtic neighbors even more so. No king ruled for long without having to crush a rebellion or lose out to one; and if the money raised from taxes could field royal troops, the private wealth withheld from the crown could raise even bigger armies. This lesson was taught by the City of London's merchants to Charles I, James's next successor. Charles underestimated the resource and resolve of the money men, and lost his head in consequence.

Oliver Cromwell sharply reduced the continuing power of the feudal nobility as he busily smashed the Scots and Irish as well as king Charles's supporters in England – and all this happened in the early decades of colonization in America. Colonists there observed and remembered.

Still one more feature of England's bellicose tradition needs notice. Englishmen insisted that they were *free* men with *rights* that governments must respect, and their colonists in America intoned a litany of "the rights of Englishmen" as rights belonging also to themselves, the colonists. They took a rather different view toward rivals, competitors, and enemies, especially those who were not English. First they dehumanized Scots and Irishmen as "savages," and therefore subject to any sort of cruelty or exploitation at the whims of their conquerors. This attitude rode also in the colonizing ships to shape tribal Indians into the mold of savage "mere" Irish, that is, those who defended their own traditional cultures against English domination. And when Virginians needed more labor than came from England, the colonists sought it in Africa. For Amerindians and Africans, English tradition was not that of freemen. This must never be forgotten, submerged though it was under the high sounding oratory of the American Revolutionaries. To Indians and Africans those uplifting phrases were nonsensical hot air. They were war propaganda.

We know how inspirational such grand utterances have been to those of us who are beneficiaries of the positive features of English tradition, and this must also be remembered; but not to the point of *disappearing* the hurt and the downtrodden (to use an anachronistic modern term). Our history should include the persons of *all* the people.

England and its colonies were all part of the same empire, and the peripheries were as imperial minded as the core. As the organization matured, the interests and ambitions of its parts diverged to some extent from each other although commerce, language, and tradition acted as cements; and the royal navy both protected the colonies and threatened them for disobedience.

The core and dominant part of this empire was England, a tumultuously bellicose land constantly at war either with its surrounding neighbors or within itself. England's colonies in America were founded while the "home" country was in perpetual uproar, burning church primates at the stake, decapitating a king, invading and massacring in Ireland and Scotland, warring with France on land and with the Dutch Status General at sea. With this sort of parentage, the colonists invaded and seized the territories of Amerindian tribes, drove Dutch imperialists away, destroyed Spanish missions to enslave their Catholic converts, and alternately fought and traded with the French of Canada.

Considering their origins, what else could have been expected of those English colonists?

There was more, of course. They occupied and repopulated lands denuded of natives by epidemic disease and dispossessed from the survivors by war. The invaders made farms and towns in the image of their homeland, and by enslaving Africans they created plantations for which no model existed in Europe. They built and manned ships of all sizes, harvested the seas, and turned Atlantic sea lanes into highways. Along the way, they gave refuge and economic opportunity to ambitious or forlorn English persons, some of whom were dumped as rejects by a hostile crown; and the colonies attracted immigrants from other European countries. So many Europeans, especially Germans, fled the wars and repressions of their own homelands that Tom Paine was to say that "Europe, and not England, is the parent country of America."[1]

But his was propagandist hyperbole, and Paine was wrong. Europeans migrating to America intended to acquire property, especially property in land, which was guaranteed to them by laws sanctioned ultimately from the English crown. The immigrants knew that they would not be taxed without their consent expressed by representatives responsible to the people. Though each colony made laws for itself, all derived from the traditional common law of England which incorporated "rights of Englishmen" as well as duties and commands.

Out of the tragic convulsions of England's religious wars had emerged traditions of tolerance for "Nonconformists," discriminatory in various degrees in the colonies, but generally following the rule of live and let live. Exceptions occurred, but there was no burning of heretics. In the colony most attractive to foreign immigrants – that is, Pennsylvania – religious toleration was positively guaranteed by charter and enforced by government.

---

1 Thomas Paine, *Rights of Man, Common Sense (1776), and Other Political Writings*, ed. Mark Philp, World Classics reprint (New York: Oxford University Press, 1995), 22.

Colonies and crown were bound together by self-interest. For instance, the colonies provided bases and naval stores for the royal navy at a time when the home islands were stripped of timber; and the crown paid. More broadly, a large commerce between the parts of the empire produced profit for substantial merchant classes and customs taxes for the royal treasury. Parliament gave rules to this commerce, largely beneficial to all the merchants, but with an edge for those in England. When the rules straitened colonials too badly, the rulers looked off in other directions while smuggling evened accounts.

We must not forget the great unifying power of the English language and its literature. It was a new language in the era under consideration. Though pockets of colonial immigrants held to other languages, most came under the sway of the King James Bible, experimental poets and playwrights, and serious essayists in science and the humanities who were suddenly appearing from newly established printing presses. Newspapers emerged also to exert their own sort of power. Even today, William Shakespeare tells Americans, Canadians, Australians, South Africans, and even many of Asia's Indians that England's traditions are their own. Contemplating London's crowds of tourists, I believe that the Bard brought more treasure to England than Francis Drake ever did.

When William the Norman had conquered England in 1066, his knights spoke French while their subjects maintained Old English. Norman culture included heritage from what France had saved from ancient Rome, considerably more sophisticated than the crudeness of Anglo-Saxon plowmen; but when William's successors lost their holdings in France they gradually gave in to those stubborn, lowly Englishmen. (While adding some polish to the language.) England's empire in the seventeenth century was better prepared for large responsibilities. Its language expanded as its jurisdictions did, and this time the empire stabilized through language in print. English was as hospitable to new, interesting words as the colonies were hospitable to immigrants. The language itself expanded with new needs. It was cohesive as well as expansive, and it incorporated new acquisitions of vocabulary into its basic grammatical structure, even as the empire fitted new peoples and territories into basic forms of government.

Thus an identity was shaped for the "British" empire, yet latitude remained and causes arose for the colonies to establish individual identities within the whole.

3

EMBRYONIC EMPIRES

It will be helpful to clarify our subject matter, which is restricted to the thirteen mainland colonies that eventually seceded from Britain. The term *colony*, for instance, is not so simple as it first appears. To be sure, English colonies started as offshoots "planted" in transatlantic shores, but they thrust in among other people who were there first. The colonists were, in fact, invaders of Amerindians. As Chief Powhatan dourly remarked to Captain John Smith, "Many do informe me, your comming is not for trade, but to invade my people and possess my Country."[1]

Regardless of "spins" put upon the process by later writers who concoct such excuses as "conquest of the wilderness," England's projectors of colonies understood very well what they were doing. Their chief propagandist, Cambridge's Richard Hakluyt, advised that forts should be built "upon the first view" by ships sent thither, "and these fortifications shall kepe the naturall people of the Countrye in obedience and goodd order." A little further on he added that the English could have "tymber to build great navies" and "without payenge for the same."[2]

From earliest beginnings, the colonies were agencies of conquest. Maps that show a colony sprawled over vast territories reflect the pretensions of the conquerors rather than actual communities of Englishmen. Still today, independent *tribal* territories are submerged within historical maps' vague boundaries because English law did not accommodate tribal rights. Colonists understood this. During the days when neighboring Indians greatly outnumbered Englishmen, the colonists pretended to recognize tribal rights as a practical necessity for negotiation, but all the while they kept in reserve their king's claims to sovereignty and the colonists' derivative claims to jurisdiction over those same Indians. Every colony thus became an empire in embryo.

1 Smith, John, *Complete Works*, 3 vols., ed. Philip Barbour (Chapel Hill: University of North Carolina Press, 1986), 1:246.
2 Richarde Hakluyt, *Discourse of Western Planting* (1584), eds. David B. Quinn and Alison M. Quinn (London: Hakluyt Society, 1993), Chaps. 13, 16.

Law's irrelevancies to fact require attention. Lawyers bury inconvenient facts in "legal fictions" that are just what the term implies. Lawyers make them up in order to handle situations that would otherwise be out of legal control. For colonials the legal fiction of royal *sovereignty* carried immense importance in several ways. It decreed that Indian peoples were subject to the king of England because earlier subjects of his had "discovered" Indian territories – had looked at their coasts from shipboard. (I am not inventing this; American courts still appeal to this rationale.)

It did not matter that the king had done absolutely nothing to found Virginia except to seal a piece of paper – a charter *donating* to the Virginia Company what he did not have, except according to his lawyers' fictions.

What he did have was a navy and an army that persuaded the Virginians that they were still his subjects though they had left his realm to cross the ocean. Accepting his sovereignty over themselves, they extended it derivatively over other territories listed in their charter, and the natives thereof, and they built fortifications to "kepe the naturall people of the Countrye in obedience and goodd order."

Rebelling natives were suppressed by superior arms, and "rights of conquest" – another legal fiction – were added to "rights of discovery."

No matter how much the colonists proclaimed their possession of the "rights of Englishmen," they had no representation in even the rotten boroughs of Parliament; the lawyers defined colonies as dominions of the king, distinct from the realm. They thus came to be supervised by the king's Privy Council instead of Parliament.[3] For many decades the colonies were content with this situation because each of them was allowed an elected assembly that it chose to conceive as its own colonial parliament. The king's lawyers thought otherwise about those assemblies, and the difference in conceptions was pregnant with future disputes.

Still one more legality: The term *colonist* applied exclusively to the king's subjects. Africans imported as plantation slaves were not colonists; they were work animals, as much property as horses or oxen. This remained true even after Africans became the majority of persons in South Carolina. (To call them persons is anachronistically factual instead of legal.)

Other persons who lived within the claimed territory of a colony – Indians in their tribal communities – were also not *colonists* and were not allowed the protection of law. If a dispute arose between an Indian and an Englishman, the Indian could not give testimony in court.

These distinctions were conceived at first in terms of religion. Colonists were Christian; Indians and Africans were heathen. This rationale ceased to

3 Joseph Henry Smith, *Appeals to the Privy Council from the American Plantations* (New York, 1950), 466–469.

function as desired when some of those heathens chose to accept Christianity. *Race*, identified by skin color, became a more satisfactory means of making essential distinctions. As in conquests everywhere, the conquerors established themselves as a privileged caste and prescribed lower castes for persons of "inferior" races.

Thus English colonies created the norms of racism that have endured throughout the history of their descendant United States. Perhaps more immediately pertinent to present concerns, Indians and Africans posed issues of grave concern when the colonists headed toward ultimate secession from Britain.

The dual nature of the colonies entailed consequences in events. Eventually it produced tensions with Britain that helped motivate the colonists to want independence. At this point, our task is analysis of the duality.

The word *colony* is ambiguous in several ways. It refers either to a clone extended from a "parent" polity or to a minority of powerful persons dominating over a larger population of aliens. Britain's mainland colonies in America fitted both descriptions. As time went on, their character evolved so as to obscure their seventeenth-century origins. They became less clonelike in two ways in the eighteenth century: Persons born in America adapted *cultures* in ways distinctively different from those of British origins, though maintaining some traditions in religion and law; and colonial *populations* changed because of immigration from Africa and from European countries other than Britain, especially Germany. By the mid-eighteenth century, Pennsylvania's people had become about 40 percent Germans who adhered stubbornly to their homeland's language and customs.[4] (Even today, the "Pennsylvania Dutch" are recognized as a distinct ethnic group.) In South Carolina, the *majority* of all the people, though decried as mere property, were persons from Africa.[5] Thus, by 1775, the persons and cultures of the colonies had achieved identities distinct from those of the founding clones and parent Great Britain, yet language, law, and religion molded the dominant people as "Englishmen."

In modern terminology, "colonial liberation" took place when the vast subcontinent of India rebelled against Great Britain's imperial rule and overthrew it. Most of the people of India differed in ethnicity, religion, and tradition from ruling Britons, whereas possibly most of Britain's American colonists shared ethnicity and religion with their rulers in London, and much tradition also. Even so, the eighteenth-century empire acted as a giant

---

4 Dietmar Rothermund, "The German Problem of Colonial Pennsylvania," *Pennsylvania Magazine of History and Biography* 84:1 (Jan. 1960), 10–13; A. G. Roeber, Chap. 6 in *Strangers Within the Realm*, ed. Bernard Bailyn and Philip D. Morgan (Chapel Hill: University of North Carolina Press, 1991), 237–244.
5 Ibid., 179.

centrifuge which, as it gained power, tended naturally to spin off the parts farthest from the center. (Even neighboring Ireland has felt that force.)

This process has been somewhat obscured by the immense contributions made by the American colonies to increases in power of the imperial centrifuge even as they tended outward. We may see the process plainly in the early years of Virginia (and we must not forget Virginia's leadership when the time came ultimately for successful Revolution).

4

DEPENDENCIES: INDIANS; THE WEST

The first objective of American empire was rule over Indian peoples and their lands. As miniature empires, the colonies evolved two distinct sets of dependencies: (1) the Indian tribes who maintained ability to govern themselves within parameters set by the colonists; and (2) after decades of growth, the western "back settlers," in tribal territories, later dubbed "frontiersmen" by historians. Relations with these dependent persons varied widely, both as compared with each other and from colony to colony. They must be noticed and described individually in each colony, but in all the colonies the Indians were recognized as aliens, fit subjects for expedient conquest and exploitation. Colonists disputed much over which of them should profit from microconquests.

The "back settlers," on the other hand, were subject to, and somewhat protected by, colonial law, and they were exploited by coastal communities according to traditional English procedures. In effect, geography established social classes, upper in the east and lower in the west. But Indians were kept in what amounted to a separate caste excluded from "civil society" and its legal structures.

In the colonial era's early years, Indians far outnumbered European colonials, but wars and cataclysmic epidemic disease diminished Indians while continuing immigration increased Europeans. So long as Indians held numerical advantage, Europeans of east and west felt obliged to stick together for safety's sake; but, as the ratios reversed, the "back settlers" pursued their economic and political interests more aggressively. This change manifested itself in demands from western counties against the dominant easterners, and these demands required political adjustments even in the midst of the American Revolution.

Even before colonies were "planted" on the continent, empires contended for supremacy off the Atlantic coasts of North America, especially to gain control of the tremendous stocks of fish then available at the Grand Banks of Newfoundland. In the seventeenth and eighteenth centuries North

Atlantic codfish fed half of Europe on religious days of fasting from meat. When fishermen landed to sun or salt their cargoes for the long voyage home, they attracted attention from native Amerindians who envied such visible European products as steel knives, copper kettles, and glistening baubles. In turn, the fishermen envied Indians' casually worn beaver and bearskin coats and robes, which would command high prices in Europe. Exchanges occurred and markets were born among both peoples.

Colonies expanded the process. European traders played a sort of leapfrog with each other to get close enough to hunting Indians to intercept them before they could reach competitors. Thus, for example, New Netherland and New Plymouth competed on the Connecticut River. Indians living close to European trade centers controlled access by hunters from other tribes, sometimes by charging tolls, sometimes by acting as brokers. The effects of intersocietal trade were felt deep in the continent's interior as they were also felt in European markets for peltry.[1]

Indians had another sort of property coveted by colonials: *land*. Colonials were determined to get lands by one means or another, sometimes violently, sometimes in trade. It was not satisfactory to colonials to convert Indian lands into generalized colonial ownership. Each colonist and each colonial government competed with all the others to get tribal lands, and sometimes the competition led on to violence between colonies, or even, as in Bacon's Rebellion in Virginia, to violence within a colony.

Indians' lands also became a bone of contention between colonials and their ruling empire. Everyone agreed that land was fundamental to all wealth, but *whose* wealth became a burning issue. Colonials wanted it for themselves, but powerful courtiers in England vied for royal grants of vast estates superseding the demands of colonials distant from court. That issue never died. At the time of the American Revolution, lobbyists in London still contended for territories being parceled out by governments in the colonies.

Several issues were at stake. Besides competition between courtier and colonist for Indian land, there was imperial competition between Britain and France for tribal alliances. In this respect the French had several advantages. French traders penetrated more deeply than the British into Indian territories, and they often settled and intermarried in Indian communities whereas racial segregation was more often the norm for the British. New France's much smaller ethnically French population was a paradoxical advantage in Indian affairs because it reduced pressure for French seizure of tribal lands. When the French proposed to build a fort and trading post in Indian terri-

---

1 For intertribal and intersocietal trade, see Francis Jennings, *Invasion of America* (Chapel Hill: University of North Carolina Press, 1975), Chap. 6; and Francis Jennings, *Ambiguous Iroquois Empire* (New York: W. W. Norton, 1984), Chap. 5.

tory, the scheme seemed much less threatening to the Indians than when the British colonials made the same sort of plans, the reason being simply that the new French establishment would be foreseeably limited in scope but the British would pour in more settlers and seize unlimited lands for their projects. Indians understood this difference.

Offsetting French advantage, British industry produced trade goods more cheaply than the French. Indian hunter/traders would travel long distances to British trading centers for cheaper prices. But never-ending immigration sooner or later created a situation in which profits from Indian trade were outweighed by profits from occupation of Indian lands. When that point was reached, the colonial embryonic empire fought or bought to acquire the lands and to force resident Indians away. Naturally, the process provoked resentment, sometimes war, and it thus created difficulties for the overall British empire in relations with its French competitor. The British crown wanted expansion into Indian territory to be gradual and controlled so as to preserve as much good will as possible with tribes whose warriors were needed against the French; but aggressive colonists were confident about managing Indian neighbors and little concerned about the crown's policies.

Sometimes this conflicting motivation produced head-on collision between colony and crown. The Powhatan uprising in Virginia in 1622 and "King Philip's War" in New England in 1675 resulted in the crown's rescission of charters for Virginia and Massachusetts. John and Thomas Penn's swindling of Delaware Indians threatened to result in the loss of Pennsylvania's charter after the Delawares rose in 1755 with lifted hatchets; and Thomas Penn had to save his legal hide by massive forgeries and fabrications of documents to exculpate himself and save his fief.[2] Friction was endemic: in relations between colonies and tribes, friction within a colony about Indian affairs, friction between competing colonies, friction between colony and crown, and friction between empires in alliance with tribes.

Until the approach of the American Revolution, colonists had to find ways to regularize relations with Indians without contravening English law's assertion of royal sovereignty. Mere dictatorial fiat would not do. Needed was a device by which trade could be carried on while Indians were persuaded peacefully and cheaply to part with their lands. The device was an adaptation of negotiations conducted between tribes. In these *treaties* both sides negotiated formally as peers. But colonials never accepted that tribal chiefs represented the kind of sovereignty delegated to them from the crown. They recognized Indian chiefs pro forma simply to achieve purposes, but constantly tried to get the same chiefs to acknowledge themselves

2 Francis Jennings, *Benjamin Franklin, Politician* (New York: W. W. Norton, 1996), Chap. 6.

as subjects of the Great King over the Water. This sometimes backfired, but it was useful to diplomats who had little else to work with, and canny Indians learned how to exploit being subjects.

In 1684, an Onondaga (Iroquois) bluntly told New York's governor, "You say we are Subjects to the King of England and Duke of York, but we say we are Brethren [i.e., equals]." The same chief later told the French governor general, "We are born free. We neither depend upon Yonnondio [of New France] nor Corlaer [of New York]."[3] But when the French and their allies chased the Iroquois out of former conquests, the Iroquois gave a "deed" to England's king for the region of Detroit. (Diplomacy worked in mysterious ways; the same king of England still claimed to be king of France also.)

The Iroquois refused point-blank to try to retake Detroit, which had a French garrison of "a hundred brisk men," and the Yorkers also preferred discretion to valor in those parts; but this "deed" was preserved in diplomacy's arsenal as a claim to "rights of conquest" by England's Iroquois "subjects."[4] Totally lacking sustained occupation in any area west of the Appalachian Mountains, English diplomats averred that Iroquois conquest in the west was their king's conquest, conveniently forgetting that the Iroquois had been beaten out of their supposed conquest.

The French were caught off guard in the 1713 treaty of Utrecht at which time they carelessly accepted England's sovereignty over the Iroquois, but the claims of Iroquois conquests were ludicrous to the French. Nevertheless, the English claim showed up again in John Mitchell's 1755 map under crown sponsorship,[5] and the claim became holy writ in histories written by American and English historians.

English colonials developed a technique for getting particular tribes to cede lands that belonged to other tribes. The Iroquois, especially the Onondagas, became adept at this ruse, for which they were well paid. (Iroquois League chiefs now try to practice it even against their "constitutional" and independent Oneida brethren.)

Religious missions became institutions for cementing alliances between tribes and colonies. One should not vaguely call them "Christian" missions because they were emphatically only Protestant or Catholic and often at war with each other as they were taught to be by their reverend teachers. A mission minimally protected its converts from attack by its sponsoring colony, but it was fair game for "Christians" of the alternate variety. Judgments about missionaries must be made individually, distinguishing very

3 Cadwallader Colden, *History of the Five Indian Nations Depending on the Province of New-York in America (1727–1747)*, reprint (Ithaca, N.Y.: Great Seal Books, 1958), 54–55.
4 Jennings, *Ambiguous Iroquois Empire*, 211–12; Chap. 2.
5 Francis Jennings, *Empire of Fortune* (New York: W. W. Norton, 1988), 128–29, 132–33.

carefully those who ventured far out into Indian country at great discomfort and hazard of martyrdom in order to save souls; in contrast were the administrative types who took charge of established communities and fed their own appetites for power by organizing converts as auxiliary troops. By and large the Roman Catholic Church made the greatest efforts at missionizing; it created financial endowments for support and maintained special seminaries to train missionaries. Until the Moravian United Brethren arrived in North Carolina and Pennsylvania in mid-eighteenth century, Protestant missions were founded mostly as means to extract donations from pious English persons. (This was certainly true of the much touted mission of Massachusetts and its "apostle to the Indians," John Eliot.)[6]

The basic institution of accommodation and mixing between colonials and tribesmen was trade.

Myth has it that Englishmen arrived in America to create colonies on "free land" as though the land's previous occupants and possessors had not existed, let alone had social and political institutions of property. Francis Parkman disposed of the land as "no property worthy the name,"[7] and with that phrase he disposed of all the centuries-long disputes and bargainings between Indians and Europeans over conveyance of land from possessions under tribal sanctions to possessions under sanctions of colonial laws.

In the late twentieth century, I have twice listened to an economic historian describe the growth of wealth in colonial America without ever mentioning either land or intersocietal trade between Indians and colonials. It will do no good to sputter and fume over such carefully preserved blindness, just as it is futile to express outrage against historians who describe America as "savage wilderness" or "virgin land." Let my single sentence serve in place of a howl against willfull denseness while we get on to the people who really did exist and whose relations with English invaders were essential to the founding and growth of English colonies.

First, when Virginia and Massachusetts and all the other colonies were founded, the colonists settled at the edge of native populations many times the size of their own numbers. The fact is obscured by demographic catastrophe that began with the introduction of European diseases to an American indigenous population that lacked the immunities painfully acquired by Europeans during their "dark ages." Indians succumbed to epidemics at fantastic rates while colonials kept adding to their own populations by continuing immigration. Precise numbers are disputed among scholars, but the general facts of epidemic loss on the one side and immigration addition on

6 Jennings, *Invasion of America*, Chap. 14.
7 Francis Parkman, *The Jesuits in North America in the Seventeenth Century* (1867; New Library Edition, Boston, 1909), 57–58.

the other now stand confirmed without cavil. Populations changed in inverse ratios. In a ballpark estimate, I have figured that the *total* population of the territories claimed by English colonials dropped sharply after first contacts, so sharply that a century elapsed before colonial immigration plus natural increase could rise to match the numbers that Indians alone had maintained prior to invasion.[8]

This picture stands in sharp refutation of the comment I have been sorry to hear made by otherwise respected economic historians that a "colony is initially unpopulated and therefore without capital, management, or labor."[9] It is a prime example of how theory can divert attention from facts. If it had been true, no trade could have arisen between Indians and colonials; but such trade not only did occur, but it largely financed the founding of identifiable colonies and perhaps of them all. For example, Captain John Smith fed starving Jamestown with food gained in trade. New Sweden and New Netherland, which became New York, New Jersey, and Pennsylvania, were established entirely in order to profit from the trade. As for functions in it, land was the Indians' contribution of capital (however unwillingly) to the institution; and as to labor, listen to Adriaen Van der Donck: "The Indians, without our labour or trouble, bring to us their fur trade, worth tons of gold, which may be increased, and is like goods found."[10] It may be added that the management of Indians' hunting for commerce and their trade between tribes, up to the point of the colonial trading post, was entirely organized by the Indians themselves.

Throughout the entire colonial era up to the American Revolution and beyond, the intersocietal trade continued powerfully to affect commerce and politics. It was at the heart of frontier conflicts between the empires of Britain and France, for the statesmen on both sides understood that alliances with Indian tribes were crucial to victory, and domination of trade was crucial to alliance. The same recognition was much evident when Britain's colonies rose in their war for independence, and it continued through the early decades of the newly founded United States of America.

From early times the colonies' interior sections resented the wealth and power of regions nearer the coast. Ordinarily this situation is called disputation between west and east, but terms of geographic direction must be modified for accuracy. As colonization usually moved upstream from river mouths, and the rivers flowed in various ways, one must often think in the

8 Jennings, *Invasion of America*, Chap. 2.
9 John J. McCusker and Russell R. Menard, *The Economy of British America, 1607–1789* (Chapel Hill: University of North Carolina Press, 1991), 27.
10 Adriaen Van der Donck, *A Description of the New Netherlands* (1653), trans. Jeremiah Johnson, ed. reprint, Thomas F. O'Donnell (Syracuse, N.Y.: Syracuse University Press, 1968), 131.

seventeenth century of inland communities versus coastal, as north versus south. Massachusetts sprawled eastward into Maine from its core, and New Yorkers from the Hudson Valley pushed eastward into violently protesting Vermont, with long-enduring consequences. In the eighteenth century, as colonial settlement oozed into open areas everywhere, maps show settled areas expanding from east to west, but there was no simple movement in a wave. Rather, highly detailed maps, made current year by year, would present fingers and projections of settlement going this way and that as opportunities offered.

To embrace all the geographical variations, one must think in chronological terms of early settlements striving for domination and advantage as against later settlements struggling for more favorable shares. Thus, to speak of west versus east is really to talk of latecomers versus predecessors. Newcoming "back settlers" or "frontiersmen" pushed for equality with established "tidewater" or urbanized communities. All of them constantly needed to be mindful of those other communities, the tribal Indians who were scheduled for exploitation and dispossession but had to be managed. "Frontier" people were in the front line of that kind of management but were rarely consulted about decisions that required it.

To conceive the colonies as empires in embryo enables the student to think of the "frontier" people as extended colonies of their established predecessors who held control and gained benefits. (They were exploited and controlled almost as much as the Indians.) "Back settlers" complained long and loud in remarkable parallels to the colonial centers' complaints against the empire's center in Britain. On one occasion, South Carolina's protesting "Regulators" raised the cry against government from Charleston: "No taxation without representation!"[11] So strong was feeling among the Regulators of the Carolinas that many of them looked to the crown to relieve them of tidewater oppression, and when war broke out between colonies and crown, many Regulators became Loyalists. Carolinians conceived Revolutionary "liberty" in fashions strange to the dictionary, not only as regarded the holding of slaves and dispossession of Indians, but even to the disfranchisement of interior settlers.

In Pennsylvania, the western counties complained of inadequate representation in the legislative assembly, and historians have made much of these complaints; but when Benjamin Franklin bossed the assembly, western members voted unanimously with easterners to support his policies. This situation will be reviewed further on.

Connecticut tried to expand westward by sending its own colonists into northeastern Pennsylvania where the Connecticut "westerners" evicted

---

11 See Chap. 17.

Pennsylvanians who had come north from Philadelphia, thus initiating a series of armed conflicts involving Indians as well as homesteaders. The situation exposes much nonsense about "frontier democracy." To speak of the Connecticut intruders as demanding greater democracy from Philadelphia is absurdity; they were an aggressive outthrust from Hartford that aimed at bringing Pennsylvania land under Connecticut's jurisdiction.

Maine was Massachusetts's farthest frontier, its inhabitants much disgruntled at having to bear the brunt of Indian hostilities caused by Massachusetts's aggressions. Eventually, long after the Revolution, Maine won independence as a separate state. Perfervid imaginations have made this easternmost state of the American Union into part of the history of the "West." No absurdity is too great for determined theorists to propagate.

These issues are noted here because they all rose to complicate the processes of the American Revolution and have all been buried under piles of semantics and abstractions. To speak of them in terms of verifiable events requires elimination of heavy burdens of obfuscation.

5

COLONIAL VARIETY I: VIRGINIA

Historians usually notice England's mainland colonies in a tripartite division: northern (or New England), middle, and southern. Virginia dominates the southern category so much that other colonies even farther south become overwhelmed by it. There are reasons, however, to distinguish South Carolina in a separate class, as will appear. West Indian influence was far stronger in South Carolina than in the Chesapeake Bay region.

Large plantations dominated economy and society in all the southern tidewater regions, but until the coming of King Cotton in the nineteenth century, Virginia's planters were a little abashed, a little uncomfortable with the slavery of Africans that made them rich. It did not seem quite acceptable in a gentlemanly code of conduct. For the South Carolinian gentry, however, slavery (of other people) was a positive good, the be-all and end-all of their society. In a later era, when *democracy* had become a word to charm with, South Carolinian John C. Calhoun rooted a philosophy in the thesis that slave society was true democracy, but colonials did not descend to that depth; they were quite content as aristocrats to enjoy the riches created by slaves. And the Carolinians were even more aggressively bellicose than the Virginians.

Virginia came first. It is much to the point that Virginia was founded by money – not by executive decision of the English crown, but by private subjects financing and organizing the Virginia Company in the hope of creating a profitable enterprise. Strictly speaking, this was not a good business for investors. Some of the "insiders" seem to have enriched themselves personally, but the Company became quicksand for investors' money. Virginia's intended purpose as an agency of conquest was very clearly understood in the organizing Virginia Company of London. The Company instructed its first emigrants about the Indian "naturals" already on the scene: "You cannot carry yourselves so towards them but they will grow discontented with your habitation."[1]

---

1 *Travels and Works of Captain John Smith, President of Virginia, and Admiral of New England, 1580–1631*, ed. Edward Arber and A. G. Bradley, 2 vols. (Edinburgh, 1910), 1:xxxiv–xxxv.

So they did, and discontent expressed itself in alternate skirmishes and negotiations, but the surrounding Powhatan Indians held off a showdown in the hope that incompetence, disease, and general shiftlessness would dispose of the colony without further action. This nearly happened. Intriguingly, some pathetic, starving settlers followed the Roanoke example by running for succor *to the Indians*. They were seized and dragged back from "savage" hospitality by the colony's masters who decreed death for them by hanging, shooting, or being broken on the wheel.[2] This civilized response had been learned from earlier experience in Ireland when Irish natives had been tolerated among English settlers and had risen by surprise in bloody revolts. Thereafter, segregation was the rule in Ireland and was carried as policy to Virginia. Racial segregation was gradually established by edict in the very first permanent English colony, and that cancer has still been preserved by gradually eroding customs.

It is quite clear in demographic statistics that Virginia was disastrous for both Indians and colonists in the founding generation – and for its venture capitalists also. Indians died in fantastic numbers by the introduction of "European" diseases. Of the colonists, 2,000 survived the first fourteen years out of a total transported there amounting to 10,000 (according to a hostile observer) or only 6,000 (according to the provincial government's defense). Of the 8,000 or 4,000 dead, 347 had been killed in a furious uprising of the Indians in 1622. At minimum, therefore, 3,600 casualties (or 6,600 by the larger estimate) occurred through the Company's maladministration, and background materials pin the blame on official neglect of bond servants dumped on shore without provision for food or shelter.[3] This was capitalism at its most primitive. It seems likely that the great majority of these "settlers" came involuntarily as indentured servants and that this low status explains the managers' indifferent attitude.

A caution must be expressed here. One must not think that the tremendous loss of human life concerned the promoters of the colonization scheme. In the seventeenth century, gentlemen with power worried little about the lives of lower-class people – there were plenty more where they had come from. (Skeptical, dear Reader? Had not the Roanoke colony been abandoned to what its founders conceived as certain death?) What did concern the investors in Virginia's Jamestown was the lack of a return on their investment.

Some investors migrated with the other settlers and took up large grants of land. Those who survived the "starving days" and the "seasoning" of

2 Nicholas P. Canny in *The Westward Enterprise: English Activities in Ireland, the Atlantic, and America, 1480–1650*, ed. K. R. Andrews et al. (Detroit, Mich.: Wayne State University Press, 1979).

3 Captain Butler, "The unmasked face of our Colony in Virginia as it was in the winter of the yeare 1622," mss. C.O. 1/3, 3637; Wesley Frank Craven, *Dissolution of the Virginia Company* (New York, 1932), Chap. 6.

feverish disease finally began to strike it rich, somewhat by coincidence. Their experiments to produce a staple crop failed to catch on in overseas markets until the Spanish crown obligingly forbade export of tobacco from colonies in Trinidad and Guiana. A huge market without competition opened for the Virginians, and it was so lucrative that they planted tobacco wherever a spot of bare earth permitted, even in the streets of Jamestown.[4] Throughout the seventeenth century, tobacco was cultivated mostly by European indentured servants, but the general labor force was enhanced by the introduction of African slaves from a Dutch nautical peddler in 1619.

Progress to wealth and power was interrupted only briefly for the First Families of Virginia by the Indian uprising in 1622 which they came to believe was a positive benefit. Suppressing it enabled a leader to gloat, "wee shall enjoy their cultivated places . . . Now their cleared grounds in all their villages (which are situate in the fruitfullest places of the land) shall be inhabited by us, whereas heretofore the grubbing of woods was the greatest labour."[5] How nicely everything suddenly fitted together in the absence of concern over lives lost.

The ministers of King James I were not ready to accept the loss of thousands of subjects through simple slackness. Seized papers disclosed beyond cavil the Company's maladministration and general crookedness. Though financed privately, the Company had been sponsored by the crown with a royal charter. This was withdrawn whereupon Virginia became one of the king's dominions instead of a private business. Thus the first serious stress between colony and imperial core ended with tighter ties than before. Instead of leaving the colony to management by a company, the crown sent out a governor to take control under terms of a new charter.

One must notice the dual nature of this colony. On the one hand, its liberties were circumscribed and limited by the crown's power. On the other hand, however, Virginia imposed its own power upon the Chesapeake Bay's indigenous people. This was not merely an extension of Britain.

The Indians were attached to their lands. Though Englishmen invaded and drove them back, they made new communities nearby and opened trade with their invaders, exchanging the peltry produce of their extractive hunting industry for goods of European manufacture. As England traded profitably with Virginia, certain privileged colonists traded with the Indians, also profitably. Despite disputes and difficulties, this trade with Indians had become by 1675 a fairly standardized and stable operation. But it was controlled and enjoyed by a small clique of the gentry associated with Governor Sir William Berkeley.

4 Joyce Lorimer in *The Westward Enterprise*.
5 Waterhouse, "State of the Colony," *The Records of the Virginia Company of London*, ed. Susan Myra Kingsbury, 4 vols. (Washington, D.C., 1906–1935), 3:556–57.

Some minor gentry, led by Nathaniel Bacon who demagogically aroused masses of common people and slaves, rebelled against their exclusion from the trade, warred against nearby Indians with peltry plunder, and finally rose against the government of Berkeley.

This bit of land-based piracy has been inflated semantically to "frontier democracy" with no visible justification except its opposition to Berkeley's autocratic rule. Nathaniel Bacon simply wanted to substitute his own autocracy for Berkeley's. For present purposes the situation reveals still another layer of structure from London on top to the tidewater planters supporting Berkeley, thence to the "back" or "frontier" colonists, and finally to the Indian communities. That extra layer of western, interior colonists, though formally subordinate to governors and bureaucrats, harbored grudges and hostility in all directions. Smoldering with resentments, the westerners perpetuated their bitter anger, sometimes justifiably, always complainingly, throughout the colonial era. The people living in western counties strove for power however they could get it, not ruling out violence as Bacon demonstrated. In 1675 they followed Bacon to attack and plunder Indians, and when Governor Berkeley intervened to protect the Indians and their profitable trade, Bacon turned his arms against Berkeley.[6]

In an interesting anticipation of events to come a century later, Bacon's "Associators" organized themselves by committees and conventions, and proclaimed revolution. It is enough here to note that they were defeated and Bacon solved by dying the problem of what to do with him. A recent historian sees the suppression of the revolt as *1676: The End of American Independence*. Certainly, King Charles II intended it that way. He sent a fleet and a thousand-man regiment to "conform [Virginians] to the bureaucratic and political requirements of the modernized English state." Stephen Saunders Webb, who wrote that, noticed the transforming effect of Oliver Cromwell's conquests in the British Isles: "Out of war and revolution . . . the imperial state . . . at last arrived in Virginia." And there it stayed.[7]

Throughout its colonial existence, Virginia's gentry sustained an attitude of autonomous rule. When England underwent the Puritan Revolution, Virginians stayed loyal to King Charles I, so much so that Parliament's Council of State let adjoining Maryland remain hospitable to Catholics – in case a base should be needed for troops to conform Virginia.

Virginia's plantation gentry established themselves as an aristocracy by classic means: increase of wealth, intermarriage, control of county court-

---

6 The best portrayal of this affair is Wilcomb E. Washburn, *The Governor and the Rebel* (Chapel Hill: University of North Carolina Press, 1957).
7 Stephen Saunders Webb, *1676: The End of American Independence* (New York, Knopf, 1984), 127–29.

houses and the vestries of the established church, and entail of landed estates. In cumulative effect, by the time of the American Revolution, three-quarters of Virginia's tidewater had come under enforced entail.[8]

With this knowledge, one can understand how a few landed gentlemen meeting in a tavern in Williamsburg could make decisive agreements over their ale and "flip." Though they were active planters, their property was maintained by laws of feudal character that excluded interlopers. In crude terms, they ran the place. For them, democracy was a very dirty word.

When these gentry became sufficiently vexed by authoritarian measures from the British crown, they could act independently for themselves and take leadership of all the rebellious colonies, and they did. The Revolution in Virginia did not overthrow and replace a ruling class. Indeed a warning is given by historian Charles S. Sydnor: "The political system of colonial Virginia warns against too much preoccupation with the mechanics of democracy."[9] Slaves, Indians, and sodbusters might have wondered if more than mechanics was involved.

8 Charles S. Sydnor, *American Revolutionaries in the Making: Political Practices in Washington's Virginia* (1952; New York: Free Press, 1966); Holly Brewer, "Entailing Aristocracy in Colonial Virginia: 'Ancient Feudal Restraints' and Revolutionary Reform," *William and Mary Quarterly*, 3d ser., 54:2 (April 1997), 307–46.
9 Sydnor, *American Revolutionaries*, 117.

6

COLONIAL VARIETY II: NEW ENGLAND

The next big colonizing campaign emerged in response to political and religious brawling in England. King Charles I disputed with Parliament, and his bishops cracked down on Puritan reformers of the king's Church of England. Feudal nobles mostly supported the king; Parliament and Puritans were strongly supported by the moneyed interests of the City of London. Though the king's side lost after a long civil war, for a while they made things so hot for the Puritans that a number of the latter decided to emigrate to escape persecution.

They organized a company and obtained a royal patent on the specious excuse that they desired to convert the heathen Indians to the worship of Christianity. (They were carefully nonspecific about what kind of Christianity.) John Winthrop Sr., a former court lawyer, joined the company's leadership and made sure that the Massachusetts Bay Company's patent should go overseas instead of remaining within reach of current court lawyers. Off went Winthrop and a great fleet of emigrants to found Boston and nearby villages in 1630, whereupon Winthrop and his partners – the magistrates called "Assistants" – promptly treated the patent as though it had become a constitution; and they paid little attention thereafter to either their parent council in England or the royal government thereof.

Mass migration made Massachusetts Bay into the aggressively dominant polity of the region called New England. Because its colonists were mostly Puritan nonconformists from the Church of England whose early contingents had fled from probable persecution by the established church, sympathetic historians have noticed their migration as a pursuit of liberty, but the Puritans of Massachusetts quickly disclosed that they were more interested in power than general liberty, and that liberty for themselves included the power to persecute people unlike them, including even supporters of the established royal church from which they had fled. These "libertarian" Puritans fined, imprisoned, and exiled on pain of death for return the believers in faiths other than their own.

Their charter claimed intent to evangelize heathen Indians, and the spe-ciousness of this claim appears from their total lack of any effort to create a mission to the Indians until forced by pressure from England. Instead of converting Indians, the Puritans attacked them to gain their lands by "rights of conquest." In place of the church established in England, the Puritans established their own and maintained its power and privileges against all challenge until well after the American Revolution.[1]

Virginia maintained the Church of England and Virginia's great planters regarded Massachusetts men as contemptible bigots and subversive radicals. There were no grand tidewater plantations in New England, where fami-lies cultivated the land in small tracts and owners labored themselves or hired "hands" for wages.

Like Virginia, Massachusetts functioned dually as a colony of England and an embryonic empire over native peoples – a situation that is masked by maps that omit to show territories under tribal jurisdiction. Unlike Virginia, New England compensated for its shallow, rocky soils remaining from glacial scouring by turning to the sea. Blessed by waters teeming with marine life, New Englanders became skilled fishermen, and their under-standing of the seas evolved easily into large-scale shipbuilding and export–import business. Whereas Virginia was dominated by the class of planters, Massachusetts came under merchant domination.

Their situation and activities confirmed Puritan policies for settling by towns rather than letting populations scatter individualistically. This mode of settlement involved substantial numbers of freemen in the town meet-ings managing community affairs. Though disputes have arisen as to how many townsmen had to qualify for church membership in order to vote as citizens, it seems clear that far more New Englanders than Virginians (or Englishmen) participated in their own government. Often only possession of a small amount of real property was required. Thus New England approached what South Africans came to call *herrenvolk democracy*. (The phrase is notable for its exclusions as well as its membership.) Whatever else may be said of this region's system of government, it emphatically was not feudal.

As Puritans had fled from the power of the English crown, so some of them broke away from government by Massachusetts. Connecticut and New Hampshire thus became colonies of a colony, and Rhode Island became a sanctuary for opponents and a hotbed of heretics and religious liberty (genuine liberty) that practiced greater democracy than any other English colony. Puritans refused to accept Rhode Island as part of New England, and they plotted to conquer it. Interestingly, protection for these heretics

---

1 Jennings, *The Invasion of America*, Chaps. 14, 11.

came first from the Parliament of English Puritans, then from King Charles II. Statesmen in Old England lacked enthusiasm for increase of power in New England.

That the Massachusetts Puritans intended independence from the start appeared from the 1635 law that all persons in the colony must swear an oath of fealty to their magistrates rather than the king, and when Roger Williams challenged this oath, they exiled him under pain of death if he should dare to return. Williams understood them and stayed away.[2]

The government of Old England was so torn by internal struggles that Massachusetts's Puritans ruled their roost very cockily until the Restoration of King Charles II in 1660. When Charles sent royal commissioners and the hint of the navy in 1664 to reestablish control, Puritan independence was curtailed, but powers continued strong until the launching of another campaign of conquest against Indians. As usual, its history was written by the conquerors so it was blamed on the victims; it was blamed on "King" Philip of the Wampanoags, and it has been King Philip's War ever since.

For all their high talk of unity of faith, the Puritans did not trust each other – with reason. With their allies in New Plymouth they encroached intolerably on Wampanoag chief Metacom (King Philip), and when he arose finally in defense, the Puritan commonwealths marched armies – *not* against Wampanoags, but against the Narragansetts. On the face of events, neither Massachusetts nor Connecticut was a party to Metacom's quarrel with Plymouth. The notion that they joined in noble unity of faith is not borne out by events; each Puritan colony intended to seize the Narragansett country for itself. Their unity consisted only in circumventing Rhode Island's (non-Puritan) charter and beating down Indians of all description. They thus united surrounding Indians against themselves as Metacom had never been able to do.

This time, however, the Puritan magistrates overreached themselves. The Indians fought back. Though they lost in the end, no stretch of imagination could call the war a great victory for the Puritans. New England's casualties were greater per capita than in any war since, and the magistrates lost territory instead of gaining it. The war was as costly as its plotting was vicious. With the indispensable help of New York's Mohawk allies, Metacom and his allies were defeated, but the Puritans failed, after all, to get their rights of conquest over the Narragansett territory despite committing Cromwellian-style massacres in the effort.[3]

As Virginia's company had lost its charter after the Powhatan uprising of 1622, so the Massachusetts company, after the Wampanoag/Narragansett bloodshed, was called to account in London and gradually reduced to

2 Ibid., 140–42. 3 Ibid., Chaps. 17, 18.

obedience. Rhode Island's feisty and heretical non-Puritans, who had carefully avoided warring against their Indian neighbors, won the English crown's grant of the Narragansett lands; and the furious Puritans were boxed in. Perhaps royal ministers had a dour sense of humor, for they compensated the bellicose New Englanders with grants of territory occupied by religious allies: The Old Colony of New Plymouth went protestingly under Massachusetts's rule. Earlier, the fiercely separatist Puritans of New Haven had been given to Connecticut, upon which many of the outraged New Havenites packed up and moved again to northern New Jersey where they strove fiercely with other Englishmen over ownership of land.

Historians have been deluded by the masses of double-talk with which Puritan apologists have loaded all blame for New England's Indian wars upon the Indians, but surviving Indians did not read the war propaganda. They preserved traditions of domination, exploitation, and cruelty in consequence of which New England was plagued thereafter by perpetual frontier horrors whenever French enemies chose to arm and instigate the tribes.

Puritans were outraged by the contrast of their own situation with New York's seeming immunity to Indian raids because its land had been acquired by negotiation and alliance. It was impossible for New Englanders to confess fault (nor will they yet) so the Puritans reviled the Yorkers with lurid inventions of demonic hostility instigating and abetting the Indians' raids. In the background was a matter of territory in the upper Hudson Valley, desired by Massachusetts but plainly in New York's jurisdiction. How could it be extracted from New York? By conquering its occupying Indians and thus acquiring *rights of conquest*.

Already in 1666, Massachusetts had launched its "praying Indians" – converts under mission control – against New York's Mohawks in the upper Hudson. That effort had come to grief with a Mohawk victory, but the desire to seize that land continued: Rights of conquest seemed to be the way to do it, but both Mohawks and Yorkers were on their guard. New England's ever-facile penmen explained away their governments' strategies and practices, and managed always to divert blame to Indian "savages." The Mohawks preserved their own memories, which were rather different. So were the records kept in New York out of the reach of editorial adjustment by Puritan propagandists. The issue of the Mohawks' lands stayed alive and rancorous until it revived bloodily in the American Revolution.

A new charter replaced the old one, and Massachusetts became a province instead of the "nation" that its magistrates had formerly vaunted. Thus ended another experiment in colonial independence – like the first, a victim of its own overweening urge to conquer.

The Puritan colonies were impelled by religion to give especial attention to their people's literacy. Originally motivated by desire and duty to equip children to read the Holy Scriptures that were the fountain of Puritan beliefs, magistrates encouraged schools for the young, and widespread literacy contributed to growth of commerce. A Bible school was founded to train ministers which, in due course, expanded its offerings and became Harvard University.

This situation contrasted especially strongly with the southern plantation colonies where masters of slaves feared their education. In the South, an opposite trend became effective. Governments discouraged public education until after the nineteenth-century Civil War. Teaching slaves to read and write was made illegal. Rich families hired tutors, but "poor whites," lacking resources, simply remained illiterate.

7

COLONIAL VARIETY III: NEW YORK

Besides colonies founded by England, that nation acquired a solid bloc by conquest. Between Virginia and New England, the Dutch had established New Netherland, which was absorbed into English jurisdiction in 1664 and again (after reconquest) in 1674. New Netherland claimed vast territories, some of which conflicted with Massachusetts and Connecticut, neither of which was ready to accept loss. King Charles II granted large parcels from the conquered Dutch territories. For present purposes, we must skip over the complications up north. In the middle, he granted New York to his brother James, the duke of York; East and West New Jerseys to court favorites; and Pennsylvania, with its appended Lower Counties of Delaware, to the great Quaker courtier William Penn.

For generations, while the colonists of New York remained more Dutch than English, this colony's central position combined with its splendid harbor and its numerous Indian peoples to recommend it as a base for crown power among unruly American subjects. A fleet based in New York harbor projected awe north and south. The Iroquois Indians living along the Finger Lakes region proposed alliance in 1675 and were made partners soon afterward in a great bicultural confederation of Indian tribes and English colonies called the Covenant Chain. At the core of this alliance system, New York and the Iroquois Five Nations (especially the Mohawks) acted as a team whose power reached southward to the Carolinas and northward to Maine. When uproars broke out in the "back country" colonial governors appealed to New York to pacify the interior through influence with Iroquois partners in the Covenant Chain. Though documentation is almost nonexistent, it appears that tribes linked to the Chain accepted Iroquois spokesmen as advantageous when treating with the colonies.

Besides their political importance, the Iroquois contributed much commercial value to New York through a large system of trade, exchanging goods manufactured in Europe for furs and peltry brought in by Indian hunters. It was not a simple system. Though its essential action was the handing over of skins for manufactured goods, the paths by which such materials reached the trading post were long and devious. Within the province of New York, the "trunk line," so to speak, of the intersocietal trade ran along the Hudson River. At its mouth, the port city received goods from Europe and transshipped them upriver to Albany where heavy trading took place. The "frontier" in New York was north before it became west.

One of the complications of this commerce was smuggling. The best furs came from the cold north in New France, and they made French merchants happy when goods were available for exchange, but the cold climate that made rich furs also froze the St. Lawrence River through long winters. It quickly occurred to French and English colonial merchants that the navigable Hudson delivered goods all year round, and they could be delivered overland in exchange for those good furs in New France's Montreal. This was a highly illegal arrangement that amounted to trading with the enemy, but both Paris and London were unable to stop it.

Smuggling as practiced in these circumstances must not be conceived as a sneaky, clandestine operation; it was a regular enterprise of highly respected and provincially powerful merchants, and it quickly gained the status of an institution. Comparison can be made to bootlegging during America's Prohibition era.

In another manifestation, the smuggling trade extended westward, through Iroquois lands out to the Mississippi Valley territories and tribes where French traders were busy. Sometimes these traders brought to their base at Detroit many more skins than the glutted French market could absorb. No problem. Detroit's commandant disposed of them via ethnically diverse entrepreneurs to Albany and Philadelphia. Again, this was strictly illegal, but who could police it?[1]

Certain New Yorkers were not content with the profits of smuggling. Iroquois alliance opened up dazzling prospects of western territorial expansion. In the 1680s, Governor Thomas Dongan observed and encouraged Iroquois efforts to conquer Indians in the Mississippi Valley, and he tried to get the Iroquois to declare themselves *subjects* of the king of England.[2] He understood perfectly well that they were independent allies, but if he could merely get words about subjection, however meaningless in fact, he could use such language in a diplomatic syllogism; to wit, the Iroquois had conquered other tribes, and the Iroquois were subjects, therefore all those conquered Indians *and* their lands were also under English jurisdiction.

1 Yves F. Zoltvany, "New France and the West, 1701–1713," *Canadian Historical Review* 46 (1965), 301–22; Francis Jennings, "Bisaillon (Bezellon, Bizaillon), Peter," in *Dictionary of Canadian Biography* 3: 65–66.
2 Jennings, *Ambiguous Iroquois Empire*, 191–92.

Dongan's effort was followed up in 1701 when Robert Livingston persuaded the badly beaten Iroquois to sign a "deed" conveying vast hunting territories in the west – lands out of which the Iroquois had been driven by the French and their Indian allies.[3] The French laughed at this nonsense, but English diplomats kept pretending it was factual until the Seven Years War when they issued the famous Mitchell map showing all those pretended Iroquois conquests as rightfully English. (The politics in that map are worthless bombast.)

In the end, New York's efforts at western expansion fell flat, but not for lack of trying. And they have led many a scholar astray who paid more attention to diplomatic claims than to demonstrable facts.

Frustrated themselves from western expansion, New Yorkers also blocked aggressive militants from Massachusetts and Connecticut who were first prevented from getting a foothold in the Hudson Valley, then forced to face it as a wall until events in the American Revolution opened a new path westward.

Among New York's legacies from New Netherland was a set of huge manorial estates in the Hudson Valley that were left intact after the conquest. Their treatment contrasted with what was done to conquered Indian tribes whose territories were seized, converted legally into provincial real estate, and sold. The property of Dutch colonials, formerly sanctioned by New Netherland, was simply accepted after English conquest and sanctioned anew under New York's law.

These vast estates endured with tremendous economic and political influence until the American Revolution and (with some changes of ownership) well into the nineteenth century. Tenants struggled perpetually, sometimes violently, against their lords over social conditions and shares of income. During the Revolution, these estates became arenas of intense conflict.

3 Jennings, *Ambiguous Iroquois Empire*, 212.

8

COLONIAL VARIETY IV: PENNSYLVANIA

New Netherland was too big to swallow in one lump. The region between the Hudson and Delaware Rivers was granted to Sir George Carteret and Lord John Berkeley in 1664 for service to the Royalists during the Commonwealth. They did little to colonize the area. From the beginning, larger, faster-growing communities in New York and Philadelphia overshadowed the gradual evolution of New Jersey.

Courtier William Penn became interested in making a refuge for his persecuted fellow members of the Religious Society of Friends (Quakers). After buying an interest in East Jersey, William Penn initiated major changes by appealing to the crown in 1681 for an immense grant of conquered territory that had become southern New York. The royal Stuart brothers were conscious of obligation to William's father, Admiral Sir William Penn, who had lent money to Charles in exile and defeated a Dutch fleet off Lowestoft (for which accomplishment the admiral discreetly stepped aside to credit Duke James). In view of such support, Charles II benevolently granted the admiral's Quaker son a territory larger than Ireland.

This was a grand gesture that the king could afford because it did not cost him even the price of his charter. William Penn paid for that.

Though Quaker William also operated on a grand scale, he rejected the peerage that might have gone with the land because religion told him that titles were vain and empty show. This was not true of all titles; young William permitted himself to become True and Absolute Proprietary of all that granted territory with original right to the soil and government of its people. Having rejected ducal title, he became nevertheless a feudal lord with rights to create manors (as he did) and to appoint governors, sheriffs, and judges (which he also did).

Pennsylvania grew fast though founded late. This colony did not get under way until 1681, but its people arrived in great numbers like the first fleet of Puritans. There, however, the resemblance ended. William Penn intended his colony as a haven of general religious toleration for all faiths, and his intention was confirmed by Quaker legislators under frequently trying circumstances. The contrast is quite precise: Massachusetts persecuted Quakers to the extremity of killing some (by law, of course), whereas Pennsylvania gave Calvinist Presbyterians (the equivalent of Boston's Congregationalists) full citizenship equal in all legal respects to that of Quakers. In plain terms, it was the difference between theocratic bigotry and – the word is accurate – *liberty*.

The difference was not lost to persons contemplating emigration from the British Isles and Europe, especially the fractured and war-plagued Rhineland. New England appeared exclusionary to them while Pennsylvania was invitingly attractive, and the result was a continued tide of immigration through Philadelphia that made the Quaker colony outgrow Massachusetts swiftly in the eighteenth century as Boston, despite its earlier beginnings, took second place to Philadelphia.

Again, one must see that money was the founding power of this Quaker colony, feudal though it was in form. In all the colonies, the cost of colonization was paid ultimately by Indians through profits to English traders and loss of lands by colonial seizures. In Pennsylvania this process became especially plain precisely because the colonizing Quakers did *not* seize lands during the first generation. Founder William Penn negotiated purchase of Indian territories and resold tracts at mark-ups that financed his colonizing. His policy lasted in substance only as long as himself; his sons maintained the form of negotiated purchase only as a cover for swindles by which they made the profits from Indian lands into a vast fortune for their family.[1]

Alike under father and sons, the crown paid nothing but retained sovereign powers. In Pennsylvania, as in the other feudal colonies, a layer of administration by a lord intervened between the crown and the colonists, but this new feudalism of the seventeenth and eighteenth centuries acquired a feature unknown in the Middle Ages – an elected assembly of freemen with power to levy or withhold taxes. In all the colonies, assemblies gave form to colonial demands for autonomy within the empire, and in all of them the assemblies represented owners of private property, landed and commercial. These assemblies were the agencies through which capitalists acquired political power that established the foundations of autonomy that developed into demands for independence – not simply or directly but ultimately unrestrainable.

1 Francis Jennings, "Brother Miquon: Good Lord!" in *The World of William Penn*, ed. Richard S. Dunn and Mary Maples Dunn (Philadelphia: University of Pennsylvania Press, 1986), 195–214; Francis Jennings, "The Scandalous Indian Policy of William Penn's Sons: Deeds and Documents of the Walking Purchase," *Pennsylvania History* 37 (Jan 1970), 19–39.

William's two great goals were to enlarge the empire and to create a sanctuary for his fellow Quakers. He blithely ignored the contradiction between empire and Quaker pacifism, and for an astonishingly long time he was lucky. William's success only seemingly disproves Steven Saunders Webb's dictum that "there are no empires without armies."[2] Though Penn's Quakers did not organize armed forces, their colony was protected by sea by the royal navy that had no pacifist scruples; and its interior was guarded by the Covenant Chain under New York's guidance. The Iroquois in the Covenant Chain were no more pacifistic than the navy. (William Penn's chief aide, James Logan, once remarked, "If we lose the Iroquois, we are gone by land." But Logan was a "defense Quaker.")[3]

There were other Indians in Pennsylvania's orbit. Delaware bands occupied precisely the ground where Penn proposed to build his city of Philadelphia. In such circumstances, Virginia and the Puritans had forcefully driven the native predecessors away. Penn acknowledged native rights and commissioned agents to buy the lands covered by them. The gratified Indians came to revere him, all the more so when he repeated the pattern of negotiation and purchase at the Susquehanna River where he proposed to build a sister city to Philadelphia. That project did not come off. Instead, the Susquehanna Valley became for many years a sanctuary for Indians where remnants of Delaware, Conestoga, Shawnee, Conoy, Tutelo, and Tuscarora communities congregated in their separate villages and governed themselves under the Quaker peace. Even some of the proud Iroquoian Senecas fled to this refuge from the casualties of the Iroquois League's perpetual wars with New France and its allies. There was no other place like it in all of England's colonies.[4]

No one who reads Penn's writings can doubt the sincerity of his intention to "do good' for the Indians and to do it with their consent. Yet a matter of strong practicality was involved in some of his negotiations. His royal charter described boundaries so vaguely that they overlapped on the south with those of Lord Baltimore's Maryland; and on the north Penn claimed so high that the Iroquois Five Nations would have fallen within this province if he had succeeded. In negotiating with Susquehannocks at the head of Chesapeake Bay, and with the Iroquois in their Finger Lakes homeland, Penn aimed to acquire for himself the Indian rights with which to face his competitors. But neither Lord Baltimore nor the duke of York retreated

2 Stephen Saunders Webb, *The Governors General* (Chapel Hill: University of North Carolina Press, 1979), xvii.
3 Benjamin Franklin, *Autobiography*, ed. Leonard W. Labaree et al. (New Haven: Yale University Press, 1964). 187.
4 Paul A. W. Wallace, *Indians in Pennsylvania* (Harrisburg: Pennsylvania Historical and Museum Commission, 1961).

before this strategy; the jurisdictional squabbles over boundaries continued for generations.

Although Pennsylvania's Indian policies distinguished it so sharply, William Penn's death in 1718 opened the way for much change. Because of the colony's feudal nature, its lord's demise created political trauma. Penn had remarried after his first wife's death and he left sons by each wife; each set of the half brothers claimed the whole estate. They went to court. Eventually, John, Thomas, and Richard, sons by second wife Hannah, acquired the province. Of these three, Thomas became executive in charge of the province, and Indians were for Thomas Penn merely a means to make money. He swindled the Delawares out of much land, made an alliance with the Iroquois to beat down Delaware protests, and acquired a colossal fortune from land sales to immigrants, adding additional income from perpetual quitrents.[5]

Thomas left his father's Quaker religion to adopt the Church of England, and he turned punishingly hostile to Quaker control of the provincial assembly. The conflict between the representative assembly and the feudal family reverberated throughout the rest of the colony's existence.

Pennsylvania grew with a great gush. It started fast with William Penn's organized fleets of colonists, picked up speed as German and Swiss immigrants fled Europe's wars and religious oppressions, and made a great spurt in the eighteenth century when English absentee landowners racked rents intolerably high in Ireland. All immigrants were attracted by the province's policy of absolute freedom of worship that contrasted so plainly with New England's Calvinist controls. Many Germans brought money to Pennsylvania with which they bought land and started family farms; they also brought knowledge of agricultural practice that had advanced in Germany beyond anywhere else in Europe. The Irish and Scotch-Irish immigrants seem mostly to have been penniless, but they found opportunity to labor for wages without competition from slaves, and many went west to squat on unbought lands beyond provincial controls. People, money, and labor gave a bonanza to preestablished merchants at Philadelphia whose import–export businesses rocketed upward.

The great flaw in this recipe for success was the power and rapacity of the feudal Penns. Under Thomas Penn's vicious leadership, they fought against measures taken by the provincial assembly, and their policies in Indian affairs eventually led to calamitous hostilities by the hitherto friendly Delawares during the Seven Years War.

Pennsylvania's history during the middle of the eighteenth century has been badly muddled because of Thomas Penn's strenuous efforts to excul-

5 Jennings, *Empire of Fortune*, 25, 28–29, 280–81, 84n36.

pate himself from responsibility for alienating the Indians. Thomas "doctored" documents and hired lawyers to destroy others and to substitute fabrications.[6] Thus, when a Quaker organization exposed his machinations, students trusting the fabrications turned the situation upside down by attributing the Quaker discoveries to spiteful invention. After my two unconfuted books and a number of well-documented articles on this subject, I can no longer respect writers who contrive alibis for Thomas. They must face the evidence.

Pennsylvania's Quaker heritage and its feudal structure delayed the colony's readiness to secede from the British empire when crisis arrived. For religious reasons, Quakers resisted the break, and others hesitated because of the need to dismantle the political structure of lordship as part of the Revolutionary struggle for independence. These problems should not mislead. When the crucial moment came, it was Philadelphia's Franklin who taught strategy to Boston, and Philadelphia's Tom Paine who preached *Common Sense* to all the colonies.

In perspective it seems to me that eighteenth-century Pennsylvania was the embodiment of what the American Revolution is supposed to have achieved, so the irony of what happened there is all the more distressing. Take, for instance, freedom of worship. In colonial Pennsylvania, no church was established by law, and religious toleration was absolute. Even Roman Catholics were permitted to celebrate mass publicly there when it was outlawed everywhere else in the British empire. Thomas Jefferson has been much praised for his achievement of religious toleration in Virginia when it was already a century old in Pennsylvania. Revolutionary Massachusetts, however, remained committed to legalized bigotry.

Politically, the members of Pennsylvania's annually elected assembly represented their constituencies so well that they were returned to office year after year, and most of their decisions were unanimous or nearly so. Hostile writers have made much of disproportionate representation of western counties as compared to the east, but such outcries ignore two rather relevant facts: For much of the century, western population fell far short of the eastern so that representation *by population* was not fairly measured by quotas for *counties*; besides which the western members of assembly usually voted along with the easterners. Indeed the "near west" of Lancaster County was a German stronghold supporting Quaker leadership. Geography was only one of the divisive issues. They were manifested as Calvinist hostility to Quaker pacifism, Quaker religious toleration, and

---

6 For itemized discussion of the false documents, see Jennings, *Ambiguous Iroquois Empire*, App. B.

Quaker accommodation with Indians who had territory desired by western squatters.

One of the more tragic outcomes of the Revolution was the destruction of Quaker middle-class democracy and the Friends' devotion to reciprocity and mutuality. Quakers did not simply decline in power; as will be shown, they were beaten down by indefensibly crooked politics engaged in by the very leaders of the Revolution.

9

COLONIAL VARIETY V: SOUTH CAROLINA

In the "salad bowl" of Britain's mainland colonies (not a melting pot), Africans mixed with Amerindians and varied Europeans. The Indians had been on the scene for thousands of years. At least a substantial proportion of Europeans came voluntarily, along with an undetermined number of indentured servants who had no choice. *All* the Africans were seized by other Africans or Europeans in their homeland and dragged in great distress and at great loss of life to serve as forced labor in European enterprises. Clearly the motives of these varied constituents were as diverse as their persons. In the categories of economic theory, Africans provided much of the labor for Britain's colonies, Indians provided land and labor, and Europeans coerced profit out of the others to create capital.

The intermixture appears exceptionally plainly in South Carolina. Charles Town, South Carolina, began in 1670 under sanction of a feudal charter granted to a set of "proprietors." Persons actually settling were an outwash from the West Indian island of Barbados with some of their African slaves – "a colony of a colony." It is highly significant that slavery had become so deeply rooted in Barbados that "Negroes outnumbered whites . . . as early as 1660."[1] Thus, at the onset of South Carolina's history, its founders were already accustomed to living as a European minority dominating and exploiting African slaves. They had not fled from the horrors of West Indian slavery; on the contrary, as Winthrop D. Jordan remarks, "by the end of the seventeenth century . . . the Barbadian example had combined to yield in South Carolina the most rigorous deprivation of freedom to exist in institutionalized form any where in the English continental colonies."[2] Mild-mannered Richard S. Dunn called it "rape's progress."[3]

---

1 Winthrop D. Jordan, *White Over Black: American Attitudes Toward the Negro, 1550–1812* 1968, reprinted (Baltimore, Md.: Penguin Books, 1969), 63.
2 Ibid., 85.
3 Richard S. Dunn, *Sugar and Slaves: The Rise of the Planter Class in the English West Indies, 1624–1713* (Chapel Hill: University of North Carolina Press, 1972), 73.

The Barbadian immigrants who congregated at Goose Creek near Charles Town were not subsistence farmers struggling against the elements to make a living. Rather, they were men of substance who had come to the mainland for greater tracts of land than were still available on the island. And they were bellicosely aggressive. Some launched into trade with Indians and quickly made themselves masters of the tribes surrounding Charles Town. Irritated by efforts of neighboring Westos to block access by distant tribes, the Goose Creek men warred destructively on the Westos, later letting the Savannahs (Shawnees) move into favored status. But the Goose Creek men aimed at bigger game.

They hired Creeks and Cherokees to raid Franciscan missions in Florida, seizing captives to sell as slaves in the West Indies and paying the hirelings with part of the booty. By 1708 they had taken ten thousand captives and had destroyed the whole mission system of Florida except for some refugees huddling under the guns of St. Augustine.[4] Their desire to save Indian souls was not prominent.

A quick look at some simple statistics reveals the overwhelming importance of those kidnapped Christian converts from the Florida missions. Our source tells us that in 1700, South Carolina held 3,300 whites, 2,400 blacks, and 200 Indian slaves. The numbers changed precipitately in 1710 to 4,200 whites, 4,300 blacks, and 1,500 Indian slaves. Ten years further on, in 1720, the colony had grown to 6,500 whites, 9,900 blacks, and 2,000 Indian slaves. Then, suddenly, in 1730 there were 10,000 whites, *20,000* blacks, and only 500 Indian slaves. It seems clear as day that selling Indians had provided the means for buying Africans, and in 1740 the picture became even more graphic. By that time all the Indian slaves had been disposed of, probably through death, and African numbers had nearly doubled to *39,200* although the number of whites had grown only 50 percent to 15,000.[5]

We need only to supplement these numbers with the information that those Indian slaves were plunder from missions; when that is understood, the figures speak as loudly as any words. The Indians were seized and sold to buy Africans who were both capital and labor in plantation slavery. The exchange was rational. Indian slaves on the mainland were hard to control because of familiarity with the terrain and nearness of refuge among kin and friends. When sold to Barbados, the Indians were as forlorn as Africans on the mainland.

The Goose Creek men thought big. Pushing the advantage of English

---

4 Jerald T. Milanich, "Franciscan Missions and Native Peoples in Spanish Florida," unpublished MS., University of Florida, Gainesville. John H. Hann, *Apalachee: The Land Between the Rivers* (Gainesville: University of Florida Press/Florida State Museum, 1988), Chap. 12.
5 Russell R. Menard, "Financing the Lowcountry Export Boom: Capital and Growth in Early South Carolina," *William and Mary Quarterly*, 3d ser., 51:4 (Oct. 1994), 660.

trade goods being cheaper than the French, they traded and treated with the big tribes to the westward, alarming the French to found Louisiana in response.[6] Consequent struggles between the Carolinians and Louisianans translated into war between English-allied Chickasaws and French-allied Choctaws, deadly to both. Cherokees and Creeks joined in at opportune moments with similar casualties. The determined French built forts and garrisoned them with regular troops to maintain territorial control.

Carolinian bellicosity and arrogance finally boomeranged on the expansionist party in 1715 when nearby Yamasees rose in bloody revolt so destructive that the British crown revoked the colony's charter and Virginia traders eased in to do business with offended surviving Indians. Hostility between the two colonies became the norm.[7] Perhaps it is needless to note that the charter's revocation became a grievance for Carolinians though their leading men seized upon it as an opportunity to grab enormous new grants of land. It is hard to find a fountainhead of devotion to liberty in this miniature empire where African slaves greatly outnumbered the colonial planters.

Other colonies (in the West Indian islands, for example) ignored the centrifugal force of urgings for independence for two more centuries after the mainland yielded to it. Central controls exerted from London through the royal navy still held them on leash, almost literally. Except for noting their difference, these colonies are beyond the scope of the present essay.

The point of this and the last several chapters has been to show diversity in the founding structures of the mainland colonies along with certain similarities in underlying motive forces. Succeeding chapters will show how mutually shared objectives drew highly diverse individuals and institutions into a common struggle.

Richard S. Dunn has paid sorrowful tribute to "the distinctive social and economic formula" developed in the West Indies. "This social mode, a small cadre of white masters driving an army of black slaves . . . shaped three centuries of Caribbean life."[8] It also sustained an arrogant and powerful ruling class in the "colony of a colony" that became South Carolina – one that has been especially virulent as a source of racism throughout its existence.

One must note and describe the real and powerful distinctions between colonies. To lump South Carolina with Pennsylvania as an imperial place of

6 Bernard Pothier, "Le Moyne d'Iberville et d'Ardillieres, Pierre" *Dictionary of Canadian Biography* 2:396–97.
7 Verner W. Crane, *The Southern Frontier, 1670–1732* (Ann Arbor: University of Michigan Press, 1929), 283.
8 Dunn, *Sugar and Slaves*, 336.

refuge for the downtrodden and persecuted is to strain the English language beyond possible tolerance. Yet both colonies grew and evolved in ways that set them eventually in deadlock with their common liege lord, and linked their highly diverse upper classes in armed revolt. Their lower classes behaved divergently, as we shall see.

Part II

———— • ————

FRICTIONS ARISE WITHIN THE EMPIRE

10

"SALUTARY NEGLECT"

Political relations between Britain and its colonies were profoundly affected by political relations and developments within Britain. In a distant echo of the way that great nobles had extracted the Magna Carta from King John, the nobles called Whigs gained a Bill of Rights after ousting James II from the throne in the Glorious Revolution of 1687. Subsequent turmoil involving the monarchy enabled those Whigs to give shaky leadership to the nation. First under Sir Robert Walpole, then under his successors, Parliament and the executive royal branch of government were dominated by an Old Whig oligarchy until kings imported from Hanover learned how to swing their weight against presumptuous nobles.

The situation conduced to easygoing government for the colonies because the Whigs needed colonial collaboration and patronage opportunities. Especially when the duke of Newcastle became head of the functioning government, he became notorious as dispenser of the patronage needed for Whig support.[1] A governor here, a customs collector there, and so on, along with their friends in Parliament and patronage in the home country gave Newcastle the votes he needed in the House of Commons; and his machine stayed strong until the duke of Cumberland "stole" the patronage of the armed forces after suppressing the Jacobite uprising in Scotland in 1745.[2]

For the colonies, Newcastle and his Whigs were easy bosses. Officials wanted posts in the colonies because they were lucrative. The crown did not pay them. Their rewards in salaries and fees came annually by vote of the elected colonial assemblies and were subject to wrangling. Sometimes they were hard to distinguish from outright bribes.

---

1 The lack of scholarly interest in Newcastle is puzzling. His papers are one of the largest collections in the British Library, but until 1974 no biography had been published. Two Americans have done book-length studies, neither fully satisfactory: Ray A. Kelch, *Newcastle, A Duke Without Money: Thomas Pelham-Holles, 1693–1768* (Berkeley: University of California Press, 1974); Reed Browning, *The Duke of Newcastle* (New Haven, Conn.: Yale University Press, 1975).
2 E. M. Lloyd, "William Augustus, Duke of Cumberland," *Dictionary of National Biography*, 342, 344.

The easy supervision intrinsic to this system, dubbed "salutary neglect," let the assemblies gradually acquire more privilege and power in their own hands until they became effectively independent in many respects. They naturally befriended the London Whigs who governed so lightly. Heavy traffic in commerce between Britain and the colonies made another strong tie between merchant classes on both sides of the Atlantic and gave the Whigs powerful support from the City of London.

On the other hand, many men of power felt uneasy because the degree of autonomy rising in the colonies seemed to be "tending toward an independency." To these men, neglect seemed anything but salutary, and they demanded that colonial "liberties" be cut back. Such men tended to cluster around the king and his associates as Tories opposed to the Whigs.

Newcastle and his Old Whigs managed to keep control until the Seven Years War against France during which the Tories, led by the duke of Cumberland, seized the patronage of the armed forces. Newcastle hung on to enough of the remaining patronage to stay in office until King George II died and George III ascended the throne.

Then, however, the patronage underwent transformation as George III took it over himself and gained control of Parliament. This third George determined to *conform* the colonists to full obedience to the royal will. Thus ended salutary neglect, and in response thus aroused the indignant spirit of colonial resistance.

Even under the regime of salutary neglect, life was not all wine and roses for the crown and its colonies, nor could it be. Both sides wanted things rejected by the other side. It is illuminating to glance, however briefly, at some of the sources of irritation. These are traceable empirically to matters of power and riches.

English interest in colonization was not altruistic. Englishmen never doubted that the function of colonies was to enrich investors and merchants in England. Occasionally, to pretend noble motives, hard-nosed men of power prated sanctimoniously about saving lost savage souls, but such remarks notably were not followed up with plans and programs. They bear the earmarks of devices to extract money and support from the gullible pious. In modern times their invokers would be televangelists.[3]

How could colonies be made to pay? In earliest days, "planting" of a colony did not seem necessary for gain from the great fisheries of the Grand Banks off Newfoundland or trade in cheap goods for Amerindian furs and skins. Planting of permanent settlements became attractive as a means of

---

3 See Wilcomb E. Washburn, "Philanthropy and the American Indian: The Need for a Model," *Ethnohistory* 15 (1968), 53–54.

establishing naval bases to harry Spanish ships and as a way to simply seize territory from weaker peoples. An extra motive came into play when Virginians learned how to grow tobacco for international commerce. Profit from this "sot weed" (as hostile James I called it) became so rich that it instantly became Virginia's staple and a specialty of great merchants in Britain. The commercial links so created expanded and strengthened until they became integral to prosperity on both sides of the Atlantic and essential to relationships between the empire's center and its rim. And, as Virginia grew, its profitability expanded.

That was well and good, but an interloper siphoned off some of the profit. The quintessentially commercial Dutch, who dominated the "carrying trade" between other countries of Europe, caught wind of possibilities in Virginia. Their ships pushed up Chesapeake Bay and made off with cargoes that English merchants regarded as property to be reserved for themselves. Indignant Parliament enacted the first Navigation Act in 1651 to require that colonial products be shipped to England in ships of Great Britain or the plantations. More Navigation Acts followed in 1660 – enumerating colonial articles to be shipped exclusively to England – and in 1663 – duties on sugar, tobacco, and other products going from one colony to another.

Parliament's anger did not reflect the Virginia planters' feeling that Dutch competition was good for their trade. Some of them, during Bacon's Rebellion, even discussed the possibility of seceding from England to put their colony under Dutch protection.[4] Virginians developed an uppity attitude toward England that did not decline as their numbers increased.

The colonies of New England also resented royal control of their commerce; and they, too, elevated themselves in concept to parity with the crown. Massachusetts's magistrates referred to their jurisdiction as a "nation" rather than a province, and they required an oath of allegiance to themselves rather than the crown.[5] For both Virginia and Massachusetts, reality intruded on daydreaming when neighboring Indians arose in arms, and the royal navy brought commissioners to demand explanations and set matters to rights.

As to sovereignty exercised through the Navigation Acts, colonial merchants discovered a peaceful, highly illicit method of adjusting their desires to Parliament's commands. They smuggled, and they shared some of smuggling's profits with merchants in England so that the proceedings became institutionalized.

4 Stephen Saunders Webb, *1676: The End of American Independence* (New York: Alfred A. Knopf, 1984), 68–69.
5 Minutes, 1 April and 14 May 1634, in *Records of the Governor and Company of the Massachusetts Bay in New-England*, ed. Nathaniel B. Shurtleff, 5 vols. (Boston: 1853–54), 1:116–17.

The colonists were quite willing to acknowledge royal sovereignty in this fashion, but not all Englishmen were happy with it. A powerful minority felt that laws were made to be obeyed. Their attitude became dominant after the enthronement of George III.

11

———— • ————

ROYAL PREROGATIVE IN AMERICA

During the reign of King George I, the first of Britain's Hanoverian kings, the great Whig families had politics generally under control. That situation changed after the 1745 rising of Highland Scots aiming to overthrow George II and to reinstate a Stuart on the throne. The frightened Whigs reacted violently by giving full support to the duke of Cumberland's suppression of the Highlanders by massacre and rapine. To Scots he became "the Butcher." To governing Englishmen, until they learned more about him, he was a savior. Loyal Scots in Parliament warded off suspicions of treason by voting the king's desires.

"The Butcher" was William Augustus, second son of the king, who moved aggressively to cut down Whig power and restore the king's power to rule by untrammeled prerogative. The startled Whig oligarchs realized too late that they had increased the power of the Hanoverian monarch by helping to suppress the Stuart pretender. Duke Cumberland first struck heavily at Whig patronage in the army which had been a major source of strength since triumphant John Churchill, duke of Marlborough, had headed the troops. Cumberland, upon being made captain general (commander in chief) took the appointment of officers into his own hands without reference, as formerly, to the ministry. So doing, he cut off a major base of support for the Whigs. Many regimental colonels were also Members of Parliament who looked to the crown for leadership and emoluments. As Bernhard Knollenberg remarks, "One of the outstanding sources of the King's dominant influence in Parliament unquestionably was his power to appoint, dismiss, replace and transfer officers of the armed services at pleasure."[1]

Cumberland took leadership of Tories who aimed at reviving war with France, and when the province of Virginia precipitated a frontier scuffle

---

1 Bernhard Knollenberg, *Origin of the American Revolution, 1759–1766*, new revised ed. (New York: Collier Books, 1961), 93.

with New France, Cumberland circumvented the Whigs' wary duke of Newcastle by sending extra troops to America ostentatiously in order to heat up the conflict.[2] British colonies abutted on tribal territories on all sides and kept constantly thrusting salients into those "dependencies of the colonies." Living among the tribes were French *voyageurs* and *coureurs de bois*, traders of European goods for Indian-processed peltry; and other Frenchmen massed in New France, New Orleans, and in towns along the Great Lakes and Mississippi Valley. South of British Georgia were the Spaniards of Florida and the tribes allied to them. By the middle of the eighteenth century, British colonials felt confidently able to handle those Indians by means of their own experienced methods. "Settlers" – mostly from Ireland and Scotland – squatted on lands in the "back country" until rich speculators caught up with them and demanded purchase money or rent, upon which the settlers moved on to repeat the process more westerly. Occasional local uprisings by Indians were charged off mentally by governments to profit and loss.

Change came quite suddenly when imperial British aggression decided the French to strike back. When the Ohio Company of Virginia moved to take control of the Ohio Valley by projecting a fort and town at the junction of the Allegheny and Monongahela Rivers, French troops drove out the Virginian builders and made the fort for themselves. They even bought the British building materials in something like a going-out-of-business sale. Thus Fort Duquesne grew up and its garrison dominated Indians over a great range.[3]

French reactions left Newcastle with no option but to go along with still more troops and a determined effort to capture French forts that seemed to threaten British colonies. Cumberland thus seized the initiative, which he turned into increased use of the royal prerogative. He made a political general – his own man – into *commander-in-chief over all forces in the colonies, with authority overriding the governments already established*. Cumberland's man was Major General Edward Braddock, a domineering, dictatorial martinet who backed demands with threats.[4]

Braddock's appointment marked the beginning of new policy by the Hanoverian kings and their Tory supporters. As Undersecretary William

2 T. R. Clayton, "The Duke of Newcastle, the Earl of Halifax, and the American Origins of the Seven Years' War," *The Historical Journal* 24 (1981), 571–603.
3 William A. Hunter, *Forts on the Pennsylvania Frontier, 1753–1758* (Harrisburg: Pennsylvania Historical and Museum Commission, 1960), 47–48; deposition of Ensign Edward Ward, 30 June 1756, mss., Etting Coll., Ohio Co., 1:110, Hist. Soc. of Pa.
4 Wm. Shirley to Morris, 23 May 1755, Indian and Military Affairs of Pa., mss., 309, American Philosophical Society, 309; Philip C. Yorke, *The Life and Correspondence of Philip Yorke, Earl of Hardwicke, Lord High Chancellor of Great Britain*, 3 vols. (Cambridge: Cambridge University Press, 1913), 2:357.

Knox would realize when he came to understand how disastrous that policy was, it arose from "zeal for making the Crown absolute in America."[5]

The so-called Seven Years War between Britain and France exacerbated all the conflicts and tensions between Britain and its colonies. Against the judgments and inclinations of Whig ministers led by the duke of Newcastle, war fever was generated by militaristic Tories led by the duke of Cumberland. Similar scheming caused French militarists to adopt a policy of ringing Britain's mainland American colonies with forts and garrisons. With these, the French purposed to control great numbers of tribal Indians and thus compensate in some degree for New France's inferior numbers of colonial manpower. Each country's war hawks aroused and stimulated the other's.[6]

British Whigs hoped to frustrate French policy by controlled local military action, but Tories sensed opportunity to seize power through war measures, and they maneuvered to escalate brushfire actions to full-scale war. Cumberland, as captain general of Britain's forces, forced the issues, seconded by Newcastle's double-crossing cousin, the earl of Halifax.

The ensuing conflict has been presented as intended to protect Americans from French expansion, but this is nonsensical. The French were entirely on the defensive and had no resources to overpower British colonials who outmanned them twenty to one. The aggressive, expanding party was Britain, and its objective, according to Secretary Thomas Robinson in 1754, was "the defence of His Majesty's just rights and dominions in those parts."[7] Robinson said nothing in this message to the governors about protecting His Majesty's loyal colonial subjects. They, however, understood him well. When General Edward Braddock, in 1755, summoned the governors to a meeting for the raising of war funds, they confessed themselves unable to satisfy his demands because of expected resistance from their elected assemblies that controlled finances. The governors could and did get some financial grants to aid His Majesty's troops, but these were not of a size to betoken fear of French aggression, let alone gratitude for defending troops. No way were the provincial assemblies going to let any Englishmen dictate as taxes what they regarded as contributions.[8] Colonists and troops regarded each other as aliens with little mutuality of interests or desires.

Thus the measures taken to support and maintain those troops, and the

---

5 Jack P. Greene, *Understanding the American Revolution: Issues and Actors* (Charlottesville: University Press of Virginia, 1995), 11.
6 Memoir of La Galissoniere, in *Documents Relative to the Colonial History of the State of New York [N.Y. Col. Docs.]* ed. E. B. O'Callaghan and Berthold Fernow, 15 vols. (Albany, N. Y.: Weed, Parsons & Co., 1856–87), 10:222–24; Etienne Taillemite, "Barrin de La Galissoniere, Roland-Michel" in *Dictionary of Canadian Biography* 3:28–30.
7 Robinson to the governors, 26 Oct 1754, *N.Y. Col. Docs.* 6:915.
8 Francis Jennings, *The Empire of Fortune* (New York: W.W. Norton, 1988), 146–47.

troops' rough and often cruel behavior toward those "foreign" colonists, soon produced frictions. The armies' commanders made no effort to win the hearts and minds of the people among whom they lived. General Braddock and his successor, Lord Loudoun, bullied and raged against colonial resistance to rule by deputized royal prerogative, and they compounded fault by incompetence that verged in Loudoun on rank cowardice. Who could respect arrogance in such losers?

Colonials still professed loyalty, but they lost respect. Actual hostility was but a step away.

General Braddock's priority mission was to conquer Fort Duquesne, but Braddock, unfortunately, was a political general lacking sense enough to accept Indian volunteers. He rejected an offer of help from the Delawares, and he was routed and killed by other Indians with whom the French had prudently allied.[9]

After that traumatic crisis, the "back country" experienced calamity. New France's Governor General Vaudreuil adopted a policy of *beaucoup de ravages* and his agents organized Indian raiding parties to descend upon defenseless backwoods families with fire and hatchet. (Each such party was accompanied by a French officer attired like the Indians. He was to make sure that they were sufficiently savage.) The result, as Vaudreuil complacently informed the French ministry, was havoc and much flight of refugees.[10]

Besides the direct effect of such northern raids, they frightened distant South Carolinians into nightmarish imaginings of forays that might release slaves to freedom or, worse yet, incite them to rise up against their masters. Such horrors dared not be risked. Thus, when appeals for troops came to South Carolina, the masters responded with money but not men because they needed all available manpower to guard against insurrection.

On another front, colonial troops from Massachusetts captured Forts Beausejour and Gaspereau on the peninsula leading from the mainland to Nova Scotia, thus guaranteeing that province against French attack. In New York, William Johnson fought the French at Crown Point, again with colonial troops but also with Iroquois Indians. The battle was a draw, but the French advance was stopped, never to advance again, and Johnson captured the French commanding general-in-chief, Jean-Armand, baron de Dieskau. The lesson was clear: The French could beat British Regulars, and colonials could beat the French.

9 Delaware chief Shingas told how Braddock rejected the Delawares' offer to help: "The Captivity of Charles Stuart, 1755–57," ed. Beverley W. Bond Jr., *Mississippi Valley Historical Review* 13 (1926–27), 58–81.

10 *N.Y. Col. Docs.* 10:410–12; *Relation De la Prise du Fort Georges, or Guillaume-Henry* (Paris: Bureau d'Adresse aux Galleries du Louvre, 18 Oct 1757), 1. Found in John Carter Brown Library.

British colonials concluded that the crown's troops could not defend them; they would have to defend themselves. Both Indians and colonials changed their minds about military power. As Benjamin Franklin commented later in his *Autobiography*, "This whole Transaction gave us Americans the first Suspicion that our exalted Ideas of the Progress of British Regulars had not been well founded."[11]

Independence from Britain, though not yet on the colonial agenda, ceased to be unthinkable.

Though the Tory militarists were getting their war, formal declaration of the expanding conflict waited until 1756. Meantime everything seemed to go wrong in 1755. Even the conquest of France's Acadian forts turned sour because of what followed in Nova Scotia.

Despite Lord Halifax's effort to populate Nova Scotia with Scottish immigrants (hence the name), most of the colonials already on the scene were Catholic *habitant* descendants of the French founders of Acadia (much intermixed with Indians) and British governors worried about the allegiance of such people. Though long conquered and ceded to Britain, could they be relied on as war approached? The Board of Trade ruled in 1754 that an unqualified oath of allegiance must be required for legal validation of land ownership. Representatives of Acadian communities refused to take the oath of allegiance in 1755, and British officials faced the question of what they would do about it.

Governor Charles Lawrence and his council decided to get rid of their problem by getting rid of its makers. Lawrence ordered deportation of the nonjuring Acadians, in doing which he aroused much ill will among the colonies upon whom he literally dumped those Acadians. Nobody volunteered to take them in. They were simply put ashore, and from that moment responsibility for shelter, security, and upkeep devolved upon their involuntary hosts. No compensation was given by the British crown or its deputy in Nova Scotia, and the receiving colonies found that Acadians in diaspora were still as bullheadedly pro-French as they had been in Nova Scotia. Added to which, they refused to work for their support on the plea that they were prisoners of war, so the hazard of disloyalty was compounded by large expense of maintenance.[12] In the midst of war!

It is a horrid story of stupidity and viciousness, but this is not the place to explain details. My point is simply that the Acadian deportation made more colonists than the Acadians – from Massachusetts to Georgia – bitter against the British government. There was no possible way of pretending

11 Benjamin Franklin, *Autobiography*, ed. Leonard W. Labaree et al. (New Haven, Conn.: Yale University Press, 1964), 225–26.
12 Lawrence Henry Gipson, *The British Empire Before the American Revolution*, 15 vols. (New York: Alfred A. Knopf, 1958–70), 6:263–85; F. Jennings, *Empire of Fortune*, 177–84.

that this episode had been contrived for the benefit of His Majesty's loyal subjects. Apart from the inherent injustice of the proceedings, it was a ham-handed imposition of royal prerogative that nobody liked even one little bit.

General Braddock was succeeded in command by Massachusetts Governor William Shirley who soon demonstrated incompetence. So it was easy for Cumberland to sack Shirley and send his own man again. This one was John Campbell, fourth earl of Loudoun and a Scot with pretensions vastly greater than his accomplishments. But loyal to the royal.[13]

Loudoun arrived at New York with a mission.[14] He was to enforce a new colonial policy adopted by the Hanoverian kings and their Tory supporters at the head of whom was Loudoun's patron, the duke of Cumberland. There was nothing subtle about this policy. It was to be effected by a commander in chief over all forces in the colonies, with royal authority overriding the governments already established.

These commanders, Braddock and Loudoun, made no effort to conciliate the people over whom they were thus given arbitrary authority. General Braddock died in battle before fully disclosing his political purpose, but Lord Loudoun left no room for doubt. Loudoun bullied and raged against colonial resistance to his rule by deputized royal prerogative. He threatened to quarter troops to punish resisters, and he did quarter men on the people of Albany, New York.[15]

Colonials still professed loyalty, but they lost respect; actual hostility was but a step away. That step would be postponed when William Pitt gained leadership of the war and sensed what was needed to get colonial collaboration. He would withdraw Lord Loudoun and change policy. Until France was defeated and New France became British, royal prerogative would lapse into latency. But it stayed very much alive and re-emerged strongly in partnership with Parliament with the Stamp Act in 1765.

Among the utterances of Tory mythology is the statement that Loudoun "created the army that won the Seven Years War."[16] How does this statement compare to empirically verified facts?

Loudoun served as commander in chief over all British forces in America from May 1756 until William Pitt could recall him at the end of December 1757. During that period, forces under Loudoun's command lost Fort

---

13 T. F. Henderson, "Campbell, John, fourth Earl of Loudoun," *Dictionary of National Biography* 8:376.

14 Incomprehensibly to me, Loudoun is missing from histories of the American colonies. I have spent six months with his papers in the Henry E. Huntington Library. See my *Empire of Fortune*, 282–311.

15 Ibid., 297–311.

16 Ira D. Gruber, "Campbell, John" in *The Blackwell Encyclopedia of the American Revolution*, ed. Jack P. Greene and J. R. Pole (Cambridge, Mass.: Blackwell, 1994), 710.

Oswego, a place essential to British relations with Indian tribes, and Fort William Henry where a second notorious massacre took place.

In America, Loudoun busied himself with exercising his deputized royal prerogative in various domineering ways. He stormed and menaced in ways that made the behavior of General Braddock seem positively polite. His only genuine attacks were made against the colonials whom he was supposed to be protecting. The colonists were to remember that he demanded winter quarters for his troops, and when they were withheld by families fearful of such boarders, he put men in with those frightened homesteaders by main force. Franklin managed to provide those winter quarters in Philadelphia barracks, but Pennsylvania simply ignored Loudoun's orders to stop negotiating with the Indians who raided the province's backwoods.

Against the French, Loudoun's "prudence" (his own term) verged close upon cowardice. (His previous record during the Highlanders' rising strengthens that judgment. William Pitt mourned his avoidance of "the least Appearance of Danger.")[17]

Loudoun embargoed colonial ports on the supposition that he thereby hid from the amused French his mobilization for a campaign against Fortress Louisbourg, and the embargo dealt a heavy blow at colonial commerce. He worsened its effect by closing a dragnet around the city of New York in order to seize and impress seamen into his fleet, after which sailors ashore hid when ships of the royal navy appeared offshore, and merchants lost their crews. He took his great force to camp in a staging area at Halifax, Nova Scotia, where he practiced and practiced and practiced; but, having made massive preparations, he dawdled until bad weather made it too late for his combined army–navy operations against Louisbourg. His hundreds of casualties occurred from illness rather than combat. Except for campaigns against British colonials, Loudoun was allergic to actual combat.

While all these preparations were going on, French General Montcalm took advantage of Loudoun's absence in order to make his own attack, a real one, against British Fort William Henry. Loudoun had left General Daniel Webb in charge, and Webb immediately *ran away* from supporting the fort's garrison. The result was a bloody massacre and a lot of alibis.[18]

So far as the colonists were concerned, Loudoun aroused feelings of strong aversion to the royal prerogative that he represented and the occupying royal army that he commanded. The most stubborn of them, though also the most militaristic, were the assemblymen of Massachusetts. Far from trembling in fear before his menaces, they locked horns and held back the men and money he demanded.

17 *Pennsylvania Gazette* No. 1525, 16 March 1758, p. 1.
18 John Entick, *The General History of the Late War* . . . 5 vols. (London: Edward Dilly and John Millan, 1763–64), vol. 2; Jennings, *Empire of Fortune*, chap. 14.

Once again, events abroad determined occurrences in America. Loudoun's sponsor Cumberland, the most aggressive advocate of royal prerogative, fell from grace. He had led an army in Europe so stupidly that he was forced, without a fight, to surrender a whole army to a French opponent. The army was intended to protect George II's beloved Hanover, and George was furious. Cumberland went into temporary retirement, and William Pitt emerged as the dynamic new, win-the-war leader of the government. Pitt learned how Loudoun had alienated the colonists, and Pitt immediately changed course. He withdrew Loudoun from America and buried the issue of prerogative for the time being. Pitt made the war effort cooperative between crown and colonies instead of imposing demands by the crown for unquestioning compliance by the colonies.

The effect was electric. No sooner did the Massachusetts assembly hear of Pitt's new policies than they voted to give all the men and money requested of them, and more besides. The newly inspired colonies turned from dutiful, grudging obedience at best to enthusiastic effort; and the doleful list of Braddock's and Loudoun's defeats soon became a series of great victories.

So the British Regular armies did win, after all, not so? And were their victories not the product of Loudoun's organizing?

No.

After a long string of defeats, the first British victory was won by Lt. Col. John Bradstreet, a native of Nova Scotia who had won rank by merit instead of purchase or political pull. Bradstreet recruited colonial boatmen and a task force of nearly three thousand troops from New York, Massachusetts, and Rhode Island, of whom fewer than 5 percent were British Regulars. On 25 August 1758 Bradstreet landed his secret force before Fort Frontenac, the key to control of Lake Ontario. He captured sixty pieces of cannon, eight hundred thousand livres worth of provisions and goods, and the entire French navy on the Great Lakes; and he sailed triumphantly home without the loss of a single man.[19] But Loudoun had excluded Bradstreet from military councils for political reasons.

Major General James Abercromby organized an attack against Ticonderoga, failed miserably, and, as the French counterattacked, Abercromby vanished from view. (Nobody knows where he hid.) Nova Scotian Bradstreet took over and prevented total disaster.

Brigadier John Forbes, also Regular, was assigned to capture Fort Duquesne where Braddock had made such a fiasco. Forbes was not the recipient of Loudoun's creativity in any respect; Forbes had to recruit most

19 "Bradstreet, John," *Dictionary of Canadian Biography* 4:85; William G. Godfrey, *Pursuit of Profit and Preferment in Colonial North America* (Waterloo, Ont.: Wilfrid Laurier University Press, 1982), 125–32.

of his own troops from colonials and to somehow produce support from politically feuding Pennsylvanians. Fortunately, unlike Braddock, he had sense enough to realize his need for Indian allies; and almost miraculously he teamed up with Pennsylvania's leading Quaker pacifist [!] to woo the Delaware Indians away from the French. The partners succeeded, the Indians changed sides, and the French abandoned and burned their fort.[20] The scourge of Indian raids was lifted from the "back country." The odd-couple partnership cannot be found in the texts.

Thus the war was turned around by no device of John Campbell, Lord Loudoun; and when the Regulars finally began to win their own victories, they had new commanders. Amherst took Louisbourg, Wolfe took Quebec, and then Amherst rolled up French defenses to the ultimate capitulation of Montreal. In all this, Loudoun's contribution was to stir up such hatred among the provincials that they perpetuated it in their litany of the sins of the monarch: The king, wrote Thomas Jefferson, "has affected to render the Military independent of and superior to the Civil power."

Let it be stressed: Loudoun stormed and botched his way through the colonies by authority of unrestrained royal prerogative and nothing else. In short, Loudoun and his activities were Tory in both the broadest and the narrowest senses of the word: He represented overweening authority dead set against the colonies' governance of themselves, and he was the direct agent of the king and the king's son Cumberland, bypassing the ministers of Britain's government.

The colonists resisted and dragged their feet until imperial policies changed under a new chief minister, William Pitt, sometimes a Tory himself but a rational one who gave priority to defeating France rather than subjecting British colonials. Instead of imitating Loudoun's bellicose arbitrariness, Pitt solicited colonials' cooperation, and got it, and together they won the Seven Years War in America.

For the time being, the ministry in London refrained from further efforts to bring the colonies to heel by general exercise of the prerogative, but the recess was only temporary. So far as the ministers were concerned, concessions had been made to colonists' autonomy only as a necessity of war. The possibility of independence weighed heavily on the ministers' minds as they mulled and debated means to forestall it. These means included exertion of the prerogative in specific instances.

Braddock's and Loudoun's forays with the prerogative have vanished almost entirely from our histories. Braddock is reported only as the loser of a critical battle; Loudoun is not even mentioned in the *Documents of*

---

20 Jennings, *Empire of Fortune*, Chap. 17.

American History compiled by Henry Steele Commager. (My copy is the seventh edition.) In general the Seven Years War is skimmed over as a sort of necessary embarrassment to be gotten out of the way with as little attention as possible.

I think the Founding Fathers remembered the time more vividly. One complaint spelled out in the Declaration of Independence was the king's grievous fault "for quartering large bodies of armed troops among us." The people of Albany, New York, had good reason to resent Loudoun's oppression in that respect.

12

---•---

WAR IN PRINCIPLE

Because the strains created by dynastic war triggered colonial resentments against Great Britain, it is necessary to realize that most colonists accepted war as a fact of life and sometimes as a very useful instrument of policy – *their* policies. War against Indians made possible the seizure of lands that was the colonists' reason for being in America. Virginians had conquered the Powhatans; South Carolinians wiped out the Yamasees; Marylanders joined Virginians to attack Susquehannocks; New Englanders massacred Pequots and Narragansetts; New Yorkers negotiated with Iroquois to war against New France. Only Rhode Island and Pennsylvania renounced war against Indians, in Rhode Island's case partly from prudence; in Pennsylvania's from principle.

Pennsylvania's Quakers and sectarian pacifist immigrants to the province preached peace; and, to the extent that circumstance allowed, they practiced what they preached. This behavior got them reviled and despised by their more belligerent contemporaries (and some historians), and it snared them into severe punishment during the American Revolution.

Why, then, did Britain's dynastic wars that revived in mid-eighteenth century arouse resistance and hostility from colonists who were in no way antiwar? The short answer is that these were not the colonists' wars as the colonists mostly understood. By mid-century these colonists had grown rich and strong and cockily confident of winning combat on land against the French and Spanish colonials who numbered not one in twenty as compared to British manpower. Britain's colonists wanted the empire's dynastic wars to serve colonial interests.

When Massachusetts men saw Franco-British war as a chance to seize Cape Breton island by capturing Fortress Louisbourg in 1745 – and thus gaining control of vast regions of fisheries – they were angered to see Britain restoring Louisbourg by treaty in 1748 in exchange for India's Madras. The point was very plain. What Massachusetts conquered was merely a counter to serve Britain's interests.

Some Virginians, however, managed to identify their own interest with the crown's. A group of the gentry lusted after land beyond the Appalachian Mountains that had hitherto served as a barrier against entry into lands occupied by Indians and claimed by France. The "fine, flaming gentlemen" of Virginia were not deterred by an additional embarrassment of the land falling within Pennsylvania's chartered bounds. Looking ahead, these Virginians set up their own counterclaim by treating with the Iroquois in 1744 when they obtained signatures to a cession of "all the lands within the said colony [of Virginia] as it is now *or hereafter may be* peopled and bounded by his said Majesty."[1] Since Virginia's charter conferred a northern boundary that, if extended in a straight line, would have brought Alaska within it, the conclusion is not hard to reach that some "pen and ink work" had been performed on the illiterate Indians.

With this grand blank check, the Virginians formed the Ohio Company of Virginia in 1750 and persuaded the very willing crown to join their enterprise. The Company sent an agent to look over the desired territory. He found it beautiful. So had the Indians who had retired there after being pushed out of the East. They correctly suspected what was afoot, and they demonstrated hostility. The crown put up a thousand pounds for an unprecedentedly lavish present to soften up the Indians at a new treaty in 1752 at Logstown (Ambridge, Pa.). At Logstown, Virginia's commissioners did some more pen and ink work and made some backroom deals to get confirmation of their 1744 deed. (The boys in the backroom were won over by time-tested methods of bribery.)[2]

All set now, Virginia sent young George Washington to tell the French to go away from Virginia's territory, but the commander who received George was not easily to be argued out of his belief that it was French territory. He besotted George and attendant Iroquois, and he sent the young emissary home with a polite rejection.

The contest was just beginning. Washington came back with a troop of provincials to compel the French to leave. They botched the mission, were surrounded and captured, and returned home to Virginia on ignominious parole. So as not to be misunderstood, the French emphasized their determination to hold the territory in question by building Fort Duquesne where the Allegheny and Monongahela Rivers meet to form the Ohio.

Thus, cooperation between Virginia's embryonic empire and Britain's bigger one created an incident that everyone knew would have to be settled by armed force. But not everyone was wildly enthusiastic at the prospect. New England nursed a grudge at having been deprived of the spoil of

---

1 Deed, 2 July 1744, mss. Original in Va. State Library, Richmond, Va. Facsimile in Iroquois Treaty Archive, Newberry Library.
2 Jennings, *Empire of Fortune*, Chap. 3.

Louisbourg. New Yorkers worried over the involvement of "their" Iroquois Indians. Pennsylvania's assembly was against war on principle, and the province's Proprietary Thomas Penn was determined to prevent Virginia from stealing "his" land on the Ohio.

French ministers desperately wanted to keep the British from "invading" the great Mississippi Valley to which they laid claim. They were well aware of the disproportionately small numbers of French colonials compared to what seemed like a British colossus; but the French ministers were determined to hold the wall of the Appalachians.

The Indians on the scene knew too well that they were powerless by themselves to defend their homes. Their only hope was to play one empire against the other.

In England, King George II and the duke of Cumberland rode roughshod over Whig hesitations that arose because Whig leaders Newcastle and Hardwicke foresaw how war would erode their own power and strengthen the Tories. They were right. What they feared came to pass.

13

———— • ————

IRRITANTS

Another of the intraimperial struggles occurring during the French and Indian War found Virginians plunging into a conflict specific to their own province. The account here given rests upon the description by Bernhard Knollenberg in Chapter 3 of *Origin of the American Revolution, 1759–1766*.[1]

A drought in 1758 drove up the price of tobacco to the point where it was worth three times normal. This posed a special question for the House of Burgesses because a ten-year-old law required that their established Church of England clergy should be paid in tobacco stipulated at 17,280 pounds per year. To conform to the old law would have cost extravagantly. Accordingly, the Burgesses amended the old law to reduce clergy compensation to normal value. The amount of tobacco due was cut back to what it would fetch in the market if sold for two pence a pound. Hence the resulting quarrel became known as the Two Penny Act dispute.

The clergy, who had been fondly dwelling on dreams of a windfall, protested loudly. They sent Rev. John Camm to lay their case before the crown, and he enlisted the strong support of Thomas Sherlock, Bishop of London.

This toughly assertive bishop assailed Virginia's Two Penny Act on grounds that it overthrew the 1748 act that "could not be repealed by a less power than made it" which was the crown's final approval. Sherlock presented the Burgesses' new law of 1758 as an attempt against a royal edict that "in some times would have been called Treason, and I do not know any other name for it in our law."[2] This was wartime, a time when *treason* is a potent curse. Sherlock's outcry pushed the dispute through official channels until the Privy Council "disallowed" Virginia's law – that is, vetoed it – and several clerics filed suit in Virginia to collect their bonanza.

---

1 Bernhard Knollenberg, *Origin of the American Revolution, 1759–1766*, new revised ed. (New York: Collier Books, 1961), Chap. 3.
2 Ibid., 59.

The performance won no love from the Burgesses for either the established clergy or the crown supporting them by royal prerogative. Influential Richard Bland argued in a pamphlet that the prerogative should be used for the people's good "and not for their Destruction."[3]

Two of the suits for damages were decided against the complaining clergymen – one by a jury, the other by judges. A third case, brought by Rev. James Maury, saw young Patrick Henry as defense counsel, and Henry was in fine form. A king who disallowed acts like the one in dispute, he cried – and his remarks were recorded – such a king "from being the father of his people degenerated into a Tyrant, and forfeits all right to his subjects' obedience." "Treason" cried out opposing counsel, but the jury sided with Henry. They settled a suit for £288 in damages by an award of one penny.[4] All of this happened seven years before Patrick Henry's more famous outburst in the House of Burgesses.

The whole proceeding highlights how the treasured independence of judges and juries was essential in the imperial system to colonial autonomy. Expanded jurisdiction of the admiralty courts, when decreed after the Seven Years War, aroused far more hostility than a mere bureaucratic reorganization because those admiralty courts functioned without juries and with judges appointed by the crown. Colonists regarded them correctly as royal power exerted directly against colonial liberties.

The means used by Virginians to struggle against royal power were less flamboyant than the riots to come in Boston's streets, but no one in Massachusetts spoke up more strongly than Patrick Henry; and his jury gave a verdict as strong as those of the defiant juries in the printers' cases in London.[5]

At about the same time that the Two Penny Act stirred Virginia's interest in independence of judges, an act of the Pennsylvania assembly brought the issue to crisis at the Privy Council. In Pennsylvania the lords proprietary appointed and dismissed all judges at pleasure. Judges were wholly dependent on proprietary favor. A pamphlet argued that "Pennsylvanians should enjoy the same valuable right belonging to Englishmen – protection from a subservient judiciary."[6]

Complications from legislative battles during the Seven Years War persuaded Governor William Denny that the Penns would recall him for being insufficiently inflexible, so he suddenly made friends with the assembly and was rewarded with a thousand pounds for passing a series of acts that pre-

---

3 Ibid., 62.   4 Ibid., 64–65.   5 See Chap. 18, below.
6 Benjamin H. Newcomb, *Franklin and Galloway: A Political Partnership* (New Haven: Yale University Press, 1972), 61.

viously he would have vetoed on instructions from the proprietaries. The new laws were conceived by Benjamin Franklin's legislative partner and assembly boss, Joseph Galloway, who discovered the opportunity and arranged the pay off.

Only one of the laws is noticed here. It ordered a change of judges' tenure to be terminated only upon application by the assembly. In legal terms this was tenure on good behavior – essentially for life – instead of being at the whim of the proprietary lords; and it followed precisely the plan that had given life tenure to British judges after the Glorious Revolution's Act of Settlement in 1701 created judges who could not be dismissed by a king unless Parliament asked him to do so. In practice, British judges had acquired life tenure with immense political consequences. The Pennsylvania assembly wanted the same right for their province. In Newcomb's words, they "demonstrated their view that the curtailment of executive privilege and the enlargement of legislative power were fundamental to the liberties of Englishmen on both sides of the Atlantic."[7]

The law passed in 1759 and was duly forwarded to Franklin to carry it through usual channels for royal approval. Lawyers for Proprietary Thomas Penn immediately challenged it. We need not follow it through the maze of official agencies. It is enough to notice that the Privy Council disagreed sharply with the act's justifications and disallowed it in June 1760. More accurately, the Council agreed with the act's reasoning but sided against it. "It was not expedient for the Interest of either the Mother Country or the Colonies, that judges in the plantations should hold their places *Quam diu se bene qesserint*" (during good behavior). Council felt it could not "give countenance" to an opinion of the act's being beneficial "least we should excite a just jealousy in the other Colonys."[8]

In short, the government wanted no more independent judges. Its unexpressed reasons were highly practical as events in London demonstrated. Independent judges there defended liberties that government was trying to suppress.

A glance may be permitted at the authorship of Pennsylvania's aborted act. Joseph Galloway contributed to the ongoing struggle for liberty despite his subsequent refusal to join the Revolution and his wholehearted adoption of the Loyalist cause. Before that traumatic crisis, Galloway, with Franklin, helped "to maintain the primacy of the legislature [and thus] strengthened the tradition of resistance to executive authority."[9] Ironically, Pennsylvania's assembly wanted independent judges as defense against the

---

7 Ibid., 39.
8 *The Papers of Benjamin Franklin* [hereafter cited as *Franklin Papers*], ed. Leonard W. Labaree et al. (New Haven, Conn.: Yale University Press, 1959–) 9:161, 162n.
9 Newcomb, *Franklin and Galloway*, 292.

executive while in England the already-established independent judges defended liberties against *both* the executive and the legislature.

The unpredictable twists and turns of history are rarely as simple as theorists make them out to be.

14

AT THE CORE

In the eighteenth century, England's social and political system coped with strong pressures, internally as well as externally. Besides colonies overseas, government was deeply concerned with the powers of Europe, especially France. Ireland and Scotland might be classed as either external or internal depending on a viewer's political assumptions. Scotland especially confuses categories: It was absorbed into the United Kingdom in 1707, and Scottish members assigned to Parliament, but in 1715 and again in 1745 Scottish Highlanders rebelled in support of exiled Stuarts claiming the common throne.[1]

Great Britain was a creation reminiscent of Dr. Dolittle's pushme-pullyou with two heads at opposite ends. Though one man served as king in both realms it had two church establishments with unreconciled doctrines. The Church of England preached passive obedience by all subjects to a king whose authority derived from God. The Presbyterian Kirk of Scotland preached that kings were responsible to their people and might be dethroned for unacceptable behavior. The king of Great Britain was at the head of both church establishments that included the anomalous intrusions of Anglican minorities in Scotland and "nonconformists" in England.

Within England, parties formed on the one hand to support the dynastic claims of Stuarts or Hanoverians; on the other hand, issues arose in regard to Whig or Tory principles of government. These are readily confused because of twists of historical circumstance. Although frequently "Jacobite" supporters of the Stuarts are noticed as Tories (as sometimes they were), the proper distinction between Tory and Whig was given by Methodism's founder John Wesley: A Tory, he wrote, was "one that believes God, not the people, to be the origin of all civil power," and Wesley iden-

---

1 See W. A. Speck, *The Butcher: The Duke of Cumberland and the Suppression of the 45* (Oxford: Basil Blackwell, 1981).

tified himself as such.[2] Wesley emphatically supported the Hanoverian regime against all Stuart pretensions, and he exhorted his followers to be loyal and obedient subjects of the king. One might think that the populist principles of Scottish Presbyterians should have thrown them into opposition in Parliament, but their members strove to avoid being suspected as encouragers of rebellion, so they became the crown's strongest bloc of support. They had reason. Much xenophobia among Englishmen was directed against the Scots who had been their hereditary enemies, so the Scottish members of Parliament had to demonstrate their loyalty beyond cavil. Regardless of religious populism, they had to toe the Tory line in politics.

As against the king and his prerogative, England had a tradition of the aristocracy's rights dating back at least as far as Magna Charta. This tradition was the basis of solidarity among the great Whig nobles who kept sharp watch on encroachments of royal prerogative. The aggressive pretensions of King James II alarmed the Whigs and momentarily gave them allies among Protestant Tories who feared James's Catholicism. The coalition overthrew James II in 1687, and powerful Whigs seized the opportunity to take charge of great offices of government. They strengthened their hold on power gradually through the reigns of William and Mary (1689–1702) and Queen Anne (1702–1714). As Anne died without an heir, the crown of Great Britain went to her German cousin George, Elector of Hanover, whose ignorance of even the English language impelled him to allow Whig nobles to conduct the government. Thus, for a while, the royal prerogative receded from prominence because the Whigs did not need it; Whigs in Parliament got along with Whigs at court, and they perpetuated their power by generous distributions of patronage to friends as well as merciless hounding of Tories. In these exceptional circumstances, the natural order of politics seemed to have reversed, but it was to revert again under later kings.

It would be wrong to assume that government thereafter fluctuated between two parties. In the eighteenth century, government in England seemed to be a game of musical chairs. Basil Williams remarks in *The Whig Supremacy*:

> The transitory union of whigs and tories which had effected the [Glorious] Revolution and its great charter, the Bill of Rights, was soon dissolved, for it had been due solely to the personality of James II. The whigs, indeed, had consistently questioned the king's claims to unrestrained authority, the tories, loyal to king and church, had joined them only when they found the two loyalties incompatible with a Roman catholic king.[3]

2 J. C. D. Clark, *English Society, 1688–1832* (Cambridge: Cambridge University Press, 1985), 237.
3 Basil Williams, *The Whig Supremacy, 1714–1760*, 2d ed. rev., by C. H. Stuart (Oxford: Clarendon Press, 1962), 3–4.

Under George II, the distinction between Whigs and Tories was often hard to see as offices were shared about among certain great noble families. Newcastle and Halifax were cousins, and Halifax owed his beginnings in high office to Newcastle's patronage, but Halifax caught the Tory winds and deserted Newcastle's Whig ship. Pitt was brother-in-law to the Grenville brothers – Tory George Grenville and whilom Whig Richard Temple Grenville, Earl Temple. Pitt was the bear who walks alone, wholly individualistic, aligning with Whigs or Tories almost by caprice. His oratorical ability to sway the House of Commons was his special political capital, and it won him vast popular acclaim, but he was not an isolate. He started in Commons as the member from England's "rottenest" borough, Old Sarum, which was "owned" by his powerful family, and never in his career did he represent more than a hundred electors.[4]

Some writers have dated the heightening of tensions that led to the American Revolution at 1763 after France was driven from eastern North America. Others put it at George III's enthronement in 1760. I have pushed it back to 1755 when the crown sent Edward Braddock as commander in chief with demands for the colonies to pay stipulated quotas toward the costs of brewing war with France. Resisting colonists equated such demands with taxes and revised their contributions sharply downward to the great displeasure of London.

Now W. A. Speck puts the date still earlier, when Franco-British warring was resumed as of 1739. He says it softly: "The war years, therefore, mark a significant shift in the importance that British ministers ascribed to the colonies, as well as the attention that they consequently gave to North America," and the process of Britain's revived wars with France "drastically altered the imperial and international context of the colonies."[5]

To support this judgment, Speck argues that imperial authorities believed the colonists had failed to support Britain's mid-century wars adequately, and the colonists resented the authorities' attitude. Ominously, the colonists had "for the first time a taste of real military government, which fed their inherited fear of the threat that a standing army posed to freedom. Things were never again to be quite the same as they had been before [war with Spain began in] 1739."[6] This judgment seems fair for the imperial side; colonial reactions become more visible after hostilities began with France in

---

4 *Dictionary of National Biography*, 15:1241.
5 W. A. Speck, "The International and Imperial Context," in *Colonial British America: Essays in the New History of the Early Modern Era*, ed. Jack P. Greene and J. R. Pole (Baltimore: Johns Hopkins Press, 1984), 400.
6 Ibid., 401.

the War of the Austrian Succession. The colonial sector (King George's War) began in 1744, after which French and British colonials plotted to eliminate each other.

In 1745 the British navy and always belligerent Massachusetts took France's great Fortress Louisbourg in combined operations. (The seeming ease of this capture is owing to a special kind of forgetfulness; in this case it overlooked the contribution to triumph made by a Mashpee Indian from Cape Cod who crawled through a hole in Louisbourg's defense wall and opened a gate to the besiegers.)[7] Most of the American conflicts in King George's War involved schemes to strike at the enemy through the victims of his conquests. Florida's Spaniards welcomed slaves escaping from South Carolina and Georgia. French and British agents instigated Indian allies to attack each other's Indian allies. South Carolinians intrigued with Choctaw chief Red Shoes to win his large tribe away from French alliance, and the French countered by arranging Red Shoes's assassination.[8] Virginians laid plans to take over the transmontane Ohio Country by first treating with the Iroquois League in 1744. New York's William Johnson persuaded the Iroquois Mohawks to attack Montreal; but the other Iroquois thought this a harebrained scheme and avoided involvement. Their correctness was proved by French Indian allies who dealt the Mohawks a punishing defeat.[9]

In short, this dynastic war threw the colonies into turmoil at the same time it convulsed the empire's center. One must remember that in the tensions between crown and nobility, the crown's pretensions were supported institutionally by bishops and colonels who had many representatives in Parliament.

In 1745 the Scottish Highlanders rose in arms to support Charles Edward Stuart, the "Young Pretender" to the throne of Great Britain. This clearly was a Jacobite rebellion, hence deemed Tory. Government troops suppressed it savagely at the battle of Culloden and in subsequent ravages, and English glory was proclaimed for the victorious commander, the duke of Cumberland, second son of George II. The victory was briefly celebrated as a Whig triumph and Cumberland was made Captain General – that is, commander in chief – of the army. He quickly demonstrated the illusory quality of appearances by defeating the Whigs in patronage almost as badly as he had smashed the Highlanders in battle. He simply took all the mili-

7 Yasuhide Kawashima, *Puritan Justice and the Indian* (Middletown, Conn.: Wesleyan University Press, 1986), 120.
8 Richard White, "Red Shoes: Warrior and Diplomat," in *Struggle and Survival in Colonial America*, ed. David G. Sweet and Gary B. Nash (Berkeley: University of California Press, 1981), 49–68.
9 Jennings, *Empire of Fortune*, 78.

tary patronage into his own hands, and with that single act he broke much of the power of the governing Whig duke of Newcastle.[10] If Jacobite Tories had been defeated at Culloden, Hanoverian Tories gained great power and a new leader with the royal prerogative as the mainstay of their strength. Only the Whigs really lost.

10 See Chap. 11, above.

15

GEORGE III

The end of the Seven Years War created a new situation – or revived an old one – about the powers of the royal prerogative. King George II died in 1760 and was succeeded by George III who fully intended to rule as well as reign. He had observed how Whig control of patronage had translated into control of Parliament, which translated further into restraint on the crown; and George III moved to restore the right given him by God. He enjoyed the votes of Parliament's Scottish contingent in the long outwash from suppression of the Highlands uprising of 1745. He had also a large slush fund of pensions, places, and honors to distribute at will. Besides these, his revered uncle, the duke of Cumberland, had seized into royal hands the patronage of the armed forces. Taken altogether, with the usual addition of trimmers moving to the side of visible, rising power, George won control of Parliament and diverted it from its former restraining role to become instead an extension of his power. He still had naked prerogative, and by 1763 he could dictate acts of king-in-Parliament. For a moment there seemed no longer to be any way of holding off what John Sainsbury has described as "the government's habitually despotic tendencies."[1]

But there was still the English constitution, unwritten though it certainly was and amorphous as it seemed; and there were subjects who idealized the constitution and the rights of Englishmen supposedly guaranteed by it. Believers in constitutional rights formed resistances of varied sorts in America as well as in England. Resistance united the American colonies as nothing else had done, and it took form as defense of existing autonomy verging gradually and ultimately to determination for independence. The English resistance centered upon reforms of Parliament by making it more responsible to its electorates rather than the ministry. (Fair representation was yet to come.) English printers fought a great battle for freedom of the

---

1 John Sainsbury, *Disaffected Patriots: London Supporters of Revolutionary America, 1769–1782* (Kingston, Ont.: Queen's University Press, 1987), 54.

press by defying administrative sanctions against them; and equally defiant juries upheld them. Violent crowds roared against the government on both sides of the ocean. Resisters gave reciprocal transatlantic support to each other. Very much involved were the merchants as a class, who opposed the government's heavy taxes and restraints of trade; those centered in the City of London protested directly to the king and indirectly by supporting his political opponents.

The parallelism of these resistances has escaped general notice by scholars who have specialized on the one side in the American Revolution, on the other side in British civil liberties. The best reason for attending to both turmoils is simply that they arose by reaction to the same stimulus which was the oppressive actions of the king. Without mentioning that fact, John Sainsbury has observed that "by 1769 inhabitants of the capital [London] were expressing in petitions that American grievances were integrally linked to their own." Those petitions were directed to George III.[2]

To accept this as fact may be hard for readers who have been exposed to many excuses for George III – that he was idealistic, that he suffered from an illness which intermittently made him "mad," that he was a loving family man, and so on. These things have been a product of Tory industry for a long time. Most recently a film called *The Madness of George III* showed the king being cheered lustily by his subjects.

That is pure invention. George was mean and harmful, and his subjects knew it. We have a report from John Wesley, founder of Methodism and ardent believer in the king's divine right to rule. By his own identification he was "an High Churchman, the son of an High Churchman, bred up from my childhood in the highest notions of passive obedience and non resistance." Wesley attacked the "poison" of radical dissidents. Yet here is what he felt impelled to report in 1775:

> I aver that the people in general all over the nation are far from being well satisfied, that they are far more deeply dissatisfied than they appear to have been even a year or two before the Great Rebellion [of 1688], and far more dangerously dissatisfied. The bulk of the people in every city, town, and village where I have been do not so much aim at the ministry, as they usually did in the last century, but at the king himself. He is the object of their anger, contempt, and malice. They wish to imbue their hands in his blood; they are full of the spirit of murder and rebellion; and I am persuaded, should any occasion offer, thousands would be ready to act what they now speak.[3]

This comment directly contradicts Benjamin Franklin's frequent expressions of idolatry about George III. "I can scarcely conceive a King of better

2 Ibid., 3.
3 J. C. D. Clark, *English Society, 1688–1832* (Cambridge: Cambridge University Press, 1985), 236–37.

Dispositions, of more exemplary Virtues, or more truly desirous of promoting the Welfare of all his Subjects," Franklin wrote in 1769.[4] One must remember that Franklin wrote this with the understanding that, as a colonial agent, his mail probably was intercepted (he had been a postmaster long enough to know about such matters). As deputy postmaster for the colonies he was a placeman subject to instant dismissal for offending the ministry. He was an applicant for a royal land grant. And he had come to England as a supplicant for the crown to take over Pennsylvania's government. Franklin can hardly be thought impartial and objective as an observer.

In the same year 1769, the king and his government became furious about the appearance of a "letter" in *The Public Advertiser*, signed by an anonymous critic calling himself Junius. Referring to the government's persecution of John Wilkes (about which more further on), Junius demanded,

> Is this a contention worthy of a king? Are you not sensible how much the meanness of this cause gives an air of ridicule to the serious difficulties into which you have been betrayed? the destruction of one man [John Wilkes] has been now, for many years, the sole object of your government; and if there can be any thing still more disgraceful, we have seen, for such an object, the utmost influence of the executive power, and every ministerial artifice, exerted without success.[5]

Junius promptly joined Wilkes as an object of royal wrath, but no one betrayed him though the government launched attacks on printers for daring to publish his scathing commentary (as was done by all the London papers). Franklin knew about such matters and the very plain hostility to the crown shown by the City of London. Among King George's other reasons for wanting a big army, he needed it for police actions against the English people.

We must not stray. Returning to the question of why the crown and imperial government reversed policies after winning the Seven Years War, we may heed one of Franklin's comments made *privately* in the margins of an anonymous British pamphlet in 1769, the same year when he poured forth the royal slush in a letter likely to be intercepted. Away from discovery by the crown's secret agents, Franklin wrote bitterly, "Had the French Power . . . continu'd at our Backs, ready to support and assist us whenever we might think proper to resist your Oppression, you would never have thought of a Stamp Act for us; you would not have dared to use us as you have done."[6]

The "new" policy was aimed at both sides of the Atlantic. Let us look first at America.

4 *Franklin Papers* 16:118.
5 [Philip Francis], *The Letters of Junius* (1783), (London: G. Woodfall, 1812), 2d ed. 1814, p. 216.
6 Jack P. Greene, *Understanding the American Revolution: Issues and Actors* (Charlottesville: University Press of Virginia, 1995), 33. Cf. *Franklin Papers* 17:343–44.

So early as 1754, Virginia had disobeyed the Board of Trade's instruction to attend the intercolonial Congress at Albany to appease the Iroquois Indians. Virginians knew that the Iroquois wanted to prevent expansion of British settlements beyond the Appalachians, which was exactly what the Virginians were intent on doing to expand their own empire over Indian territory. Though no Virginians attended the Albany Congress, its delegates received news of George Washington's capitulation at his jerry-built Fort Necessity.

The Indians wanted a boundary line between tribal territories and provincial settlements. Such a line was promised to them at Easton, Pennsylvania, in 1758. It swayed French-allied Delawares to change sides and made possible General John Forbes's capture of Fort Duquesne at the head of the Ohio River. But British military men interpreted the Easton promise differently from the Indians. Definitely, the Indians wanted *all* Europeans and colonials to stay on the east side of the boundary line, but British officials insisted on maintaining garrisoned forts in the Indians' territory.[7]

Royal policy otherwise agreed with the Indians that settlers should be held back. Reasons differed, however. The Indians wanted the west for themselves forever. Crown officials wanted only to restrain western settlement long enough to get the land under control and suppress tendencies to independence that would become likely among subjects distant from organized bases of power.

In 1763, under Seneca and Delaware leadership, the Indians exploded in the misnamed "Pontiac's War." They captured some forts, but Detroit, Niagara, and Fort Pitt held out; and while the fighting continued, the crown's clever officials bethought themselves of a political ruse to soften up the warriors. It emerged as The Royal Proclamation of 1763 which revived the promise of a boundary line. This did indeed pacify the warring Indians who were told that "lands *reserved* to the Indians" had become accepted as lands *belonging* to the Indians.[8]

What pacified the Indians angered the Virginians because those *reserved* lands were clearly designated as *crown* lands, and Virginians coveted them for Virginia. The Proclamation line carved right through Virginia's chartered territory and did so by simple royal prerogative. What good was a charter if the king could chop it up at his pleasure?

For the time being, gentlemen speculators in western lands refrained from making trouble because they believed the crown was only fooling the Indians. George Washington wrote that "the nominal line, commonly called the Ministerial Line . . . seems to have been considered by government as a temporary expedient . . . and no further regard has been paid to it by the

---

7 Jennings, *Empire of Fortune*, 461–62 and n 10. 8 Ibid.

ministers themselves."[9] Speculators went to London to lobby for large grants in those reserved crown lands.

Attitudes changed sharply after ten years during which antagonisms between crown and colonies increased harshly. When George III, now fully in control of Parliament, gained passage in 1774 of the Quebec Act, Virginians roared hostility. The Quebec Act was a much stronger instrument of policy than the Royal Proclamation. Whereas the Proclamation was subject to administrative rescission at any time, an Act of Parliament could only be undone by another Act of Parliament, and the Quebec Act made permanent the Proclamation's boundary line. Worse, the Act put lands beyond the boundary into the jurisdiction of the newly conquered Province of Quebec which was still under military government. Now the line had become serious and permanent. The governor of Quebec could enforce it with troops directly under his command. No patents for real property could issue except with his approval from his headquarters remote from Virginians' influence.

Thomas Jefferson came to the fore in 1774 with an utterance typically oblivious to any suggestion of rights for Indians. In *A Summary View of the Rights of British America*, Jefferson asserted that possessions in America were "undoubtedly of the allodial nature." This was a typical Jeffersonian twist of words to make them seem to say what he wanted (à la Humpty Dumpty). *Allodial* means land held in original ownership, time out of mind, without obligation of service to any feudal overlord. "From the nature and purpose of civil institutions," Jefferson continued, "all the lands within the limits which any particular society has circumscribed around itself are assumed by that society, and subject to their allotment only." Perhaps Jefferson suppressed Indian rights by limiting his dictum to "civil institutions." Whatever the meanderings of his arcane reasoning, he neatly suppressed with one phrase any rights to be claimed by king *or* aborigines.[10] He had a knack.

Some historians have argued that British controls over colonial commerce resulted in such huge indebtedness to the metropole that the colonists finally rose in revolt. In this scheme, the Navigation Acts play a villainous role. Plausible on the surface, it fails to account for the tremendous growth and success of the colonies up to and through the Seven Years War.

John J. McCusker and Russell R. Menard have surveyed colonial commerce from its beginnings; they found that "the costs imposed on the

9 Clarence W. Alvord, *The Mississippi Valley in British Politics* (1916), reprinted (New York: Russell and Russell, 1959), 2:186; Chap. 3.

10 Thomas Jefferson, *A Summary View of the Rights of British America* (1774), in *Tracts of the American Revolution, 1773–1776*, ed. Merrill Jensen (Indianapolis: Bobbs-Merrill Co., 1967), 273.

colonies by the restrictions on trade were small, certainly less than 3 percent of colonial income, perhaps less than 1 percent" and such costs "were largely offset by the benefits: naval protection; access to a large free-trading area; easy credit and cheap manufactures; and restricted foreign competition."[11]

One wonders how such prosperity could have come about while specie was drained to England and paper money was discouraged by law. No doubt is possible about these facts, regardless of theories; colonial complaints in the sources are loud and clear.

How could such apparently contradictory phenomena be reconciled? It seems plain that colonial merchants had traded heavily *outside* the restrictions as well as within the permitted area. Much documentation establishes regular trade to the French and Spanish West Indies, from which the profits constantly renewed the supply of specie in British colonies. We do not and cannot know the full extent of smuggling, which took place overland as well as on the seas, because it was strictly illegal. In wartime, it was trading with the enemy, and it did not stop. Records are neither adequate nor trustworthy. But, to judge by its consequences, smuggling must have been much more than a supplementary by-product of colonial trade. There are signs that it was intrinsic and necessary to the system.

As an example, I can cite the exchange of trade goods from Albany or Philadelphia for rich furs from Montreal or Detroit, often involving Indian intermediaries. This was outlawed by both France and Britain, but maintained by arrangements of merchants on both sides against all efforts to suppress it. I feel certain that merchants engaged in export–import overseas trade were just as expert in evading controls.

My conclusion stands in contradiction to McCusker and Menard's judgment that "by the eighteenth century smuggled goods accounted for a tiny fraction of all goods handled," which should be qualified as all goods *recorded* as having been handled.[12] Is it really necessary to argue that few illegal entrepreneurs keep incriminating records to assist the cops? If smuggling had been really insignificant, the colonists would have been less furious over its suppression. Better than by columns of figures from dual sets of account books, the extent of smuggling is measurable by the intensity and magnitude of the campaigns waged against it.

McCusker and Menard also note that the Sugar Act of Minister Townshend "was objectionable not only because it levied a tax, but also because it threatened to damage seriously the North American–West Indian trade" – which was "customs racketeering."[13] John W. Tyler has found that Boston's merchants, headed by John Hancock, were so heavily involved in

---

11 John J. McCusker and Russell R. Menard, *The Economy of British America, 1607–1789* (Chapel Hill: University of North Carolina Press, 1991), 77, 354.
12 Ibid., 77.   13 Ibid., 355–56.

smuggling that customs officers could not get a jury to convict when a smuggler was seized. Parliament responded by creating a new vice-admiralty court at Halifax, Nova Scotia, and by authorizing prosecutors to sue in jury-less vice-admiralty courts.[14]

Even in staid Pennsylvania, the mayor of Philadelphia was "deeply concern'd in the French trade" during the Seven Years War. On the authority of Proprietary Thomas Penn's collector of rents, everyone knew about this scandal.[15] An anonymous pamphleteer charged that proprietary men monopolized the trade in provisions to enemies of the French and Spanish West Indies.[16]

One of the best gauges of smuggling was what happened when Parliament finally decided by the Townshend Acts to stop formerly tolerated illegal trade. Henry Steele Commager notes that "prior to 1767 the American customs had brought in some two thousand pounds annually . . . from 1768 to 1774 the American customs brought in an average of thirty thousand pounds annually."[17]

Smuggling could not have operated without a rather debonair attitude toward the laws and officials of the empire. If a Boston merchant was unlucky enough to encounter an honest naval officer, he needed not to worry overmuch. He would be brought to trial in a court where judge and jury were on his side. Indeed the naval officer might be punished for performing his duty. R. C. Simmons notes how "commonplace" it was for colonial courts "not only to find against customs officers but to admit counter-claims for false arrest and the like and award substantial damages against them, even to imprison them." He adds: "Considerable Parliamentary attention was given to the seizure in June 1768 of the *Liberty*, owned by John Hancock of Boston, which led to threats to the American Customs Commissioners and their flight from the city."[18]

A climax was reached in 1772 when the revenue cutter *Gaspee* ran aground in Narragansett Bay. Eight boatloads of armed, reputable citizens, headed by merchant John Brown, overpowered the crew, wounded the commander, and set the ship on fire. No one was ever punished.[19] This incident requires a moment of thought to comprehend its enormity. Suppose the

---

14 John W. Tyler, *Smugglers and Patriots: Boston Merchants and the Advent of the American Revolution* (Boston: Northeastern University Press, 1986); R. C. Simmons in *The Blackwell Encyclopedia of the American Revolution*, ed. Jack P. Greene and J. R. Pole (Cambridge, Mass.: Blackwell Publishers, 1994), 164.

15 R. Hockley to T. Penn, 25 Oct. 1755, mss., Penn Mss., Off. Corr., 7:133, Hist. Soc. of Pa.

16 *An Answer to an invidious Pamphlet, intituled, A Brief State of the Province of Pensylvania* (London: S. Bladon, 1755).

17 *Documents of American History*, ed. Henry Steele Commager, 2 vols., 7th ed. (New York: Appleton-Century-Crofts, 1963), 63n.

18 Simmons in *The Blackwell Encyclopedia*, 167.

19 *Encyclopaedia Britannica*, 15th ed., 1993, 5:139.

Chicago police close down a shop selling untaxed cigarettes and liquors, upon which the Chamber of Commerce organizes a march against the police station and burns it to the ground. That would surely arouse law-and-order citizens to outrage, yet the same citizens will look back on the burning of the *Gaspee* with approval for the revolutionary spirit of the arsonists. Ministers of the crown thought otherwise.

It must be added that some of the naval officers looked on colonial ships as prey. Reputedly, Admiral Lord Colvill, naval commander in chief from 1763 to 1766, "hoped to make his fortune from customs seizures."[20] Robert Middlekauff reports that Philadelphia merchants in 1760 "lost thirty vessels with cargoes valued at £100,000 to the navy."[21] This was in wartime, but it is doubtful that the merchants thought they deserved the loss. The attacks on trade were not confined to any region. They outraged "otherwise conservative merchants such as Henry Laurens of South Carolina, whose experiences with the customs service led him to radical pamphleteering and ultimately to revolution."[22]

Let us backtrack a bit to follow different trails that head in the same direction.

Before and during the Seven Years War, Bostonians and New Yorkers acquired hostility to the royal navy on grounds other than its actions against smuggling. Though the navy protected coastal cities from French attacks, its regular practice of unrestrictedly impressing seamen for naval service hurt commerce as well as the sorrowful men who were thus conscripted into a status like slavery, differing mostly in being legally "free" instead of being property. Bostonians rioted in November 1747 against the press gangs, after which twenty-five-year-old Samuel Adams and others founded the *Independent Advertiser* as America's first antiwar, protest newspaper.[23]

Whole cities were crippled by the press gangs' seizures of likely young men. In the midst of the Seven Years War, in 1757, the crown's commander in chief Lord Loudoun threw a cordon at night around New York City and picked up eight hundred men who were more than a quarter of the city's adult male population. Historian Jesse Lemisch remarks that impressment "pervaded and disrupted all society."[24] Benjamin Franklin remarked

20 Simmons in *Blackwell Encyclopedia*, 166.

21 Robert Middlekauff, *The Glorious Cause: The American Revolution, 1763–1789* (New York: Oxford University Press, 1982), 60.

22 Simmons in *Blackwell Encyclopedia*, 168; Merrill Jensen, "Introduction" to *Tracts of the American Revolution, 1773–1776*, xliv–xlvi.

23 William Pencak, "Warfare and Political Change in Mid-Eighteenth Century Massachusetts," in *The British Atlantic Empire Before the American Revolution*, ed. Peter Marshall and Glyn Williams (London: Frank Cass, 1980), 60.

24 Jesse Lemisch, "Jack Tar in the Streets: Merchant Seamen in the Politics of Revolutionary America," *William and Mary Quarterly* 3d ser., 25:3 (1968), 383.

in 1759 that impressment often hurt trade "more than the Enemy hurts it."[25] It was justified as "a prerogative inherent in the Crown."[26]

Under George III, colonials quickly learned that an imperial army's functions matched those of the royal navy. The army was in America to surround, intimidate, and discipline those too-autonymous colonists and to reduce them to proper obedience.

As that policy would have been too harsh for blunt statement, the crown presented its troops in America as being there to protect the colonists from the savage Indians, just as impressment was supposed to be "for public service," and when Pontiac's War broke out in 1763, the excuse seemed to have some validity. We must remember that the smoke of burning cabins and the screams of their occupants were not detected in pleasant, comfortable London. The crown was much concerned to prevent settlement out of control beyond the mountains, so its army was intended in fact not so much to protect the colonists as to protect the Indians! Secretary Shelburne's papers include one recommending that "the Indians be everywhere encouraged to support their own sovereignty," and it notes significantly that the provinces were "now surrounded by an Army, a Navy and by hostile Tribes of Indians."[27]

John Shy has found that "the decision to maintain a garrison in North America had been accepted without scrutiny or criticism, primarily for reasons that had nothing to do with North America."[28] Those reasons will be noted a little further on here.

However the ministry might have balanced its aims, the colonists became immediately suspicious. (So did many Englishmen.) Englishmen had long hated standing armies as instruments of oppression, and Englishmen in America remembered the attitude and the reasons therefor. Connecticut's Eliphalet Dyer told a friend that the government "seems determined to fix upon us a large number of regular Troops under pretence for our Defence; but rather designd as a rod and Check over us." Pennsylvania's John Dickinson feared the "formidable force established in the midst of peace to bleed [America] into obedience."[29]

Alarmed Pennsylvanians took no stock in the excuse that the army was intended to protect them. Philadelphians had seen the raggle-taggle remnants of Edward Braddock's troops retreating from Fort Duquesne in 1755, after which the province had to defend itself from French-led Indian raids.

25 *Franklin Papers*, 8:315–16.
26 "Impressment," *Encyclopedia Americana* (1974), 14:829.
27 Knollenberg, *Origin of the American Revolution*, 92.
28 John Shy, *Toward Lexington: The Role of the British Army in the Coming of the American Revolution* (Princeton, N.J.: Princeton University Press, 1965), 78–79.
29 Knollenberg, *Origin of the American Revolution*, 90.

When a provincial militia was formed, the assembly, sans Quakers, waged a fierce political battle over its command. Proprietary Thomas Penn urged his placemen to get control so as to turn the militia into an auxiliary of his political machine; and the Penns' henchmen were fought and defeated by populists led by Benjamin Franklin. (*Not* by Quaker pacifists, as is so often asserted by writers who don't feel a need to consult source materials.)

Pennsylvanians had been well prepared to suspect the real functions of the crown's army after the war. Benjamin Franklin's hatred of feudal domination by the Penn family, however, blinded him to the crown's purposes. He kept quiet on the standing army issue because he was in the midst of a campaign to have the crown take over Pennsylvania. (Great issues are rarely simple.) But Franklin's friend and neighbor Charles Thomson, who was also a kinsman of Dickinson, objected strenuously to being "burthened with a standing army and subjected to insufferable Insults from any petty officer.[30]

Such antagonisms were confirmed by the redistribution of troops in 1766 when they were taken out of western garrisons to be stationed in eastern cities. The process is very plainly stated in the catalog of the British Library's commemoration of the American Revolution. Picturing how the forces were moved, the text commented: "During the Stamp Act crisis, 1765–66, Thomas Gage, Commander-in-Chief in North America began to withdraw troops to the Atlantic colonies, with the evident intention of using military force to support civil rule . . . Troops were withdrawn from all but the largest forts in the interior, and quartered on the unwilling colonists in the provinces of New York and Pennsylvania."[31]

One must not think from this that Boston had been overlooked. General Gage landed troops there in September 1768 under the guns of a line of warships with cannon trained on the "mutinous" city. Neither troops nor cannon scared Bostonians into being less mutinous. Far from reducing tensions, the troops exacerbated them.

One of the reasons for thinking of the American Revolution as a civil war was the strong inheritance on both sides of the Atlantic of traditional hostility to standing armies. Colonists and Englishmen thought alike on that subject, and both reached back in history for proof of their logic.[32]

The editors of *Cato's Letters* note that King William III, who had been

30 Shy, *Toward Lexington*, 141–42.
31 *The American War of Independence, 1775–83* (London: British Library Publications, 1975), 17. Cf. maps in *Atlas of Early American History: The Revolutionary Era, 1760–1790* ed. Lester J. Cappon et al. (Princeton, N.J.: Princeton University Press, 1976), 41.
32 Cf. Don Higginbotham, *The War of American Independence: Military Attitudes, Policies, and Practice, 1763–1789* (Boston: Northeastern University Press, 1983), 16.

enthroned in the Glorious Revolution against James II, ran into determined resistance in the House of Commons when he tried to get a standing army in 1697 after peace with France.[33] He so antagonized Parliament that he had factional difficulties "during the remainder of his troublesome reign." Whigs then controlled Parliament in the interests of their great noble families, and they protected themselves (and incidentally the nation) from unchecked royal prerogative.

Reflecting on the event in 1722, "Cato" – that is, John Trenchard and Thomas Gordon – observed, "It is certain, that all parts of Europe which are enslaved, have been enslaved by armies; and it is absolutely impossible, that any nation which keeps them amongst themselves can long preserve their liberties." This thought was still current in 1754 when the seventh edition of *Cato's Letters* was published – an edition that speaks loudly of the attitude's widespread acceptance while George II was still on the throne.[34] Bernard Bailyn pays respects to the writings of Trenchard and Gordon as "the most authoritative statement of the nature of political liberty."[35]

When George III took office and insisted on maintaining the bulk of the wartime army after peace once again with France, the political opposition took alarm. Not only the colonists were to be brought under royal control. One opposition English pamphleteer fretted over the "infinite Dependance upon the Crown" created by the war and its aftermath. "Too many" of the crown's servants, civil and military, "might be tempted to assist in extending the Influence of the Prerogative to the Prejudice of public Liberty." He lamented to see the nation "so amazingly reconciled" to a large standing army in peacetime."[36] The newly retired duke of Newcastle wailed privately that "such an Extensive Plan of Power and Military Influence was never thought of before in this Country."[37]

Among other things, George's army required for Englishmen an era of exceptionally high taxes, not only to pay war debts, but, more painfully, *new taxes* to support *new* royal policies. These included costs of the corruption called patronage by its supporters. John Wilkes put his finger on one item of uncountable many. He pointed to the government's loan of £3,500,000, a huge sum in an era when a penny was often equivalent to a modern pound sterling and when the taxpaying base of population was a small fraction of today's. Wilkes noted that an *immediate advance* of 7 to 11

33 John Trenchard and Thomas Gordon, *Cato's Letters* (1720–23), ed. Ronald Hamowy, 2 vols. (Indianapolis: Liberty Fund, 1995), 2:670n.
34 Ibid., 2:682.
35 Bernard Bailyn, *The Ideological Origins of the American Revolution* (Cambridge, Mass.: Harvard University Press, 1967), 36.
36 *A Letter Addressed to Two Great Men on the Prospect of Peace* (London: A. Millar, 1760), 43–46.
37 Knollenberg, *Origin of the American Revolution*, 35.

percent (which he rounded off to an even 10 percent) was paid to the loan's subscribers. "Consequently," wrote Wilkes, "in the period of a very few days, the minister gave among his creatures, and the tools of his power, £350,000 which was levied on the public."[38] Wilkes named the recipients of this handout. He carefully observed the legal taboo against attacking the king directly, but any gentleman or businessman would understand how the king was bribing supporters.

Maintaining the standing army was one of the more expensive of the new royal policies. Its cost for the regiments in America was estimated by the ministry at £225,000 per year, but this was soothing syrup to disguise the taste of harsh reality. As desired, the army was approved with the promise that "after the first year the colonies themselves would pay for the American army." The promise was as false as the estimate. Between 1763 and 1775, the army's actual cost came to £384,000 annually, and the colonials immediately denounced and rejected any tax levied upon them by Parliament.[39]

Englishmen were appalled by the new *postwar* taxes that were heavier than those imposed during the Seven Years War. A new excise tax on cider fell most heavily on commerce because land taxes were already at maximum. This new "cyder" tax naturally aroused special resentment in the southern, apple-growing shires and among the merchants of the City of London. Ardent though the merchants had been in support of the preceding war, they grew angry at increased taxes afterward, and especially at the means used to collect the excise. Collectors were given power to enter and search any householder's premises, business or domestic, and to seize whatever the searcher chose to call suspect.[40]

Among Englishmen on both sides of the Atlantic, such practices were hated and opposed. (They would be forbidden by the basic law, the Constitution of the United States, in its Bill of Rights, Amendment IV.)

---

38 *North Briton* #42, cited in George Nobbe, *The North Briton: A Study in Political Propaganda* (New York: Columbia University Press, 1939), 190.
39 Peter D. G. Thomas in *The Blackwell Encyclopedia*, 107.
40 *The Gentleman's Magazine* 33 (1763), 447.

16

———— • ————

REACTIONS BECOMING REVOLUTION

Colonials could not simply refuse to accept imposition of rule from Britain. They had to determine exactly what they wanted and how to get it. Each new assault from London demanded new adjustments to existing goals and institutions.

At the end of the Seven Years War, few colonists, if any, contemplated independence in the sense of secession but most agreed on the desirability of autonomy; and popular support was strong for assemblies that had stood up against the batterings of Braddock and Loudoun wielding royal prerogative. Plenty of history-minded leaders remembered how Parliament had extorted rights and privileges from kings who needed money for their wars, and the assemblies had held successfully to that pattern during the war against France.

With the peace, new issues arose. Yearners after western expansion were taken aback by the Royal Proclamation's ban on expansion by colonial initiative in 1763, especially as the ban was maintained by a standing army in western garrisons. The expansionists temporarily refrained from strong protest because they counted on the ban being merely an expedient, even after a limiting boundary line was surveyed when royal superintendents of Indian affairs negotiated with tribes. Instead of arousing rebellion, the Proclamation incited lobbying in London for new grants of western lands *from the crown* instead of the provinces, and prospects seemed favorable. The metropole buzzed with projects for new colonies in the west. (Benjamin Franklin joined one.)[1] The crown's image became more attractive for many important colonists responding to the lure of western lands.

The crown maintained initiative as the Sugar Act (1764) and royal instructions to the navy cracked down on smuggling. When customs agents brought contraband into court, they could choose vice-admiralty courts

---

1 Carl Van Doren, *Benjamin Franklin* (New York: Viking Press, 1938), 394–95.

without the local juries that had made officials miserable, but jury trials were sacred in the British constitution and tradition.

Protest was prompt, and not only from Massachusetts. Indeed the elected *governor* of Rhode Island, Stephen Hopkins, wrote a pamphlet, *The Rights of Colonies Examined*, which his assembly approved and sent on to London. This attracts attention now on two scores: It was the voice of the whole government rather than a wild-eyed minority, and it immediately raised the issue of *rights*.

> The British subjects in America have equal rights with those in Britain; that they do not hold those rights as a privilege granted them, nor enjoy them as a grace and favor bestowed; but possess them as an inherent indefeasible right; as they, and their ancestors, were free-born subjects, justly and naturally entitled to all the rights and advantages of the British constitution.[2]

Editor Merrill Jensen may raise an eyebrow with his introductory comment that "the corruptness of Rhode Island politics during this period has seldom been equaled in all of American political history." He adds that nevertheless most Rhode Islanders joined forces.[3] It is a thought to remember as one reads the innumerable invocations of *virtue* attributed by colonials to themselves intending sharp contrast to the corruption in Britain. Libertarian struggles can be and often have been fought by persons who lacked conventional respectability. When power is the issue, it may be reached for by persons who are not very nice. Power does corrupt – both its possession and the grasping after it. The writer who refuses to recognize corruption among his own people will miss a lot of history.

We have already seen in these pages how merchant smugglers resented and resisted Parliament's Sugar Act of 1764. In March 1764, Minister Grenville announced consideration of a stamp tax. As the Stamp Act was to generate outrage throughout all the colonies, its gestation requires detailed examination. Alibis and excuses for that law were concocted to distract attention from its basic purpose; from its inception it was intended to reduce the autonomous powers of the colonial assemblies.[4]

Ostensibly it was to support an army of seventy-five hundred men to protect the colonists from Indians and the possibility of a French return to America. These suggestions carried no weight in America, where the proclivity of regular army soldiers to run away from Indians was too well understood, and where the notion of a French uprising was ludicrous. Garrisons

---

2 Stephen Hopkins, *The Rights of Colonies Examined* (1764), in *Tracts of the American Revolution, 1773–1776*, ed. Merrill Jensen (Indianapolis: Bobbs-Merrill Co., 1967), 47.

3 Introduction, *Tracts*, ed. Jensen, xxv.

4 Peter D. G. Thomas in *The Blackwell Encyclopedia*, 110; Edmund S. Morgan and Helen M. Morgan, *The Stamp Act Crisis: Prologue to Revolution* (1953), reprinted (Chapel Hill: University of North Carolina Press, 1995), 64–65.

posted in the west, as was quickly noticed, were protecting *the Indians* from advancing European settlers, by enforcing the Royal Proclamation and the boundary line drawn in 1768 at Fort Stanwix.

From first announcement, the colonists feared presence among them of a standing army. British tradition warned them against the uses of such troops to suppress popular movements. As recently as 1745, the army had devastated the Scottish Highlands, and troops sent from England during the Seven Years War had created hostility everywhere. While losing battles against the French, they had domineered over colonial assemblies and seized quarters in civilian homes. In 1765 the colonists wanted to protect themselves. Nevertheless, when the ministry decreed that army, the colonists accepted an imperial obligation to help pay for it, and they offered to tax themselves in response to royal requests.[5]

A delegation from the Massachusetts assembly called on Governor Francis Bernard to discuss how this might be done, and he turned them aside because he had no advice from London about the quotas expected from each colony.[6] In England, colonial agents consulted with Minister Grenville – twice – for guidance about how much revenue was desired and how responsibilities might be shared out. Grenville shuffled them off, and in retrospect it is clear that his intent went further than raising a revenue. He meant to demonstrate beyond question Parliament's power to *rule* the colonies however it pleased, regardless of how their assemblies felt about the matter. As Edmund and Helen Morgan concisely observe, "The main issue was no longer raising a revenue, but putting the Americans in their place."[7] When the act was finally passed on 22 March 1765, the colonists were "taxed without consent for purposes of revenue, their rights to common-law trial abridged [by omission of juries], the authority of one prerogative court (admiralty) enlarged, and the establishment of another (ecclesiastical) hinted at."[8]

Not surprisingly, the Stamp Tax provoked an uproar in the colonies.

Protest against the Stamp Act was strong from Britain's commercial classes and irresistible in America. Parliament backed down grudgingly as a matter of expediency. To make sure that its retreat did not abandon basic principles, Parliament accompanied the Stamp Act repeal with the enactment of a new Declaratory Act asserting the right of the king-in-Parliament to make binding laws for colonial Americans "in all cases whatsoever."[9]

Whatever else this might be called, it was not ambiguous, and it expressed precisely what the colonists had found most objectionable in the hated

5 Theodore Draper, *A Struggle for Power: The American Revolution* (New York: Times Books, 1996), 263–64.
6 Morgan and Morgan, *Stamp Act Crisis*, 62–63.   7 Ibid., 65.   8 Ibid., 74.
9 *Documents of American History*, ed. Commager, 1:60–61.

Stamp Act, but optimists saw it as merely a way for Parliament to save face after defeat by those disobedient "subjects" in the colonies. "This is merely to save Appearances," advised Franklin to the Pennsylvania assembly, "and I think we may rest secure notwithstanding such Act, that no future Ministry will ever attempt to tax us."[10] He could not have been more wrong.

The first official reaction against the Stamp Act came from Virginia's House of Burgesses in May 1765 when a fiery new member named Patrick Henry seized political leadership with a speech and a set of proposed Resolves of protest and defiance. Garbled reports made them more subversive than they seem actually to have been. Everyone "knows" the doubtful story that Henry climaxed his speech with "if this be treason make the most of it," but fewer persons know that he was admonished by the Speaker for the violence of his remarks, upon which he sensibly apologized. Similarly the Burgesses rejected his most extreme Resolves. The reports circulated about the event omitted such nice distinctions. They purported defiance greater than the actuality, and aroused radicals in other colonies to actions stronger than the Burgesses' own.[11]

In September, Rhode Island's assembly, like Virginia's, denied Parliament's authority to tax and went beyond Virginia by ordering colonial officers "to proceed in the execution of their respective offices in the same manner as usual [without stamps]; and that this Assembly will indemnify and save harmless all the said officers, on account of their conduct, agreeably to this resolution."[12]

Other colonies took up the cause, though none went so far in resistance as Rhode Island. In June the Massachusetts House of Representatives (the lower house of a two-chamber legislature) sent a circular letter to other assemblies inviting delegates to a congress at New York City in October. Nine colonies responded to this Stamp Act Congress.[13] It became more important for what it was than for what it did which was just another petition for relief. Its true significance lay in its precedent for the quite varied colonies to act jointly after mutual discussion. Nothing like it had ever happened among them till then; previously the nearest thing to colonial unity occurred when agents in London joined to lobby Parliament together.

Important men in all the colonies began to wonder what means were possible to get relief from a Parliament that would not even consider their petitions. After legal channels had been closed off, only extralegal, forceful actions were left, whereupon Boston came to the fore. As Edmund and

---

10 *Franklin Papers* 13:186–87 and n2.
11 Knollenberg, *Origin of the American Revolution*, 210; Morgan and Morgan, *The Stamp Act Crisis*, 94–100.
12 Ibid., 103.   13 Ibid., 108.

Helen Morgan remark, "Bostonians sometimes seemed to love violence for its own sake."[14] A number of highly respectable gentlemen, knowing that mob violence broke out among the city's gangs at regular intervals, gave guidance to the gangs to put political messages in their vandalism – just as in London. First, on 14 August 1765, they vented wrath on the house of Provincial Secretary Andrew Oliver who reputedly had been appointed distributor of stamped paper. Their destruction was thorough but not so complete as their masterwork on 26 August when they attended to Lieutenant Governor Thomas Hutchinson. "They destroyed windows, doors, furniture, wainscoting, and paintings, and stole £900 in cash, as well as clothing and silverware. They cut down all the trees in the garden, beat down the partitions in the house and had even begun to remove the slate from the roof when daylight stopped them."[15]

It is hard to square the downright thievery of this affair with an image of noble patriotism. Some of the very proper (and highly anonymous) instigators of the gangs' actions worried that they had let a genie escape from its imprisoning bottle, but the officers in charge of law and order confessed themselves unable to suppress the riots or even to venture near them. The gang leader, a man named Ebenezer McIntosh, was later arrested without resistance, but the judges did not know what to do with him. McIntosh let it be known that if he were charged he would name the riots' respectable instigators, and his followers threatened destruction of the customs house. On urging from the customs agents, McIntosh was released.[16]

For modern romanticists who envision revolution as the common people rising in outrage, it is scandalous that colonial resistance to Britain's repressions started among merchants and lawyers and the owners of great slave plantations. (And to think that Nikolai Lenin praised the American Revolution extravagantly!)

The bourgeois gentlemen of the colonies adopted a strategy of squeezing commercial partners in Britain on the assumption that British merchants would compel Parliament to rescind the Sugar Act and the Stamp Act. This was sound strategy; the City of London merchants actively opposed their government's repressive measures. Colonials banded together to boycott British goods by nonimportation agreements, and some of them withheld payment for bills past due, to the anguish of their creditors.

Southern planters were as involved as northern merchants because the planters had the habit of buying British luxuries on a large scale. The planters drove slaves to produce their tobacco staple (the largest single colo-

14 Ibid., 127.   15 Ibid., 133.   16 Ibid., 134–35.

nial commodity), but they became great merchants when they took tobacco to market.

Sanctioned by the most respectable men in the colonies, less respectable types used violence and intimidation to prevent distribution and use of Parliament's stamped paper. Mobs guaranteed the effectiveness of the commercial boycott by threatening and attacking merchants who held back from participation. This was in the pattern of London's contemporary mobs. These popular actions tapped a deep well of anti-British resentment especially among recent Irish and Scotch-Irish immigrants who had been forced out of their homelands by the rapacity of English absentee landlords.

The resistance of the eastern urban merchants was joined by immigrants who had gone west in search of lands. Their resentments festered also because of the Royal Proclamation line barring further western settlement. Joining them, many veterans of the Seven Years War had been promised bonus lands as rewards for service, but colonial governments were forbidden by the Proclamation from fulfilling their engagements. Only the crown could now grant lands west of the Proclamation line, and the crown adamantly refused to do so. Cheated soldiers blamed the crown and joined hotly in antiroyal demonstrations.

The merchants and lawyers who launched the earliest resistance acquired followers in great numbers and at nearly all levels of Euro-American society; but the leaders of the resistance began to find their followings too much to handle as newer, more violent spokesmen came to the fore.

One must distinguish sharply between the outlooks of Euro-Americans and the blacks and Indians also living in America and claimed by the colonies. It is essential from this point in the narrative to recognize this distinction constantly. The *society* of Euro-Americans was part – a large part – of the total *population* that included rigid castes imposed by conceptions of race. Southern planters never for a moment forgot the possibility of slave uprisings against *them*, and because the westerners who are often called frontiersmen demanded full freedom to seize tribal lands at will, the tribes conceived *them* instead of the crown as their enemy.

Writers from New England tend to monopolize the history of the American Revolution and to treat it somewhat as the history of Massachusetts writ large. Their obsessive belief that Massachusetts was the heart and soul of that great event is demonstrably erroneous. Perhaps the mistake appears most clearly in the way that after ultimate victory the new United States was taken over by a "Virginia Dynasty" that ran the government in the interests of slave owners for more than thirty years with only a brief interruption from Massachusetts's John Adams. Let that thought be whatever it is worth; the consensus among New England's historians needs empirical correction on several counts.

They all mix up the coming of the Revolution with the squabbles and intrigues of Boston's local politics, playing down the groundswell in other colonies of hostility to Britain. This confuses a gun's trigger with its ammunition. Massachusetts's assembly took leadership from Pennsylvania's Benjamin Franklin.[17] Virginia originated the intercolonial committees of correspondence and sent out the call to the Continental Congress that coordinated the Revolution – after Franklin advised it.[18]

On the other hand, inexplicably, no credit is given to Massachusetts for what had been in fact a toughly effective resistance against royal prerogative during the Seven Years War. In 1757 the assembly had held out against commands by the agent of royal prerogative, Lord Loudoun. He commanded them to provide money and men in stipulated amounts, and they risked his furious anger by evading his demands until William Pitt in England *solicited* their aid in return for reciprocal benefits. Pitt did this on advice from Governor Thomas Pownall (who is sneered at by the historians), and on those terms the assembly immediately voted more help to the crown than Pitt had asked for.[19] This has all sunk below the level of historical recognition in favor of much attention to the personal ambitions and enemies of Thomas Hutchinson who became governor in 1774.

There is praise for Hutchinson's integrity as an upright servant of the crown, and much deploring of the wild men in the assembly who supposedly were manipulated by Samuel Adams as creatures of passion rather than reason. The assembly's earlier principled struggle against Loudoun and the prerogative is overlooked, as also is the not so negligible support, equally principled, given by Hutchinson to Loudoun and the prerogative. Boston's radicals and middle-of-the-roaders had a bone to pick with Hutchinson that had more meat on it than their aversion to his holding of multiple offices. One can concede readily that their treatment of him was too vicious (as will be shown), but it was not insensate rage. It was rage with reasons. Hutchinson's flaunted uprightness had a sneaky quality; he secretly advised the ministry to curtail Massachusetts's liberties, and he got caught at it.[20]

Always behind events in Massachusetts was its living legend as the offspring of England's Puritan revolution of the 1640s. Those Puritans had chopped a king's head off; and, when the tide turned, two of his sentencers found refuge and *protection* in New England. The founders of Massachu-

---

17 See Chap. 21 below.
18 David W. Conroy in *The Blackwell Encyclopedia*, 225; Francis Jennings, *Benjamin Franklin, Politician*, 189–90.
19 Pitt to governors, 30 Dec. 1757; Pownall to Pitt, 14 March 1758, *Correspondence of William Pitt, Earl of Chatham*, 4 vols. (London: John Murray, 1838–40), 1:136–40; 1:203–4.
20 *Franklin Papers*, 20:550, 551.

setts had governed without deferring to the king until Roger Williams exposed how they demanded an oath of loyalty only to their own magistrates and not to the king.[21] In Massachusetts, *revolution* was a respected word. In this respect, certainly, Boston was far out in front of other colonies, but they made their own judgments about their own interests in their own good time. This is not the same as accepting leadership of a dozen independent polities. Certainly, Virginia's and South Carolina's slave-owning elites wanted no part of New England's ranting, canting social radicals. What united the varied colonies was the repressive activity of king and Parliament, not the fulminations of some noisy agitators though such persons became active everywhere. To call Samuel Adams "the father of the Revolution" shows only political narrow-mindedness to match his bigotry. Patrick Henry roused Virginia. Philadelphia's Thomas Paine sounded the clarion to all the colonies after John Dickinson had warmed them up. Massachusetts attracts notice as bubbles announce champagne, but the bubbles do not make wine; wine makes the bubbles. The Revolution fermented through all the colonies.

21 Minutes, 1 April and 14 May 1634, *Records of the Governor and Company of the Massachusetts Bay in New-England*, ed. Nathaniel B. Shurtleff, 5 vols. (Boston: 1853–1854), 1:116–17; 3 September 1635, 1:160–61.

17

A VARIATION ON THE THEME OF
LIBERTY IN THE CAROLINAS

Much high-sounding oratory about colonial virtue versus British corruption tends to homogenize the colonists in ways that simply were not true. At the same time that colonial assemblies and their civil spokesmen denounced the crown's minions for assorted measures of repression, the same measures were being used in the Carolinas, and by many of the same men, to uphold the power of slaveholding tidewater aristocrats against complaints of freemen in the backcountry.

John Richard Alden tells of vain efforts by the interior settlers to get the attention of indifferent aristocrats. "The South Carolina frontier, like any American frontier was a refuge for outlaws, rascals, and ne'er-do-wells as well as a land of opportunity for the honest and industrious."[1] Yet, despite repeated pleas by the frontier's law-abiding folk, protection was denied to them by both the crown's appointees and the elected assembly.

After 1764, the English placeman Richard Cumberland was supposed to keep order as provost marshal, but Cumberland held to the pattern of sinecure holders: He stayed in England and deputized his duties to Roger Pinckney. It is worth noting that Pinckney belonged to a family that would become notorious soon as protestors against being "enslaved" by the crown. His libertarian outlook was highly directional. He gave no comfort to the westerners, and he had reasons of pounds and pence. If he were to send sheriffs up-country, the fees for their services would go to them instead of coming through Charleston's court to the provost marshal and his deputy. There were no backcountry courts because Charleston's legal fraternity wanted none of the discomforts of travel.

Instead of creating new counties in the backcountry, the loudly libertarian assembly simply ran existing county lines westward so that interior settlers had to journey to Charleston for even the routine legal work of

---

1 John Richard Alden, *The South in the Revolution, 1763–1789*. A History of the South III. (Baton Rouge: Louisiana State University Press and Littlefield Fund of University of Texas, 1957), 147.

counties; and doing this might require the expense of travel demanding a week of time.

So, while colonists elsewhere protested the Stamp Act, backcountry settlers formed local vigilante groups in 1767 to drive away outlaw bands. Instead of responding to the westerners' need, Governor Lord Charles Montague ordered the "Regulators" to disperse and asked the assembly to restrain them. Some of these people desirous of law and order were hauled into court and punished as though they were the criminals they had tried to suppress.[2]

The protesters grew more angry and said so in a "Remonstrance" by four thousand of them. At last Charleston began to pay attention, but before policing could be reformed, placeman Cumberland had to be bought off expensively. He demanded five thousand pounds for his sinecure property. At length, the money was found and six new circuit courts and judges were enacted, but with a catch. The judges were to serve during good behavior rather than at the crown's pleasure, and the assemblymen probably understood that the Privy Council would disallow this measure, which it did. The Privy Council was not about to tolerate any more independent judges. So the South Carolina backcountry remained as distressed as before.

Unrest grew worse until people met to defy the tidewater government with a declaration that its writs and warrants would be nullified until approved by the Regulators. Lord Montague made a couple of comic opera efforts to put down the Regulators in 1769 by using militia troops more in sympathy with the Regulators than with the government. Relief came when Lord Montague returned to England, leaving the government to native-born Lieutenant Governor William Bull II, who conciliated the Regulators, pardoned their leaders, and established order in the backcountry.[3] By that time the Regulation in South Carolina was caught up in the near approaches of the American Revolution.

Hostile though they were to the western settlers of their own province, the Commons of South Carolina recognized an identity of interest with Wilkesite resisters against royal domination. When the London society of Supporters of the Bill of Rights solicited help from colonials, the Carolinian House of Commons responded (8 December 1769) with a gift of fifteen hundred pounds sterling; and it thereby precipitated conflict with the crown and its colonial officers.

No one disputed that Commons had the right to *originate* money bills, but in this instance they *consummated* the transaction by sending the money before their governor realized what was happening. Lt. Gov. William Bull II indignantly reported it to Secretary Hillsborough, the London press pub-

2 Ibid., 148–49. 3 Ibid., 149–50.

licized it, and ministers were furious about Commons ordering money out of the treasury without the consent of the executive. It did not mollify them that the money had been given for their most violent and effective critic, John Wilkes.[4] The Privy Council sent an "additional instruction" to Lt. Gov. Bull specifying that any treasurer who should issue money without Bull's signature would be sacked and heavily fined. With that, the two sides took up combat positions from which they did not stir during the next five years.

Commons refused to originate a tax bill except on terms satisfactory to themselves, and the crown's officers refused to consider any bill except one that complied with the "additional instruction." Commons lobbied vainly to get the "additional instruction" revoked, and devised several innocent-seeming bills that ran into an executive stone wall. For Henry Laurens traveling in London, the issue was identical with resistance to the Stamp Act. It was nothing less than the "Right of the People to give and grant voluntarily in mode and in Quantity free from the Fetters of ministerial Instructions, restrictive, or obligatory."[5] Benjamin Franklin, also in London, received news of the struggle from his printing partner Peter Timothy, whose *South Carolina Gazette* supported Commons.[6]

King and ministry were as intransigent as Commons, and when the assembly passed defiant bills, it was dissolved by executive order. Twice. Governor Lord Charles Montague tried to circumvent the radicals centered in Charleston by calling the assembly in 1772 to meet at Beaufort, seventy miles south of the city. He guessed wrong. City radicals appeared in force, and when Montague saw what was happening he prorogued the session after three days of doing nothing; and they reassembled again at Charleston. Montague gave up and returned to England bequeathing the mess to Lt. Gov. Bull.

Issues ramified as the governor's Council took up the fight in 1773. Pre-arranged income from a tax law passed for a term of years in 1769 had kept the province going before the locking of horns. Now this income was due to expire, so the Council's majority stopped action on all other legislation until the tax should be renewed on the crown's terms. Two Council members dissented and one, William Henry Drayton, asked printer Thomas Powell to publish their dissent. Powell assented, but his act amounted in law to printing part of Council's journals without its consent, for which he was jailed for "a high Breach of Privilege and a Contempt of this House." The order to jail him was signed by Egerton Leigh, president of the Council. In that era of multiple office holding, Leigh was involved also as Attorney General.

---

4 *The Nature of Colony Constitutions: Two Pamphlets on the Wilkes Fund Controversy*, ed. and comp. Jack P. Greene (Columbia: University of South Carolina Press, 1970), 7–11.
5 Ibid., 19. 6 *Franklin Papers*, 18:233–35.

Two judges associated with the Commons majority released printer Powell with a writ of habeas corpus, whereupon he sued Sir Egerton Leigh for damages. Printer and judges in South Carolina paralleled remarkably the experience of printers and judges in London, yet how different were their circumstances.

In 1774, Commons devised a new scheme to invent a substitute for money. It issued certificates of indebtedness to pay the government's bills, and its members pledged to accept them as currency. They carried a promise of payment in legal tender when a new tax bill should be passed. It worked. Commons and crown came to a stalemate, and their local issues soon were swamped by uproars from Britain's Coercive Acts and pan-colonial resistance generated by committees of correspondence.

This section rests heavily on Jack P. Greene's Introduction to his reprint of two pamphlets generated in 1774 by the political brawl. Sir Egerton Leigh wrote a justification for the royal prerogative, attacking the House of Commons's actions as "unconstitutional." Leigh's interest in the case was plain. "I am a downright *Placeman*," he wrote, and so he had been. From that standpoint, he demanded, "What could influence Men to step forth, and, by an unconstitutional and unwarrantable stretch of Power, to misapply the Public Money, and at the same time offer so gross an insult to His Majesty's Government both at home and abroad?"[7]

I shall make no effort to dive into the arguments and invective of these pamphlets, but some interest attaches to author Arthur Lee who responded to Leigh. Lee was not a South Carolinian. He was a Virginian in London and clearly he had affiliated with the Supporters of the Bill of Rights. He may have written that society's appeal for funds to which Commons responded in the first place. Lee had also become deputy agent for Massachusetts's lower house, working as Benjamin Franklin's teammate before Franklin returned to Pennsylvania. Thus, the spokesmen for radical Massachusetts were a Pennsylvanian with multiple colonial agencies and a Virginian embroiled as the champion of South Carolina's House of Commons.[8]

As a marker of evolving conceptions, it is interesting to see how Arthur Lee (like opponent Egerton Leigh) appealed to that amorphous English "constitution," and how differently he conceived it. Egerton Leigh argued that colonial charters had been granted by royal prerogative and could be altered or abolished by the same prerogative. Arthur Lee contradicted this, point-blank. We see him invoking a higher law that was one step short of outright revolution.

7 *The Nature of Colony Constitutions*, 78.   8 See *Franklin Papers*, Vol. 21.

> The Rights and Privileges of the Commons House spring from the Rights and Privileges of *British* Subjects, and are coeval with the Constitution. They were neither created, nor can they be abolished by the Crown. The Charter recognized, but could not create them. The Right of being represented in that Legislature, by whose Acts they are bound, is the unalienable Birthright of *English* Subjects. This Claim is prior and paramount to any royal Grant.[9]

How incident evolved into Revolution! There is no need to speculate about the influence of John Locke or any other theorist. Commons made a gift. The crown ordered revocation. Commons defied the order. Both sides worked up rationalizations that reached ever deeper into basic assumptions pro or anti prerogative; and at last only force could settle the argument.

But while the abstractions in all these appeals to the rights of men sound grand, where is there any thought of the majority of South Carolinians enslaved by the passionate defenders of liberty?

North Carolina's Regulation went a different way from South Carolina's. The piedmont region underwent excitement and protest against exploitation by tidewater rulers, but historian Marvin L. Michael Kay attributes it to resentment by a social class rather than a region. He shows much display of working farmers against the wealthy, and a difference in *kind* of property where slavery was concentrated in the eastern tidewater region (as in South Carolina also); but whatever the explanation of theoretical analysis may be, the site of unrest was in the piedmont, and repression came from the coast.

There was much substantial reason for unrest. Unlike South Carolina, its neighboring colony had created inland counties with the usual county apparatus of sheriffs, courts, and offices. Unhappily, they demonstrated to the South Carolinians that there may be worse fates than lack of officials. In North Carolina the local officials were appointed by the provincial governor and council, and their sins were many. Professor Kay's catalog requires quotation.

> Officials pursued policies which added to private fortunes in many ways: by the awarding of public contracts to favorites; by locating and building roads, bridges, harbors, ferries, and towns to convenience the rich and powerful; by issuing licenses for mills to favorites; by insuring that the public offices the wealthy controlled were remunerative; by granting compensations to masters for executed slaves; and by awarding exorbitant commissions to a favored few to handle the mechanics of currency emissions.

So far, it sounds familiarly like patronage everywhere, but there is more.

9 *The Nature of Colony Constitutions,* 186.

Affluent officeholders also exploited more directly their poorer and weaker constituents. They collected unlawful taxes and fees and corruptly handled public monies. Such actions not only stole money . . . but also increased the tax levels that had remained high after the French and Indian War. . . . A regressive tax system that depended primarily upon poll taxes, duties, fees, and work levies . . . disproportionately and harshly burdened the poor. . . . Moreover, creditors, merchants, lawyers, and public officers brought an increasing number of court suits against indebted farmers, while lawyers and officers charged exorbitant or extortionate court fees. All these groups cooperated in distraining exorbitant amounts of property from moneyless farmers and corruptly selling the property at public auctions below its value to members of the in-group – with nothing returned to the victims. The wealthy and powerful were able to maintain these conditions both by passing biased laws and by manipulating the application of these statutes."[10]

Difficulties concerning land tenure accompanied exploitation by officeholders. Between 1758 and 1770, corrupt practices of proprietor Lord Granville caused such disturbance that his land office closed so that no purchases could be patented. Petitions to the assembly were met by county officials parroting the assemblymen's invocation of the *constitutional rights* of Englishmen, but with a small twist. The officials sued in court for their constitutional *prerogatives*. The English constitution had more than one aspect.[11]

The situation deteriorated until the Regulators' association organized in April 1768 and quickly gained adherents in the piedmont region centered on Orange County. Armed followers assembled at Hillsborough. (Ironically, Hillsborough had been the home location of the friendly Occaneechee Indians massacred by the frontier rogue Nathaniel Bacon in 1675.)[12]

Governor William Tryon, another English placeman, determined to suppress the Regulators' "insurrection" by force. He marched militiamen from other counties to Hillsborough where he intimidated the Regulators into dispersing; but their agitation continued, and it now included a complaint that farmers averaged a twelfth of the year on unpaid militia musters or road work.[13] (This corvée inheritance from feudal England smells at today's distance of patrols to control slave property among other things. Militias did not ordinarily drill so often otherwise.)

Considering the assembly's policies toward the piedmont, another of its actions becomes especially interesting: In 1769 the North Carolina assembly adopted the Virginia Resolves proposed by Patrick Henry against Parliament's Townshend Acts.[14]

10 Marvin L. Michael Kay, "The North Carolina Regulation, 1766–1776: A Class Conflict." In *The American Revolution: Explorations in the History of Radicalism*, ed. Alfred F. Young (DeKalb: Northern Illinois University Press, 1976), 75–76.
11 Ibid., 83–84.   12 Jennings, *The Ambiguous Iroquois Empire*, 147nn.
13 Kay, "North Carolina Regulation," 96.   14 Ibid., 97.

In 1770, the Regulators turned violent, harassing some of the wealthy officials who had been exploiting them. In January 1771, the assembly authorized Governor Tryon to suppress the Regulators with an act "to prevent riots and tumults," an act so severe that the crown later disallowed it. In May 1771, Tryon marched once more into the piedmont and was met by more than three thousand assembled Regulators at the Battle of Alamance (near present-day Chapel Hill). The Regulators were routed with casualties, and Tryon vented his displeasure by hanging one summarily. Six more were hanged later, after trial, and the Regulation ended.

However, it achieved some reforms in its backwash. Governor Tryon was succeeded by Josiah Martin who took the trouble in 1772 to investigate Regulator complaints on a peaceful trip to the piedmont. The assembly rejected Martin's proposals for reform, and the county clerks disobeyed his instructions to end exorbitant fees.[15]

Historians dispute whether the Regulators resentfully became crown Loyalists in the imminent outbreak of revolution. Perhaps the Revolutionaries' strongest lure was a guarantee of the land titles that had been jeopardized by the closing of Lord Granville's land office. However, one must remember Professor Kay's wry remark that the Tidewater Whig elite, as always, "kept reform to a minimum."[16]

In the Carolinas, liberty was not easy to define.

15 Ibid., 104.   16 Ibid., 107.

18

———— • ————

REPRESSION AND RESISTANCE

George III and his Parliament waged repression against the people of Britain as well as those of the colonies. If he never succeeded in becoming a complete tyrant, it was not for lack of trying. The British resistance against his policies is an inspiring story in its own right, another episode in the long history of struggle for the rights of Englishmen, and one that achieved substantial victories in Britain comparable to those of the gains toward autonomy in the colonies. To present the American Revolution validly, tribute must be paid to Englishmen striving toward liberties important to them. These were not so spectacular as the Americans' secession, but were genuine popular advances in what T. H. Breen has called "the supreme example in the western world of a State organized for effective war-making."[1]

In 1771, a society was formed of Supporters of the Bill of Rights. These were rich Londoners who proposed to pay John Wilkes's debts while working for a broader program. Their preamble was direct: "Whoever seriously considers the conduct of administration, both at home and abroad, can hardly entertain a doubt, that a plan is formed to subvert the constitution." Among other specifications, they tell, "we have seen a House of Commons infringing . . . the freedom of election; erasing a judicial record; committing to the Tower, and threatening with impeachment, the friends of the people, and the defenders of the law . . . [Commons had become] an engine of oppression in the hand of the crown." Looking abroad, the Supporters directed political groups. "You shall endeavour to restore to America the essential right of taxation, by representatives of their own free election."[2]

In 1777, Edmund Burke protested in an Address to the King that the establishment of military power in America "will become an apt, powerful,

---

1 T. H. Breen, "Ideology and Nationalism on the Eve of the American Revolution: Revisions *Once More* in Need of Revising," *Journal of American History* 84:1 (June 1997), 16.
2 [Junius], Philip Francis, *The Letters of Junius* (1783), "Preliminary Essay" by George Sackville, 2d ed. 1814, 91–93nl.

and certain engine for the destruction of our freedom here."[3] Virginian Arthur Lee, writing from England in 1774, observed that "the great Foundations of Freedom are the same on both Sides of the Atlantic, nor can they be subverted in the one, without being shaken in the other."[4]

In one respect, Britons were way ahead of the Americans. While chattel slavery increased under the regime established by the Revolution, British abolitionists and judges (and eventually even Parliament) set a course toward emancipation. But to acknowledge the contrast, a historian must assume that slaves by law are human persons by physique. This acknowledgment is sometimes hard to find in the Revolutionary fairy tale.

John Wilkes was as unlikely a popular hero as can easily be imagined. To begin with, he was not a handsome and virtuous young man on a white horse – no St. George or Galahad he. Wilkes was cockeyed and downright ugly from birth, and he became as squanderingly dissolute as any privileged lord limned by Hogarth. Inheriting wealth from his father's distillery, he married more money that came with an heiress. This was an arranged union rather than a love match. The couple quickly tired of each other and arranged a permanent separation. Wilkes's only domestic rectitude was his tender love for their daughter whom he cared for throughout a profligate, swashbuckling life. He compensated for personal ugliness by great charm of manner (when he cared to), so that a number of women succumbed to his easy advances; and, in addition to ordinary womanizing, he frequented Sir Francis Dashwood's Hellfire Club orgies at Medmenham Abbey. Wilkes fought two duels and at one point had to flee to France to escape threats of prosecution. He threw money about without reckoning, and went deeply into debt, yet always seemed able to borrow more or be rescued by a patron. What he could do better than anyone else in the kingdom, and what made him valuable to a patron, was to win elections.[5]

In our modern day when a single out-of-wedlock escapade can destroy a political career, it is bewildering to read of Wilkes's openly scandalous goings-on that seemed only to enhance the public's admiration for him. How did he do it?

To some extent it was a case of the man arriving on the scene at just the right moment, seemingly by happenstance, and seizing Fortune by the forelock (or anything else grippable). Englishmen were in ferment. Prices of necessities were rising at the same time as taxes, and the government seemed

---

3 Edmund Burke, *On the American Revolution: Selected Speeches and Letters*, ed. Elliott Robert Barkan (New York: Harper and Row, 1966), 158.
4 *The Nature of Colony Constitutions*, ed. and comp. Jack P. Greene, 137.
5 Raymond Postgate has written a fascinating biography, *"That Devil Wilkes"* (1930, rev. ed. London: Dobson Books, 1956).

indifferent to the woes of ordinary people, many of whom sought relief in Hogarth's Gin Lane. King George demanded and got a Scot, Lord Bute, as his leading minister, to the great dismay of common men who feared a reign presided over by what seemed to them an enemy. Ousted Whig lords schemed to regain power, and one of them, Earl Temple, discovered in John Wilkes a willing and skillful agent to smear the administration. With Temple's ample financial backing, Wilkes founded a weekly paper called *The North Briton* that regularly tore into the ministry's misdeeds which was the easier because they were so many.

In 1757, Wilkes had gained the seat for Aylesbury in the House of Commons by the usual method of buying voters at two pounds to five pounds each for a total of seven thousand pounds. It cannot be doubted that he had direct, personal knowledge of corruption. He learned more about the depravity of high officials when he became one of twelve "Monks of St. Francis" in the Hellfire Club. Their saint was Sir Francis Dashwood who organized orgies and black masses involving ministers and prostitutes on his estate at "Medmenham Abbey." Dashwood seems to have been England's foremost roué at a time when competition was keen. Supposedly Lord Bute joined his fun and rewarded Dashwood by making him Chancellor of the Exchequer in which capacity he has been called "probably the least competent minister ever to hold that office."[6] Very clearly sainthood for John Wilkes got no further than Dashwood's estate.

Wilkes had played the game of climbing from one showy place to another by appointment in 1754 as High Sheriff of Buckingham and as Colonel Dashwood's aide in the Buckinghamshire militia. But Wilkes's Parliamentary service was unobtrusive until 1762 when he founded *The North Briton*. Suddenly, with much help from the king and ministry, Wilkes became a celebrity.

Though he certainly was a rabble-rouser – none better – he carefully determined the legal limits of insult and epithet against the government, and he stayed just within the limits. He never attacked "the best of kings" while lambasting the king's chosen ministers. He hinted at royal scandals and roared against a presumed conspiracy of the Scots directed by Lord Bute to rule over honest, loyal Englishmen. He assailed tolerance for Catholics in Quebec. Until the colonies actually seceded, he spoke out in their behalf as victims of misrule.

In the House of Commons, Wilkes denounced coercion of the colonists, and between 1775 and 1780 "he delivered ten set speeches" in favor of peace. His biographer remarks that "every friend of the constitution saw early in

---

6 J. Steven Watson, *The Reign of George III, 1760–1815* (Oxford: Oxford University Press, 1960), 92.

the support of the American cause a vindication of the rights of Englishmen against an old exploded usurpation of the Stuarts, revived under the third prince of the House of Brunswick."[7] Naturally, Wilkes had to modify his approval of the Americans' cause when war broke out, but he never trimmed or switched.

Yet Wilkes never originated a set of principles to become inspiration for a movement; rather, he became the focal point of a campaign for "English liberties" by defending in his own person against the crown's measures to curtail such liberties. Wilkes was the visible actor in behalf of the Whig faction ousted from government; more or less covertly, they worked with him and through him to regain power.

It is curious to see that in some respects the most principled man in all these struggles was George III, but his righteousness lacks allure. George belonged to the class of virtuous rulers who are determined to conform subjects to what is good for them whether they like it or not. In his mind he had to save Britain from the "tyranny" of the Whig nobility. It was a mind not always well balanced, eventually becoming clinically insane. Until that traumatic day of revelation, one can only guess about his decisions in particular matters. In some cases, however, and punishment of Wilkes was one of them, George was seemingly half-mad, certainly obsessed and implacable. He insisted on attacking Wilkes even when his ministers hesitated to arouse the London mobs for whom Wilkes had become an idol. Theodore Draper found that the king "persistently took the hardest line against the Americans."[8]

One must recognize this plainly because of so many smooth portrayals of George as just a virtuous family man, confused by factional politics, who had the misfortune to fall victim to a disease. (The disease is very carefully described as *physical*.) In this sort of apologia, what George *did* gets lost behind what his tragedy was. Londoners knew better. The mobs roaring through London's streets were not anarchic; their targets were George's friends and associates. Happily expressing their own variety of political action, the mobs broke windows, smashed carriages, pulled down houses, and walked off with their contents. Even the troops were afraid of them.

This is not the place to repeat the saga of Wilkes, but his career can shed light on how London mobs, printers, and judges put limits on royal domination within England even as armed colonials ended it abroad. Wilkes used the courts successfully in some matters of politics, but he could not escape punishment for printing his pornographic poem "An Essay on Woman."

7 Horace Bleackley, *Life of John Wilkes* (New York: John Lane Co., 1917), 302, 314, 315.
8 Draper, *A Struggle for Power*, 478.

The same judges who found in his favor on political issues put him in prison for twenty-two months for the pornography. He emerged from prison more idolized than ever by the London crowds and he was reelected Member of Parliament for Middlesex County three more times despite George's insistence that he be expelled and replaced by a losing candidate. Finally, in 1774, Wilkes took his seat, having won for the people the "liberty" that Parliament could not reverse their election.

Along the way, he was elected Lord Mayor of the City, in which capacity he became a very polite spokesman to the crown for commercial and mercantile interests, after which the City made him its Chamberlain in December 1779, with a fat annual income of fifteen hundred pounds, enough to pay off his large debts. No martyr he, Wilkes behaved very circumspectly thereafter. In his own words, he became "an extinct volcano."[9]

It is his adoption by the City that reveals much about his former ability to arouse the masses in London and its surrounding counties. Powerful resentments against the government's policies pervaded the "middling" business classes that had long been informally allied to the Whigs in government. Supporting Wilkes served to express their anger, and the mobs in London's streets served to remind the government of how the City had turned against King Charles I. Despite his notoriety, John Wilkes was not so much the leader as an agent of one side in an internal struggle for power that paralleled the struggle between Britain and its colonies.

Ian R. Christie remarks that "the proud, vigorous, thrusting society" of the City of London "was in almost constant collision with the national government."[10] Supporting Wilkes was one way of expressing the City's anger. These moneymen showed hostility also by giving sanctuary and support to printers refuging from governmental persecution. Two major issues precipitated trials in court. The first concerned publication of "A Letter to the King" by an anonymous author calling himself Junius. (He has been identified as Philip Francis.) Junius's biting critiques were stronger than Wilkes's comments in *The North Briton*, and they reached a much larger reading public because they were picked up and reprinted in all the London papers.[11] Exasperated officials could not identify Junius, so they moved against his printers for "a most wicked, scandalous, seditious, and malicious libel" upon both the king and Parliament. Curiously, the first case was brought against a *re*printer, one John Almon, who was found guilty by a "special jury," 2 June 1770. We are obliged to guess about what made that jury "special."

9 George Rudé, *Wilkes and Liberty: A Social Study of 1763 to 1774* (Oxford: Oxford University Press, 1962), 171.
10 Ian R. Christie, *Wilkes, Wyvill and Reform: The Parliamentary Reform Movement in British Politics, 1760–1785.* (London: Macmillan, 1962), 8–9.
11 Watson, *Reign of George III*, 145–46.

Almon was fined and required to post heavy bond "for his good behaviour, for two years." When the original printer and others were tried, 13 June 1770, "each by a Jury of independent citizens of London," all were acquitted.[12]

The details of the case reveal much about those printers and the public's attitudes toward the government. Junius had provided substantial grounds for the prosecution of his "letter" to the king although anonymity precluded suit against his person. The "letter" dripped polite venom against George III. Though the "letter" made a thin pretence of attributing all the king's elegantly described nastiness to his ministers, its real target was very plain. And Junius's parting shot omitted even the pretence. "The prince who imitates [the Stuarts'] conduct," he wrote, "should be warned by their example; and while he plumes himself upon the security of his title to the crown, should remember that, as it was acquired by one revolution, it may be lost by another."[13]

When the printer of the *Public Advertiser* was sued by the crown, Law Lord Mansfield instructed the jury to decide two points: the printing and publishing of the paper, and the sense and meaning of it. They brought in a verdict of "Guilty of printing and publishing *only*." Tumult ensued in Parliament.

A new trial was ordered with hilarious and inspiring results. For this second trial, the attorney general needed a copy of the original publication, but this had been forethoughtedly removed by the foreman of the first jury, who destroyed it. What happened then opens a wide window into public feeling. Though the paper had been so popular that its entire issue sold out within hours of publication despite five hundred extra copies being added to the usual number, *not a single copy could be found by the attorney general's office to serve as essential evidence in the second trial*. Whereupon the judge threw out the case.[14]

Those printers were a sturdy lot. Two of them, John Wheble and R. Thompson, defied a ban against reporting actions in Parliament. They were summoned before the House of Commons, but fled to sanctuary in the City. George III offered rewards of fifty pounds each for their arrest, and six more printers were summoned to Commons. Of these, one was arrested, but the City's Alderman Oliver arrested the arrester (official messenger). King George flew into a rage. In actions that do not seem entirely sane in the circumstances, he ordered commitment to the Tower of the defiant alderman *and* the City's Lord Mayor. Whereupon the City's Common Council voted thanks to alderman, lord mayor, and John Wilkes who

---

12 *The Trial of John Almon, Bookseller . . . For Selling JUNIUS's Letter to the K——* (London: J. Miller, 1770); Francis, *Letters of Junius*, 117–25 and long note.
13 Francis, *Letters of Junius*, 221–22.   14 Ibid., 117–25, 213n.

had protested. What happened then gave warning to king and Commons to back down.

> The two magistrates were released from the Tower to a salute of twenty-one guns of the Hon. Artillery Company and escorted in a triumphal procession of fifty-three carriages by almost the entire Common Council, and saluted with loud and universal huzzas. At night, the City was illuminated in their honour and angry crowds smashed [Commons's] Speaker Norton's windows.[15]

There was no punishment for the printer heroes, the newspapers resumed reports of Parliament's debates, and Commons abandoned the issue. The upshot was that the printers made ministers responsible for the king's speech from the throne when opening a session of Parliament. Thereafter the ministers could no longer hide behind the king's immunity from challenge.

This does not mean that Parliament now began to champion democracy or the common people, not at all. The rotten boroughs still stank. Corruption still polluted. Whig lords as well as Tories were as lordly as ever. But now there were some limits that arrogance prudently observed, and courts enforced them. Though it has often been said that the king-in-parliament held absolute power, the law lords and the mobs kept it within limits set by that exasperatingly amorphous thing, the English constitution.

John Wilkes made a greater contribution to responsible government (not democracy) than he had originally intended because action by government forced him to defend himself. Unlike anonymous Junius, Wilkes had been known as the publisher of *The North Briton* when its strong criticism of the ministry appeared in Number 45. Although Wilkes carefully avoided attacks on the king, the earl of Halifax, as secretary of state, issued a *general warrant* to arrest Wilkes and seize all his papers – at the least, to put him out of business, but with the further intent to find him guilty of criminal libel, sedition, treason, *anything* to punish him hard. The limitless range of what was sanctioned under a general warrant alarmed even the law lords.

Wilkes counterattacked with an action for trespass (6 December 1763), and Lord Chief Justice Pratt took note of the breadth of a general warrant when he instructed the jury.

> The defendants [government officers] claimed a right under precedents to force persons' houses, break open escrutores, seize their papers, &c. upon a general warrant, where no inventory is made of the things thus taken away, and where no offenders' names are specified in the warrant, and therefore a discretionary power given to messengers to search wherever their suspicions may chance to fall. If such a power is truly invested in a secretary of state, and he can delegate this power, it certainly may affect the person and property of every man in the

15 Rudé, *Wilkes and Liberty*, 164.

kingdom, and is totally subversive of the liberty of the subject. . . . Precedents which had been produced since the [Glorious] Revolution, are no justification of a practice in itself illegal, and contrary to the fundamental principles of the constitution.

The jury took less than half an hour to return a verdict for Wilkes with a thousand pounds damages.[16] [I cannot resist noticing the contrast between Justice Pratt's instruction and the practice today of certain agencies of the United States government.] London's tough printers understood what general warrants were about. They blacklisted the man who had turned Wilkes's printed proofs over to the government.[17]

Chief Justice Pratt's strong judgment put him out on the end of a long limb, but the other judges came around to his belief in 1765, and even the House of Commons in 1766 resolved general warrants to be illegal and obnoxious.[18] But they were still used in Massachusetts under the name of Writs of Assistance.[19]

Despite his prominence in the histories, Wilkes was not a solitary hero. Behind his flamboyance, a group of Whig nobles, led by Earl Temple, used him to forward their own, more conservative opposition to the king.[20] On the other hand, a more radical Society of the Supporters of the Bill of Rights was formed in 1769 and raised twenty thousand pounds toward Wilkes's huge debts. The Society members kept active during his stay in prison, and they seem to have been involved in some of the demonstrations by London mobs against the crown.[21] In Massachusetts a group of excited citizens picked up the name from a speech by one of Wilkes's parliamentary supporters and adopted it for themselves to become the Sons of Liberty. Connecticut settlers in Pennsylvania's Wyoming Valley named their town Wilkes-Barré after Parliament's leading champions of colonial interests.

Historian George Rudé has come closer than other writers to telling the story of English battles for civil liberties under George III, but hints suggest that much more remains to be told. It seems to me that Tory devotees of royalty have tried to save George III's reputation (and the stability of the crown) from the full implications of his policies. This has required omitting or underplaying the breadth and size of the *movement* – not merely a limelit man – opposing the king. A substantial literature has piled up to decry "the Whig interpretation of history" as though the Tory interpretation is objective and trustworthy. We need a better.

16 *English Historical Documents*, Vol. X: *1714–1783*, ed. D. B. Horn and Mary Ransome (London: Eyre and Spottiswoode, 1957), 256–57.
17 Rudé, *Wilkes and Liberty*, 36.   18 Ibid., 30.
19 Edmund S. Morgan and Helen M. Morgan, *The Stamp Act Crisis: Prologue to Revolution* (1953), (Chapel Hill: University of North Carolina Press, 1995), 46, 219.
20 Rudé, *Wilkes and Liberty*, 21.   21 Ibid., 61–62, 107.

But to speak of *the* Tory interpretation is a little misleading. One writer with fair credentials as a Tory has remarked that as a result of the Wilkes campaigns and jury verdicts:

> The letter of the law [concerning press freedom] was thus subjected in each case to the discretion of a jury, and in the last year of the eighteenth century, it could be said that "a man may publish anything which twelve of his countrymen think is not blameable." History will not deny some share in the credit for this achievement to Alderman John Wilkes.

Thus Winston Churchill in *Age of Revolution*.[22]

---

22 Winston S. Churchill, *A History of the English-Speaking Peoples*, 4 vols.; III: *The Age of Revolution* (New York: Dodd, Mead and Co., 1957), 169.

19

A BATTLE FOR BISHOPS

In the eighteenth-century colonies, as in their parent country, religious organizations functioned as political parties. In New England governmental power, though exerted by laymen, responded and conformed to what was in fact an established church of "nonconformists." In Virginia, the Church of England was also the colonial establishment, though dissenters were tolerated. In Rhode Island and the "Middle" colonies (formerly part of New Netherland), church organizations existed independently of government. An apparent qualification is required for Pennsylvania where Quakers regularly were elected to control the provincial assembly until 1756, but the Quaker faith stressed religious toleration as inherent in its creed; thus the Quaker-dominated assembly protected the right of even despised Roman Catholics to conduct public worship. Until the conquest of French Canada, Pennsylvania was the only place in the entire British empire to extend toleration so far.

It followed that church rivalries became political campaigns with control of governments as objectives. In Virginia, clergymen struggled with the lay gentlemen who constituted their controlling vestries. It was not much of a battle because the vestrymen also controlled county and provincial governments. When some of the clergy demanded larger incomes, they could only appeal to the crown (as in the Two Penny dispute), and Virginia's gentry made short work of edicts from London. Except for royal controls over outreach to the west, Virginia had become effectively autonomous well before opting for independence, and the gentry liked to keep clergy on leading strings. When the Archbishop of Canterbury proposed to send bishops to America, Virginians bridled.

The proposal aroused absolute fury in Massachusetts where the established "nonconformists" saw it as an attack upon their true faith. In the middle colonies, Quakers opposed bishops as a means of introducing a church establishment, and Presbyterians opposed them as agents of the wrong establishment.

In 1763 (that pregnant date), Archbishop Thomas Secker declared, "We must try our utmost for bishops."[1] Secker was a man with strong personal connections among the powerful; he had baptized, confirmed, crowned, and married George III, who held him in high respect.[2] But the government held back; issues enough were rising between colonials and crown. Boston's fire-eating minister Jonathan Mayhew attacked the Society for the Propagation of the Gospel (SPG) for its record of sending missionaries to Protestant dissenters instead of Indian heathens.[3] Very soon the issue heated up as nearly all the Anglican clergy "actively opposed any resistance to the Stamp Act by counseling passive obedience and branding any other conduct as disloyal."[4]

With their record of support for government (which was natural enough for an established church), the Anglican clergy antagonized dissenters on political grounds even more strongly than in matters of creed. Long after the triumph of the Revolution, John Adams would remember that "the apprehension of Episcopacy contributed . . . as much as any other cause, to arouse the attention not only of the inquiring mind, but of the common people, and urge them to close thinking on the constitutional authority of parliament over the colonies."[5]

On the American side of the Atlantic the bishops were urged by the SPG's missionaries in the northern colonies who convened in 1765 to petition "warmly" for them. Southern clergymen, however, held different views. "They are their own pastors," wrote Samuel Auchmuty, by which he meant they had no desire for new supervisors to impose unwanted personal discipline.[6]

When "commissioner" James Horrocks summoned a meeting of Virginia's Anglican clergy in 1771, only eleven responded (of more than a hundred). Only seven of them, plus the commissioner, voted to petition for a bishop, and four voted strongly against. As historian Carl Bridenbaugh remarks, "The Southern Anglicans, especially in Virginia, enjoyed through their vestries a virtually congregational form of church polity, which neither they nor the majority of their parish clergy had any remote desire to change."[7] Charles S. Sydnor confirms: "Throughout the eighteenth century, the vestry was a self-perpetuating body . . . [and] ecclesiastical as well as political government was conducted by a dozen or so men who had the power to choose their own successors."[8] Devout layman Richard Bland

---

1 Carl Bridenbaugh, *Mitre and Sceptre: Transatlantic Faiths, Ideas, Personalities, and Politics* (New York: Oxford University Press, 1962), 220.
2 *Dictionary of National Biography*, 17:1110.
3 Bridenbaugh, *Mitre and Sceptre*, 223–27; Knollenberg, *Origin of the American Revolution*, 79–80.
4 Bridenbaugh, *Mitre and Sceptre*, 255.
5 Ibid., 233.   6 Ibid., 248–49.   7 Ibid., 323.
8 Sydnor, *American Revolutionaries in the Making*, 83–84.

favored the church's doctrines "without approving of her Hierarchy, which I know to be a Relick of the Papal Incroachments upon the Common Law."[9]

In contrast with the passive opposition in the establishment South, a very excitedly active opposition to bishops arose in the *un*established colonies farther north, and it became more passionate as the proposals for bishops seemed to gather likelihood of success. One must note the implications of bishoprics to grasp the emotions aroused by proposals to establish them. Bishops held separate ecclesiastical courts with jurisdiction over wills and weddings, the sins of sex – that is, fornication and adultery – and defamation. Bishops were expensive: they lived in grand "palaces" and maintained large retinues. Financial support for them would have to come from tithes or taxes.[10]

Not least, bishops were executives of the established church from which nonconformists had fled to the colonies. There was little sympathy for the Anglican clergy's complaint of being discriminated against because religious young men could not be ordained in their faith except by journeying to the Bishop of London at a cost of a hundred pounds for the trip. Supposedly, then, some who lacked the price simply turned nonconformist and accepted the easy local ordaining available at home. There are no statistics for this complaint, but it was repeated often and loudly to very deaf ears.

The nonconformist clergy, led by Massachusetts's Jonathan Mayhew, denounced Anglican plots against their faith that supposedly were evidenced by the SPG's missionaries and the hostility of the crown. When Church of England clergy openly and actively supported the Stamp Act hated by everyone else, nonconformists concluded that "no distinction between religious and civil liberties any longer existed; LIBERTY itself faced extinction, and they rushed to its defense." English nonconformists agreed that "stamping and episcopizing our colonies were understood to be only different branches of the same plan of power."[11]

Royal bias showed in a series of actions. In 1763, the Massachusetts General Court chartered "The Society for Propagating Christian Knowledge [SPCK] among the Indians of North America," ostensibly to counter Catholic influence among tribes formerly governed by French Canada. Anglicans saw this, however, as competition for their SPG, and the Privy Council responded to their opposition by disallowing the act. The veto came after active lobbying by Thomas Secker, Archbishop of Canterbury and President of the SPG, assisted by Philadelphia's Provost William Smith.[12]

In 1766, New York Presbyterians applied for incorporation so that they

9 Bridenbaugh, *Mitre and Sceptre*, 319.
10 Knollenberg, *Origin of the American Revolution*, 82–83.
11 Bridenbaugh, *Mitre and Sceptre*, 257, 259.
12 Knollenberg, *Origin of the American Revolution*, 79–80.

could build churches and own property as a body. (They had been bonding individuals for such legal purposes.) The Privy Council disallowed.[13]

In 1759 and 1763, Anglicans in New York opposed incorporation of Lutherans and other applications for such legal status by Huguenots and Dutch Reformed congregations.[14]

In 1773, the Privy Council disallowed the charter of Presbyterian Queen's College in North Carolina's Mecklenburg County.[15]

The disputation spread into frontier regions through agencies concerned with Indian affairs. Massachusetts intended its SPCK as a spur to missions among Indians. Presbyterian Samuel Kirkland toiled among the Iroquoian Oneidas. Congregationalist Eleazar Wheelock founded Dartmouth College ostensibly for Indian instruction. These actions threatened the ambitions of Sir William Johnson, Superintendent of Indian Affairs for the Northern Department, who was strongly Anglican and hoped to embrace all Indians in his church.

Johnson observed developments from his manor among the Mohawks and offered twenty thousand acres of land to support a bishop if the SPG could persuade the crown to match his gift.[16] Pennsylvania's Provost William Smith joined Johnson's efforts for Anglican missions, and Archbishop Secker approved.[17]

Johnson's status was that of a great frontier lord though he was titled deceptively as only a bureaucrat. Provost Smith was at least as imperialist as Johnson. This is what he preached (anonymously) almost as soon as he arrived in America: "The Statesman has always found it necessary for the Purposes of Government, to raise some one Denomination of religions above the Rest to a certain Degree. . . . [If] all Sects and Persuasions be equally favor'd . . . how shall they be influenc'd or how rul'd?"[18]

Smith hated Quakers and strove mightily to overthrow their power in Pennsylvania. With Thomas Penn he conspired to make the College of Philadelphia (of which he became provost) into a sort of executive committee for Anglican politics in Pennsylvania.[19]

Pennsylvania's Presbyterians also hated Quakers, but politics in that province threw men into strange, befuddling relationships. In 1764, Benjamin Franklin proposed to overthrow the province's status as a Penn family fief and to return it to direct government by the crown. Whereupon Presbyterians and Quakers, in fear of religious establishment, opposed Franklin, and Smith joined the effort to overthrow him. This seems weird until one

13 Bridenbaugh, *Mitre and Sceptre*, 260–61.
14 Ibid., 253.	15 Ibid., 322.	16 Ibid., 264–65.
17 Smith to Johnson, 16 March 1767, mss., SPG Papers Lambeth Palace Library, 15:185–87, London.
18 Bridenbaugh, *Mitre and Sceptre*, 152.	19 Jennings, *Empire of Fortune*, Chap. 11.

learns that Smith was Thomas Penn's hired man for undercover dirty work, and Penn wanted to keep his vast provincial estate.[20]

In the face of so much fear about religious establishments, Franklin had to explain that his proposal for direct royal government was innocuous for religions.

> A Bishop for America . . . probably from the apparent Necessity of the Thing will sooner or later be appointed . . . And the Spiritual Court, if the Bishop should hold one, can have authority only with his own People, if with them, since it is not likely that any Law of this Province will ever be made to submit the Inhabitants to it, or oblige them to pay Tithes.[21]

It is necessary to correct a much-repeated, highly confusing error. Emphatically, the assembly that supported Franklin's project was NOT a "Quaker assembly" nor was it "dominated by Quakers." It was Franklin's assembly, almost to a man, and the Quakers *opposed* it and his plans with all their enfeebled strength.[22] This fact is unambiguously plain – incontrovertibly so – in public records, and the constant repetition of falsehood does no honor to historians who keep it up out of mindless bias.

The net effect of these twists and turns on the Anglican campaign for bishops was to eliminate Pennsylvania from the opposition; but Quakers and Presbyterians wrote to their counterparts in Britain, and another odd twist took place. Nonconformists in Britain threw their weight against appointment of American bishops, but British Quakers, for reasons of their own, kept quiet.[23] For Pennsylvania, the tortuous evolution of events confirms the finding of Owen S. Ireland that the ethnic–religious conflict transcended section and class and was the most salient characteristic of the contending political forces.[24]

In all the colonies, Congregationalists and Presbyterians realized that they must put aside their traditional individualism to unite their churches for effective political action.[25] They became aware also that the pulpit was not the only place to influence public opinion. Some of them started newspaper campaigns: a series called The American Whig that started in Andrew Bradford's *Pennsylvania Journal* and was reprinted elsewhere; and a new paper called *The Centinel* which was founded by a triumvirate destined to

---

20 Smith's retainer from Thomas Penn for what we now call covert operations is confirmed by ltr., Penn to R. Peters, 21 Feb. 1755, mss., Peters Mss., 4:4. Hist. Soc. of Pa.
21 *Franklin Papers* 11:168–69.
22 Jennings, *Empire of Fortune*, 233, 242–43.
23 Bridenbaugh, *Mitre and Sceptre*, 285, 287.
24 Owen S. Ireland, "The Ethnic-Religious Dimension of Pennsylvania Politics, 1778–1779," *William and Mary Quarterly*, 3d ser., 30 (1973), 425, 442; Owen S. Ireland, "The Crux of Politics: Religion and Party in Pennsylvania, 1778–1789," *William and Mary Quarterly*, 3d ser., 42:4 (Oct. 1985), 454.
25 Bridenbaugh, *Mitre and Sceptre*, 271–82.

loom large in the Revolution. These were Francis Alison, John Dickinson, and Judge George Bryan. Naturally Anglican forces responded. Was it significant that their paper appeared in New York instead of Philadelphia? Timothy Tickle, Esq., vented indignation with "A Whip for the American Whig" in Hugh Gaines's *New York Mercury*.[26]

The uproar died down after Archbishop Secker died in 1768. The American defense against bishops was victorious. One may see in that battle, however, some foreshadowings of the full-scale Revolution yet to come, especially in the lessons for nonconformists about how to organize politically and sway general public opinion.

26 Bridenbaugh, *Mitre and Sceptre*, 299.

Part III

———————— • ————————

AN AMERICAN CLONE BREAKS OFF

20

———— • ————

IMPERIAL AND COLONIAL FRONTIERS

"There is some inherent tendency to write American history as if it were a function of white culture only."

Bernard De Voto, *The Course of Empire*

In North America, the empires of Britain and France competed directly in several great regions. Outpost "factories" of the Hudson's Bay Company faced against the French reaching across the tops of the Great Lakes. New France and New England frequently warred or prepared for war. On the western flank of the Appalachian Mountains, French traders and political agents took pains to keep British competitors east of the mountains, but some of the latter made smuggling arrangements with French Detroit. Britain's southern colonies of Georgia and the Carolinas faced against French Louisiana, and Virginia thrust outward both to the northwest and the southwest against territories claimed by the French.

Imperial crowns schemed constantly against each other, usually (not always) through the agency of their colonies, which also competed for advantage against each other without regard for imperial affiliations. And the traders to the Indians looked out for themselves as individuals. Commercial struggle continued incessantly; military combat broke out in a series of wars climaxing with Britain's victory in the Seven Years War. Considering the legal fiction of "savage love of war," note the list of *civilized conflicts*: 1687–1697, King William's War; 1701–1713, Queen Anne's War; 1744–1748, King George's War; 1754–1763, Seven Years War.

At all times, the Indian tribes were caught between the great powers grinding against each other. The situation provided some advantages and much grief for the Indians. They learned how to run between the competing empires, playing them off against each other to gain more favorable prices in trade and bidding up tribal services as allies. In the long run, however, repeated imperial wars created disastrous Indian casualties. All this turmoil of factuality has been caricatured in popular histories as The Frontier, "a line between civilization and savagery." Such wholly imaginary abstractions are ignored herein in favor of empirically identifiable persons and events.

For victory in the Seven Years War, Britain acquired the territories of New France. (Louisiana and its frontiers west of the Mississippi went to Spain.) Victory was sweet, but what was the British crown to do with the spoils? Indians were among the acquisitions but they did not accept the role of spoils. As we have seen, many tribes rose in arms in the so-called Pontiac's War of Britain's northern frontier region. Disturbances occurred in the south also, which were promptly suppressed by militias of ever-bellicose South Carolina aided from Virginia and North Carolina. The British crown's most pressing problems rose in the north, and in plain truth the British crown did not know what to do about them. Certainly the tribal uprising had to be beaten down, but what then? How were the tribes to be kept quiet after troops were moved from the west to the eastern towns? How was the former New France, newly created as the Province of Quebec, to be governed with its alien institutions, including the Roman Catholic religion? How long could its people be ruled by a military governor? For a decade the British dithered.

Britain's first effort at a comprehensive frontier policy was the creation of George Montagu Dunk, 2d earl of Halifax. From long, active service as president of the Board of Trade, Halifax understood the colonies probably as well as any Englishman, but this is not to say he sympathized with them; he was a prerogative man through and through.

He has earned a moment's summary. He had heavily subsidized Nova Scotia and patronized emigration to it, which is memorialized in the name of its chief city. He had connived with the duke of Cumberland to circumvent the peace-minded duke of Newcastle, and he patronized the warmongering map of John Mitchell with its flagrant lying about Iroquois conquests in Canada.[1] Having helped to bring on the Seven Years War, Halifax turned a blind eye to the dispossession and deportation of about nine thousand Acadian peasants.[2] In 1763, though he had left the Board of Trade, Halifax was called to act when the new president died, and he "hastened to put the final touches to the drafting of the Royal Proclamation."[3] We have seen his approach to domestic policy as he prosecuted John Wilkes in London, so arbitrarily that Wilkes won heavy damages in a court suit.[4] Halifax, in short, sided with authority, especially his own.

1 Jennings, *Empire of Fortune*, Chap. 6.   2 Ibid., Chap. 8.

3 Pierre Tousignant, ". . . From the Royal Proclamation to the Quebec Act," in *Dictionary of Canadian Biography*, 4:xxxv.

4 Postgate, *"That Devil Wilkes,"* 56–58, 60.

A Canadian scholar remarks that, in Halifax's drafting of the Royal Proclamation, "he implemented a strategy of imperial control that he had long since entered upon. . . . A serious political error, for although the urgency of pacifying the Indians demanded an official declaration from the crown, there was no need to put through on the same occasion an imperial programme for the whole of British North America."[5]

Thus by royal prerogative alone, a vast territory was reserved temporarily as Indian hunting grounds, colonials were forbidden to settle west of a line on the map while colonial charters were arbitrarily curtailed at that line, and new colonies were decreed in East and West Florida and the Province of Quebec. Not surprisingly, the new officials of these new colonies were to be all royal appointees. Even for the traditionally jerry-built structure of the empire, Halifax's edict over the royal signature was too rickety to last.

For the time being, the new colonies were controlled by occupying troops. Indian tribes were too numerous and scattered for that sort of solution to last very long. In 1764 the Ministry considered a plan forwarded by the Board of Trade which proposed in effect to bureaucratize the Iroquois League by putting British residents in the villages. All would be supervised by Sir William Johnson, northern superintendent of Indian affairs, and an interesting historical question arises as to how the tribes might gradually have been converted into a province assimilated to the British bureaucracy. But the scheme was too expensive for that era, so it was dropped,[6] and the Iroquois were managed as before through treaties, subsidies, and selective favoritism.

Colonists viewed the Royal Proclamation's boundary line rather cynically. George Washington called it a temporary measure and added to his western investments; he conspired with a frontier agent "to secure some of the most valuable lands in the King's part [i.e., the reserved territory] which I think may be accomplished after a while notwithstanding the Proclamation that restrains it at present and prohibits the Settling of them at all."[7] In the same letter, Washington suggested that agent Crawford "evade" Pennsylvania's law by a device of registering an illicitly large tract of land in small parcels, this to be done with the connivance of "an Acquaintance of mine" in the land office. Washington also "infringed" Virginia law; seizing lands to which he was not entitled, surveying them illicitly through a man unqualified by law who laid them out in violation of legal stipula-

5 Tousignant, *Dictionary of Canadian Biography*, 4:xxxv.
6 Lords of Trade to the King, 7 March 1768, *Documents Relative to the Colonial History of New York*, 8:24.
7 George Washington, *Writings*, ed. John C. Fitzpatrick, 39 vols. (Washington, D.C., 1931–44), 2:468.

tions as to size and location, and all to the detriment of Washington's Virginia comrades-in-arms for whom these lands had been intended. "The more he got of the allotted 200,000 acres, the less was available for the enlisted men to whom it was promised."[8]

"Pioneers" continued to invade and seize Indians' lands. It soon became apparent that there was no sound reason for western Indians to believe that the Royal Proclamation had guaranteed their territorial or jurisdictional integrity. Some settlers simply squatted, built blockhouses, and dared the Indians to try to force them out. Others anticipated eventual introduction of efficient government by the legal device of quitclaims from Indians – any Indians – based on the premise of an Indian right in property exclusive of jurisdiction. This adoption of the moral high ground had been tried repeatedly in colonial times, and had always been struck down by governments that required formal cession of tribal lands to the governments prior to recognizing individual titles to real estate. There was no end to irony. Practically and politically, direct purchase by a colonial from an Indian, no matter how valid it might be in Indian eyes, was disobedience to the commands of government, which fell little short of rebellion. For the time being, governments had little power to enforce laws in frontier lands. Washington's example shows willful pursuit of personal gain in violation of colonial governments as well as the crown, and even by embezzling the property rights of the men he had commanded in the Seven Years War. Some writers have equated such lawless enterprise with "frontier democracy." Washington's soldiers, had they known what was going on, might have defined democracy somewhat differently. The Indians did understand fairly well how they were victims instead of participants in this sort of democracy.

One must recall that frontier troubles bubbled up at the same time as Stamp Act riots made havoc in the eastern towns. It became evident to the empire's Ministry that something authoritative must be done, and that meant bringing western garrison troops east to awe the dissidents. Without garrisons, what would happen to authority in the west? The Indians must be made to feel that the Royal Proclamation's boundary line was genuine, so orders went forth to the northern and southern superintendents of Indian affairs to hold treaties with the tribes to determine exactly where the boundary should be and get the tribes to confirm it.[9]

Let us set aside the southern theater for separate treatment. In the north, relations between colonies and tribes had long been dominated by the Covenant Chain confederation in which the Iroquois acted as spokesmen

---

8 Bernhard Knollenberg, *George Washington: The Virginia Period, 1732–1775* (Durham, N.C., 1964), 93–100, quotation at 99; Willis Van Devanter, *The Virginia Soldiers' Claim to Western Lands Adjacent to Fort Pitt* (New York: privately printed at Spiral Press, 1966), short, unpaged.

9 Jennings, *Empire of Fortune*, 461–62 and n10.

for the tribes and increasingly as a sort of woodland police acting for Sir William Johnson. When the Board of Trade ordered a definite boundary, Johnson summoned the Iroquois to the treaty of Fort Stanwix in 1768. As realists in diplomacy, the Iroquois agreed to a line that protected their own territories, by "ceding" much land of their allies. In the course of this gratifying process, Johnson gained "grants" from the Iroquois of vast tracts of land for himself and General Thomas Gage. This was not difficult because Iroquois title to these tracts existed only in Johnson's recognition.[10]

The tribes so lightly pilfered could only simmer in resentment, but they counseled much together. Gradually (the precise date is not clear) a new Western Confederation came into being, much influenced by experienced Delawares, Shawnees, and Hurons, who deliberately conceived their new association as a counterbalance to the Iroquois Covenant Chain.

While some land grabbers were so busy in frontier regions, others strove for bigger prizes in London. George Croghan had used his former prominence as a trader to obtain a quitclaim from the Iroquois for two hundred thousand acres near Fort Pitt, and he lobbied for validation of this "grant" under British law. As head of the "suffering traders" claiming compensation for prewar expulsion by the French, Croghan prevailed on Sir William Johnson to push the Fort Stanwix boundary as a deep salient into Indian territory. Johnson did nothing for nothing; "grants" for himself were also part of the package.

Croghan then joined his claims with the petition of the syndicate headed by Philadelphia merchant Samuel Wharton, who took them all to London. Wharton's strategy included co-opting Benjamin Franklin as a shareholder in the projected colony of Vandalia. To grease the project through channels, some influential British politicians also received share donations. Wharton was an energetic wheeler-dealer. Encountering obstruction from the Ohio Company of Virginia that had been formed in 1750, but had run out of steam, Wharton simply assimilated it in his own venture.[11]

His more serious difficulty centered in the new Secretary of State for American Affairs, Lord Hillsborough, who disliked the Vandalia scheme (and Americans generally) and blocked Wharton at every turn. Hillsborough dragged out the proceedings to the point where rebellion in America forestalled any new royal grant.[12]

In Virginia, George Washington had plenty of competitors for speculation in western lands. A new royal governor, John Murray, earl of Dunmore,

10 Jack M. Sosin, *The Revolutionary Frontier, 1763–1783* (New York: Holt, Rinehart and Winston, 1967), 84.
11 Jennings, *Benjamin Franklin, Politician,* 181; Sosin, *The Revolutionary Frontier,* 34–35.
12 Peter Marshall, "Lord Hillsborough, Samuel Wharton and the Ohio Grant, 1769–1775," *English Historical Review* 80 (1965), 717–39.

outranked them all and used all their devices along with some of his own. Stimulated by the western curve of the Indian boundary and the withdrawal of royal troops from Fort Pitt, Lord Dunmore connived with squatters in that region led by an adventurer named John Connolly. Claiming the Ohio River headwaters as part of Virginia, Dunmore established the "district of West Augusta," and commissioned Connolly as captain of Virginia's militia. With superior force, Connolly seized Fort Pitt and renamed it Fort Dunmore early in 1774.[13]

Dunmore was insatiable. When his henchman Connolly picked a fight with Shawnees, Dunmore declared war on them. Though the Shawnees appealed for justice to the Iroquois Grand Council, they were rebuffed because the Shawnees had protested against Iroquois sale of Shawnee lands; the Grand Council saw Dunmore's war as an opportunity to discipline those dissident Shawnees. In consequence, they fought alone against Dunmore's militias. They put up a good fight, but they were outnumbered and they ran out of ammunition. They had to capitulate and withdraw from their territory in what became Kentucky.[14] As Jack M. Sosin comments, "The war between Whig frontiersmen and the Indians during the Revolution [soon to break out] was but the culmination of the tension between the two races that had been mounting during the previous decade."[15]

The southern frontier region had been dominated before the Seven Years War by competition between the British Carolinas and Georgia on the one side, and French Louisiana and Spanish Florida in opposition, with the intervening Indian tribes allied. By the 1763 Treaty of Paris, France ceded Louisiana to Spain and West Florida to Britain. Tribal allies stayed in the same patterns, partly because of their own reasons for opposing each other as well as allying with colonials.

This complex situation was highly unstable, but networks of commercial exchange continued to operate, with this difference: The tribes formerly accustomed to playing off Englishmen against the French now found themselves deprived of that strategy. Like it or not they had to deal with the British. This was disturbing because British traders tended to be rough and abusive. Nothing like a pan-Indian revolt developed, but, as Daniel H. Usner Jr. reports, "Indians in both West Florida and Louisiana resorted more frequently to stealing livestock, pillaging supplies, and other forms of intimidation in order to win demands from colonial governments."[16] The

13 Sosin, *Revolutionary Frontier*, 58–60.
14 Ibid., 85–87; Jack M. Sosin, "The British Indian Department and Dunmore's War," *Virginia Magazine of History and Biography* 74 (Jan. 1966), 34–50.
15 Sosin, *Revolutionary Frontier*, 87.
16 Daniel H. Usner Jr., *Indians, Settlers, and Slaves in a Frontier Exchange Economy: The Lower Mississippi Valley Before 1783* (Chapel Hill: University of North Carolina Press, 1992), 127.

situation worsened from "excessive consumption of alcohol" as British traders poured rum into the villages.

Still more tensions arose as increasing numbers of African and Indian slaves fled to Spanish jurisdictions where freedom could sometimes be attained. Others escaped into the woods and formed separate "maroon" communities that functioned independently of all empires and constituted a threat to slave plantations everywhere.[17]

No authority could exert control, so turbulence continued throughout the interwar years and the Revolution.

The big tribes of Cherokees and Creeks regarded the Appalachian Mountains as their own territories but were forced on the defensive by massive invasions of colonial settlers from farther east. Louis De Vorsey Jr. attributes the surge to two fundamental reasons: a passion for productive lands because of soil exhaustion in older settlements and the strategic requirements of empire.[18] The royal Board of Trade added a third reason: "the monopoly of lands in the hands of land jobbers from the extravagant and injudicious grants made by some of Your Majesty's governors."[19]

In an effort to gain control, the crown first made its famous Proclamation in 1763. Finding this inadequate, it ordered in 1768 the superintendents of Indian affairs to treat with concerned tribes for a definite boundary line. The advancing companies of squatters paid no attention to either line.

In 1774, the Transylvania Company was organized with Daniel Boone's advice, and it summoned the Cherokees (or the most malleable of them) to Sycamore Shoals for a big land grant. Superintendent John Stuart and North Carolina's Governor Josiah Martin denounced the operation as illegal. Only royal officials had the right to treat for land. But in 1775 the newly organized Continental Congress appointed commissioners to oversee the Transylvania project.[20]

It was not hard to see trouble shaping up. Superintendent John Stuart presented Cherokees with twenty loads of ammunition, the Cherokees ordered several companies of settlers to withdraw back east, the settlers rejected the order and armed themselves. In May 1776, northern Indians (probably Iroquois) exhorted the Cherokees to fight, and raids were made.

Unlike the British crown, the colonial Congress supported the squatters. Congress coordinated campaigns by militias from Virginia, the Carolinas,

17 Ibid., scattered refs.; see index under *Maroon camps.*
18 Louis De Vorsey Jr., *The Indian Boundary in the Southern Colonies, 1763–1775* (Chapel Hill: University of North Carolina Press, 1966), 53, 55.
19 Ibid., 30–31.
20 Sosin, *Revolutionary Frontier*, 36–38; Shaw Livermore, *Early American Land Companies: Their Influence on Corporate Development* (New York: Octagon Books, 1968), 92–97; *Atlas of Early American History*, 16, 93.

and Georgia. Cherokee villages were scorched. The tribal government fell apart into villages struggling for individual survival. Peace was made with much loss of Cherokee lands at the treaty of Long Island of Holston in 1777, and the surge of invading settlers renewed.[21]

In this region, the striving for liberty and property by the Revolutionaries very clearly overthrew the liberty and property of the Indians. The pattern of herrenvolk democracy is strictly limited to an ethnic caste.

---

21 See James H. O'Donnell III, *The Cherokees of North Carolina in the American Revolution* (Raleigh, N.C.: Dept. of Cultural Resources, 1976).

21

CHANGING SIDES

Stung by inability to enforce the Stamp Tax, Parliament rescinded it, but instead of recovering credit for goodwill, it exacerbated colonial tempers by a new act that amounted to an ultimatum. This Declaratory Act purposed to be "for the better securing the dependency of his Majesty's dominions in America upon the crown and parliament of Great Britain" and it asserted that the king-in-Parliament "had, hath, and of right ought to have, full power and authority to make laws . . . to bind the colonies and people of America . . . in all cases whatsoever." Explicitly, any colonial actions denying this power "are hereby declared to be, utterly null and void to all intents and purposes whatsoever."[1]

Though Franklin thought this splutter merely a face-saving gesture without serious intent at enforcement, Parliament meant its assertion of unqualified sovereignty so deeply that it discussed and effectively decided upon the Declaratory Act *before* repeal of the Stamp Act.[2] It seems that Franklin could not believe that responsible rulers could be so stupid as to rave in the manner of the Declaratory Act, so he continued to hope for reconciliation; but part of the character of preeminent power wielders is the belief that all opposition can be disposed of by being firm. One must exert power, and more power, and still more power until opposition is wiped out. To this end, Parliament baffled incredulous Franklin by striving with a vigor that should have been reserved for better, more attainable goals.

These observations, harsh though they be, are solidly grounded in the most direct kind of documentation: Franklin was called as a witness before Commons's Committee of the Whole at a time when the Declaratory Act was still being considered by the House and the Stamp Act was still in force. A questioner asked, "Considering the resolutions of parliament as to the right, do you think, if the stamp-act is repealed, that the North Americans will be satisfied?"

1 *Documents of American History*, ed. Commager, 1:60–61.
2 Peter D. G. Thomas in *Blackwell Encyclopedia*, 120–22.

Franklin responded, "I think the resolutions of right will give them very little concern, if they are never attempted to be carried into practice."[3]

He was asked by an adversary, "If the stamp-act should be repealed, would it induce the assemblies of America to acknowledge the rights of parliament to tax them, and would they erase their resolutions [of opposition]?"

Answer: "No, never."

An ominous question: "Is there no means of obliging them to erase those resolutions?"

Answer: "None that I know of; they will never do it unless compelled by force of arms."

Besides the thrusts and parries about sovereign rights, the Members worried about a more mundane matter that Franklin struck at shrewdly. If the Stamp Act was not repealed, asked one questioner, "what do you think will be the consequences?" To which Franklin answered, "if the act is not repealed, they will take very little of your manufactures in a short time."[4] He caused a flutter and a series of further questions on the issue of commerce that showed he had struck a nerve. What, after all, was the empire for if not to profit the homeland? Merchants of the City of London were already protesting and demonstrating against government's policies as much as the colonials were doing.

It is thought-provoking to notice that it was entirely owing to Londoners' dedication to a free press that Franklin's interrogation became public. Parliament's ban against reporting its proceedings was still in effect. Franklin's printer friend William Strahan obtained a copy of a clerk's journal "with great Difficulty, and with some Expense" – which probably means by bribery – and he sent the document to David Hall, Franklin's partner in Philadelphia. Hall printed it rather circumspectly just in time to influence the next assembly election, and other printers in America and London picked it up. Far from being suppressed according to Parliamentary rule, it gained an immense, widespread audience. It had powerful influence for repeal of the Stamp Act and for rehabilitation of Franklin's reputation that had suffered severely because of his too-ready accommodation to the passage of the Stamp Act.[5]

Some Members of Parliament were friendly to the colonials, many City merchants wanted commerce smoothed and restored, and Franklin's direct, well-informed responses to the House of Commons added a special effect. *But* before the Stamp Act's repeal, Parliament did pass the Declaratory Act; and, contrary to Franklin's expectation, Parliament did intend to enforce it.

Proof came soon with the Townshend Revenue Act.

---

3 *Franklin Papers*, 13:141.   4 Ibid., 13:158, 143.   5 Ibid., ed. n. 124–29.

In the musical chairs of ministries trying to cope with turmoil at home and abroad, Charles Townshend took charge in 1767 and determined to bring those fractious colonists to heel. His Revenue Act passed in June under the guise of taxing external commerce only and defraying "the charge of the administration of justice" besides "defending, protecting and securing" the dominions. It sounded proper and innocent. On the surface it responded to critics who had distinguished between external and internal taxation. (Franklin had testified that the colonists had "never" objected to external taxes by Parliament.) But, beneath the surface Townshend hit sharply at one of the colonial merchants' most cherished "liberties," that is, the tacit license to smuggle. Townshend's devices for suppressing smuggling were highly effective, and they "excited the liveliest dissatisfaction in the American colonies."[6]

Why should this have been when Townshend had taken such care to meet the colonists' expressed objections? There was fine print in his revenue act. It spelled out not only the kinds and amounts of taxes, but the means used to collect them. The device used in the colonies was the same in principle as the "general warrant" that kicked up an unholy row in London. This was the "writ of assistance" (to be banned in future by Article IV of the United States Constitution's Bill of Rights). In Minister Townshend's legislation, it was

> lawful for any officer of his Majesty's customs, authorized by writ of assistance . . . to take a constable, head-borough, or other public officer inhabiting near unto the place and in the daytime to enter and go into any house, shop cellar, warehouse, or room or other place and, in case of resistance, to break open doors, chests, trunks, and other pakage there, to seize, and from thence to bring, any kind of goods or merchandise whatsoever prohibited or uncustomed.[7]

Officers enforcing the act could bring their cases before a vice-admiralty court in Halifax, Nova Scotia, far from the defenders' habitations and friends, and in courts without juries where judges were royal appointees."[8] In such circumstances, verdicts were practically predetermined. Not surprisingly, American customs revenue zoomed. So did American tempers.

We have it from Edmund Burke that when Minister Townshend proposed in Parliament his new plan of taxation for American, "the reasons he gave were that it was in order to establish a police in America – to strengthen and fortify the government of America."[9]

6 *Documents of American History*, ed. Commager, 1:63; *Franklin Papers* 13:156; *Documents of American History*, ed. Commager, 1:63–64.
7 *Documents of American History*, ed. Commager, 1:63–64.
8 *Blackwell Encyclopedia*, 164, 10.
9 Edmund Burke, *On the American Revolution: Selected Speeches and Letters*, 18 Nov. 1768, ed. Elliott Robert Barkan (New York: Harper and Row, 1966), 2–3.

Franklin failed to notice the oppressive writs of assistance clause in this revenue act. He was "rather pleas'd" with the continuance of Townshend's ministry because, he thought, possible alternatives would likely be worse. In consideration of Franklin's expansive ego, I think he was pleased also with Townshend's seeming attention to Franklin's testimony before the House of Commons. To the colonials, Franklin advised conciliation of British friends and avoidance of "rash Proceedings on our side."[10] In short, his Anglomania blinded him again to how colonials felt and would respond. A reminder came soon. His old Pennsylvania adversary John Dickinson published a series of "Letters from a Farmer in Pennsylvania." (Dickinson was a lawyer.) The "letters" attacked each and all of the provisions of the Townshend Revenue Act, and some others for good measure, and denied the legal assumptions on which they were based.

Though Dickinson maintained a polite, argumentative tone instead of fulminating, his conclusion could not be mistaken: "I hope the people of these colonies will unanimously join in this sentiment, that the late [Townshend] act of parliament is injurious to their liberty, and that this sentiment will unite them in a firm opposition to it, *in the same manner as the dread of the Stamp-Act did.*" This was not a voice crying out in the wilderness. Dickinson's "letters" were reprinted so widely that "their popularity and circulation surpassed that of all other publications in the revolutionary war period save Thomas Paine's not yet published *Common Sense.*"[11]

Even Royalist Franklin picked them up and published them with his own foreword that presented them as the "general sentiments of the Inhabitants." But Franklin held back from full endorsement: "How far these Sentiments are right or wrong I do not pretend at present to judge."[12] He was not simply being stubborn in this instance; he struggled with problems in logic. To son William he confessed bewilderment about Boston's acknowledgment of "subordination" to Parliament while denying Parliament's power to make laws governing the colonies. Nor could he make clear sense of the Farmer's Letters' distinctions between duties for regulation and those for revenue.

> If the Parliament is to be the judge, it seems to me that establishing such principles of distinction will amount to little. The more I have thought and read on the subject the more I find myself confirmed in opinion, that no middle doctrine can be well maintained, I mean not clearly with intelligible arguments. Something might be made of either of the extremes; that Parliament has a power

---

10 *Franklin Papers*, 14:228–30.
11 Robert J. Chaffin in *Blackwell Encyclopedia*, 132. Dickinson, in *Tracts of the American Revolution 1773–1776*, ed. (Merrill) Jensen (Indianapolis: Bobbs-Merrill Co., 1967), 160 (emphasis added).
12 *Franklin Papers*, 15:110–12.

to make *all laws* for us, or that it has a power to make *no laws* for us; and I think the arguments for the latter more numerous and weighty than those for the former.[13]

Intellectually, Franklin had become more daringly radical than the colonial agitators whose violence he deplored, but he harbored emotions as well as intellect, and he still yearned for royalty. He dreamed of an association of states, each governing itself, but united by a common king. As of 1768 when he wrote the foregoing quotation, he still had faith in George III.

Generally, London's merchants opposed the government's colonial policies, not only because of restrictions on trade, but also because of concerns over debts owed by colonials. Long before disputing with armed force, colonials waged commercial war with the simplest of weapons: They stopped payment on credits that amounted in 1766 to more than £4,450,000.[14] After repeal of the Stamp Act, they resumed payments, but the Declaratory Act aroused antagonisms once more and the Townshend Acts exacerbated them.

Townshend's acts passed in June 1767. Colonial reaction came swiftly.

A gentry-led mob in Charles Town, South Carolina, attacked a British sea captain. The mayor of Norfolk, Virginia, led a similar attack.[15]

The Sons of Liberty, who had diminished after repeal of the Stamp Act, reorganized.

Massachusetts's Samuel Adams picked up the purported Resolves of the Virginia House of Burgesses that had been launched by firebrand Patrick Henry, and acted upon John Dickenson's advice. Adams adapted them to the new circumstances and composed a circular letter to all the colonies to protest the Townshend Acts; the letter was adopted and sent by the Massachusetts assembly, and it aroused fury among officials in London.[16]

New York's assembly buckled under Parliament's threat to close it down. The Yorkers decided to obey the Mutiny Act's orders to pay costs of troops quartered among them; but this was an orderly retreat rather than a rout. They drew up a bill of colonial rights that denied Parliament's power to suspend the legislature as unconstitutional.[17]

South Carolina's assembly refused point-blank to provide supplies for troops passing through the colony to Florida. The Townshend Acts were illegal so "we are constrained to refuse making the desired provision during the existence of those acts – acts which strike at the very root of our constitution, by taking our property without our consent, and depriving us of the liberty of giving to our sovereign."[18] Perhaps we may be permitted a smile over the Carolinians' great sorrow at being deprived of such a liberty. It did not seem funny in London.

13 Ibid., 15:75–76.   14 Draper, *A Struggle for Power*, 341.
15 Robert J. Chaffin in *Blackwell Encyclopedia*, 140.   16 Ibid., 132.   17 Ibid., 134–35.
18 Ibid., 136.

For a brief while, Parliament stepped aside to let the crown's executive officials take up the battle. A new Colonial Department opened with Wills Hill, earl of Hillsborough, as its first secretary of state, and Lord Hillsborough threw down a gauntlet. He ordered all the governors to prevent their assemblies from acting on Massachusetts's circular letter, and he demanded that Massachusetts's Governor Bernard *order* his assembly to rescind the letter.[19] Only three thousand miles of distance could make Hillsborough's demands seem feasible. The governors tried, but they were outgeneraled by increasingly angry opponents. For a crown officer to command what an elected assembly representing the people must do!!!

When an assembly was dismissed by its governor to prevent it from acting on Massachusetts's circular letter, the assembly met extralegally to respond to the letter. This was far more damaging to royal authority than any sort of action in official channels would have been because it showed colonists beginning to act independently of constituted authority.

Under Sam Adams's prodding, the Massachusetts assembly in 1769 raised defiance to a new stage by asserting that it need not abide by any legislation in which it had not participated.[20] This followed Rhode Island's previous initiative against the Stamp Act and it got Massachusetts's assembly prorogued. Troops had already arrived in Boston in 1768.

Merchants met publicly to renew the nonimportation agreement of Stamp Act days.[21] Very privately, Lt. Gov. Hutchinson wrote to Thomas Whately in London (who had been an official in the Treasury and who had worked directly under Minister Grenville). Hutchinson appealed for "measures . . . to secure this dependance" of Massachusetts on the crown. If there should be nothing more than "some declaratory acts or resolves, *it is all over with us.* . . . There must be an abridgment of what are called English liberties." One must remember that this was written while troops were garrisoned in Boston. Hutchinson begged his correspondent "to keep secret every thing I write."[22] He was understandably apprehensive about reaction from the populace if they were to discover his covert campaign against their most cherished rights.

It seems plain to me that he was angling for appointment as governor which he did get for these covert services to the crown. Respect to his "integrity" nowadays must somehow explain his secret actions against those English liberties. Hutchinson smoothly deplored the necessity of force, but he stressed the political reality of that necessity. As to that, no responsible public official would think otherwise than that force should be a last resort; Hutchinson differed only in advising that its time was at hand. Bernard Bailyn, in his hearts-and-flowers grieving over what was to happen to

19 Ibid., 132–33.   20 Ibid., 134.   21 *Franklin Papers*, 20:545.   22 Ibid., 20:550, 551.

Hutchinson, pulled out all the stops with the statement that Hutchinson's letters "contained no statement that he had not elsewhere, and publicly, expressed."[23] This would be more persuasive if any of those public expressions had been quoted. When and where had Hutchinson *publicly* advocated abridgment of English liberties? Innocent remarks would not have needed Hutchinson's slithy tove admonition to "keep secret every thing I write."[24]

Hutchinson and his colleague Oliver were well-informed conspirators working hand in glove with British officials. They reaped rich rewards for their dirty work until they were exposed, as will be shown, by Benjamin Franklin.

I do not share much of the common idolatry of Samuel Adams, but he had the measure of Thomas Hutchinson.

In 1767, Charles Townshend had died and had been succeeded as Chancellor of the Exchequer by Frederick North who also became leader of the House of Commons in January 1768. This and other changes signaled a government line even harder than Townshend's. Its policies were those of George III, and Lord North was to faithfully fulfill the king's desires.[25]

The hard issue that became harder, month by month, was the sovereignty of king-in-Parliament. As each party in any negotiation has bargaining demands that may be dropped to get other values, but also has a rock-bottom, nonnegotiable position; so the British empire's crown and colonies had arrived by 1768 at their respective bottom demands. Colonials rejected alternatives for their own autonomies, and the king-in-Parliament refused absolutely to give up sovereignty defined as power to override colonial assemblies.[26]

There still seemed to be a little room for maneuver in 1770 when Lord North moved to repeal some of the Townshend taxes. He excepted the tax on tea. North assured the colonists that his ministry would not further tax them for revenue, but he insisted that Parliament should not give up its *right* to tax. As Robert J. Chaffin cautions, a trick was concealed in North's repealing. "In fact," writes Chaffin, "the modification of the Townshend Duties Act was scarcely any change at all." North kept the act's provisions to pay colonial officers from the royal treasury and thus to make them independent of the assemblies with which they previously had had to negotiate for their salaries. "By 1772 the tea duty supported almost every important civil office in Massachusetts. Similarly, New York's governors obtained their salaries from those funds, as did the Chief Justice of New Jersey."[27]

23 Bernard Bailyn, *The Ordeal of Thomas Hutchinson* (Cambridge, Mass.: Harvard University Press, 1974), 227.
24 *Franklin Papers*, 20:551.   25 Draper, *Struggle for Power*, 312.   26 Ibid., 318–19.
27 Chaffin in *Blackwell Encyclopedia*, 138–40.

It is another little twist of historical irony that the colonists should have resented and resisted losing the expense of official salaries. When we hear tax haters demanding cuts in all sorts of government activities, it seems strange to come across this example of demands to shoulder the cost of government, but the colonials had not gone daft. Experiment and experience had shown them that officials accommodated their paymasters, and colonies relieved of that responsibility would be treated according to the crown's policies rather than their own. For colonials, as indeed for other people, the responsibility to pay was the power to influence. With this proviso: that the responsibility should carry with it the power to withhold payment.

The irony became heightened in 1773 when Lord North stirred up a hornet's nest by an act to make tea *cheaper* in the colonies! He really meant to save the East India Company from bankruptcy by reducing its vast stores of tea through sales to Americans at prices below possible competition by colonial merchants. But those merchants were smugglers. From 1769 to 1771, "five-sixths of the tea consumed in Massachusetts . . . was judged to have been illegally imported, nine-tenths in Philadelphia and New York." Thus the estimate of Massachusetts's Governor Hutchinson. Lord North's Tea Act, by cutting the East India Company's monopolistic prices from two shillings seven pence per pound to an even two shillings, was supposed to cut out the competition from Dutch suppliers, but as Theodore Draper remarks, "The only ones to be cut out were the smugglers."[28]

Lord North had seriously underestimated the dimensions of the smuggling business (as a number of writers still do). It was *big* business. The men engaged in it refused to let go of a good thing, so they used their multitude of resources, which included a multitude of employees and business associates, to mount a furious offensive against the law. Previously the opposition to tea duties had been real but diffuse. Now it became intense and focused.

How could the colonists attack a device for saving them money? That was not their ostensible target. Instead, they revived and magnified resistance against Townshend's *duty* on tea, which had been maintained in North's law. Fireworks resulted.

During all the rows about the Townshend duties, Benjamin Franklin had guarded expression of his private views because of the likelihood that his writings would be monitored by spies.[29] His need for diplomatic tact increased with his authority as an American spokesman. In 1768 he added agency for Georgia to his representation of the Pennsylvania assembly. In

28 Draper, *Struggle for Power*, 390.   29 *Franklin Papers*, 18:127.

1769, New Jersey commissioned him and, in 1770, Massachusetts's lower house did also. He became, in Carl Van Doren's phrase, "an ambassador from America before America had the right to send one."[30] Perhaps his income from four agencies slowed his development as a spokesman for protest and dissidence. At fifteen hundred pounds per year it was substantial, and tradesman Franklin understood profit and loss.

But he was also philosopher Franklin. As Parliament's harassment of the colonies increased, so did Franklin's disagreement with its policy assumptions. And all of his efforts to bring the government to reason failed.

To follow his concerns we must make a distinction of analysis that was not clearly delineated at the time. Most colonists wanted autonomy from British rule, but not separation from the empire. King George, Lord North, and their colleagues could not see that distinction. To them, what the colonists wanted was *independence*, and in their determination to suppress autonomy they drove the colonists toward the defensive goal of secession.

Despite sentimental affection for a British empire embracing many autonomous "distinct states" under a joint king, Franklin came logically to reject Parliament's right to legislate for the colonies in all cases whatsoever. He no longer counseled patience but still advised that protest be decorous. To Massachusetts's Thomas Cushing in 1771, Franklin hoped that "the colony Assemblies will show, by frequently repeated resolves, that they know their rights, and do not lose sight of them." He added ominously, "There is no doubt of the [ministry's] intention to make governors and some other officers independent of the people for their support."[31]

Cushing agreed about the need for pressure. On being chosen Speaker of the Massachusetts House of Representatives, he responded to Franklin with a declaration of "our Duty to declare our Rights, and our determinate Resolution at all Events to maintain them." Governor Thomas Hutchinson had "repeatedly refused to accept of the usual Grants for his Support. . . . Such an Independency [by the governor] threatens the very Being of a free Constitution."[32] How curious it is in this empire to see each contending side worrying about the other's "independency."

Franklin began to change his adulation of the crown after becoming agent for Massachusetts. Writing to Speaker Thomas Cushing on 13 January 1772, Franklin declared his sentiments to be "for the most part" like those of the province's people. "I think the Revenue Acts should be repealed . . . ; that the Commission of the Customs should be dissolved; that the Troops (Foreigners to us, as much as Hanoverians would be in England

---

30 Van Doren, *Benjamin Franklin*, 360.   31 *Franklin Papers*, 20:437, 18:27, 29.
32 Ibid., 18:147, 149.

. . .) ought to be withdrawn, . . . that the General Court should be return'd to its ancient Seat [in Boston], and the Governor's Salary put upon its ancient footing."[33]

In July 1772, the Massachusetts lower House voted a petition to the king opposing a royal salary for its governor that would make him independent of the general assembly. Speaker Cushing wrote to enlist Franklin's "best Endeavors" to get this grievance redressed. Franklin agreed to do so. Then Franklin lit a long fuse. In December, he informed Cushing "that there has lately fallen into my Hands Part of a Correspondence, that I have reason to believe laid the Foundation of most if not all our present Grievances."[34]

The enclosed letters had been sent from Massachusetts by Thomas Hutchinson and Andrew Oliver, advising the crown to do just the hateful things that the ministry, in fact, was doing. These letters had been secret, and Franklin had acquired them by means never admitted. One must wonder if his provider had also given the "reason to believe" their importance.

Apart from their notoriously explosive effect in Massachusetts, these letters stirred Franklin to personal outrage. Ordinarily case-hardened to the devious ways of politics, he was moved to untypically emotional response. Indeed, this seems to have been the moment when Benjamin Franklin stopped being the easygoing philosopher who tried to understand the out-looks of men on different sides of the big issues. There is no genial impar-tiality in his outburst to Cushing. Listen to his denunciation.

> When I find them bartering away the Liberties of their native Country for Posts, and negociating for Salaries and Pensions, for which the Money is to be squeezed from the People; and, conscious of the Odium these might be attended with, calling for Troops to protect and secure the Enjoyment of them; when I see them exciting Jealousies in the Crown, and provoking it to Wrath against a great Part of its faithful Subjects; creating Enmities between the different Countries of which the Empire consists; occasioning a great Expence to the new Country for the payment of needless Gratifications to useless Officers and Enemies; and to the old for Suppressing or Preventing imaginary Rebellions in the new; I cannot but doubt their Sincerity even in the political Principles they profess; and deem them mere Time-servers, seeking their own private Emolument thro' any Quan-tity of Publick Mischief; Betrayers of the Interest, not of their Native Country only, but of the Government they pretend to serve, and of the whole English Empire.[35]

Franklin requested that the papers be shown privately to some persons in Massachusetts who might thus be convinced of the secret misdeeds of Hutchinson and Oliver. Perhaps if they understood this, there might yet be

33 Ibid., 19:23.   34 Ibid., 19:209, 364, 411.   35 Ibid., 19:412–13.

hope for a rapprochement with London where some important persons sympathized with the colonies. Secrecy, however, became impossible. The letters were printed and a torrent of abuse poured out on Hutchinson and Oliver. Historian Bernard Bailyn presents Hutchinson's defense that they were only public-spirited officials trying, according to their understandings, to serve the people beneficially by preserving government from raving, radical excess, of which there was plenty.[36] (In a long note, the editors of the valuable *Franklin Papers* suggest that Hutchinson and Oliver did not "instigate repressive measures, as Franklin says they did; they argued that such measures were necessary, but in these letters they did not specify any."[37] Can this be more than a quibble? My *American Heritage* dictionary defines *instigate* as "1. to urge on; to goad. 2. To foment; stir up." Certainly Hutchinson and Oliver did exactly that, and we must not forget Franklin's "reason to believe" it. But the conscientious editors of the *Franklin Papers* let readers judge for themselves by the complete text of "The Hutchinson Letters" in Volume 20:539 ff.)

The letters did advocate an abridgment "of what are called English liberties" and did urge that governors and judges be supported by the crown instead of having to negotiate their salaries with assemblies. True, such proposals were already under consideration by ministers, but the letters did say those things, decisively, as it seemed to Franklin, and those things meant TYRANNY to Bostonians.

From this moment of revelation for Franklin, consequences flowed along three tracks: Franklin's own further development in England; uproar in Massachusetts; and decision in Virginia. To follow the direction of events we must alternate attention on these interacting stages. For the moment, let us stay with Franklin.

By the end of 1772, Franklin had cause to despair. His hopes for a fortune to be gained by a royal grant of western lands had been blasted. His goal of turning Pennsylvania into a royal province had led to defeat at the hands of his bitter enemy Thomas Penn. Now the Hutchinson letters revealed that officials in royal colonies were as self-serving and indifferent to general welfare as those of proprietary colonies. He had to face not only complete defeat but the knowledge of his own starry-eyed foolishness that had

---

36 Bailyn, *Ordeal of Thomas Hutchinson*, 251. In an appendix, devoted to "The Historiography of Loyalism," Professor Bailyn makes Hutchinson into a "scapegoat." As my book shows, my own sympathies with the Loyalists are strong, but not with the Hutchinson kind. I share Franklin's outlook: "When I find them bartering away the Liberties of their native Country for Posts, and negociating for Salaries and Pensions, for which the Money is to be squeezed from the People; and, conscious of the Odium these might be attended with, calling for Troops to protect and secure the Enjoyment of them . . . I cannot but doubt their Sincerity even in the political Principles they profess" (More in *Franklin Papers*, 19:412–13).

37 *Franklin Papers*, 19:403n1.

absorbed his time and energies for eight years. But Franklin was unsuppressable. He set himself new purposes.

He began to think in terms beyond the interests of individual provinces. Having served Massachusetts so powerfully with the Hutchinson letters, he fitted that province with a role in a larger political arena. "Perhaps it would be best and fairest," he wrote to Speaker Cushing in July 1773,

> for the Colonies in a general Congress now in Peace to be assembled, or by means of the Correspondence lately proposed, after a full and solemn Assertion and Declaration of their Rights, to engage firmly with each other that they will never grant aids to the Crown in any General War till those Rights are recogniz'd by the King and both Houses of Parliament; communicating at the same time to the Crown this their Resolution.

Thus in one sentence this retired printer reduced British taxes to voluntary "aids," proposed to make both crown and Parliament dependent on the colonies, suggested the means to accomplish this, and even named the organization that was to take charge of the Revolution! "Such a step," he imagined, "will bring the Dispute to a crisis," and indeed it did.[38] "Or by means of the Correspondence lately proposed" was a reference to a packet of letters previously sent him by Cushing, who had described it as "a Number of Resolves appointing a standing Committee to Correspond and Communicate with their Sister Colonies in America . . . and request them to appoint similar Committees."[39]

Thus we find Sam Adams's role somewhat diminished. The resolutions to initiate a network of committees of correspondence were made in Williamsburg, Virginia, 12 March 1773.[40] They were passed on to Franklin by Speaker Cushing. Franklin mulled over them and proposed to use the committees to create a Congress of all the colonies. That suggestion was passed back to Virginia, and within a year the Virginians summoned the first Continental Congress. The process throughout was the work of conservative gentlemen accustomed to power. Frenetic Samuel Adams had little to do with it. (Cf. Chapter 22.)

Franklin anticipated the crisis with arguments in the London press. Governor Thomas Hutchinson, whom Franklin had come to detest, asserted in a speech to the General Court that the colonists had taken Parliament's jurisdiction with them when they emigrated to America. Printed in the London *Public Advertiser*, the speech started a controversy concerning the king's right to own and grant American lands. Franklin denied the very basis of royal sovereignty in America. Royal land grants, he asserted, meant no more than "an Exclusion of other Englishmen from the respective

38 Ibid., 20:282.   39 Ibid., 20:172–73.
40 Chaffin in *Blackwell Encyclopedia*, 807; Gipson, 209.

Boundaries of each Grant. Grantees, to obtain some Title, were obliged to purchase of the Indians or conquer them *at their own Charges*" (italics in original).[41]

We must make an effort to remember Franklin's own share in a land grant project that had failed to get royal approval. Like others among the Revolutionaries, he had a great gift for rationalization.

Once launched, he carried on with "Rules by Which a Great Empire May be Reduced to a Small One" (11 September 1773) and "An Edict by the King of Prussia" (22 September 1773). These were bitter satires that attest to the freedom that London newspapers had won. Their like from an antigovernment source would not be printed in any American general newspaper today. Franklin's outlet, the *Public Advertiser*, had previously published the "Letters" of pseudonymous Junius attacking George III and had fought governmental censorship to complete victory. Like the Junius papers, the issue containing Franklin's "Edict by the King of Prussia" sold out immediately.[42] We are reminded here, as elsewhere, that rebelliousness was alive on both sides of the Atlantic.

41 *Franklin Papers* 20:120. Franklin was wrong about this. The general rule, including Pennsylvania, was for the colonial government to acquire land by cession from the owning tribe, then to patent tracts to individual colonials as real property. William Penn showed the rule very clearly.

42 Ibid., 20:390, 413.

22

·

DEFIANCE AND CRACKDOWN

Samuel Adams aroused Massachusetts's House of Representatives in January 1768 to protest the Townshend Acts by a circular letter sent to all the colonies to propose an exchange of views through correspondence.[1] He wanted to organize widespread nonimportation agreements, but Philadelphia's merchants declined to join.[2] Their tepid response was more than outmatched in London where Lord Hillsborough saw Adams's device in terms of treason, and the Ministry decided to send troops to calm Boston down.[3]

Virginia wakened in response to established and important gentry. When the Burgesses heard of the Ministry's crackdown, they condemned Parliament's ruling that Massachusetts radicals should be tried for treason, in England; and the Burgesses averred further that the Massachusetts House of Representatives was within its rights to appeal for joint action by all the colonies. In 1769, Virginia's House of Burgesses adopted "resolves" prepared by George Mason and introduced by the great planter George Washington.[4]

Naturally Sam Adams was gleeful, but other colonies did not respond to his invitation to correspond, and Governor Thomas Hutchinson outmaneuvered him in the General Court where a conservative lull set in. Even John Hancock, who marched always with the winning drummer, had distanced himself from Adams until Franklin's actions stirred up new agitation.[5]

Adams had had no direct contact with Franklin who was much too conservative for the firebrand's taste, but after Hutchinson's letters converted Franklin, Adams praised him. Franklin's advice, in the view of the editors of his papers, "was what American radicals were looking for."[6] They surged

---

1 Ralph Volney Harlow, *Samuel Adams: Promoter of the American Revolution: A Study in Psychology and Politics* (New York: Henry Holt & Co., 1923), 109.
2 Ibid., 113–18. 3 Ibid., 124–26. 4 Alden, *The South in the Revolution*, 110.
5 Harlow, *Samuel Adams*, 165–67. 6 *Franklin Papers*, 20:282n7.

forward. Handicapped by the disclosure of his secret letters, Hutchinson no longer could stop them. He could only hope that "many of the other Colonies will not join if the proposal was made by this."[7]

Perhaps that might have happened because Massachusetts was widely distrusted, but this time Hutchinson was outflanked. Franklin's proposal was sent on to Virginia. There, on 27 May 1774, eighty-one members of the House of Burgesses met at Williamsburg's Raleigh Tavern and voted for a Continental Congress. They met again, 1 August, and chose delegates. These meetings were extralegal because the Burgesses were locked out of their regular hall as was the case also with other colonies where voluntary and unofficial "conventions" chose delegates. They could not be official because governors dissolved their assemblies, but many assemblymen appeared as citizens in the conventions.

Virginia's gentlemen had no need, like Sam Adams, to convince the provincial power elite; they *were* the power elite, and they intended to keep on being that regardless of politicians in England.

Let me anticipate some events, to which we shall return. The Virginians observed the menace of troops in Boston and General Thomas Gage's proclamation, with heavy penalties, against political activity. Virginia's gentry declared, "this *odious* and *illegal* proclamation must be considered as a plain and full declaration that this *despotic viceroy* will be bound by no *law* . . . and therefore, that the *executing* or *attempting to execute* such proclamation will justify RESISTANCE and REPRISAL."[8]

They understood precisely the implications of such words, and so should modern readers. These gentlemen held themselves above the vulgar brawling in the streets that Bostonians seemed to delight in, but the orderly, methodical processes of making decisions in Virginia were actually far more hazardous to crown and Parliament than Boston's flamboyant antics. Boston obsessed the crown precisely because it was indeed flamboyant.

Boston forced the issues to extremes. If Sam Adams pushed matters from one side, Governor Thomas Hutchinson foolishly pushed back from the other. Late in 1772, Adams persuaded Boston's Town Meeting to publish a pamphlet about colonists' rights "as men, as Christians, and as subjects," and circulated the pamphlet throughout the province requesting statements of support. These started to come in and Hutchinson took alarm, seeing that "a local controversy was thus being used to instigate a general revolt."[9] So Hutchinson summoned the assembly to hear his speech on constitutionalism. Instead of being overwhelmed by his logic, the radicals were delighted. They responded, point by point, in both the Council and the

7 Ibid., 20:278.   8 *Documents of American History*, ed. Commager, 1:79–80.
9 Bailyn, *Ordeal of Thomas Hutchinson*, 206.

House of Representatives. He rebutted, and the whole exchange was published in newspapers and a pamphlet; and Hutchinson capped his foolishness of being drawn into this hopeless dispute by sending all the papers to Lord Dartmouth who had replaced Hillsborough as American secretary of state. Dartmouth despaired.

Dartmouth had been friendly with Franklin and had hoped that if things quieted down – if Boston would only shut up – some way might be found for English friends of the colonies to smooth matters over. How could that be when Hutchinson had provoked utterances "subversive of every principle of the constitutional dependence of the colonies upon this kingdom"? An aghast Hutchinson read Dartmouth's instruction to be quiet and not to "press either the Council or the House of Representatives to a declaration of their sentiments upon points that cannot be kept too much out of sight."[10] This letter arrived about 13 June.

Franklin's packet of Hutchinson's secret letters to Thomas Whately arrived in Boston in the same month and was also published.[11] In one word, Hutchinson was ruined.

So were the hopes of Franklin and Dartmouth to create reconciliation. Hutchinson applied for leave to go to England, but approval was delayed in transit until 13 November, and by that time he was head over heels in trouble again. In December 1773, Bostonians staged one more circus, more flagrant than anything that had gone before. This Boston Tea Party was so crude that it distressed Franklin and the Virginians, and so violent that it destroyed the last vestiges of possibility for Franklin's hopes to renew the empire as a federation of states under one crown.

The Boston Tea Party is beloved by historical writers for the romantic color with which it brightens their prose. To treat it more seriously, three vessels with cargoes of tea docked at Boston and were forbidden by radicals to unload. A militia guard under smuggler John Hancock enforced the ban. (One must not succumb to the romantic notion that radicals are always poor and outcast. Hancock reputedly was one of Boston's wealthiest and most prominent merchants.)

Hutchinson insisted on the law requiring customs duty on the tea. "It is time this anarchy was restrained and corrected by some authority or other." The radicals opposing taxes on tea forbade payment. The owner of one

10 Ibid., 205–19.
11 How those incriminating letters came to Benjamin Franklin has remained mysterious. There is no substantial reason to suspect Thomas Pownall; he was not very friendly with Franklin. More likely was Francis Dashwood, Lord Le Despencer who, as Chancellor of the Exchequer, would have had access to documents in the Treasury where Thomas Whately had worked. Dashwood was a warm friend of Franklin's, whose intellect he admired and who became Dashwood's guest for prolonged visits at the lord's country estate. And Dashwood would stand by Franklin through his worst troubles. Was he afraid that Franklin might spill what he knew?

vessel, who saw the mood of the townsfolk, begged for permission to take the tea back to England, but Hutchinson adamantly refused. Whereupon crowds of men, flimsily masquerading as Mohawk Indians, forced themselves into the ships and dumped the tea into the harbor, all of which was done under the guns of Castle William.[12]

It makes a lively tale, but English authorities were not amused. For Hutchinson it was a no-win situation. Bernard Bailyn comments that Hutchinson would discover criticism later in London "not for having been too rigid, and taking too many risks in enforcing the law, but for having been too lenient . . . that he should simply have sent in the troops to seize the tea and hold it until the situation cleared. But this he had never considered doing."[13]

Now a succession of actions, as though driven by doom, split the British empire. On 20 August 1773, Franklin in London received instruction from Massachusetts's outraged House of Representatives to demand the removal of Governor Thomas Hutchinson and his kinsman and aide Lt. Gov. Andrew Oliver. Though Franklin immediately passed this on to the Ministry, it stayed in committee, apparently deliberately stalled by Lord Dartmouth who kept trying to concoct ways out of the government's dilemma. Dartmouth earnestly consulted Franklin and even took the unprecedented step of writing as a private citizen to Speaker Thomas Cushing. Could there not be some acceptable basis for reconciliation?[14]

Franklin sympathized with Dartmouth's evident goodwill but had nothing to offer. The Boston politicians to whom Cushing showed the letter simply laughed at it. (The Adamses do not seem to have been among them.) The situation indicates that Parliament had a certain representative quality, rotten as was its proportioning; for Dartmouth could not concede colonial demands for fear of being put out of office by opponents. He was ready to let issues simmer down by stalling and apparently hopeful of making concessions quietly in practice while stoutly maintaining Parliament's sovereignty in principle. In this respect, Secretary Lord Dartmouth shared the outlook of his leader Lord Frederick North, head of government since 1770 and inclined to approach problems as they came along rather than to deal with them in terms of fixed policy. If the Ministry had really been despotic, they could have decided whatever they pleased.[15]

Events relieved Dartmouth and North of the need to make hard choices. Franklin confessed his role with the Hutchinson letters on Christmas Day 1773 in a letter to the *London Chronicle*.[16] Soon afterward, 20 January 1774,

12 Bailyn, *Ordeal of Thomas Hutchinson*, 261–71.   13 Ibid., 263.

14 Ibid., 214–16: see also Dartmouth's correspondence with Philadelphian Joseph Reed, cited in Draper, *Strugggle for Power*, 405–7.

15 Watson, *Reign of George III*, 147.   16 *Franklin Papers*, 20:513–16.

news arrived in London about the Boston Tea Party.[17] All possibility of dealing quietly with disputes went up in smoke, and Franklin's utility as a colonial agent blew away with it.

The Privy Council appointed 29 January to hear Massachusetts's petition against Hutchinson and Oliver. Agent Franklin attended and was seared by the worst invective of his life as Solicitor General Wedderburn tore into him for thievery and treachery in an hour-long harangue. Rather incidentally, the Council decided against his petition.[18]

Then government turned to the serious work of teaching Boston a lesson. The crown sent a new governor to relieve harassed and weary Hutchinson, and this new man had power at command. He was General Thomas Gage, commander in chief of all the royal forces in America, who arrived in Boston 13 May 1774.[19] Gage thought to end the hatching of conspiracies by moving the provincial capital from Boston to Salem, and he forbade town meetings. This did not work as intended. Salem's selectmen promptly posted announcements of their intended meeting. Gage issued a special proclamation to prevent it. The proclamation was ignored, and the meeting was held despite his presence with two regiments of soldiers. What to do? He arrested seven conspicuous leaders, but refrained from punishing them unless he could get more troops.[20]

Parliament was as busy as the crown. It enacted the Boston Port Act, 31 March 1774, scheduled to go into effect on first June. This was an embargo on all commerce into and out of the port until the drowned tea should be paid for and "reasonable satisfaction" made to revenue agents who had suffered in the performance of their duties.

The Port Act was followed, 20 May 1774, by the Massachusetts Government Act to "regulate" the legislature and judiciary. It made the Council (upper house) members and all judges appointive to serve "during the pleasure of his Majesty"; and it banned all town meetings unless approved in advance by the governor.

At the same session, 20 May, Parliament enacted the Administration of Justice Act providing for criminal trials to be transferred to Britain or "any other colony" (which meant Nova Scotia where royal control was strong).[21]

Parliament also took up the long-festering issue concerning quartering of troops, and it provided explicitly that troops need not be restricted to barracks but might be assigned by order of the governor to uninhabited houses, outhouses, barns, "or other buildings." It passed on 2 June.[22]

17 Ibid., 21:38.   18 Ibid., 21:37–70.   19 Bailyn, *Ordeal of Thomas Hutchinson*, 271.
20 Harlow, *Samuel Adams*, 247.   21 *Documents of American History*, ed. Commager, 1:71–74.
22 Lawrence Henry Gipson, *The Coming of the Revolution, 1763–1775* (New York: Harper and Brothers, 1954), 225.

Parliament called these laws "Coercive." Colonials denounced them as Intolerable Acts and aroused resistance everywhere. Although other colonies had kept aloof from Massachusetts, suddenly it became the focal point of widespread complaint against royal "tyranny." Unified action became the new watchword.

In view of the prominence given to John Adams in the historiography of the Revolution, we may notice how this resentfully envious man later protested against ascribing the Revolution to Benjamin Franklin. John C. Miller has reprinted Adams's spiteful remark, "The History of our Revolution will be one continued Lye from one end to the other. The essence of the whole will be that *Dr. Franklin's electrical Rod smote the Earth and out sprang General Washington.*"[23]

It is on record that during the eventful struggles reported herein, "John Adams dropped absolutely out of the political circle." Thus Ralph Volney Harlow. He dropped out of the House of Representatives in 1771, declared privately his intention to be "more retired and cautious," and he avoided all "politics, political clubs, town meetings, General Court, &c." throughout 1771 and 1772.[24] The crucial documents of 1773 do not mention him in the coterie of Speaker Thomas Cushing. Adams emerged to historical attention again as a delegate to the First Continental Congress in 1774 (see Chapter 23).

In short, while Franklin was braving the lions in London, John Adams watched to see how the big cats would jump. When Adams climbed onto the bandwagon, he became the loudest tooter of his own horn. He must be credited also, however, with becoming the most diligent, almost fanatically so, member of the Continental Congress, and unswervingly dedicated to the cause of independence.

If regulating the frontiers baffled the British Ministry, an even greater difficulty faced them in governing the new province of Quebec. Six years after the conquest, the Board of Trade found that Quebec's makeshift military government was "very imperfect, inadequate and defective."[25] The usual provincial pattern of governor and assembly could not be used there because most of the population, including nearly all the leaders, were Catholic, and Catholics could not take office anywhere in the empire. In 1764, no more than two hundred British householders lived in the entire province, of

23 John C. Miller, *Origins of the American Revolution* (Boston: Little, Brown and Co., 1943), 333.
24 Harlow, *Samuel Adams*, 165.
25 Peter Marshall, "The Incorporation of Quebec in the British Empire, 1763–1774," in *Of Mother, Country and Plantation*, ed. Virginia Bever Platt and David Curtis Skaggs (Bowling Green, Ohio: Bowling Green State University Press, 1971), 59–60.

whom only a dozen were from New England and New York.[26] However, this aggressive minority clamored that military government held back the colony's economic progress (they seem to have been mostly merchants), but Governor James Murray rejected an assembly for which only such a small minority could be eligible.

Which legal system, French or English, should be established, and what should be done about privileges formerly exercised by the Catholic clergy?[27] Successive ministers struggled with a constitution for the colony until the Boston Tea Party forced them to decide on measures "to secure the Dependance of the colonies on the Mother Country."[28]

It could not be considered a routine problem. Peter Marshall observes:

> The issues and problems which emerged in the years after 1763 were constantly to recur as the Empire reached its greatest extent: on the one hand beliefs in assimilation, the authority of the imperial Parliament, the supremacy of Parliament and English law, and the power of the prerogative; on the other, respect for the existence of non-British cultures, the need for local representative institutions, the recognition of diversity in laws and religions, and an Englishman's right to assert and transmit his liberties throughout the Empire.[29]

This all has a very modern ring though we would use different terminology today with reference to multiculturalism. Today, as then, bigots rave propaganda to force repressive responses to libertarian problems.

In 1774, Parliament enacted the Ministry's recommended Quebec Act, which had immediate repercussions throughout the colonies. By two main provisions, its effect was to set off Quebec distinctly from the tumultuous colonies farther south. Internally it legalized the Roman Catholic religion and permitted its professors to hold office, thus authorizing the governor to appoint Catholics to his governing council to the frustration of the tiny Protestant minority scheming to take rule into its own hands. Externally the Act affected the frontiers by fixing the boundary line of the 1763 Royal Proclamation as Quebec's boundary south to the Ohio River.

Both provisions worked well for Quebec. The majority population achieved its desired freedom of religion and was grateful. Despite the outcries of the Protestants, Quebec's people did not miss an elected assembly because they had never known one under French rule. Trade with the Indians, Quebec's only staple trade, was brought under control. Troops

26 G. P. Browne, "James Murray," in *Dictionary of Canadian Biography* 4:573; Pierre Tousignant, "Integration of the Province of Quebec . . ." in ibid., 4:xli.

27 Marshall, "Incorporation of Quebec," 59–60; Tousignant in *Dictionary of Canadian Biography* 4:xlv; L. H. Thomas, "Walker, Thomas," in ibid., 4:758–59.

28 Tousignant, *Dictionary of Canadian Biography*, 4:xlvii.

29 Marshall, "Incorporation of Quebec," 61.

needed to pacify the frontier region and enforce royal edicts about land ownership were on hand and under command.

However, so far as the rebellious colonies were concerned, the Quebec Act was one more outrageous "Coercive Act" emanating from London.[30] In one stroke, the Quebec Act made worthless all the speculators' grasping for western lands, and they were furious. Thomas Jefferson wrote hotly that a people had the inherent right to circumscribe their own boundaries. Thus, omitting Indians from the ranks of people as he soon would omit Africa's descendants, he proclaimed Virginia's gentry's defiance of Parliament and king.[31]

Liberties for Catholics, which were so gratifying to French Canadians, aroused special rage in New England. In the opinion of one proper New Englander of modern times, Henry Steele Commager, "the Quebec Act was one of the most enlightened pieces of colonial administration in the history of European colonial expansion."[32] What should we think, then, of contemporary Mercy Otis Warren's downright falsehood that "this act cut the Canadians off from the privileges of English subjects," a piece of word magic that equated *Canadians* with the Protestant minority. Her readers did not need to be told that the asserted privileges had included political and religious monopoly for Protestants.[33]

Modern historian John C. Miller, who knew better, repeated Mrs. Warren's line of denunciation. Securing an escape hatch with "in essentials," Miller opined that "the Quebec Act continued the undemocratic government over the province of an appointed governor and council." Two pages later he conceded that the Act "acknowledged Canadians' natural right to enjoy their own laws and religion."[34] He failed to note that the alternative demanded by rebellious colonists farther south was a different variety of undemocratic government in which an assembly elected by a religiously qualified few would rule over the religiously unqualified many. Democracy can be a very elastic concept.

Miller correctly classed the Quebec Act as a matter of practicality and power rather than a sudden conversion by the crown to virtue. "The British government made no effort to apply its new-found liberalism to Ireland, where there was as great a need for justice and toleration as in Canada." For

30 *Documents of American History*, ed. Commager, 1:74–76.
31 Thomas Jefferson, *A Summary View of the Rights of British America* (1774) in *Tracts of the American Revolution, 1773–1776*, ed. Merrill Jensen (Indianapolis: Bobbs-Merrill Co., 1967), 273.
32 *Documents of American History*, ed. Commager, 1:74.
33 Mercy Otis Warren, *History of the Rise, Progress, and Termination of the American Revolution* (1805), reprint ed. Lester H. Cohen, 2 vols. (Indianapolis: Liberty Fund, 1989), 1:137.
34 Miller, *Origins of the American Revolution*, 373.

the rebels, the Act was an evil device to win Canadian Catholics against the disaffected Protestant colonies. Members of Parliament (Protestant without exception) agreed that tolerance might curb "those fierce fanatic spirits in the Protestant colonies."[35]

Like the Stamp Tax, the Quebec Act united the rebellious colonists, whether motivation was religious or expansionist. Even before they declared themselves independent of Britain, they organized armies to invade Canada. If the west was to be within Quebec's boundaries, the Revolutionaries intended that Quebec should be within theirs.

35 Ibid., 373–75.

23

———— • ————

UNITING FOR LIBERTY, TENTATIVELY

The individual colonies had protested and petitioned against being deprived of autonomous rights. They had battered against London's stone wall. Gradually they came to accept the analysis of their situation that Franklin had suggested, and when General Gage arrived in Boston armed with both the civil powers of provincial governor and the military powers of his command, political leaders knew they must either surrender or raise resistance to a new level. It was time to sink provincial differences and unite for American liberties.

Gage arrived on 13 May. Four days later, feisty Rhode Island issued the first call for a "Grand Congress" of the colonies.[1] Seemingly by coincidence, Virginia's Burgesses met privately on 27 May to discuss a congress and returned at a subsequent meeting, 1 August, to choose delegates.[2]

This was treasonous activity in the eyes of imperial officials; but radicals in Massachusetts contrived to flout their governor by locking the General Court's doors while they organized a call for a congress, and the transaction was complete before Gage could dissolve their session. The date was 17 June. This was in the best tradition of romantic revolution, and it has attracted much gleeful attention. As the dates show, however, Massachusetts acted later than Virginia. Mercy Otis Warren had a little difficulty squaring the dates with her local pride. She thought there was a "remarkable coincidence of opinion" between Virginia and Massachusetts, and she noted delicately an initiative not led by Boston: The Virginians had agreed for a general congress "before they were informed of the resolutions of Massachusetts."[3] It seems that she had not been informed of the signal sent by Franklin to produce this "remarkable coincidence."

Nova Scotia, Quebec, and Georgia stayed away from the First Continental Congress, which had delegates otherwise from all the continental

---

1 *Blackwell Encyclopedia*, 811.
2 *Documents of the American Revolution*, ed. Commager, 1:78–79.
3 Warren, *History of the . . . Revolution*, 1:75n.

colonies. (No West Indian colony was represented.) The Congress's chief result was to convince the provincially proud delegates that they really could cooperate effectively. To get to that end, however, was not so easy as the statement makes it seem.

First, the opposition of governors had to be overcome. As they saw the issue of participation coming forward, they tried to stop it by dissolving assemblies. To counteract this, the radicals gathered in extralegal "conventions" to choose delegates. Thus the gathering of the Congress justified royal fears; by creating a new, competitive source of legislative power, it *was* treasonous, no matter how fulsomely the delegates professed loyalty. (In this legal aspect, it seems much like the later soviets of the Russian empire.)

A different sort of obstruction was posed in proprietary Pennsylvania where Governor John Penn shrewdly permitted his assembly to choose six delegates on the assumption that their conservatism would offset the wild men. But Pennsylvania also had radicals. They gathered in convention while the assembly met, and the convention chose a set of delegates different from the assembly's.[4]

The delegates from other colonies converging on Philadelphia had not realized the complexity of Pennsylvania's politics. This proprietary colony's assembly had long been a battleground since Quakers resigned from it in 1756 when Franklin took it over with the hope of persuading the crown to resume direct government. While Franklin was in England, his political partner Joseph Galloway built a political machine with the assembly, but when Franklin turned against the crown Galloway continued loyal and kept the assembly in line.

Pennsylvania's radicals, led by lawyer John Dickinson and merchant Charles Thomson, aroused strong opposition to the assembly party's program as they aligned a new provincial party with the rebellious policies of Virginia and Massachusetts. They were elected to the assembly even as they organized local committees and a provincial convention to compete with it.[5] Dickinson was also chosen as a delegate to the Congress. Thomson never became a delegate but went on to greater office as Congress's secretary.

These two conspired with Massachusetts's Adamses. When assembly Speaker Galloway offered to host the Congress in Pennsylvania's State House, the radicals rebuffed him by choosing nearby Carpenters' Hall instead to demonstrate their opposition to everything official. When Congress met, 5 September, they succeeded in electing Charles Thomson as secretary despite his not being a delegate. The act was portentous. Thomson would remain secretary during the entire existence of the Revolutionary Congress, and he did much more than take minutes. He became what is now

---

4 Newcomb, *Franklin and Galloway*, 246.   5 Ibid., 258.

called an executive secretary, always second in authority to the president of congress pro tem, but always the enduring visible symbol of the organization's perpetuity.[6]

Regrettably, historians cannot praise Thomson's disposition of the official papers in his care. At the end of his tenure he destroyed them, and his motive is illuminating: "I could not tell the truth without giving great offense. Let the world admire our patriots and heroes. Their supposed talents and virtues (where they were so) by commanding imitation will serve the cause of patriotism and our country."[7] Thus he reduced himself to "the Sam Adams of Philadelphia" instead of revealing himself to be the national leader that Sam never became.[8]

It was instantly predictable from Charles Thomson's election as its secretary that the Congress would reject the program offered by Joseph Galloway. This amounted to what later became the British Commonwealth, a federation of colonies and realms united under the same king, but self-governing by its constituents in all important matters. Ten years earlier, Benjamin Franklin could have endorsed it, but too much had happened in that decade. Congress's delegates were full of resentment against imperial government. Though they deferentially declared, "We wish not a diminution of the prerogative," they set themselves the task of doing just that – and of diminishing Parliament's power too.[9]

Congress urged support for Boston in response to the Suffolk Resolves.[10] These emanated from Suffolk County, Massachusetts, where a convention of delegates from the county's towns took up the burden of government, 9 September 1774, by unanimously renouncing the authority of a legislature sponsored by General Gage. As Mercy Otis Warren reports, "They recommended to the people to resist by force of arms, every hostile invasion," and they resolved direct physical action against officers of the crown.[11] Paul Revere galloped to Philadelphia with this voice of a determined people, arriving at Congress with the Resolves on 16 September. On the seventeenth, Congress endorsed the Resolves, and next day Revere headed back to Boston with this inspirational action.[12] He was a very busy silversmith. (And a very good one.)

6 Boyd Stanley Schlenther, *Charles Thomson: A Patriot's Pursuit* (Newark: University of Delaware Press, 1990), 156, 165.

7 *Congress at Princeton: Being the Letters of Charles Thomson to Hannah Thomson, June–October 1783*, ed. Eugene R. Sheridan and John M. Murrin (Princeton, N.J.: Princeton University Library, 1985), xxii.

8 Cf. John J. Zimmerman, "The Sam Adams of Philadelphia," *Mississippi Valley Historical Review* 45(1958): 464–80.

9 Gipson, *Coming of the Revolution*, 230; Newcomb, *Franklin and Galloway*, 254–57.

10 Middlekauff, *The Glorious Cause*, 246–47.

11 Warren, *History of the . . . Revolution*, 1:89.

12 David Hackett Fischer, *Paul Revere's Ride* (New York: Oxford University Press, 1994), 27.

David Hackett Fischer compels recognition that the Suffolk Resolves were not mere rhetoric. General Gage had tried to disarm the men of Massachusetts by seizing their magazine of gunpowder. His first effort, 1 September 1774 (before the meeting at Suffolk), seized without warning the Provincial Powder House northwest of Boston with the largest stock of powder in New England. The unanticipated outcome of this perfectly executed capture was an eruption of the countryside so ferocious that Gage ordered Boston closed and fortified. "The whole country was in arms and in motion," he reported to London. This was the news that Paul Revere brought, along with the Sussex Resolves in response, to the Continental Congress in Philadelphia, and it was in the delegates' minds as they endorsed the Resolves' recommendation to prepare for war.[13]

But not yet to launch it. Other colonies did not yet feel the rage of Massachusetts because they did not yet have to deal with direct suppression by the royal army. Provincial special interests at odds with each other dampened the Congress's enthusiasm for united action. By compromising on economic weapons, Congress ordered an Association to curtail exports and imports with British merchants, and a petition to the king for redress.[14] Nothing new there, but the delegates had actually met and had come to respect each other, and they agreed to meet again in May 1775. By that time, Gage and the Massachusetts farmers imposed a new agenda on Congress. As the delegates' ancestors had learned long before in England, there could be no compromise with a royal standing army.

Before adjournment an incident occurred that awakened some delegates to one significance of their meeting in "the Quaker city." Israel Pemberton Jr., "the king of the Quakers," invited John Adams to a Quaker meeting at Carpenter's Hall where Pemberton launched an attack on Adams's religion and provincial institutions. No issue was more important, he said, than "liberty of conscience." New England's laws "not only compelled men to pay to the building of churches and support of ministers, but to go to some known religious assembly on first days, etc." Pemberton demanded assurance that such laws would be repealed.[15]

Pemberton had never been known for tact, and John Adams was not the sort of Christian to turn the other cheek. In retrospect, the situation is hardly credible. Here was a leading neutralist pacifist assailing the province occupied by an active royal army and desperately organizing to defend its right to self-government. Pemberton's charges were true enough, but not

---

13 Ibid., Chap. 3.   14 Middlekauff, *Glorious Cause*, 241–49.
15 Theodore Thayer, *Israel Pemberton, King of the Quakers* (Philadelphia: Historical Society of Pennsylvania, 1943), 209; *The Spirit of 'Seventy-Six*, ed. H. S. Commager and R. B. Morris (New York: Harper & Row, 1967), 395–96.

very relevant to the circumstances. Adams can be forgiven for responding irately. Less forgivably, he carried a grudge against Quakers that he vented without scruple three years later.

Israel Pemberton's behavior with John Adams was not typical of most Quakers, who were generally stuffy but mild mannered. Pemberton was exceptionally aggressive and militant among his brethren of the Society of Friends. The Friends certainly and adamantly opposed wars and measures that might lead to war, but they relied on persuasion rather than provocation.

They have been subjected to much false malignity because of their neutrality during the Revolution, so it will be well to check some facts behind that inflammatory rhetoric by turning to the dealings of London Quakers with Benjamin Franklin. Neutrality did not mean for them a disengagement from great issues; they sought actively to promote peace and reconciliation. Great merchant and banker David Barclay and preeminent physician Dr. John Fothergill tried to find compromises acceptable to Franklin and certain ministers who wanted to prevent rupture of the empire.

This seems the more surprising because Franklin's earlier effort to make Pennsylvania a royal colony (instead of proprietary) had been resisted strongly by Quakers. They greatly valued the religious tolerance guaranteed by William Penn's Charter of Liberties, which they had steadfastly defended, not only for themselves, but even for the right to worship of despised Roman Catholics. If Franklin had succeeded in making the province royal, the crown would have been able to establish its own religion as in England.

Now in 1774, after having opposed royalization of Pennsylvania, the same Quakers were resisting Franklin again, but this time as he opposed the crown. They had great influence with powerful aristocrats. Fothergill was physician to some statesmen (and apparently discussed state issues with them). Barclay was prominent in the merchant community of the City of London, and he had acted as host to the family of the king, no less, for viewing the festive Lord Mayor's Day parade. It appears that these two approached Franklin as unacknowledged agents for certain ministers of government, not merely as kindly gentlemen seeking uplifting conversation. They hinted plainly what they might be able to do.

What transpired has been told in detail and with clarity in Carl Van Doren's *Benjamin Franklin*. I give only a précis.[16]

16 Van Doren, *Benjamin Franklin*, 495–519; Jacob M. Price, "The Great Quaker Business Families of Eighteenth-Century London," in *The World of William Penn*, ed. Richard S. Dunn and Mary Maples Dunn (Philadelphia: University of Pennsylvania Press, 1986); Jennings, *Benjamin Franklin, Politician*, Chaps. 15, 16.

Franklin and the Quakers exchanged position papers. Then he was introduced for direct interviews with several lords, among them William Pitt, Earl of Chatham. Pitt wanted to help the Americans but could not give up the doctrine of Parliament's sovereignty.

By a delightful device, Franklin was inveigled into playing chess with the sister of Lord Howe who just happened to be nearby, close enough to join the talk – even to continue after she departed. Howe showed great sympathy for the colonists and hinted at a bribe for Franklin (who contemptuously ignored it), but the same obstacle of Parliament's supremacy could not be circumvented.

There were limits to what the men of goodwill (or just sanity?) could achieve, for there were other ministers like Lord Sandwich whose power as first lord of the admiralty was augmented by a system of personal patronage and bribery. Sandwich's hostility toward the colonies was as notorious as his personal corruption, and he could not be ignored. So the limits were reached but not transcended, and when news arrived of the Continental Congress's doings, the government responded with more troops.

Sadly Franklin learned of his wife's death while the threat of trial in the Hutchinson letters affair came closer. There was no point in staying longer in England.

He advised Americans that the Congress's Association for boycotting trade with England must be maintained unwaveringly. He thought that the City's merchants could force government's reversal of policy. If Congress could sustain the boycott weapon, "a year from next September, or to the next session of Parliament, . . . the day is won."[17]

In fairness to the Quakers who have been so badly mauled in the war propaganda, Franklin's report about Barclay and Fothergill illuminates much.

> I met them by desire at the Doctor's house, when they desired me to assure their friends from them that it was now their fixed opinion that nothing could secure the privileges of America but firm, sober adherence to the terms of the Association made at the Congress, and that the salvation of English liberty depended now on the perseverance and virtue of America.[18]

17 Van Doren, *Benjamin Franklin*, 520.   18 Ibid., 519.

24

———— • ————

SHOTS HEARD ROUND THE WORLD

The structure of Boston's revolutionary movement, and Paul Revere's place within it, were very different from recent secondary accounts.

David Hackett Fischer

While Congress's delegates searched for means to unite, and London Quakers, Franklin, and friendly politicians groped for means of reconciliation, armed men faced against each other in Massachusetts. Rationalizations and excuses notwithstanding, men acquire weapons with intent to use them. It was only a matter of time until General Gage's troops and the rebellious militias should be precipitated into combat.

The time came, and it has been splendidly described in a book that arouses the rare pleasure of warranting recommendation without reserve. *Paul Revere's Ride* by David Hackett Fischer is as near to being definitive as a book can be; its evidence is copious and authentic; and it is enjoyable to read. It is my source for this chapter.[1]

In brief, General Gage worried much about the militias' stockpiling of munitions and, as we have seen, he captured one magazine by surprise. Hearing of another accumulation at the town of Concord, he determined to take that also, but the rebels were ready this time. Their intelligence system included virtually the entire population of Boston, and it marked precisely the day when the troops were to march: 18 April 1775. An elaborate system of couriers was readied to carry warnings ahead of the troops. Gage's men had also a secondary objective to seize leading rebels Samuel Adams and John Hancock who were known to be hiding in Lexington.

As Professor Fischer points out, the ride of Paul Revere, so greatly famed in verse and story, "was not a solitary act. Many people helped him on his way . . . [it] was truly a collective effort."[2]

---

1 New York: Oxford University Press, 1994.   2 Fischer, *Paul Revere's Ride*, 98.

Before Revere even got started on his mission to warn Adams and Hancock, a tanner named William Dawes made his way across Boston Neck with the same message, and Dawes got through just before the Neck was closed to passage. Revere went by a different route. He waited for the famous signal from the spire of Old North Church to tell which way the troops would start – "one if by land, two by sea" – and when two lanterns flashed, Revere's watchmen notified him and he was rowed over to Charlestown where a fast horse had been found for him.

General Gage was a systematic man. Many British patrols were on the roads that night. Revere was nearly caught by one of them, but he was as good a horseman as a silversmith, and he detoured sharply in time. He got to Lexington about midnight where he aroused the people and was joined by William Dawes. They rested briefly, then rode on to Concord.

These two never got there because they were ambushed by another patrol; but they had picked up young Dr. Samuel Prescott, of Concord, who had been courting his fiancée at Lexington until late at night. Prescott dashed away from the ambush, leaped a wall, and made good his escape – and fulfilled Revere's mission to Concord. Dawes was less fortunate. His horse bolted and threw him, but he could only hide. Revere was surrounded and faced with cocked pistols on all sides. He could only surrender.

But Revere spoke up boldly, and when distant shots and Lexington's bell frightened his captors, they decided to hurry back to warn the advancing troops. To make better speed, they freed Revere and other captives.

Still other couriers were on the roads that night. Before Revere left Charlestown, he had dispatched a man to ride north to arouse the militias in that direction. Another went northeast, and still another directly eastward to Malden. Relays picked up the message and fanned out in all directions. The total operation was far more effective than one man's dramatic ride could possibly have been. This was not the work of a lone hero; it was a whole people as angry and ready to sting as a disturbed hive of hornets.

Fischer's comment is worth repeating.

> The midnight riders went systematically about the task of engaging town leaders and military commanders of their region. They enlisted its churches and ministers, its physicians and lawyers, its family networks and voluntary associations. Paul Revere and his fellow Whigs of Massachusetts understood, more clearly than Americans of later generations, that political institutions are instruments of human will, and amplifiers of individual action. They knew from long experience that successful effort requires sustained planning and careful organization.[3]

3 Ibid., 139.

True enough, and the essential fact was that the people were already united in support. That was why they could be wakened in the middle of the night to face certain hardship and possible death.

Freed by his captors, Revere walked back to Lexington and a sequel combining low comedy and high drama. He found Sam Adams and John Hancock still arguing as Hancock mouthed off about how he personally would face down the Regulars. But as the troops came nearer the braggadocio evaporated. He "insisted on traveling in high state" in his heavy coach, taking Sam Adams along but abandoning Aunt Hancock and his fiancée to the mercies of the Regulars.

One must notice more about this leader's valor. He had abandoned a trunk full of important papers that "contained the innermost secrets of the Whig cause, and written evidence that could incriminate many leaders."[4] But he hungered for the delicacy of a freshly caught salmon given to him at Lexington, so he sent back for it and incidentally for Aunt Hancock and Dolly Quincy.

Revere went for the trunk with the papers. While Lexington's trainband mustered on the Common, Revere and young John Lowell found the trunk and carried it off to hiding, for which purpose they had to pass directly through the ranks of the tense minutemen watching approaching Regulars.[5]

Hancock's salmon joined him in Woburn, and his aunt and fiancée also. By command, the salmon was cooked; but (woe!) another alarm caused it to be abandoned and the fleeing hero had to make this sacrifice for his cause.

As to Mr. Hancock's personal peculiarities, it must be observed that even a revolution of a whole people must be financed, and Hancock was probably the richest man in Massachusetts.

At Lexington, the Regulars advanced and ordered the patriots to disperse. Revere and Lowell hurried faster with their trunk. A shot was heard. It may have been "an accident that was waiting to happen"; no one has ever confirmed the shooter's identity. Alarmed, the troops volleyed with the roaring sound of their black powder – as loud as cannon shots. Horses bolted. Militiamen fired back. Revere and Lowell ducked with their trunk as bullets whizzed overhead.

The odds were far from even. Two militiamen were killed in line formation, 6 more as they fled. Only 1 Regular was wounded. But the countryside was not intimidated. Whereas 60 armed farmers had stood up to the Regulars before the skirmish began, 160 gathered nearby after the troops marched off, and these men did not go home. Like the troops, they headed toward Concord.

4 Ibid., 179.　5 Ibid., 188.

There the numbers of militiamen had been growing all morning. Still not enough to challenge the troops, they retreated from the town while soldiers ransacked it for the munitions that were their objective; but most of the munitions had been scattered to other towns, and much of what remained was hidden underground. One engagement took place at Concord Bridge where the superiority of aimed fire over volley fire was demonstrated. As the militias continued to increase, Lt. Col. Smith ordered retreat, but he did not thereby escape the aroused country people. They deployed along his road behind stone walls and trees. The minutemen who had been chased out of Lexington now took revenge. British casualties were so heavy that the thought of surrender rose until the wretched troops found reinforcements from Boston awaiting them at Lexington.

New officers took charge on both sides. Lord Hugh Percy commanded the troops from Lexington back to Boston. General William Heath took over the militias. Each had a rational strategy, but Heath had the advantage of terrain and numbers, and the militiamen aimed their shots. The fighting turned very ugly. The Regulars had observed an atrocity in Concord when a colonial hatcheted a wounded, fallen soldier to death. Furiously now, they declared and practiced no quarter when coming upon unwary civilians.

With heavy losses, the battered troops managed to get through to Boston, but safety was only temporary as thousands of militiamen surrounded the town. While they prepared entrenchments, Revere's couriers took off again to all the colonies with news of the events; and a fast schooner took it to London where newspapers printed it before Gage's dispatches could arrive. Professor Fischer summarizes:

> In strictly military terms, the fighting on April 19 was a minor reverse for British arms and a small success for the New England militia. But the ensuing contest for popular opinion was an epic disaster for the British government, and a triumph for American Whigs. In every region of British America, attitudes were truly transformed by the news of this event.[6]

John Adams had hoped for success from appeals to reason, but he became convinced "that the Die was cast, the Rubicon crossed."

Tom Paine was to recall "the moment the event of that day was known, I rejected the hardened, sullen-tempered Pharaoh of England forever."

George Washington asked rhetorically, "Can a virtuous man hesitate in his choice?"[7]

The nineteenth of April 1774 was one of those rare days that mark decision beyond cavil. But what decision?

6 Ibid., 279.   7 Ibid., 279–80.

Certainly it unified colonies for armed rebellion transcending talk. Yet one must note carefully that New England distinguished itself from the others on that day. For the others, in a military sense, the Revolution was now beginning; it is possible, however, to think of it as near to consummation in Massachusetts. Though all the colonies united to resist the crown, they were far from identical in what they would do with victory when, or by what means, it should come.

New Englanders viewed events through a filter of memories special to their region. Their Puritan forefathers in England had risen against a king only a little more than a century earlier and had committed an ultimate sacrilege by executing him.

In Pennsylvania, however, large numbers of Quakers also had memories of the same era when those triumphant Puritans had persecuted Quaker forefathers.

And in Virginia, many of the gentry were descended from the Cavaliers who had fought so bitterly against the Puritans. They, too, had memories.[8]

Need it be added that enslaved descendants of Africans had aims of their own; and the colonies/states wanting to expand beyond their western boundaries were watched closely by still other peoples with tribal territories to defend.

With all honor to some real heroes, the Revolution in New England must not be put forward as though these varied peoples, and others as well, were only tails to Massachusetts's kite. It is grave fallacy to confound the part with the whole.

8 David Hackett Fischer, *Albion's Seed: Four British Folkways in America* (New York: Oxford University Press, 1989), 783–88.

25

MULTIPLE REVOLUTIONS

We must pick up the First Continental Congress again to show especially how it began organizing the Revolutionary militants even before a decision could be made feasibly for independence. The Congress's location was all-important. Radicals understood well that their cause could not be successful without Pennsylvania. Naturally enough, therefore, as Lynn Montross comments, "Without concerning themselves too much about ethics, the delegates of other colonies did not hesitate to dabble in the troubled waters of Pennsylvania politics."[1]

In perspective, one can see that the First Congress's most important single decision was its recommendation to the provinces to create Associations of citizens with multiple functions. Overtly they were to prevent trade with British merchants on the assumption that the merchants would clamor to change the crown's policies. Had that been all, the Associations would have faded off into insignificance when the British shrugged and opened trade in other directions, especially eastward. But the Associations took on police functions also; they publicized and punished recalcitrant merchants. And they were also to arm themselves and operate as militias outside the authority of former provincial officers.[2]

It was a heavy load of responsibilities for volunteers, and in this respect one can see the emergence of genuine democracy *within the movement* though an indeterminate number of persons either refused to join or were excluded. Such persons were not overlooked by the Associators; they were punished and exploited with such force as seemed necessary. Paradoxical though it sounds, a new political society was being created, a broad oligarchy made up of democrats.

In view of later developments, one may note that the senior colonel of these Associators in Pennsylvania was John Dickinson – lawyer, author of

---

1 Lynn Montross, *The Reluctant Rebels: The Story of the Continental Congress, 1774–1789* (New York: Harper and Brothers, 1950), 149–50.
2 Ibid., 56–60.

the *Farmer's Letters*, and kinsman by marriage to Charles Thomson. Though often excoriated as a conservative because he tried to hold back the decision for the colonists to secede from the empire, Dickinson was a major leader among rebellious Pennsylvanians. He, too, wanted autonomy, but he also wanted more time to exhaust all possibilities before the ultimate decision to secede. This attitude was different in substance from the Quaker desire to stay within the empire even on terms imposed by the crown.

The Germans must not be overlooked. They composed a very large component of the whole population – at least a third and perhaps as much as 40 percent. Their religions ranged widely. There were "high church" Lutherans, Dutch Reformed, and even a few Roman Catholics. The "low" churches included Moravians, Mennonites, Schwenkfelders, and other sects. Little love was lost between the Germans and the Scotch-Irish Presbyterians, and the "peace sects" felt strong kinship with Quakers; but overwhelmingly the Germans were hostile to noble and royal classes in society. Some of them seem to have joined the Revolutionary Associations and to have armed themselves with the best weapon for infantry on either side of the conflict – the Pennsylvania rifle which was itself the product of German immigrant craft.

In this conglomeration of ethnicities, the Congress met and thrust forth its "recommendation" to form Associations. Presbyterians seized upon the initiative thus offered. They certainly could not have been the only Associators, but authorities agree that they were foremost and most active.

The Revolution appears in greatest complexity in Pennsylvania. It required overthrow of the Penn family's feudal propriety as well as the ultimate sovereignty of the crown, and this meant rescission of William Penn's Charter of Liberties as well as the royal charter. The two charters warranted contradictory powers: The royal grant from Charles II empowered the Penns to own, sell, and rent every square foot of the province, and to appoint governors and judges; but William Penn's grant to his colonists guaranteed freedom of worship that was integral to the creed of his Quaker faith.

Because of Quakers' devotion to William's guarantee of freedom of worship, they opposed politically the rebellion that threatened to abolish this freedom along with feudal trappings and royal sovereignty; but because Quaker faith demanded pacifism, the Friends did not and could not act like Loyalists who fought for the crown or aided its armed services. There were exceptions such as Rhode Island's General Nathaniel Greene who were swayed by enthusiasm for the Revolution into joining it. Men like Greene had to leave their traditional religion or be "disowned" – that is, excommunicated. Orthodox Quakers opposed secession in words and strove to be neutral in conduct, but Revolutionaries ruled broadly that every Pennsylvanian must join them or be regarded as an enemy. Opposition was not tolerated and neutrality was not recognized in the struggle for "liberty or death."

In this province, the most ardent Revolutionaries were Presbyterians who had an old feud with the Quakers. Presbyterians in that era did not share the Friends' devotion to religious tolerance, and they deeply resented the devices by which they had been held off from offices of political power. Until 1756, Quakers dominated the provincial assembly and shaped its policies to their beliefs. As far back as 1755, the Quaker Speaker of the assembly, Isaac Norris Jr., had jovially accounted for Quakers' leadership despite their people being a minority in the whole population. Norris wrote that fearful Church of England people supported the Quakers "to keep the others out."[3] This was less amusing to the Presbyterians than to Norris.

Other cleavages split the two religions over militarism and Indian policy. Indian attacks of 1755 and 1763 had especially ravaged the Scotch-Irish Presbyterians far out in the backwoods that coincidentally were territories being defended by Indians as their own. Quakers tried to negotiate with those hostile Indians for peace, and the backwoods settlers interpreted this as taking the Indians' side against themselves. Such logic followed an ancient pattern: The friend of my enemy is my enemy. The logic intensified when pacifist Quaker assemblymen voted against forming and arming a protective militia.

Much of the Presbyterians' hatred of Quakers arose from misunderstanding what actually had happened, but this is not the place for clarification. (See my book *Empire of Fortune*.) It is enough here to recognize the hatred, for which some natural reciprocity arose on the Quaker side. It will be well also to stress that these issues and feelings existed as of *then*, and must not be attributed to present-day descendants whose attitudes have changed greatly.

That said, one may add that the Presbyterians were not wholly homogeneous. "Old Lights" of the learned variety tended to live in the city, to be prosperous, and to be more respectful of Quakers than the excitable, unlearned "New Lights," mostly based in western counties and among working poor. The William Allen family of Old Lights even turned Loyalist, to the horror of their coreligionists.

Rebellious Anglicans at first went along with Presbyterian radicals, then became alarmed at their dictatorial, extremist measures. Much conflict ensued, but it was restrained by the need to unite against Britain.

---

3 Norris Letter Book, 1719–56, mss., 5 Oct. 1755, 83–85, Hist. Soc. of Pa.

One must remember also that formally organized political parties did not exist in the eighteenth century. Their functions were performed by churches, so that it is not possible to write candidly about politics in that era without noting the positions and programs of competing churches and their spokesmen. Because of Pennsylvania's justified reputation for tolerance, the province had attracted a greater number and variety of religious immigrants than any other. The Revolutionaries' method of dealing with this variety was not tolerance.

When the Second Continental Congress convened in Philadelphia, 10 May 1775, Pennsylvania's proprietary government still functioned as prescribed by charters. Governor John Penn held office by appointment from the proprietary lords, and the elected assembly functioned under William Penn's Charter of Liberties. John Penn was shrewd enough to avoid head-to-head conflict with his province's rebels; he let the assembly send delegates to the Second Congress, like the First, without obstruction, and one of the delegates was newly returned Benjamin Franklin, who was promptly given much committee business by the Congress.

By this time, Franklin and his old political partner Joseph Galloway faced in opposite directions. The First Congress that owed so much to Franklin's conceptions and actions was assailed by Galloway in what Benjamin H. Newcomb characterizes as a "vindictive tirade." Galloway's own terms for this Congress accused it of inciting the "unthinking, ignorant multitude" to ravish the wives and daughters of the loyal element of the Americans.[4] Galloway directed his epithets particularly against Presbyterians who had opposed his following of varied upper-class gentlemen since 1770. Frustrated in his hopes and defeated in the assembly by old opponents John Dickinson and Charles Thomson, Galloway retired from politics on 12 May, at the moment when Franklin surged forward to national leadership in the Second Congress.[5]

The two men tried unsuccessfully for reconciliation, and Galloway went on to become a Loyalist whose former friendship "was perverted into vindictiveness and open hatred."[6] In view of later developments, it is well for clarity to note that he was not a Quaker, nor was he associated in any way with Quaker policies of neutrality. Statements that put him at the head of an imaginary "Quaker Party" need correction.

The provincial assembly continued to function, and Franklin was chosen to membership in it at the next election. Meantime, however, rebels organized extralegal committees throughout the province, apparently based on local militia companies and Presbyterian congregations. These were voluntary associations, campaign groups, that included only persons of like mind.

4 Newcomb, *Franklin and Galloway*, 272.   5 Ibid., 278.   6 Ibid., 289.

News of armed clashes in Massachusetts and Virginia aroused bitter anger that searched for means of expression. This found an eloquent spokesman in a recent immigrant from Britain to Philadelphia (who had borne a letter of introduction from Benjamin Franklin). This journalist was asked by the militant physician Dr. Benjamin Rush to open discussion of possible independence from Britain. When Thomas Paine obliged with the pamphlet that Rush titled *Common Sense*, they found a printer willing to risk his neck for publishing its plainly treasonous contents. He was the "notorious" Scot Robert Bell, whose views were as republican as Paine's.[7]

Common Sense was a clarion call sounded in January 1776, and it found instant response throughout all the colonies. It has been called the most influential pamphlet ever published in the English language, for it aroused action as well as thought. Men who had hardly dared to consider independence even hypothetically suddenly became its most ardent champions. Still today, the powerful rhetoric stirs emotion, so much so that a modern reader may not permit himself to question the doctrines of that rhetoric. How often my pulse has stirred at the rhythm of its phrases: "Government, like dress, is the badge of lost innocence"; "the fate of Charles the First hath only made kings more subtle – not more just"; "To the evil of monarchy we have added that of hereditary succession; and as the first is a degradation and lessening of ourselves, so the second, claimed as a matter of right, is an insult and an imposition on posterity"; "Why is the constitution of England sickly, but because monarchy hath poisoned the republic, the crown hath engrossed the commons?" "Of more worth is one honest man to society, and in the sight of God, than all the crowned ruffians that ever lived." And on and on.

It is poetry. Such lines scan and reverberate. They entranced a generation, and they still cast such a spell that criticism seems almost like sacrilege. Yet one must consider the implications of Paine's remark in the "Appendix" that was added after the first edition. Seen from one angle, it is a plea for unity: "Let the names of Whig and Tory be extinct; and let none other be heard among us than those of *a good citizen, an open and resolute friend, and a virtuous supporter of the* RIGHTS *of* MANKIND *and of the* FREE AND INDEPENDANT STATES OF *America*." Events were to disclose this plea as somewhat equivocal. Paine was to demonstrate that "let none other be heard" meant "none other will be permitted." Despite exhortations about principles, the underlying message of *Common Sense* is a demand for power.

---

7 Eric Foner, *Tom Paine and Revolutionary America* (New York: Oxford University Press, 1976), 74.

It was simultaneously a superb rallying cry and a warning to dissidents. Paine ended his Appendix with strong condemnation of a Quaker statement of the "wrong" principle. "Because it tends to the decrease and reproach of all religion whatever, and is of the utmost danger to society, to make it a party in political disputes."[8]

This was hardly candid from a man who aligned himself with Presbyterian radicals intending to do great harm to those Quakers. Their method and Paine's association with them are reported below.

May I be permitted a personal note? In my youth, I, too, joined a revolutionary party – one that advocated the dictatorship of the proletariat which, in practice, became the dictatorship of men controlling the party. I survived its ultimate collapse in disillusion. Though I had and still have respect and admiration for the political foot soldiers who sacrificed so selflessly for that party's inspiring professed goals, I came to acquire strong distaste for authoritative government by persons considering themselves to be holders of the only true faith *whatever it may be*. It is that insight (or cynicism?) which has led me to question the implications of so really inspiring a piece of literature as *Common Sense*, and of a number also of other utterances that will appear in succeeding chapters. Is it too trite to say that things were seldom what they seemed?

8 Thomas Paine, *Rights of Man*, ed. Mark Phils, 59.

26

DECISION

A desire for independence from Britain gained few converts until events of 1775 and 1776 forced the issue. "It was a restoration to the state of things before the contest began that almost all Americans wanted."[1] Defensive combat in Massachusetts and Virginia aroused much strong feeling, and (it must be admitted) so did offensive combat against the province of Quebec. The most effective recruiter to the cause of independence was George III. When Congress, on 8 July 1775, sent the king an "Olive Branch Petition" asking him to "direct some mode" for "a happy and permanent reconciliation," he refused even to look at it. He was "determined to listen to nothing from the illegal congress."[2]

Instead, on 23 August 1775, he proclaimed his demand for suppression of rebellion and "condign punishment [for] the authors, perpetrators, and abetters of such traitorous designs."[3] In fairness, one must admit that he might have been responding to Congress's invasion of Quebec, which had been launched two weeks before the Olive Branch Petition.

Tom Paine's *Common Sense* exploded like a bomb on Americans' minds. Sensing a new tide in politics, Congress hesitantly took one tentative step after another. As of 18 February 1776, it authorized privateers to prey on British shipping. On the twenty-sixth it embargoed exports to Britain and its islands. In March it sent Silas Deane to prospect for help from France. In the same month, it voted to disarm all Loyalists, and in April it violated the Navigation Acts by opening American ports to all nations *except* Britain.

Then the individual colonies began to act. In April, North Carolina instructed its delegates to support independence. (North Carolina had also suffered from an armed attack by its governor.) Rhode Island followed suit in May, and the ever-legalistic Massachusetts Provincial Council asked the towns for their views, getting positive responses in May and June. In May, also, Virginia's convention called on Congress to vote for independence.

1 *Spirit of 'Seventy-Six*, ed. Commager and Morris, 271.   2 Ibid., 278–80.   3 Ibid., 281.

Following that instruction, Virginia's Richard Henry Lee moved in Congress for independence on 7 June 1776, and his motion was debated, but voting was postponed for three weeks while laggard colonies were pressed hard to join the rest. Despite postponement of the issue, a committee was set up to draft a declaration of independence. Was this a gesture of confidence? A device of pressure? Or perhaps a delay caused by poor communications with the provinces? Whatever, New Hampshire voted independence on 15 June, and Maryland and New Jersey on 28 June.[4]

The motion for independence came to a preliminary vote on 1 July, but with results disappointing to the radicals. South Carolina and Pennsylvania voted *nay*! and Delaware's two delegates split. That night, cancerous Caesar Rodney forced his sick frame on a ride of eighty miles from Dover, Delaware, to burst in on the Congress and cast Delaware's vote in favor. South Carolina, for unexplained reasons, changed from nays to yeas. Pennsylvania's recalcitrant delegates John Dickinson and Robert Morris walked abroad while their colleagues voted yea. Instructionless New Yorkers simply refrained from voting so that Congress could proclaim the vote to be unanimous.

(Some trickery must have been involved. Later, when the Declaration was signed, Pennsylvania's nine signers were not the same men as the nine delegates sent by Pennsylvania's assembly, and John Dickinson never signed. How much of the unanimity for independence was cosmetic, and how much derived from hidden pressures?)

Pennsylvania's delegates to Congress, chosen by the assembly, 9 November 1775, compared to the signers of the Declaration of Independence.[5]

Delegates	Signers
John Morton, Speaker	John Morton
John Dickinson	Benjamin Rush
Robert Morris	Robert Morris
Benjamin Franklin	Benjamin Franklin
Charles Humphreys	George Clymer
Edward Biddle	James Smith
Thomas Willing	George Taylor
Andrew Allen	George Ross
James Wilson	James Wilson

4 Ronald Hamowy in *Blackwell Encyclopedia*, 264–66; also 814–15.
5 See Chap. 27, below. The delegates are listed in *Pa. Archives*, 8th ser., 8:7347. Their instruction to vote against independence is at ibid., 8:7353. On 15 May, the assembly changed its instruction and ordered its delegates to vote *for* independence (ibid., 8:7535, 7539).

Five of the *delegates* did not sign, compared to four who did. A question is very pertinent: If Delaware could not be recorded for independence until Caesar Rodney rode to break a tie, why was Pennsylvania recorded for independence when a majority of its delegates were opposed?

It is a curiosity that Congress appointed a committee to draft a declaration of independence before the motion for independence was voted on. Before *Common Sense* made its tremendous impact on opinions, much sentiment still existed outside New England against secession from the empire. Even George Washington opposed secession early in 1776.[6] But though there was no certainty of its being decided, Congress's militants wanted to have a declaration on hand *in case*. And it was entrusted to some of the most important members: Benjamin Franklin, John Adams, Robert Livingston of New York, Roger Sherman of Connecticut, and (of course, Virginia must be represented) young Thomas Jefferson. The committee gave the drafting job to Jefferson, and he was mortified by how thoroughly his draft was criticized and edited by both the committee and the whole Congress. Still it emerged substantially as his own work.

In its final form, now rating capital initials, the Declaration of Independence has been analyzed and celebrated a hundred ways. Its power cannot be doubted. It was a magnificent statement of principle and fact that shows how strongly minds can be swayed by mere words when crafted by a master. My discussion herein will not try to study it comprehensively. Rather, fully accepting its overwhelming importance and effect, I attend to its propagandistic presentation of fact and to certain problems in its philosophical treatment of liberty.

Let us look first at the recital of facts. Jefferson understood that no arguments could sway American opinions as well as the actions of George III. "The history of the present King of Great Britain is a history of repeated injuries and usurpations, all having in direct object the establishment of an absolute Tyranny over these States."

The king became the whipping boy, not without reason. Though colonial rebels had sometimes tried to evade Parliament's rule by insisting they were exclusively in the king's domain, it had become clear that Parliament did what George III wanted done. So the Declaration complained that, "*He* had assented to Parliament's 'acts of pretended Legislation,'" besides refusing to assent to proper laws, "the most wholesome and necessary for the public good." *He* had dissolved colonial legislatures "for opposing with manly firmness his invasions on the rights of the people." *He* had "made

6 *Spirit of 'Seventy-Six*, 271.

Judges dependent on his Will alone." *He* had harassed the people with "a multitude of New Officers" and "swarms of Offices." *He* had sent standing armies "to render the Military independent of and superior to the Civil power."

This was just warming up. After reciting other offenses involving trade, taxes, and juries, the Declaration assailed the king "for taking away our Charters . . . and altering fundamentally the Forms of our Governments." This royal criminal had "abdicated Government here, by declaring us out of his Protection and waging War against us. He has plundered our seas, ravaged our Coasts, burnt our towns, and destroyed the Lives of our people" and "He is at this time transporting large Armies of foreign Mercenaries to compleat the works of death, desolation and tyranny . . . with circumstances of Cruelty and perfidy scarcely paralleled in the most barbarous ages."

Even as propaganda, that last was a bit shrill. Jefferson knew history, and circumstances of cruelty and perfidy are among history's most common phenomena. But propaganda aims at effect rather than accuracy. So perhaps we must not criticize Jefferson too harshly for twisting the Quebec Act's tremendous freedom of religion provisions into something else. In the Declaration this was presented as "abolishing the free system of English Laws in a neighbouring Province [which would have suppressed Catholicism], establishing therein an Arbitrary government [instead of imposing a tiny minority of Protestants on the multitude of Catholics], and enlarging its Boundaries." The new boundary was indeed offensive to Virginians who craved the territory within those enlarged boundaries.

Maybe one should not raise questions about great propaganda documents. Despite its power, the Declaration was not perfect even in its bill of complaints. It is hardly necessary to note again the abysmal fault in its "self-evident" truth "that all men are created equal" coming from the pen of a slaveholder. But in a kind of justice to Jefferson, he must be credited with noticing the evils of slavery albeit allegedly as the fault of George III. Congress eliminated this section, the self-serving logic of which must be seen in its own phrasing. He, the king:

has waged cruel war against human nature itself, violating it's [*sic*] most sacred rights of life & liberty in the persons of a distant people who never offended him, captivating & carrying them into slavery in another hemisphere, or to incur miserable death in their transportation thither. This piratical warfare, the opprobrium of *infidel* powers, is the warfare of the CHRISTIAN king of Great Britain, determined to keep open a market where MEN should be bought and sold, he has prostituted his negative for suppressing every legislative attempt to prohibit or to restrain this execrable commerce, and that his assemblage of horrors might want no fact of distinguished die, he is now exciting those very people to rise in arms among us, and to purchase that liberty of which *he* has deprived them, by murdering the people upon whom he also obtruded them, thus paying off former crimes committed against the *liberties* of one people, with crimes which he urges them to commit against the *lives* of another.[7]

Perhaps someone in Congress was bold enough to suggest that this horror could be turned into a revolutionary asset by simply emancipating all those poor people from captivity. Probably not; more likely the members simply spotted how vulnerable to criticism the passage appeared. Slaveholding members understood very well how they violated the "most sacred rights of life and liberty." They never left off crying that the king would never make slaves of *them*.

Jefferson had much reason to be grateful to the Congress that saved him from his excess of rhetoric. Its inclusion would have made the Declaration the laughingstock of Europe.

7 Ibid., 316–17.

27

RELIGION THEN AND NOW

At the time of the American Revolution, religious organizations dominated political developments. Churches often doubled as political parties. It is essential, therefore, to recognize responsibility by organized religions for what happened in politics – the bad as well as the good. It is just as essential, however, to recognize explicitly that churches have evolved during subsequent centuries in both formal creeds and social actions. The description of their political activities herein must not be applied to present-day identities, despite continuation of the same names.

This is easy to see in the case of the Roman Catholic church whose devotees in mid-eighteenth century were much maligned and powerless in the American colonies. No one at that time could have foreseen the election of a Catholic President (from Massachusetts!) and the membership of three Catholic justices of the Supreme Court at one time.

Jews were so few as to be statistically negligible.

Quakers then had been powerful in the government and politics of Pennsylvania; but, as we shall see, they were suppressed in politics, and the orthodox Friends determined to purge their meetings of politically involved types in order to fend off evident persecution.

Members of the Church of England were obliged to maintain special loyalty to the king who was head of their church, but one must not sort them out too sweepingly as opponents of the Revolution. They were also citizens of their provinces/states, and many of them came to be important Revolutionary leaders. In Virginia the Revolution was conducted by members of Anglican vestries. In Pennsylvania, as an example, General Anthony Wayne was an Anglican rebel.

Dominant roles in the Revolution were assumed by Congregationalists in New England and related Presbyterians in other regions – "dissenters" with traditions of hostility to the crown that reached back to the Puritan Revolution of seventeenth-century England and Scotland. Especially to the point here, those traditions included intolerance and suppression of pietists such as the Quakers; and as the dissenters of Revolutionary times seized power in state after state, they used legal and extralegal means to exclude pietists from civic affairs. These dissenters boasted much about their "democracy," and they have been much praised for it by historians. It was an ambiguous sort of democracy, real enough within the dissenters' own ranks, but sometimes becoming what I have called "the dictatorship of the presbyteriat" over outsiders. (The phrase was too apt to be resisted.)

The dissenters also have changed, and it is erroneous to project backward what they have since become. Furiously exclusionary in the eighteenth century, their good works of hospitals, colleges, and retirement institutions today are multiracial, multiethnic, and often nonsectarian. This would be heresy by the standards of 1776, but it reflects a broader conception of democracy than prevailed among dissenters then.

A reader must therefore keep constantly in mind that statements and descriptions of political involvement by organized religions in the Revolution are no more than that. The names must be used, but attitudes then were as different from today's as those of grandparents are from those of their children's children.

In some respects at least. For others, a different book will be needed than this one. True enough, religiously motivated barbarians are horribly prominent in modern American politics, but they must be sorted out by today's standards. In this book, it is enough to describe facts as they were in the eighteenth century.

In 1775–76, Pennsylvanians resisted the movement for American independence. It is misleading to suggest that they were slow in making up their minds. Quite to the contrary, the minds of a great many were determined for liberty within the empire but against secession from it. This attitude posed great problems for the Congress and stimulated it to actions that, in a manner of speaking, became the Revolutionaries' *conquest* of Pennsylvania – their first armed conquest.

To support this statement, attention must be given to the province's varied and competing religions and to their geographical distribution. A very knowledgeable guide is available in a 1784 letter of Dr. Benjamin Rush. He sorted out the state's population at "about 350,000 souls," of whom the English were most numerous and wealthy, consisting of "chiefly Quakers and Episcopalians." Germans were divided among Lutherans, Calvinists [Reformed], Mennonites, and Roman Catholics. The Irish, who constituted about a sixth or an eighth of the state, "are in general Presbyterians." (These were the Scotch-Irish from northern Ireland.)[1]

1 *Letters of Benjamin Rush*, ed. L. H. Butterfield, 2 vols. (Princeton, N.J.: Princeton University Press, 1951), 1:335.

Rush did not like those Scotch-Irish people though he was also Presbyterian. He slurred them as "not very remarkable for industry." But "the *passive* conduct of the Quakers and the moderate conduct of the Episcopalians threw our government wholly in the hands of . . . Presbyterians in the year 1776," and the "uninformed" Germans "submitted to their usurpations and formed a principal part of their strength."[2]

Rush had more to say – he was never taciturn – but we must look into the process by which such arrangement of power came about.

Pennsylvania had been founded by Quakers who kept a majority in the assembly until 1756. The Presbyterians who immigrated massively after the 1720s opposed Quakers on several grounds. Geography was one: Quakers mostly lived in the older, eastern communities whereas Scotch-Irish Presbyterians, who came later, mostly settled farther out, especially congregating in the west and north though some remained in Philadelphia.

It followed that the Presbyterian "backcountry" settlers were more vulnerable to Indian raids in 1755, and angrily resentful against Quaker assemblymen who opposed military measures against those Indians. Quakers wanting to negotiate against hostile Indians discovered that they had been defrauded of lands. The backcountry Presbyterians who had settled on the lands in question were not inclined to discuss moral issues. For them, Quaker justice to Indians was Quaker enmity to Presbyterians.

Quakers were forced out of the assembly in 1756 by the threat of test oaths regarded as violations of religious principles.[3] (Such oaths kept English Quakers out of Parliament.) Benjamin Franklin took leadership of the lawmakers to initiate militias, but they were of such a defensive nature that the westerners were not happy. They wanted Indian blood. They also wanted much more regional power in the assembly where eastern counties' members outnumbered those of the western counties. Even under Franklin's leadership this ratio was maintained, and for good reason. As our quotation from Benjamin Rush shows, the westerners' populations were much smaller than those of the east.[4] Rush was confirmed by the census of 1790. But power-hungry politicians wanted assembly voting *by counties* rather than *by persons*. This is understandable as political strategy by contemporaries, but why have historians failed to note the disparity of popula-

---

2 Ibid., 1:336.
3 Ibid.; David Freeman Hawke, *Benjamin Rush, Revolutionary Gadfly* (Indianapolis: Bobbs-Merrill, 1971) 159–160, 273.
4 Charles H. Lincoln, "The Revolutionary Movement in Pennsylvania, 1760–1776," Ph.D. diss., (Philadelphia: University of Pennsylvania, 1901), 266–67. The Federal census of 1790 gave proportions as follows: English 35.3; German 33.3; Scotch-Irish 11; Mere Irish 3.5; Scotch 8.6. Cited in Robert L. Brunhouse, *The Counter-revolution in Pennsylvania, 1776–1790* (Harrisburg: Pennsylvania Historical Commission, 1942), 2.

tions? Instead of speaking plainly about a power play, they bleat about "frontier democracy" being demonstrated by the few westerners trying to dominate the many.

Though Franklin's assembly of mixed religions continued to withstand the westerners' demands, they blamed Quakers for their frustration, and the histories label it the "Quaker assembly" though it contained not one Quaker in good standing and was opposed by all such. It is edifying to see how Franklin demonstrated his "teflon" quality in this as in other matters.

It is directly relevant to present concerns that the Revolution gave opportunity to Presbyterian westerners to re-form government to their desires by creating institutions in which voting was done by counties rather than by persons, with the result that the "one sixth or one eighth" governed the rest.[5] By means of this trick and other suppressive devices, especially test oaths, the Presbyterians fastened on the newly fledged State of Pennsylvania a constitution under their firm control.[6] By means of smoke and mirrors, this has become Holy Writ in histories as "the most democratic" constitution of all the Revolutionary states.[7] (See Chapter 28.)

Presbyterian Benjamin Rush did not think so, nor did thousands of Philadelphians who demonstrated against it. Why would Rush, who was one of the most democratic agitators in America, oppose the reputedly most democratic constitution? We must look at the whole process step by step. One must attend carefully. The details are complex.

In June 1774, faced with Governor John Penn's refusal to summon the assembly to choose delegates to the Continental Congress, John Dickinson proposed the extralegal action of a provincial convention of county delegates to name them. Governor Penn tried to forestall it by inventing an Indian threat to the frontiers that would require a special session of the assembly after all; but the convention invitation had gone out so seventy county delegates appeared in the city, and on 15 July they met in Carpenter's Hall. Charles Thomson became their secretary. Voting was decreed by counties so that the seven newer and more radical counties controlled the total of eleven. They suggested that the assembly choose particular nominees for the Congress.[8]

The assembly, still dominated by Joseph Galloway, met and chose six Congress delegates *other than* the convention's nominees. Notably, John Dickinson had been proposed by the convention and was ignored by the

5 Lincoln, "Revolutionary Movement," 266–67.
6 *Letters of Benjamin Rush*, ed. Butterfield, 1:336.
7 Cf. Richard Alan Ryerson, *The Revolution Is Now Begun: The Radical Committees of Philadelphia, 1765–1776* (Philadelphia: University of Pennsylvania Press, 1978), 252.
8 Ibid., 47–64.

assembly. Pennsylvania thus became the only colony to have its assembly and a convention functioning at the same time.

In October 1774, the Philadelphia rebels John Dickinson and Charles Thomson were elected to the assembly, and they immediately pushed for strong measures opposing royal rule. In November, the assembly launched a Committee of Observation and Inspection to enforce the Continental Association banning trade with Britain. This "committee" was a body of volunteers rather than a structural part of the assembly; they functioned by personal pressures on recalcitrant merchants. Richard Alan Ryerson reports that the committee's controls during the winter of 1774–75 were "both strict and successful."[9]

A *second* provincial convention met in January 1775. Although it ignored calls for an armed militia, it resolved to resist force exerted by Britain.

Quaker elders took alarm. The Philadelphia Monthly Meeting recommended that local meetings admonish Friends to resign from the rebel-sponsored committees, and that they disown Friends who disobeyed. A "testimony" was issued against independence, and in March "began the reprimands, contrite confessions, and disownments that would swell to a flood of Quaker soul-searching and disorder in the next twelve months."[10]

Congress was meeting in the midst of this turmoil. Then came news of Lexington and Concord on 24 April, arousing feverish determination. "All opposition to congressionally directed armed resistance became covert – and treasonable." The Philadelphia Committee of Observation organized a new Association, a military one, to train militia; and by 10 May over thirty companies had formed, "including one of young Quakers."[11] John Dickinson was made senior colonel, and the assembly appropriated some funds.

We begin to see the Revolution's organizational structure forming up. On 30 June 1775 the assembly endorsed *local* militias throughout the province, issued thirty-five thousand pounds in paper currency for them, and appointed twenty-five persons as a Committee of Safety;[12] and a new Committee of Observation sprang up with an assumed function of "suppressing dissent and preparing for war."[13]

Let us remember that in January 1776 Tom Paine's *Common Sense* struck like a thunderbolt. Yet, when special assembly elections were held as of 1 May 1776, the result was "a defeat for the advocates of independence."[14] More people than Quakers must have favored staying in the empire. Then came news a week later that the crown was hiring foreign mercenaries.

The atmosphere in Philadelphia became thick with tense preparations for war. John Adams smote the provincial assembly with a resolution in Congress for provinces to establish governments "sufficient to the exigencies of

9 Ibid., 91–96.   10 Ibid., 104.   11 Ibid., 117, 118.   12 Ibid., 122.   13 Ibid., 131.
14 Foner, *Tom Paine*, 127.

their affairs." To leave no doubt of what that might mean, he added a "pre-amble" several days later: "authority under . . . crown should be totally suppressed."[15] His target was plain enough. No one could doubt that Pennsylvania's assembly derived its authority from the crown.

But the assembly stubbornly refused to roll over and play dead, so the radicals gave it a push. In mid-June, the Board of Officers of the Philadel-phia battalions of Associators, and the Committee of Privates of the city's Military Association, both informed the assembly of refusal to serve under officers appointed by the assembly.[16] (It is incorrect to mention only the pri-vates.) In itself, such notice had precedent in the province. During the Seven Years War, Franklin's new militia (then) had insisted on electing their own officers. In 1775, however, the action was ominous of political purpose. Armed militias (Associators) throughout the province were controlled by radicals intent on independence. In contrast, empire loyalists were unarmed.[17]

Suggestively, Virginia's Richard Henry Lee made his Congressional motion for independence on 7 June 1776. It is not hard to see a connection between this motion and the Pennsylvania armed forces' actions one week later. Yet a majority of the stubborn Pennsylvania delegates to Congress still voted against independence on 1 July. Immense pressures must have been exerted before the final, decisive vote on 2 July, to make John Dickinson and Robert Morris absent themselves so that the resultant majority of Pennsyl-vania's delegates could vote with all the other provinces for independence from the old empire. (They were not yet ready to integrate themselves into a new empire.) Morris later signed the formal Declaration, but Dickinson never did.

Pennsylvania's *second* convention was just beginning to meet. Now, with royal authority rejected and a new authority to be derived from Congress, the second convention assumed the task of writing a constitution for the new Commonwealth of Pennsylvania. As Eric Foner notes, the convention delegates "were chosen by the county and city committees (not by direct popular vote)."[18]

For the sake of simplicity of presentation, let us stay with the assembly a little longer. It did not die, as often averred, for lack of a quorum. Rather, it held its last session on 26 September 1776, well past the Declaration of Independence, with twenty-three members present. Respect is deserved

---

15 Marc W. Kruman, *Between Authority and Liberty: State Constitution Making in Revolutionary America* (Chapel Hill: University of North Carolina Press, 1997), 24–25.

16 *Pennsylvania Archives*, 8th ser., 8:7545–48.

17 In July, the Council of Safety ordered militia officers to take away the arms of non-Associators and give them to Associators. Traditionally this device had been used by colonials before attack-ing Indians. *American Archives*, comp. Peter Force, (Washington, D.C.: M. St. Clair and Peter Force, 1851), 5th ser., 2:5.   18 Foner, *Tom Paine*, 128.

for the responsible way it wound up its business, and even more respect for its principled defense of civil liberties against onslaughts from the convention.

Pennsylvania had a long-standing reputation as the most reliable in business of all the colonies, and it sustained that reputation to the last. The assembly paid all its obligations, including the wages of armed Associators who were busy attacking it. It did not pass away with either a whimper or a bang. Rather, in its other business of this last session, the assembly challenged the convention's assumption of powers without consulting the freemen entitled to vote about government. The assembly's accusation was true. In the manner of all revolutionaries, the convention purportedly had spoken *for* the people, but as is too often the case it had taken power *by* a minority who never permitted their actions to be voted on by the whole people.

Considering the convention's assaults against liberty (to be noticed next chapter), the assembly's defense of liberty is remarkable. It asserted that the convention

> has no authority from the good People of Pennsylvania to levy Taxes and dispose of their Property: And therefore, that the late Ordinance, imposing a rate of Twenty Shillings per Month, and Four Shillings in the Pound [one Fifth] on the Estates of Non-associators is illegal, and the said Sums ought not to be paid. . . . The late Ordinance of the Convention, impowering two or more Justices of the Peace to imprison, for an indefinite Time, at their Discretion, all Persons whom they shall judge to be guilty of the Offences therein specified, is, in the Opinion of this House, a dangerous Attack on the Liberties of the good people of Pennsylvania, and a Violation of their most sacred Rights; and therefore ought not to be considered as obligatory.[19]

But the convention had armed forces, and the assembly had none, so we must note regretfully the demise of the assembly that had contended mightily for liberty during its entire existence. It amuses me to see how it is cried down pejoratively as *wealthy* and *conservative* by historians who are certainly conservative and usually fairly prosperous and who have screamed in rage at revolutionaries in their own time. Let it not be said that the favored revolutionaries of the eighteenth century were democratic; they were no such thing as will be apparent when we examine their behavior. They strove to overthrow the power of the crown in order to assume it themselves, not to transmit it to the people in general. They can be compared to the "people's democracies" of the twentieth century with considerable justice, although the comparison must not be pushed too far. Procedures varied. Nevertheless, power was the issue.

19 *Pennsylvania Archives*, 8th Ser., 8:7586.

The subject must not be abandoned lightly because writers for a century have smeared this agency as "the Quaker assembly," supposedly run by a tyrannical "Quaker party," and have used these terms in much the same spirit as nowadays writers speak of "Commie" organizations. The obvious bias and malicious intent of this practice emerge from the slippery explanation of Charles H. Lincoln who wanted to call names but escape odium for doing so:

> By the use of the term "Quaker party" the author would by no means assert the identity of the religious body with the conservative easterners who controlled the Assembly after 1756. The dominant faction was bound by no religious lines. It was drawn from Episcopalians and other sects as well as Friends – the term is used as a convenient designation for *the group of politicians in Philadelphia . . . whose object was the control of the colony for their own ends.*[20]

That is, if they were nasty, they should be called Quakers.

This misleading practice still continues, perhaps thoughtlessly in some instances, probably viciously in others. It is false to recorded fact, and should be stopped *now*.

Thomas Paine worked closely with the radicals in Pennsylvania and participated in the process by which the new constitution was created. There can be no question about Paine's dedication to liberty and democracy. His strongest testimonial was given (much later) by John Adams: "Such a mongrel between pigs and puppy, begotten by a wild boar on a bitch wolf, never before in any age of the world was suffered by the Poltroonery of Mankind to run through such a career of mischief."[21] The outburst reveals much about Adams. So does his fuming silence while Paine was assisting the drive for independence contributing to Adams's personal drive for power.

We learn more about Paine after the Declaration of Independence was achieved. Then, as Alfred F. Young declares, a new issue arose "as to what kind of a republic should replace British rule and this debate continued through the revolutionary era and into the 1790s."[22] Thereafter Adams opposed Paine's democratizing principles. (See Chapter 44.)

Tom Paine stayed true to his ideals. Famously, when Benjamin Franklin opined, "Where liberty dwells, there is my country," Paine responded, "Where liberty is not, there is my country." With the success of the Revolution in America, he turned back to Britain and stirred up such a movement that he had to escape the government by running off to France to join

---

20 Lincoln, "Revolutionary Movement," 25n.
21 Quoted by Alfred F. Young in *Science, Mind and Art*, ed. K. Gavroglu et al. (The Netherlands: Kluwer Academic Publishers, 1995), 433.   22 Ibid., 417.

the Revolution there. He was acclaimed, but he had not reckoned on the volatility of French politics. He went to jail in France and lived in the shadow of the guillotine until Thomas Jefferson rescued him for return to the Revolutionaries of America. His former comrades there withheld gratitude for his immense services, but let him stay out of jail.

A student must brush aside the rhetoric of myth to realize that the leaders of the Revolution were not all devoted to ideals cherished today. It was by no means a Golden Age of general striving for general welfare. Paine was one of the most self-sacrificing men of any age in pursuit of that goal, as his life testifies even more than his writings. Adams's life and writings show different goals.

28

—— • ——

A "PEOPLE'S DEMOCRACY"

It is Holy Writ among American historians that the Pennsylvania constitution was the most *democratic* in all the new American states.[1] This judgment is arrived at by uncritical acceptance of the pretense put forward by the document's passages concerning rights, and by overlooking the associated devices by which a major fraction of the former electorate was disfranchised. Once again, it confirms that actions must be examined for the validity of words.

It will do no good for me to rant and rave about historians' faults in this matter because too many of those who write books would have to be refuted page by page. Let John C. Miller stand for all of them: "The democratic movement achieved its greatest triumph during the Revolution not in New England but in Pennsylvania" and so on and on.[2] Miller's statement equates the *text* of the Pennsylvania constitution with a triumph of the democratic movement. What follows herein refutes this nonsense by a straightforward description of how the Pennsylvania constitution came into being, how it was imposed upon the new state, and how the government under it functioned repressively. (For this topic, chronological limits must be slightly subordinated to clarity of exposition.)

When the radicals summoned the first provincial convention, they wanted to be sure of outvoting the substantial numbers of conservatives, so they installed a pattern of one vote per *county*, thus assuring control to the newer, more numerous, and more radical counties though they were much less populated than the older counties.[3] This pattern was maintained by the second convention that drew up the constitution, and the advantage was seized by a party led by Timothy Matlack and James Cannon,

1 Text of the constitution is in *American Archives*, comp. Force, 5th ser., 2:22–24.
2 Miller, *Origins of the American Revolution*, 503. More recently, in Eric Foner, "the most democratic state constitution," *Tom Paine*, 108.
3 Each county had one vote, and seven of the eleven counties were new – i.e., "frontier" counties – with power of decision. Ryerson, *Revolution Is Now Begun*, 57.

newcomers to provincial politics. In the background as president of the convention hovered Benjamin Franklin who, of course, was anything but a newcomer.

This convention taught radicals like Dickinson and Rush that there is more than one kind of radicalism. Horrified by the Matlack-Cannon variety, Benjamin Rush suddenly turned conservative.

To begin with, the convention's membership was highly selective, indeed, highly discriminatory. It was not the product of general elections. Instead, delegates were chosen by county "committees" that excluded dissidents and neutralists at gunpoint.[4] These committeemen had assumed local power by force and intimidation as well as persuasion. Most were armed Associators of the new militias. This was a coup d'état.

The convention produced a new constitution in two parts – a Declaration of Rights and a "Frame" of Government. The Declaration of Rights is unassailably high-minded except for its religious and oath-taking requirements that aroused outrage even in that era. Deist Benjamin Franklin simply shrugged and signed; who would prosecute *him* for falsehood? But Pennsylvania under the Quakers had avoided such requirements. Indeed, swearing oaths was intolerably sinful under the Quaker creed. A mass meeting in Philadelphia expressed immediate, strong revulsion against the constitution and specifically rejected the requirement for taking oaths in order to vote, but the "back counties" enforced oaths. In the first election under the constitution, only two thousand votes were cast by fifty thousand qualified citizens. This highly undemocratic situation has been attributed by Robert L. Brunhouse to "the detested oath."[5]

Instead of analyzing the new constitution abstractly, I shall pick up key clauses and show how they were interpreted to achieve effects of power. Overall, it must be said at once, the constitution was presented by fiat as the Commonwealth's fundamental law, *never* subjected to approval by the people, and alterable only by a complicated process rigged against change.

To withhold allegiance to this constitution could be defined as treason. To speak or write against "the American cause" opened a culprit to being jailed by a justice of the peace. (So early historically, the expression of a minority viewpoint made a man "unAmerican.") To fail to report knowledge of a traitor made a man guilty of "misprision of treason" punishable by forfeiture of a third of his property and imprisonment for the war's duration. In blunt terms, this was solicitation for informers under threat.[6] There was more.

---

4 Foner, *Tom Paine*, 128.   5 Brunhouse, *Counter-Revolution*, 19, 21.
6 *American Archives*, comp. Force, ser. 5, 2:34–35, 37–38.

The constitution's full effect was felt in the processes created to enforce its proclaimed rights. For example, section 12 of the Declaration of Rights guaranteed freedom of speech and press, but the convention enacted an "ordinance" providing that any person speaking or writing against "the American cause" must give security or be jailed by a justice of the peace. The Rights section 9 would seem to have protected dissidents because it endowed them with rights to counsel, to be heard, to be told the causes of their accusation, to confront witnesses, to an impartial jury, to a speedy public trial, and to be excused from giving evidence against themselves. It sounds like an eighteenth-century version of the American Civil Liberties Union.[7]

Events cannot be squared with these rights. Scanty records reported by Anne M. Ousterhout sent at least 58 persons to jail between 4 July 1776 and 11 February 1777, their crimes being "damning Congress, being an enemy of the United States, uttering disrespectful expressions, and behaving in an inimical fashion. Only one man was specifically accused of high treason. Most were detained by either a local county committee or by Council of Safety or both. *None of these persons ever had their day in court.*"[8]

Section 5 of the Rights provided "an indubitable, unalienable, and indefeasible right to reform, alter, or abolish government," but militia officers were ordered to take arms away from non-Associators and give them to Associators.[9] Anyone wanting to alter Pennsylvania's new government would have no weapons to do so violently and would get jailed quickly for nonviolent behavior such as advocating change "in an inimical fashion."

Such provisions need not surprise when we consider how the convention was chosen. The conference of county committees that laid down ground rules decreed that no man could vote who had "been published by any committee of inspection or the committee of safety, in this province, as an enemy to the liberties of America," which automatically disfranchised any man hostile to the committees if he had "not been restored to the favor of his country." As all these committees were exclusively radical, it was easy to see what would happen, and it did. In the restrained language of Marc W. Kruman, "During a revolution, commitment to the cause itself becomes a measure of one's faithfulness to the community's interests.[10]

Section 7 of the constitutions' Rights declared that "all elections ought to be free; and that all free men having a sufficient evident common inter-

---

7 Ibid., 2:22–24.
8 Anne M. Ousterhout, "Controlling the Opposition in Pennsylvania During the American Revolution," *Pennsylvania Magazine of History and Biography* 105:1 (Jan. 1981), 9 (italics added).
9 *American Archives*, comp. Force, ser. 5, 2:5.
10 Kruman, *Between Authority and Liberty*, 101, 98.

est with, and attachment to, the community, have a right to elect officers, or be elected into office." Refining the right of suffrage, section 8 provided that persons conscientiously scrupulous about bearing arms could not be compelled to do so, *but* they must either yield personal service or pay an innocently identified "equivalent." This was a heavy fine. Men sixteen to fifty years old were fined twenty shillings (one pound) each month, in addition to a levy of four shillings in the pound (one-fifth of it) on the annual value of estates of men over twenty-one years old. Commissioners were named in each county to enforce this ordinance. This was directed at Quakers and Mennonites. One may note for comparison that teachers' salaries ranged between ten and twenty pounds annually.[11]

The constitution was carefully contrived as an instrument of power for which its proclaimed rights were only eyewash. It put all governmental authority in a single chamber legislative assembly, which elected an executive body consisting of a council with the assembly's president. A Council of Censors was provided, with the functions of amending the constitution, but a catch-22 attached to it. The Censors were to be elected every seven years, with the first election scheduled for 1783. When elected, they were to sit for a term of *one* year, after which six more years must pass before constitutional change could even be considered. Looking ahead, we see that when the first (and only) Council of Censors was elected in 1783, it voted *by counties* rather than by populations, and it stalled until its year had expired. As obviously intended, it made no change in the constitution.

Whether or not one approves the objective of secession from the British empire that was the "American cause" program, it is simply ludicrous to call these shenanigans *democratic*.

Owen S. Ireland summarizes: "Firmly in control by 1778, [the Revolutionaries] defended the constitution under which they had come to power, and then turned on their enemies, punishing Tories and traitors, disenfranchising pacifists and neutrals (especially Quakers and German Sectarians) and replacing the Anglican-controlled College of Philadelphia with the Presbyterian-dominated University of Pennsylvania."[12] These actions had a strong effect on the membership of the state assembly. "In the first assembly elected after Independence, 58 percent of the representatives were Calvinists, and the next year, in the fall 1777 election, this proportion increased to 82 percent."[13]

When rhetoric is bypassed, it is instructive to compare Virginia's Declaration of Rights, composed by George Mason and Patrick Henry for that

---

11 *American Archives*, comp. Force, ser. 5, 2:42–46.
12 Owen S. Ireland, *Religion, Ethnicity, and Politics: Ratifying the Constitution in Pennsylvania* (University Park: Pennsylvania State University Press, 1995), 39.
13 Ireland, "The Crux of Politics," 471.

state's constitution, adopted 12 June 1776.[14] Virginia granted the right of suffrage to all men (slaves not qualifying as men) and added that none might be taxed or deprived of property without their own consent "nor bound by any law to which they have not . . . assented for the public good." This makes an interesting comparison with Pennsylvania's old assembly's protest against the actions of the government replacing it.

Further, Virginia directed that "all men are equally entitled to the free exercise of religion, according to the dictates of conscience; and that it is the mutual duty of all to practise Christian forbearance, love, and charity towards each other."

One cannot ignore the exclusion of slaves from the ranks of men – it was not a trifling oversight – but, as limited to the *herrenvolk*, Virginia's constitution was plainly more libertarian than Pennsylvania's. The reason seems to be that Virginia's gentry were not at feud with Quakers as was the case in Pennsylvania.

Although the Pennsylvania constitution was never submitted for popular approval, its opponents called a mass meeting of fifteen hundred Philadelphians on 21 October 1776. Having no formal, legal way to change the document, they hoped to cripple its machinery beyond practical use by persuading voters to refuse to take oaths required for qualification.[15] Presbyterian Benjamin Rush denounced the constitution's demand that assemblymen must swear belief in one God and the divine inspiration of the Bible's Old and New Testaments.[16] Quaker governments had been free of such tests. Thomas McKean and John Dickinson spoke against the new constitution.[17] A second meeting rejected oaths for voters, but this was in Philadelphia whereas the "back counties" maintained oaths. Not strangely in the circumstances, assembly candidates who held the views of persons actually voting were elected rather than those who boycotted the elections, with the result of legislation by the elected assemblymen harsher than the edicts of the constitutional convention.

Treason and misprision of treason were defined more broadly by this first Revolutionary assembly, and penalized more fiercely. A Test Act passed in June required

> all males over the age of eighteen to take an oath of allegiance to the state, to renounce their allegiance to the King, to promise not to do anything prejudicial to the freedom and independence of Pennsylvania, and to report all treasons or conspiracies which they might discover. Anyone refusing the oath would be incapable of holding office, serving on juries, suing for recovery of debts, electing or being elected, buying, selling, or transferring lands, or owning arms. A nonjuror

14 *Documents of American History*, ed. Commager, 1:103–5.
15 Lincoln, "Revolutionary Movement," 284; Brunhouse, *Counter-Revolution*, 19.
16 Hawke, *Benjamin Rush*, 159–60.   17 Brunhouse, *Counter-Revolution*, 19.

traveling out of his usual home territory might be suspected of being a spy because
he lacked a certificate saying that he had taken the oath. If he persisted in his
refusal to take the oath, he could be put in jail and kept there without bail until
he did swear or affirm his allegiance to Pennsylvania.[18]

Persons suspected of disaffection who did "any other thing to subvert the
good order and regulations, that are or may be made" might be confined,
and judges were forbidden to issue a writ or habeas corpus in such cases.
No limits were placed on the confinement, no process of law was allowed
the prisoner.[19]

The Council of Safety was empowered to seize and punish "either capi-
tally or otherwise . . . *in a summary mode*" persons "who from their general
conduct or conversation may be deemed inimical to the common cause of
Liberty, and the United States of North America." As Anne M.
Ousterhout comments, this Council of Safety could have been "a very dangerous group." This seems like the mildest possible judgment. Even the
Revolutionaries were scared. The Council was abolished, 6 December 1777,
by proclamation of the Supreme Executive Council.[20]

In passing, one may note that these supreme councils operated by prerogative in ways denied to George III. The contrast is sharpened by Henry
J. Young's observation: "It is paradoxical that, during the Revolution,
neither prosecutions for treasonable offenses, nor acts of attainder, were initiated against Pennsylvanians by the British government, while in the same
period headstrong Pennsylvania Whigs proscribed, or prosecuted as traitors,
hundreds of citizens who had never deviated from the allegiance in which
they were born."[21]

Though the Council of Safety was abolished, the test laws remained in
force, and persons refusing to swear allegiance "could be deprived of their
civil rights, kept from practicing their professions, and forbidden to move
freely throughout the state." Such laws, in Professor Ousterhout's judgment, "made a mockery of the state constitutional guarantees" of due
process for accused persons.[22]

As far as highly inadequate records permitted, Professor Ousterhout
made a careful tabulation of cases, and she was struck by the general public's
reluctance to enforce extreme measures. "The harshness of the laws . . .
tended to operate against their enforcement. There is evidence that juries
were loath to indict or convict on a charge of treason because of the manda-
tory execution." There were even instances of sudden sanity revealing to

18 Ousterhout, "Controlling the Opposition," 13.   19 Ibid., 14.   20 Ibid., 15.
21 Henry J. Young, "Treason and Its Punishment in Revolutionary Pennsylvania," *Pennsylvania
Magazine of History and Biography* 90 (1966); reprinted in *Patriots, Redcoats, and Loyalists*, ed.
Peter S. Onuf (New York: Garland Publishing, 1991), 288(orig)/352(reprint).
22 Ousterhout, "Controlling the Opposition," 16–17.

the powerful that "Tories might be made serviceable in many respects . . . induced by gain . . . [to have] indirectly and undesignedly promoted our affairs. If then they carry on any business, that may be eventually advantageous, in God's name let them go on."[23] I have to wonder which God was being invoked.

Nevertheless, dissidents lived at constant hazard of being worked over by superpatriots. "Peace people" Mennonites, refusing for religious reasons to sign test oaths, were seized in Northampton County in June 1778. Their personal property was seized and sold, their real property was ordered over to their heirs, and they were ordered to leave the state. The startled government became aware of what had been done to these nonpolitical persons when their wives appealed for subsistence help. The assembly alleviated some of the harsher penalties for nonjurors, but nothing was done for the victimized wives except to give them doles.[24]

It would seem from Professor Ousterhout's study of recorded incidents that the laws often escaped execution in full rigor because of sympathy from friends and neighbors of accused persons. Nevertheless, it is plain that many other incidents escaped being recorded, and one must remember that neighbors can be vicious as well as sympathetic. Among other things, tarring and feathering of victims was not regarded as important enough (except to the victims) to be legally recorded. Whatever palliations may be considered, it becomes impossible to conceive Pennsylvania as a democracy under such rule, even when it was conducted with misdirected goodwill; and one must doubt the frequency of goodwill. For instance, what happened to property seized from nonjurors or from persons accused of crimes against the state? Knowing that power corrupts, as indeed it does, must we innocently assume that accusing patriots turned confiscated property over to the state instead of keeping some or all for themselves? To do so stretches credulity. We have the enlightening example of General Moses Hazen who sent out prisoners of war to ask farmers for food or directions so that Hazen could charge the farmers with one of the many varieties of misprision of treason and, as informer, collect half the fines levied against convicted persons.[25] A sweetheart, that patriotic general.

On a larger scale were the profits made by informers naming candidates for attainder in 1777. First the assembly, then the executive proclaimed names of persons required to surrender and stand trial for treason within a set period. Failure to comply would attaint the publicly named persons as traitors forfeiting all property and doomed to be hanged if captured.

Legal historian Henry J. Young observes,

---

23 Ibid., 27, 29.   24 Ibid., 30.   25 Ibid., 24–25.

The carelessness with which the council prepared attainder proclamations increased the damage to reputations, as the record clearly shows. The names of persons supposed to have joined the enemy were sent to the council by the agents for forfeited estates. These agents, *who profited by receiving a percentage on sales of estates*, all too often based their reports on hearsay and assumption, since not even sworn information was required before a proclamation was posted."[26]

A total "certainly close to 500" of conditional attainders reduced finally to 386 persons absolutely attainted after 113 of the proclaimed persons surrendered. Of these, fewer than 20 came to trial "for the evidence was in most cases too flimsy for prosecution." Of the 386 convicted absolutely of attainder, circumstances spared all but one from hanging. "He was probably the first American ever legally executed untried, under the provision of a bill of attainder. It were well had he been the only one."[27]

Professor Young is silent about what happened to the property of the attainted persons. I must assume that their property was forfeited and sold, with the legally specified percentage reverting to informers.

When proclaimed persons fled, their wives and children remained behind to face the hostility of righteous neighbors. Some of the more rabidly patriotic Whigs forced a number of these women to seek refuge from vigilante action in 1779, well after British troops had retreated from Philadelphia. A mob laid siege to the sanctuary provided by no less a person than James Wilson, who was a signer of the Declaration of Independence.[28]

Students who dig into source materials concerning civil liberties during the Revolution are clearly embarrassed by what they find. Professor Ousterhout acknowledges that, for victims, "the declaration of rights in the state constitution of 1776 must have seemed a cruel hoax," but she adds they were a "relatively small" number.[29] I am reminded of the case that came before Henry Fielding in London when a woman charged with bearing an illegitimate child pled that it was such a small one.

Professor Young explains that "extreme penalties were barbarous and likely to invite reprisals; the tendency therefore was to find some excuse for clemency."[30] That clemency should require an excuse sheds a harsh light and dark shadows on the Revolutionaries' noble aspirations.

It seems to me that American historians generally are reluctant to face the fact that the American Revolution operated very much like other revolutions. If it was not so gory as some, it drove vast numbers of people into permanent exile. Devotion to the mythology of nationalist democracy causes some writers to say things flagrantly contradictory to demonstrable

---

26 Young, "Treason and Its Punishment," 305/369 (italics added).   27 Ibid., 307/371.
28 Ibid., 311/375; Brunhouse, *Counter-Revolution*, 75.
29 Ousterhout, "Controlling the Opposition," 33–34.
30 Young, "Treason and Its Punishment," 313/377.

fact. Thus Richard Alan Ryerson alleges that "under the Constitution of 1776, Pennsylvanians enjoyed the broadest franchise of any large polity in the world."[31]

Benjamin Rush, who was in the thick of the struggles, thought otherwise. In 1784, after plenty of opportunity to judge the effects of that constitution, Dr. Rush denounced it for "precluding two-thirds of the state from voting, by means of the most disgraceful test laws."[32] As we have seen, the test laws were only one of the devices by means of which an active, unscrupulous minority seized and used power. Professor Owen S. Ireland has examined the character and dimensions of that determined party.

Although much interpretation of Pennsylvania's Revolution has centered on opposition of western counties to the long-established domination of the more urban east, Professor Ireland has found that "in Pennsylvania from 1778 through 1789 conflicts based on religious differences formed the most persistent and predictable component of political partisanship."[33] The constitution aroused support and opposition that shifted geographically over time. In 1778–79, the Constitutionalists were strongest in the southeast (apparently by being backed by "leather apron" workmen resenting the former controls of conservative merchants). But by 1788–89, opposing Republicans came to dominate again in the counties that had exerted power throughout the colonial period.[34]

Constitutionalists continued to control in the newer, less populous, western and northern counties by a combination of factors to be noted further on. For the duration of the shooting war with Britain, Constitutionalists rigorously enforced the test laws by means of which they disfranchised their opponents. Thus the Scotch-Irish Presbyterians and their Calvinist allies dominated over the Republican coalition of Anglicans, Quakers, and German sectarians (i.e., pietists). One issue became especially fierce when the assembly simply abolished the College of Philadelphia, which had been an Anglican political stronghold, and replaced it with the (Presbyterian) University of Pennsylvania.[35] Outraged Anglicans suddenly remembered why they had teamed up with Quakers for decades "to keep the others out."

We must not get too far ahead of events. Arguments aside, the evidence of statistics shows how the 1776 constitution and associated legislation transformed political relations in the new state by a revolution within the Revolution. Regionalism, though powerful, was not decisive.

---

31 Ryerson, *Revolution Is Now Begun*, 252.
32 *Letters of Benjamin Rush*, ed. L. H. Butterfield, 2 vols. (Princeton, N.J.: Princeton University Press, 1951), 1:335.
33 Ireland, "Crux of Politics," 454.   34 Ibid., 459.
35 Ibid., 455; for background, see Jennings, *Benjamin Franklin, Politician*, 67–70, 140.

Calvinists from Philadelphia voted Constitutionalist [in the assembly] with Calvinists from nearby commercial-agricultural areas as well as from Lancaster on the east side of the Susquehanna River, from York on the west side, and from the western and northern frontiers. Non-Calvinists, whether urban or rural, east or west, north or south, commercial agriculturalists or frontier farmers, voted together in the Republican party.[36]

The sudden rise to power of Presbyterians goes far to explain the special handicaps and punishments imposed on Pennsylvania's "peace peoples" by the Revolutionaries. The colony had been founded by pacifist Quakers, and their long administration of tolerance had attracted other pacifists, especially pietists, to a place of refuge. Latecoming Scotch-Irish Presbyterians lacked sympathy with pacifists, to say the least. Ever since Oliver Cromwell's conquest of Ireland and colonization of its northeastern region by Scots (hence "Scotch-Irish"), that unhappy island had been rent by religious and ethnic conflict, and the immigrants from there to Pennsylvania were a bellicose lot at political feud with the Quakers.

Yet they were small enough in numbers so that they could not have achieved their wartime dominance without allies. The allies arose from men who resented the Quaker persistence in pacifism during wartime that alienated many more persons than Presbyterians. Indeed it caused many younger Quakers to turn against the faith of their fathers. While the old provincial assembly still sat, it received indignant protests from its Association troops of volunteers. Why? demanded the Associators, why should those pacifists be allowed to benefit from the sacrifices of men who were risking their lives and losing the income from their peacetime occupations? Meantime the pacifists seemed to be profiting greatly. It was an outcry that soldiers of any religion, any ethnicity, any generation can respond to; and circumstances permitted seizure of political power by the militarists – who then devised methods to keep it.

Our old friend Dr. Benjamin Rush explains that "the *passive* conduct of the Quakers and the moderate conduct of the Episcopalians threw government wholly in the hands of . . . Presbyterians in the year 1776. The Germans, who are an uninformed body of people, submitted to their usurpations and formed a principal part of their strength."[37] Rush, himself a Presbyterian of the learned variety, became so disgusted by the wartime domination that he turned Episcopalian.

To a degree then, what has been touted as the rise of democracy in Pennsylvania may validly be seen in part as a program of revenge against Quakers. However, one must look beyond the general laws, oppressive as they were. A particular episode of persecution exposes more of the vengefulness. A "frame up" of leading Quakers meanly involved some of the most

36 Ireland, "Crux of Politics," 458.   37 *Letters of Benjamin Rush*, ed. Butterfield, 1:336.

prominent Revolutionary "heroes." On 25 August 1777, New Hampshire's General John Sullivan pretended to have found a paper from the Friends Meeting of Spanktown, New Jersey, which gave treasonous information to the British army. Unsigned and anonymous, this was an obvious fabrication from a nonexistent source; there was no Quaker meeting in Spanktown. But the president of Congress was John Hancock of Massachusetts, and he promptly referred this sensational discovery to a committee of three men of whom one was John Adams, also, need it be said, of Massachusetts, and we may remember that Quakers had taunted Adams three years earlier about bigotry in Massachusetts. Now, as historian James Donald Anderson remarks, the deliberations of Adams's committee "were short and perfunctory."[38] The committee reported its horrified concern to the whole Congress, and President Hancock called attention to it by the Pennsylvania Supreme Executive Council with a recommendation to arrest named Quakers as well as others who "evidence a disposition inimical to the cause of America." None of these reputable leading citizens of Philadelphia had been named even in Sullivan's fabricated "document."

The Supreme Executive Council regarded Hancock's recommendation as "a direct order," and it ordered seizure of forty-one individuals with all their papers and the records of the Philadelphia [Friends] Meeting for Sufferings.[39] Thus began John Adams's revenge on "King of the Quakers" Israel Pemberton Jr. John Adams carefully distanced himself from the dirty work of persecution carried out by the Calvinist coreligionists of his Congregationalists. As a veteran lawyer he understood very well how due process of law was being violated in its most basic principles, but Adams was also highly conscious of public relations for posterity as well as contemporaries. He was an ostentatiously *virtuous* man.

The tale of the victims' tribulations was told in 1848 by Quaker chronicler Thomas Gilpin and again in 1981 by James Donald Anderson. It is missing from standard national texts that rave about the democracy of Pennsylvania under the 1776 constitution.

In brief, twenty-one leading members of Philadelphia's religious and commercial community were sentenced without trial to exile though no specific charge was made against any one of them. When magistrate Benjamin Paschall tried to get information in order to secure a hearing for the internees, he was rebuffed.[40] They were offered freedom if they would sign oaths of allegiance to Pennsylvania "as a free and independent state," but

38 James Donald Anderson, "Thomas Wharton, Exile in Virginia, 1777–1778," *Virginia Magazine of History and Biography* 89:4 (1981); reprinted in *Patriots, Redcoats, and Loyalists*, ed. Peter Onuf, 426(orig)/380(reprint). I had independently researched my text before coming upon Dr. Anderson's thoroughly researched article of confirmation. It now serves as a convenient and reliable source for the episode. 425(orig)/379(reprint) – 447(orig.)/401(reprint).

39 Ibid., 427/381.   40 Ibid., 429–30/383–84.

they had never sworn allegiance to British kings for religious reasons and they refused to deviate from their creed.[41] Indeed it is hard to sympathize with their adamantine stubbornness, though their right to it was "guaranteed" by the constitution.

Congress and the state Council disputed responsibility for dealing with them, but the Council eventually rounded them up and sent them off to Winchester, Virginia, still without any sort of charge or hearing. Justice Thomas McKean sent habeas corpus writs that reached the prisoners on the road at Pottsgrove. The Supreme Executive Council ignored the writs, and the sitting assembly enacted a law legalizing the prisoners' arrests as "an imminent danger to the state."[42] Regardless of methods, this has at least an appearance of justification as a British army was marching on Philadelphia.

After traveling twenty-eight days, the prisoners crossed borders into Virginia. As Governor Patrick Henry had known some of them personally, they hoped for help from him, but Virginia Congressman Richard Henry Lee (the mover for independence) wrote to warn Governor Henry against these "mischievous People." His phrasing is odd. He blamed the Quakers for intending to "make disturbance and raise discontent" in Virginia as though they had invaded the state to make propaganda.[43]

In the meantime their businesses were ruined, and they were charged outrageous prices for food and shelter, not a penny of which was paid by their persecutors. And the nonjuror fines against their property at home kept being collected. No relief was allowed for them until after the British army evacuated Philadelphia, but it is evident that much unrecorded protest had been directed toward the Supreme Executive Council which notified Congress on 7 March 1778 that the exiles could be allowed to return without danger to the state.[44]

By this time, so much popular sentiment had been whipped up against these "enemies" that they needed an escort for their return journey. Arrived at Lancaster where the Council had moved during the British occupation of Philadelphia, the Quakers demanded exoneration, but were denied an audience with Council. *At no time* was any single constitutional guarantee of due process afforded them. Evidently there were some sore consciences among their persecutors who did not even try to defend their actions.

Two Quakers died in Winchester. Israel Pemberton Jr., an old and broken man, lived only a short time more. All of these victims of arbitrary fiat suffered terribly in property. Even the excuse of the British army approaching Philadelphia looks feeble in comparison with the liberties permitted to persons of other religions who emerged as Loyalists during the

41 Ibid., 431–32/385–86.   42 Ibid., 435/389.   43 Ibid., 438/392.   44 Ibid., 444/398.

occupation. The whole affair seems to me to have been inexcusable *religious* vengeance; and what motives have caused it to be hushed up in the histories?

That master of public relations Benjamin Franklin presided over the convention that produced Pennsylvania's constitution, and he took a copy of it to France when sent there as an ambassador. He had it copied and distributed widely to show how advanced Pennsylvania had become in the sort of Progress advocated by Enlightenment philosophers. (Voltaire paid him a visit and was introduced to his grandson.) Franklin did not take to France copies of the test oaths and other repressive procedures patronized under the constitution. He did not tell the enthusiastic Enlightenment thinkers how the voting franchise had been chopped down and limited to religious partisans.[45]

As in so many other matters, Franklin established an orthodox mythology that has resisted exposure by fact. For a historian the lesson is repeated and confirmed: What protagonists *did* supersedes what they merely *said*.

The Quakers' victimization and suffering stand in the way of an award of *democracy* to the state's Revolutionary tyrants. The problem is solved in our histories with the utmost ease by simply omitting all reference to it.

The question cannot be blinked: What sort of history are such accounts?

45 Van Doren, *Benjamin Franklin*, 605–6; 656–57.

29

LIBERTY; VIRTUE; EMPIRE

For popular support, both sides of the American Revolution had to justify themselves morally. Put bluntly, they had to generate war propaganda. Today, it is possible, of course, to simply accept the propaganda at face value, and this has been done, which is why so many fat volumes recite the Revolution as an unacknowledged fairy tale.

This is no way to discover what happened and why. To clarify what the Revolution was all about, one must make a strong distinction between motives and rationalizations; or, as it once was put, between real reasons and good reasons. We know pretty clearly that the king and Parliament intended to establish beyond question their sovereign right over the colonies; and that the colonists struggled to maintain and expand self-government. Why?

Since tradition and legality were on the king's side, the rebels had to justify themselves with appeals to inspiring abstractions. These included natural rights, rights of Englishmen, love of liberty, hatred of slavery, and American virtue versus English corruption. Some historians profess to see also devotion to democracy. With such words as weapons, the rebels presented themselves as St. George versus the dragon.

These were rationalizations. Only in recent years has the independent, nonacademic writer Theodore Draper asserted baldly that the Revolutionaries' overriding goal was simply power, with an implication that all those other supposed aims were propaganda contradicted by conduct.[1] I think he is right, but let me itemize.

Democracy is an invention of historians. No Revolutionary of any account believed it. Many expressed overt hostility. As one example among many we may cite "Mr. Revolution" Benjamin Franklin. He looked on the increasing numbers of German immigrants in Pennsylvania with abhorrence, and he tried to stop more from being admitted. He held several black domestic slaves until he was converted late in life to abolitionism. He was no friend

---

1 Draper, *Struggle for Power*, xiv, 517–18.

to Indians; for many years he devoted much effort to plans for a new colony to be founded on Indian territory. Quite apart from ethnic considerations, he proposed about people generally, "If we provide encouragement for Laziness and supports for Folly, may it not be found fighting against the order of God and Nature, which perhaps has appointed Want and Misery as the proper Punishments for, and Cautions against as well as necessary consequences of Idleness and Extravagancy."[2] This sour attitude of 1753 was repeated in 1764 in a letter to Dr. John Fothergill. "Half the Lives you save are not worth saving, as being useless, and almost the other Half ought not to be sav'd as being mischievous. Does your Conscience never hint to you the Impiety of being in constant Warfare against the Plans of Providence?"[3]

It takes a kind of ambidexterity to transform such views into a belief in democracy, but some modern writers have found democracy where the Revolutionaries condemned it because a term that then implied social evil has now become the very definition of utopia. An English writer has narrowed the concept: "The American Revolution was not in its origin or intention a social revolution, its aims and ideals having been purely political; nevertheless a revolution must of necessity have social consequences." So far, sound enough, but he showed his own social assumptions with an addition that neither blacks nor Indians could accept: "It is, I think, impossible to deny that the revolution involved a forward movement, all along the line, in the direction of democracy."[4] This reads more truly if qualified for the *herrenvolk democracy* of white men. More on that point further on.

A major way of explaining the American Revolution has been to analyze it by the sources and methods of what is called intellectual history. These procedures demonstrate the thinking of writers contemporary with the events and thus enable a modern reader to see and conceive the events as contemporaries did rather than by imposing present-day notions upon them. Such advantage is obviously valuable, but certain disadvantages need notice: Were those conceptions of contemporaries satisfactory from our perspective? Did they express "good" reasons for motives other than good? Must we accept the ethnic and religious hostilities of the eighteenth century? How skewed were concepts not balanced by writings from nonliterates – such people as Indians, Africans, and unschooled lower-class persons?

Of course it is important to know how events appeared to articulate, literate persons who usually held high status, often wielded considerable

---

2 *Franklin Papers*, 4:480.   3 Ibid., 11:101.
4 Daniel Parker Coke, one of *The Royal Commission on the Losses and Services of American Loyalists, 1783 to 1785*, ed. Hugh Edward Egerton (1915), reprinted (New York: Burt Franklin, 1971), xxvi.

power, and were involved in events. It is equally important to know their
boundaries, morally, intellectually, and physically, and to compensate as well
as possible from other sources. Thus, as the Revolutionaries declaimed pas-
sionately that they struggled for *liberty*, it will be useful to examine what
they meant by that word and how they used it. It must not be waved aside
as "merely" a word. The philosopher Ernst Cassirer has observed "that all
verbal structures appear as also mythical entities, endowed with certain
mythical powers, that the Word, in fact, becomes a sort of primary force, in
which all being and doing originate."[5]

As the word *liberty* occurs so frequently, and in such diverse contexts, we
are fortunate to have a thoroughgoing and sophisticated scholarly analysis
of it: John Phillip Reid's *The Concept of Liberty in the Age of the American
Revolution*. Its beginning makes distinctions: "On the *western* side of the
Atlantic both parties to the revolutionary controversy could use the word
'liberty' in the same yet opposite ways – one invoking American liberty, the
other British liberty – to support opposing causes."[6]

Worse for clarity, "British liberty" was a mantra intoned also on the *east*
side of the Atlantic. Mr. Reid dutifully reports a British boast that "We are
a free, generous, and brave people, and cannot enslave or oppress others."
This was a little hard to swallow; indignant Irish ancestors protested sar-
castically through Mr. Reid "that generous, benevolent Great Britain was
the ruler of Ireland."[7] For the most part, however, he seems to accept the
claim that Britons had more liberty than other Europeans. It is a fault of
this way of doing history that he does not include Highland Scots whose
rebellion had been suppressed by massacre and rapine as recently as 1745.[8]
Their opinions might have made another discordant note in the raptures
about British liberty. Allowing for the truth of certain "rights of Englishmen," a retrospective view sees them being won by rebellions and
revolutions.

Still, the historian must puzzle over the peculiar rebellion of American
colonists against what they themselves acknowledged were "British liberties" and "the rights of Englishmen." How could they have fought against
the constitution that no less a person than John Adams once described as
"the most perfect combination of human powers in society which finite
wisdom has yet contrived and reduced to practice for the preservation of
liberty and the production of happiness"?[9]

---

5 Ernst Cassirer, *Language and Myth* (1924), tr. Susanne K. Langer, reprinted (New York: Dover
Publications, 1946), 45.
6 John Phillip Reid, *The Concept of Liberty in the Age of the American Revolution* (Chicago:
University of Chicago Press, 1988), 11.
7 Ibid., 16.
8 See W. A. Speck, *The Butcher: The Duke of Cumberland and the Suppression of the 45* (Oxford:
Basil Blackwell, 1981).   9 Quoted by Bernard Bailyn, in *Ideological Origins*, 67.

Despite the many examples of high praise for that ill-defined constitution, admiration was not universal. Again, a flaw in intellectual history obtrudes. The fact is plain enough that in politics expressions of sycophancy and toadyism are always encouraged by agents of power; mental reservations and outright dissent are discouraged, to say the least. In the eighteenth century, dislike of that "most perfect" English constitution must have been accumulating a long time when Tom Paine blasted it in *Common Sense*.

That "so much boasted" constitution was only brag, he wrote. "The prejudice of Englishmen, in favour of their own government by king, lords, and commons, arises as much or more from national pride than reason." Far from keeping England peaceful, it had created constant violent turbulence. "Thirty kings and two minors have reigned in that distracted kingdom since the [Norman] conquest, in which time there have been (including the [Puritan] Revolution) no less than eight civil wars and nineteen rebellions." In a phrase destined to echo through generations, he denounced the English constitution as "an house divided against itself." Present purposes preclude full analysis of *Common Sense*. It is enough that the *liberties* so highly praised by "interested men . . . weak men . . . and prejudiced men" were *miseries* for Paine.[10] Certainly his powerful polemic did not strive for objective fairness. Paine aimed to replace *English liberties* by *independence* as the proper goal for American colonials, and he wrought so well that the mantra of American liberties thereafter became subordinate to the idea of independence.

Like his opponents, Paine argued in terms of abstractions, but he empowered his side of the arguments with enough factuality from English history and society to deflate opposing abstractions, and he swept the field. Modern critics call him, with the exception of Karl Marx, "the most influential pamphleteer of all time."[11]

It is all the more important, therefore, to establish the dimensions and limitations of his powerful message. It was aimed rather narrowly. He did not champion Africans oppressed in slavery though he had written elsewhere against existing slavery. Paine did not praise Indians defending their homelands. Instead he wrote of "unoccupied land" that could become "the constant support of government."[12] In *Common Sense*, Paine denounced the British government as "that barbarous and hellish power, which hath stirred up the Indians and Negroes to destroy us."[13] For Paine, liberties were the property of Europeans. He did not use terms of skin color, but his physical referents were the same as those spelled out more bluntly by later generations. Bluntly, Paine was racist, and so were the libertarians who took up

10 Thomas Paine, "Common Sense" in *Rights of Man*, ed. Mark Philp, 10, 18, 9, 25, 5.
11 Bailyn, *Ideological Origins*, 286.   12 Paine, "Common Sense," 41.   13 Ibid., 35.

his cry for independence. Given their deep-seated motives for conquering a continent, they may have had no alternative.

Within a century, they would bitterly regret the Civil War implied by their variedly shared motive, but it was not the only limitation of Paine's battle cry. Though he praised "above all things, the free exercise of religion," he attacked at length the "pretended scruples" of Quakers who had been almost alone among the colonists in patronizing and protecting religious tolerance.[14] Paine joined the party that disenfranchised Quakers and pietists in Pennsylvania. His notion of tolerance included all, and only, religious persons who were on his side in the Revolution.

Despite their admiration for liberty, the Revolutionaries permitted less dissent than the British government allowed its critics and opponents in England. As Theodore Draper so cogently has demonstrated, the central issue of the Revolution was power rather than liberty. The questions cannot be evaded: "power for what and for whom?"

There was long precedent for using *liberty* with such precision. During Europe's Middle Ages, kings sometimes repaid towns for providing services or goods; the king granted a charter specifying that particular privileges had been guaranteed as irrevocable liberties. A liberty was what today we call a right. In the Revolutionary era, *liberty* seems to have been in transition to its more abstract modern sense.

The sanctimonious prating by the Revolutionaries that they were *virtuous* – coming from such political bosses, bootleggers, financial tricksters, and slavers – is too disgusting for detailed discussion here. The Revolutionaries correctly ascribed corruption to the British ruling class, but pretended falsely that they did not do the same things for the same reasons. Indeed, they added an extra kind of corruption that the British were systematically eliminating: The Revolutionaries bought and sold human cattle. Let Thomas Jefferson describe the effect of this practice on virtue.

> The whole commerce between master and slave is a perpetual exercise of the most boisterous passions, the most unremitting despotism on the one part, and degrading submissions on the other. . . . The man must be a prodigy who can retain his manners and morals undepraved by such circumstances. And with what execration should the statesman be loaded, who permitting one half the citizens thus to trample on the rights of the other, transforms those into despots, and these into enemies, destroys the morals of the one part, and the amor patriae of the other.[15]

14 Ibid., 33, 56–59.
15 Thomas Jefferson, *Notes on the State of Virginia* (1787), ed. William Peden (Chapel Hill: University of North Carolina Press, 1954, reprinted 1982), 162–63.

Yet the Americans' belief that their people were virtuously contending against the corruption of Old England must be noticed because morale depended upon it to some extent. The war for independence lost support as evidence mounted of war profiteering.[16] Charles Royster asks the key question: "If American independence depended on public virtue, how could one resolve the conflict between the demanding ideals and the sharp practice that betrayed them?"[17]

Not only a few starry-eyed idealists asked that question. The general populace adopted "a vivid and precise vocabulary" referring to profiteering in commerce while soldiers suffered and sacrificed: "*Smart money* was a recruiter's illegal take; 'horse-beef' was soldiers' rations of dubious origin; 'CUSTOMHOUSE OATHS' were perjury; '*mushroom* gentlemen' were the newly prosperous Revolutionaries; 'jockeying' was getting rid of paper money before it lost value. As Washington's aide Tench Tilghman wrote in 1779, 'We Americans are a sharp people.'"[18] Private George Morison wondered, "Did they not know that their doings were crimes – that they were cheating their country, and exposing its defenders to additional sufferings and to death?"[19]

A historian must notice that these things happened and were done by these people. It follows like the night the day that this war was like other wars in many respects.

A historian has written that "in the United States it is almost a heresy to describe the nation as an empire. [But] the founders so regarded it."[20] Euphemisms are so common that some empirical data are required to give meaning to them.

In 1750, some Virginia gentlemen formed the Ohio Company to sell and settle lands in the Ohio Valley. They sent young George Washington as their troop commander against French resistance that flamed into the Seven Years War and was succeeded by "Pontiac's War." In 1783, the same George Washington conceived his newly fledged nation, newly triumphant against Britain, as a "rising empire."[21]

This was more than a flight of rhetorical fancy. The treaty of peace with Britain would give to the United States vast territories extending westward to the Mississippi River. Washington personally claimed large tracts of land in the West (as it was then), and when he later became president, his policies aimed straight at legalizing and organizing them.

---

16 Charles Royster, "'The Nature of Treason': Revolutionary Virtue and American Reactions to Benedict Arnold," in *Patriots, Redcoats, and Loyalists*, ed. Onuf. Originally published in *William and Mary Quarterly*, 3d ser., 36:2(1979). This note paged 173(orig.)/329(reprint) – 179/335.
17 Ibid., 178/334.   18 Ibid.   19 Ibid.
20 Van Alstyne, *The Rising American Empire*, 6.   21 Ibid., 1.

So early as 1754, Benjamin Franklin proposed *A Plan for Settling Two Western Colonies* "between the Ohio and Lake Erie." His much-noticed Albany Plan of Union was motivated in part by the less-noticed purpose of establishing "one or more new colonies," which could be supported jointly by the old colonies "united under one governor general and grand council, agreeable to the Albany Plan."[22]

During his years in London, Franklin lobbied in behalf of a company in which he shared, to secure a charter for the western colony dreamed of in 1754. As negotiator of the peace treaty with Britain in 1783, he secured the western boundary of his new nation at the Mississippi River.

While the statesmen wrangled over legalities, hordes of lesser folk streamed westward. The histories speak of them as "settlers" in a customary dismissal of that category for "Indians," but the Indians conceived otherwise and they took up arms to resist the *invaders* of their territories. In Europe, when one nation pushes successfully past the boundaries into a second nation, the event is dubbed "conquest." In America, "territorial expansion was primarily opportunist and defensive."[23] Whether a conflict is defensive depends on the standpoint of the observer. As the United States expanded, Indians thought that *they* were being defensive. (It is relevant that the Virginia gentry regarded the *settlers* as *squatters*.)

A wry historian has remarked:

> American foreign policy has a vocabulary all its own, consciously – even ostentatiously – side-stepping the use of terms that would even hint at aggression or imperial domination, and taking refuge in abstract formulae, stereotyped phrases, and idealistic cliches that really explain nothing. . . . Parrot-like repetition of these abstractions and other generalities produces an emotional reflex which assumes that American diplomacy is 'different', purer, morally better than the diplomacy of other powers. There is a strong pharisaical flavour about American diplomacy, easily detected abroad but generally unrecognized at home. No doubt it is a part of the cult of nationalism.[24]

It needs only be added that the same comments apply to nationalist American histories.

It follows that one must look past such comments as Jack M. Sosin's "The early history of America is the story of the peopling of a continent"[25] or Bernard Bailyn's title *The Peopling of British North America*. What the Revolutionaries intended, regardless of the skittishness with which they

---

22 *Franklin Papers* 5:456–63; quote at 459.
23 Reginald C. Stuart, *United States Expansion and British North America, 1775–1871* (Chapel Hill: University of North Carolina Press, 1988), 5.
24 Van Alstyne, *The Rising American Empire*, 7.
25 Jack M. Sosin, *The Revolutionary Frontier*, 1; Bailyn, *The Peopling of British North America: An Introduction* (New York: Alfred A. Knopf, 1987).

approached the subject in phrases like "the conquest of the wilderness," was conquest of the native peoples who had previously *settled* and *peopled* the continent, and acquisition of their lands.

Colin G. Calloway says it concisely: "The American revolutionaries who fought for freedom from the British Empire in the East also fought to create an empire of their own in the West."[26]

---

26 Colin G. Calloway, *The American Revolution in Indian Country* (Cambridge: Cambridge University Press, 1995), xv.

30

CONQUEST; SLAVERY; RACE

Feelings of antagonism between peoples of competing countries are universal among humankind; in a relatively mild manifestation they are classed as ethnocentrism. When this feeling is strengthened in relations of conqueror to the conquered, it acquires rationalizations to offset other feelings of pity or mercy and to justify the use of power to exploit the conquered. In the Americas, such rationalizations multiplied to sanctify the oppressors' superiority as *natural* or even divinely ordained (for which there was plenty of authority in the Holy Bible written by barbarians millennia ago). With such authority the extreme case of ethnocentrism became racism branded by gradations of skin color.

It seems important to note that racism was produced, or at least encouraged, by official policy. As Oscar Hammerstein so concisely summarized in *South Pacific*, "it has to be carefully taught." Although racism was to become an important factor in the American Revolution, it owed more to religion than to skin color in the earliest colonial times. The colonists conceived themselves as Christians, and all others were contemptible pagans or infidels, but with the saving grace that they were capable of being converted to Christianity. As non-Christians, they were available for enslavement without strain on the Christian conscience, but when converted they had to be made free.

It was also accepted that "wild" people – those not under Christian, civil government – could be killed if they seemed to present danger to God's chosen people, and in the seventeenth century Englishmen were not embarrassed to say that God was an Englishman. Jamestown's authorities faced a dilemma: Their wild Indian neighbors were needed to feed the colonists, but the authorities feared fraternizing between colonists and Indians because they remembered how such mixing in Ireland had made English colonists there vulnerable to Irish uprisings.

One must not be misled by the marriage of Pocahontas and John Rolfe, beguiling as it seems today. It was an extremely exceptional case, perhaps unique, for reasons of diplomacy. The general rule was racial segregation, which was made official first by Virginia and then by Massachusetts and Connecticut. When starving colonists at Jamestown fled to hospitable Indians, they were captured, drawn back to the colony, and tortured horribly to death to deter emulation.

(French policies differed. Louis XIV encouraged intermarriage as a means of multiplying his subjects, and French traders traveled from one tribal village to another even as Indian traders were welcomed to "fairs" at Quebec. Not strangely, the French thus acquired much more influence with Indians than the English could hope for.)

After African slaves arrived in Virginia, some confusion existed for a while about how to treat them. They were welcome as manpower during a shortage of labor, and at first they seemed to be like unfree indentured servants from England. With time, this situation changed drastically. Laws gradually prescribed social distance between colonists and their chattels, and the mystique of race gathered form and force. Its foundation in policy rather than nature is well attested by notorious illegitimate coupling between masters and slaves that continued throughout the entire life of slavery.

Slave-owning planters were not at all enthusiastic about converting their lost souls to Christianity because that would mean emancipating them. Rationalizations quickly changed from religion to race which was much more convenient. Race, as conceived, was supposed to be innately absolute and unchangeable; it was ideal as a stable basis for property.

Although slavery was legal in all the colonies throughout the colonial period, it grew massively in the Southern tidewater regions of large plantations cultivating staple crops for export. Especially in South Carolina, whose colonists immigrated from the harsh slave culture of West Indian Barbados, African slaves quickly came to outnumber descendants of Europe, and this disparity required the colonists to behave with great discretion when imperial governments requested wartime support. Planters dared not loosen controls for fear of slave uprisings.

Ethnicity clearly was a factor in rationalizing slavery. The Germans who came to central Pennsylvania rejected it and its great plantations in favor of family farms cultivated by their own labor in accordance with pietist religions. Certain Mennonites lectured Quakers holding slaves. A meeting in Philadelphia's Germantown preserves the tradition.

New England had religious beliefs similar to those of the tidewater South planters, but New England's soil was rocky and broken, suitable only for cultivation in small farms. The culture of slavery became identified as Southern.

When Benjamin Franklin went to England in 1764 to argue that the crown should dispossess the Penn family of their fief in America, he arrived at about the same time that a movement against slavery began. Slavery was immoral, the campaigners charged; it was sinful for anyone to hold or traffic in slaves and for the government to sanction such practices. Franklin had held domestic slaves himself and had bought and sold some in business. Biographer Van Doren recites that, during Franklin's 1757 trip to London, he had "lived handsomely with two servants he had brought from Philadelphia."[1] Those "servants" were slaves and one ran away.[2] Franklin was made uncomfortable in 1764 by the taunts of Englishmen who jeered at colonists' outcries that the British government was reducing them to slavery. "You Americans make a great Clamour upon every little imaginary Infringement of what you take to be your Liberties; and yet there are no People upon Earth such Enemies to Liberty, such absolute Tyrants, where you have the Opportunity, as you yourselves are."[3]

Thus Franklin quoted the charge against the colonial people for whom he was a spokesman in London. The complaint put this master of public relations into a bad bind from which he wriggled to free himself. He did not confess his own dealings with slaves. He acknowledged the "Zeal for Liberty, in general" of an Englishman who had written a book for the abolition of slavery, but Franklin disapproved of the writer's conclusion that "therefore our Claim to the Enjoyment of Liberty for ourselves, is unjust. . . . He is too severe upon the Americans." Distinguishing the mass of colonists as freemen and nonholders of slaves, Franklin went over to the "you're another" style of argument. "Remember, Sir, that [England] began the Slave Trade." And when the colonies tried to stop it, their laws "have been disapproved and repealed by your Government here, as being prejudicial, forsooth, to the Interest of the African Company." This was true.

Furthermore, in Scotland, coal miners were "absolute Slaves by your Law . . . [who were] bought and sold with the Colliery, and have no more Liberty to leave it than our Negroes have to leave their Master's Plantation." But that was Scotland. When Franklin tried to find slavery in England, he was reduced to attacking the conditions of service of soldiers and sailors.[4]

Had Franklin looked more closely, he might have found some thousands of slaves in England as events were to disclose. But he had been stimulated enough to correspond with Quaker Anthony Benezet, a tireless antislavery crusader who told him of hopeful progress in public opinion

1 Van Doren, *Benjamin Franklin*, 128–29, 197–98, 272.
2 Gary B. Nash and Jean R. Soderlund, *Freedom by Degrees: Emancipation in Pennsylvania and Its Aftermath* (New York: Oxford University Press, 1991), 11, 13, 20.
3 *Franklin Papers*, 17:37.   4 Ibid., 17:37–44.

but who added, sadly, "there is now eight hundred and fifty thousand negroes in the English Islands and Colonies; and an hundred thousand more yearly imported by our Nation, about a third of this number is set to perish in the passage."[5]

In the same year, 1772, an event occurred that was to be a "turning point" for English abolitionists. Even as Franklin was reading Anthony Benezet's letter, a slave called James Somersett became embroiled with the law for escaping from the Virginian master who had brought him to England. Somersett was retaken and put in irons for shipment to the slave market in Jamaica, but three abolitionists obtained a writ of habeas corpus for him, and his case came before the Court of King's Bench.

The outcome of the case was epochal. No drums or trumpets proclaimed its significance, but four robed and bewigged gentlemen, in decorous and dignified surroundings, set off a land mine. William Murray, Chief Justice Lord Mansfield, observed that the condition of slavery is "so odious, that nothing can be suffered to support it, but positive law." Whereupon he made the startling discovery that *no law in England authorized the holding of slaves.* "Whatever the inconveniences, therefore, may follow from the decision . . . the black must be discharged."[6] And James Somersett walked out of that courtroom a free man.

Much higgling and legalistic haggling have wrangled over whether Lord Mansfield's decision constituted real abolition of slavery, and indeed nasty episodes of kidnapping continued to occur thereafter because Mansfield had not made slavery *against* law; he had only declared that a slave owner had no property right supported by English law. Nevertheless, his biographer reports, "as a result of this decision 14,000 or 15,000 slaves were in fact freed."[7] Those were persons not inclined to chop the fine points of law. Better yet, the decision heartened English abolitionists to campaign harder, first to outlaw the slave trade and finally to outlaw slavery in Britain's dominions (1834).

Americans knew about Justice Mansfield's decision regarding slaves in England. Philadelphia's Dr. Benjamin Rush was in touch with Granville Sharp, the leading British abolitionist. Rush appealed to American politicians: "You cannot show your attachment to your King, or your love to your country better, than by suppressing an evil which endangers the dominions of the former, and will in time destroy the liberty of the latter."[8] New laws

---

5 Ibid., 19:112–16.

6 *English Historical Documents*, gen. ed. David C. Douglas, Vol. X: 1714–1783, ed. D. B. Horn and Mary Ransome (London: Eyre and Spottiswoode, 1957), 264.

7 Edmund Heward, *Lord Mansfield* (Chichester, West Sussex: Barry Rose, 1979), 147.

8 A Pennsylvanian [Benjamin Rush], "An address to the Inhabitants of the British Settlements in America Upon Slave-Keeping" (1773), in *American Political Writing During the Founding Era,*

were needed "after the Spirit of Religion – Liberty – and our most excellent English Constitution."

It seems impossible that this should have been written by the same Dr. Rush who, within three years, would recruit a printer for Tom Paine's trumpet call in *Common Sense* of a complete break from that "most excellent English Constitution," and it becomes even harder to understand in the light of the Revolutionaries' attitudes toward slavery. Every effort of the humanitarians was smashed by the powerful slaveholding planters who prevented even a ban on the importation of new cargoes of slaves.[9]

So far were the planters from manumitting their human chattels that the colonies' (and new states') slave population increased faster than the free population.[10]

The acclaimed historian of *The Ideological Origins of the American Revolution*, Bernard Bailyn, found spiritual uplift and moral comfort in the struggles of some Revolutionaries against slavery. Drawing attention to them, he declared that the institution "had been subjected to severe pressure as a result of the extension of Revolutionary ideas, and it bore the marks ever after."[11] That such struggles took place is indisputable. Antislavery actions before and during the Revolution are detailed in Chapter 3 of Benjamin Quarles's *The Negro in the American Revolution*.[12]

Another prize-winning "mainstream" historian has found comfort because

> the Revolution suddenly and effectively ended the cultural climate that had allowed black slavery, as well as other forms of bondage and unfreedom, to exist throughout the colonial period without serious challenge. . . . The Revolution in effect set in motion ideological and social forces that doomed the institution of slavery in the North and led inexorably to the Civil War.[13]

Thus Professor Gordon Wood when searching for *The Radicalism of the American Revolution* and apparently being unaware of the lessons taught and laws won by British abolitionists. And, to judge by the absence of *slavery* from Mr. Wood's index, that issue was irrelevant to *The Creation of the American Republic, 1776–1787*.[14] The mainstream sometimes flows over rocky cataracts.

1760–1805, ed. Charles S. Hyneman and Donald S. Lutz, 2 vols. (Indianapolis: Liberty Fund, 1983), 1:226, 228.

9 Paul Finkelman, *Slavery and the Founders: Race and Liberty in the Age of Jefferson* (Armonk, N. Y.: M. E. Sharpe, 1996), 27–29.

10 *Blackwell Encyclopedia*, 95.   11 Bailyn, *Ideological Origins*, 246.

12 Benjamin Quarles, *The Negro in the American Revolution* (1961), reprint (Chapel Hill: University of North Carolina Press, 1996), Chap. 3.

13 Gordon S. Wood, *The Radicalism of the American Revolution* (New York: Alfred A. Knopf, 1992), 186–87.

14 Gordon S. Wood, *The Creation of the American Republic, 1776–1787* (Chapel Hill: University of North Carolina Press, 1969).

Because of being looked at in sidelong glances (when at all) slavery leaves the impression of a minor issue in the midst of great concerns such as independence, liberty, and democracy. It was rather more important. To begin with, slavery was an empirical, verifiable institution rather than an abstraction. Morally speaking, as a British writer states firmly, "The transatlantic slave trade was a human atrocity that has yet to be duplicated."[15] The stern-faced believer in realpolitik who disdains moral issues might consider the eighteenth-century judgment of Malachy Postlethwayt that the African slave trade was "the great Pillar and Support" of British trade with America and that the British empire was "a magnificent superstructure of American commerce and [British] naval power on an African foundation."[16]

When the slaveholding American Revolutionaries maneuvered to keep the slave trade in being, their war aims had nothing to do with virtue, liberty, or democracy. Wealth and power summed them up.

It must be added that some other Revolutionaries aimed differently. In the observable creation of the new American republic, these idealists lost advantage to the superior ruthlessness of the slaveholders; but we shall see that they did gradually free the slaves *north* of the Mason-Dixon line. It is, of course, possible to interpret that fact as what led inexorably to the Civil War. Other interpretations suggest themselves.

Northern freedom was defensive. After the Revolution, bondage was extended *west*. Ostensibly the Northwest Territory was guaranteed against slavery, but Paul Finkelman has shown the devices by which slaves were introduced into that region.[17] The "slave power" sought aggressively to preserve and extend the advantages it had gained during the Revolution.[18] Texas was admitted to the Union as a slave state long past the year 1834 when emancipation began throughout the British empire. While England had no law supporting slavery, and did not make one, the American Revolutionaries locked the institution into the Constitution of their new nation. It cannot be blinked that one of the products of *their* work was the American Civil War.

---

15 Jennifer Lyle Morgan, *Transatlantic Slavery Against Human Dignity*, ed. Anthony Tibbles (Liverpool: National Museums and Galleries on Merseyside, 1994), 60.
16 David Richardson, in *Transatlantic Slavery Against Human Dignity*, 26–28.
17 Finkelman, *Slavery and the Founders*, Chap. 2.   18 See Chap. 43.

31

———— • ————

COMBAT: MULTIPLE OUTBREAKS

Who ever said that dates are unimportant in the study of history? The battle of Lexington and Concord occurred on 19 April 1775. News of it had reached Philadelphia by the twenty-fourth. Benjamin Franklin debarked at Philadelphia on 5 May. On the sixth, the Pennsylvania assembly chose him to be a delegate to the Second Continental Congress that convened on the tenth. Quickly the Massachusetts assembly asked Congress to manage the siege of Boston. Congress began raising an army and commissioned George Washington as commander in chief on 14 June, and he immediately rode to take charge of the siege.

Meantime, Connecticut rebels targeted the cannon of Fort Ticonderoga, and they asked the Green Mountain Boys to choose a commander to take the fort. Ethan Allen took charge. An ancient comedy was reenacted when suddenly Col. Benedict Arnold showed up, purporting to have been given command by Massachusetts, insisting indeed that he was "the only person who has been legally authorized to take possession of this place." Allen's men were not impressed, and they charged right on to accomplish what Arnold reported as "*we* had taken the fort."[1] Allen wrote, "*I* took the fortress. . . . Colonel Arnold entered the fortress with me side by side."[2] It was an omen of many struggles for personal rank and glory clogging the Revolution's progress.

Self-serving reports aside, the Green Mountain Boys swarmed over a stupefied garrison. The aroused captain, "with his breeches in his hand," confronted Allen to ask the authority for his demand to surrender. Allen roared out one of the immortal phrases of American history: *In the name of the great Jehovah and the Continental Congress!*[3] How it rolls off the tongue. Allen was reputedly an atheist, but he understood drama.

---

1 *The Spirit of 'Seventy-Six*, ed. Commager and Morris, 104–5.
2 Carl Van Doren, *Secret History of the American Revolution* (New York: Viking Press, 1941), 147 (emphasis added).
3 *Spirit of 'Seventy-Six*, ed. Commager and Morris, 103 (emphasis added).

The outcome of this sideshow was capture of the fort's cannon, which were freighted to Boston when winter ice made hauling possible across the waters. Washington had them at hand by February 1776, and "Shells we got from the king's store at N. York."[4]

British troops had stormed the besiegers in the battle of Bunker's Hill (actually nearby Breed Hill), sustaining serious casualties. Though they took the hill, they could not raise the siege, and those casualties discouraged them from forcing the issue. Both sides settled down to watch and wait until Washington got the Ticonderoga cannon and deployed them on Dorchester Heights, from which they menaced royal ships in the harbor and killed some troops in the town. (Civilians were frantic.)

General Howe, convinced that Washington's new fortifications were impregnable, offered a bargain. He would not burn the town if Washington would let him evacuate without harassment. The bargain was accepted and kept, and the Regulars sailed off to Halifax, 17 March 1776, taking a thousand Loyalists with them. (This General Sir William Howe had replaced Gage as commander; he was the brother of the admiral who had labored with Franklin in London.)[5]

Thus George Washington and the Congress, with more than a little help from the wholly independent Green Mountain militia, gained their first victory. Perhaps it went to their heads.

The First Continental Congress had addressed the French people of Quebec Province with a plea for alliance. It argued that the Quebec Act of 1774 condemned Canadians to a government without the great British liberty of an elected assembly. To achieve liberty the Canadians should join with the rebel provinces farther south.[6]

This failed to produce the desired result, so the Second Congress considered more direct ways of acquiring Canadian cooperation. The delegates worried much about the royal troops based in Quebec as a kind of sword poised over the rebels so it seemed sensible to strike at Quebec before the crown could mobilize extra forces there. If the French inhabitants did not understand the wonders of a British constitution, they would have to be made to listen.

Ticonderoga's capture opened the way along the traditional invasion route of Lakes George and Champlain and the Richelieu River. Benedict Arnold busily promoted himself as the captor of Ticonderoga (his greatest feats were his triumphs of self-advancement); and Arnold agitated for command of an expedition to Canada. Congress hesitated. As David Ramsay

---

4 Ibid., 175–76, 178.   5 Ibid., 173–83.
6 David Ramsay, *The History of the American Revolution*, 2 vols. (1789), ed. Lester H. Cohen (Indianapolis: Liberty Fund, 1990), 1:131; Higginbotham, *The War of American Independence*, 107; *Documents of American History*, ed. Commager, 1:91–92.

remarked, "They were sensible that by taking this step, they changed at once the whole nature of the war. From defensive it became offensive, and subjected them to the imputation of being the aggressors. It could be a great disservice to forfeit the good opinion of friends in Britain."[7]

Perhaps the ease with which Howe's Regulars had been chased out of Boston decided the issue. On 27 June 1775, Congress authorized invasion, "if practicable and . . . not . . . disagreeable to the Canadians."[8] As Don Higginbotham remarks, "already expansion, if not Manifest Destiny, was in the air."[9] It could hardly have been worse planned or executed.

Congress commissioned General Philip Schuyler to command an expedition along the traditional war path, but Schuyler got sick so Brigadier Richard Montgomery took charge. These arrangements did not suit Benedict Arnold who prevailed on George Washington to let him take a second expedition along a different route *without* authorization from Congress. Arnold obviously intended to win laurels for a surprise attack that the British would not foresee, but there were good reasons for their not fearing the direction he took. Certainly he chose a route that no sane man would have undertaken: up the Kennebec River and through woods for 350 miles. The six-week ordeal "saw the men stumble along formidable portages, struggle against swollen streams, wade snow-covered swamps, and, when provisions gave out, eat their dogs and make gruel from shaving soap."[10] Incomprehensibly to me, this is touted as "magnificent leadership," despite the arrival of these haggard troops in no condition to conquer anything. Arnold had started with eleven hundred men and arrived with six hundred before doing battle.[11] If not for being guided by Abenaki Indians, they probably would never have arrived at all.[12]

Montgomery captured Montreal, and Congress sent reinforcements. Arnold did not capture Quebec City despite much braggadocio. Montgomery took a detachment of men to join him, and they plotted an assault in a blinding snowstorm (to surprise the enemy). Montgomery was killed, Arnold took command with a leg wound, and their men surrendered in droves. After this fiasco in May, British reinforcements arrived, and nothing was left to do but to pull out of Canada. Even that cost casualties. Don Higginbotham calculates that five thousand men had been lost from battle, disease, and desertion, besides huge amounts of money and goods. Arnold departed before his troops.[13]

7 Ramsay, *History*, 1:213–14.
8 Stuart R. J. Sutherland, "Montgomery, Richard," in *Dictionary of Canadian Biography*, 4:545.
9 Higginbotham, *War of American Independence*, 108.
10 Ibid., 110.
11 Sutherland, *Dictionary of Canadian Biography*, 4:547.
12 Calloway, *American Revolution in Indian Country*, 70.
13 Higginbotham, *War of American Independence*, 114–15.

The political effort also became a dead loss. When invasion began, most French Canadian *habitants* could hardly care less about supporting the great British king who had conquered them only a dozen years previously. The seigneurs, clergy, and French bourgeoisie responded loyally to the Quebec Act's religious freedom for Catholics, but a small coterie of British and American Protestant merchants rejected that law for precisely the same reason. They wanted an elected assembly for which only Protestants – that is, themselves – would be eligible.[14]

So long as the Americans paid in hard money, the *habitants* shrugged and sold what was wanted, but when coin turned to inflationary paper money, attitudes changed, and the Catholic clergy's natural leadership reasserted itself.

In the spring of 1776, while Quebec was still under siege, three Congressional commissioners arrived in Montreal to woo the populace. One was Benjamin Franklin. Another was Charles Carroll, a Catholic intended to reassure the Canadians about the Protestant Congress's intentions. This political mission foundered as badly as the military invasion.

Don Higginbotham's comment is pertinent: "As Benedict Arnold soberly noted, 'the junction of the Canadians with the Colonies' was 'now at an End.' It was time to 'quit them and Secure our own Country before it is too late.' Congress could not have been given better advice."[15] Arnold himself was the first to act upon it.

It is worth notice that already this early, Indians were involved on both sides of the fighting. Some fought with the Americans in the siege of Quebec; others helped the British to defend the city. Abenaki Chief Swashan brought four warriors to join George Washington at Boston, and offered more.[16] Events were to prove that such impulses were misguided. They caused great loss and gained no gratitude. In measurable terms of life and property, the Revolution cost Indians more than it took from any other ethnic group.[17] (The invasion's atmosphere is caught in *Spirit of 'Seventy-Six,* Chapter 6.)

Britain's rulers suddenly had to face the fact that this colonial uprising differed sharply from the Scottish Highlanders' effort to restore the Stuart dynasty thirty years earlier. That had been suppressed by the slaughter at Culloden and subsequent ravaging of the Highlands. But Massachusetts was more formidable in every way. It had better weapons, better-trained soldiers

---

14 Lewis H. Thomas, "Walker, Thomas," in *Dictionary of Canadian Biography* 4:758–59.
15 Higginbotham, *War of American Independence*, 115.
16 Calloway, *American Revolution in Indian Country*, 69–70.
17 "The American Revolution was a disaster for most American Indians . . . the new America had no room for Indians and their world" (ibid., 291).

and more of them, and a multitude of allies adopting the rebellion as their own.

In Britain also, the rebellion wore a different aspect. Whereas the Highlanders had threatened Parliament's establishment of the Hanoverian dynasty and had seemed to open Scotland to invasion by French enemies, Massachusetts raised neither of those menaces – yet. The American colonists were on the defensive, and they seemed to be defending the "constitution" that Englishmen cherished highly. Friends of Massachusetts existed within the realm of England, within the halls of Parliament as well as in America.

George III was not certain even of how much he could depend on his own army. Commander in chief of the army General Jeffrey Amherst refused to command the troops in America. Lt. Gen. Frederick Cavendish, a veteran of the Seven Years War, refused to serve, as did also Gen. Henry Conway, Admiral Keppel, and the earl of Effingham. General William Howe kept striving to find means of reconciliation. Unrest among ordinary people led George to doubt their trustworthiness for the job he wanted done, so he hired thirty thousand troops from German princes.[18]

The siege of Boston moved the king to issue a proclamation, 23 August 1775, against subjects "traitorously preparing, ordering and levying war against us." By the same document, George tried to suppress opposition within the realm, and he demanded that "loyal and obedient subjects" should transmit "due and full information of all persons who shall be found carrying on correspondence with, or in any manner or degree aiding or abetting the persons now in open arms or rebellion."[19] Thus the contentions became a civil war within England as well as between the realm and its colonies.

The royal navy shelled Bristol, Rhode Island, and ceased only when bought off with payments in sheep and cattle. On 18 October, the navy shelled and burned the fishing village of Falmouth, Maine, without provocation. Perhaps with greater consequences, Virginia's governor Lord Dunmore destroyed the city of Norfolk with naval fire in January 1766.[20]

Such events testify to the vindictive spirit of the king and some officers of his armed forces; yet, when the whole scene is surveyed, one is struck by how little carnage was inflicted at this stage of the conflict. The rebels could not possibly have stopped the navy from reducing every coastal town and city to ashes *if* that had been policy. What restrained the destruction? Why was the ravaging of the Scottish Highlands not repeated on a larger scale? It seems plausible to attribute the difference to the sympathy in Britain for

18 *Spirit of 'Seventy-Six*, ed. Commager and Morris, 239–41, 265.
19 *Documents of American History*, ed. Commager, 75–76.   20 Ibid., 106.

the rebels which manifested itself even in Parliament despite the royal ban on "aiding or abetting" the rebels.

One is drawn by the inference that this was the king's war rather than the nation's. He cannot escape responsibility by making Parliament equally culpable because this Parliament was his purchased property, "singularly corrupt, even by the genial standards of the eighteenth century." The king had almost a million pounds sterling for bribery in his civil list which he disposed of entirely by prerogative. "He fought elections, bought seats, bailed out insolvent members, dispensed patronage and pensions, sold military offices, and in countless other ways assured himself a loyal following."[21] One of those other ways was the solid support of the Scottish members who were still concerned to avoid imputations of disloyalty arising from the 1745 uprising in the Highlands. George *owned* that Parliament.

Why did he act as he did? He was not a clod; he collected art objects with a keen eye for quality. He was not lazy; he consulted daily with his prime minister during Parliament's sessions. But he was capable of obsession as he demonstrated in his hounding of John Wilkes. More to the present point, he forced issues with the rebel colonists whenever his ministers were inclined to slack off.[22] We know that his mind became progressively more unbalanced until he finally had to be institutionalized and relieved of government. That came late in life, so how much of his actions against the colonies were due to his disorder must remain an enigma. Whatever the reasons, he *was responsible* as much as any one man can be for great historical motions. The judgment of Henry Steele Commager and Richard B. Morris cannot be refuted: George's "methods were those of influence, intimidation, and corruption, and his tools were for the most part beneath contempt."[23]

It was the king's war. Not until France came into it did the nation rally wholeheartedly. This, I think, goes far to explain why the British fought this war against the colonial rebels comparatively genteelly. It may explain also why the British treated opponents of the war rather differently than the Americans treated Loyalists. More of that later.

In Virginia, political power was not seized by new rebels; it was kept by the old ones. From the time of that colony's founding, its landed gentry functioned as an autonomous power within the empire, constantly at odds with royal governors and usually winning their disputes. The reasons for their success had become organic and institutional long before the Revolution. Great estates were held intact by semifeudal laws of entail.[24] Members of

---

21 *Spirit of 'Seventy-Six*, ed. Commager and Morris, 229.   22 Draper, *Struggle for Power*, 478.
23 *Spirit of 'Seventy Six*, 227.   24 Holly Brewer, "Entailing Aristocracy," 307–46.

interlocked gentry families presided in county courts, commanded militias, acted as vestrymen in the established churches, and functioned as members of the provincial House of Burgesses. Whatever a royal governor wanted to do had to be done by them. If they withheld cooperation, he was helpless.

The Virginia gentry resented royal exertions of power in regard to taxation, and westward-yearning speculators particularly detested the Quebec Act that banned their expansion and profit. In greed to profit from western lands, a new governor had colluded with bellicose "frontiersmen" to start war with the Shawnee Indians and try to seize abandoned Fort Pitt with its adjacent tracts of Pennsylvania territory. The Revolution interrupted his rapacity when Virginians sent delegates to the First and Second Continental Congresses. This was John Murray, Earl Dunmore, who took office in 1771. Most governors of the province had learned to adjust to the facts of gentry power, but Dunmore "was but ill fitted to be at the helm in this tempestuous season." The judgment was that of an early historian from South Carolina who found that Dunmore's "passions predominated over his understanding, and precipitated him into measures injurious both to the people whom he governed, and to the interest of his royal master."[25]

Like General Gage in Boston, Dunmore used armed forces to seize gunpowder from a magazine in Williamsburg and to store it in a naval vessel on the James River. Was there some planned coordination? Gage sent his troops to Lexington, 18 April, and Dunmore acted on the twentieth. However, the outcomes were different. At this stage, Virginia did not resist like Massachusetts. But Dunmore alarmed Virginians who began to think that he intended to deprive them of the ability to defend themselves.

There was contrast between these two governors. Gage was a gentleman soldier who restrained his troops from excessive bloodshed and pillage. He had a nasty job to do, but he did it without malevolence. Dunmore, on the other hand, could not be properly described without descent into the argot of the streets that is forbidden to professional discourse. In one polite word, he was *vile*.

Virginians reacted to Dunmore's initiative by holding many meetings, and they organized a system of patrols (probably by extension of preexisting patrols to guard against escape by slaves). Patrick Henry recruited militiamen for a march to Williamsburg to regain the powder, seemingly rather melodramatically as was Henry's wont. Crisis was averted when he accepted a face-saving gesture of payment for the powder, which was not returned. Tensions relaxed until Dunmore aroused them all the more by fortifying his palace with cannon and sending his family to safety on the schooner *Fowey*.

25 Ramsay, *History*, 1:229.

Persons previously doubting his intentions became convinced he meant no good.

When the prime minister Lord North in London offered a plan for reconciliation, Dunmore summoned the House of Burgesses to respond to it, but they concluded, "it only changes the form of oppression without lightening its burthen."[26] The Burgesses were no less devoted to empire than Parliament and the crown, but they intended it to be their own sovereignty rather than Britain's.

On this assumption they continued with the normal business of legislation, but Lord Dunmore fled to the river and the navy's cannon. A comedy ensued. Dunmore assured the Burgesses that he could sign their laws on the *Fowey*. No way, was the response, he must come ashore and act in the capital. He offered to receive them on board ship, but they deemed that a high breach of their rights and privileges. At this impasse, the Burgesses ended their session, "and royal government in Virginia from that day ceased."[27]

Dunmore gave way to rage, and launched attacks from shipboard against the people he was supposed to govern. He recruited Loyalists to improvised forces, ravaged plantations, and burnt houses. At the extreme of enmity he decreed freedom for slaves and servants, not out of solicitude for their circumstances, but on condition that they join his armed forces.[28] Thus he woke the ultimate nightmare of the slave society, and response came quickly.

Dunmore was stupid as well as vicious. By previously threatening, without action, to free the slaves, he had caused their owners to take special precautions while most slaves saw no practical approach to freedom and much hazard of terrible punishment. In one estimate, eight hundred slaves rallied to Dunmore's banner.[29]

The gentry-led Virginians boiled up as Massachusetts's town militias had risen after Lexington and Concord. Every Virginia county armed and drilled its able-bodied men. An observer estimated that an army seven thousand strong could be raised at an instant's notice. Sharpshooters lined the banks opposite Dunmore's ships to prevent cannon from being used. An engagement took place in December at the Great Bridge spanning the river at Norfolk.[30] A participant called it "a second Bunker's Hill in miniature with this difference, that we kept our post and had only one man wounded in the hand."[31] As historian Ramsay delicately expressed it, "the Americans who had joined the king's standard, experienced the resentment of their countrymen."[32]

26 *Spirit of 'Seventy-Six*, ed. Commager and Morris, 110.   27 Ramsay, *History*, 1:232.

28 Christopher Ward, *The War of the Revolution*, 2 vols., ed. John Richard Alden (New York: Macmillan, 1952), 2:847.

29 Middlekauff, *Glorious Cause*, 556.   30 Ramsay, *History*, 1:231–32

31 *Spirit of 'Seventy-Six*, 112–14.   32 Ramsay, *History*, 1:234.

Dunmore's resentment was powerful, ruthless, and ultimately futile. His fleet reduced Norfolk to ashes.[33] It did not seem to concern him that Norfolk harbored more Loyalists than anywhere else in Virginia – until then. Dunmore had a sizable fleet at command but could not provision it or prevent disease from breaking out. He finally burnt some ships and sent thirty to forty off to Florida, Bermuda, and the West Indies. The "unhappy Africans" who had risen to Dunmore's bait "are said to have almost universally perished."[34] One must wonder how that happened. The gruesome probabilities reflect no credit on Virginia's high-minded aspirations. Nor to Dunmore's honor. Slaves who had taken refuge on his ships were "sent to Florida and the West Indies where 'a great number of negroes' were sold into slavery."[35]

Thus Virginia shared with Massachusetts the natural outrage of people attacked by their own governors. Virginia chased its governor away while General Howe still held Boston. It was natural for Virginians to feel euphoric about their power and success. They were ready to challenge the world.

But not without differences among themselves. In the overall context of reactions to Lord Dunmore's assaults, it is odd to notice that Thomas Jefferson "remained secluded" at his great estate of Monticello. Was it to guard his own slaves? Or perhaps rejection of the lead of firebrand Patrick Henry whom Jefferson would later call "avaritious and rotten hearted"?[36]

However that may have been, the expulsion of Lord Dunmore was none of Jefferson's doing. His surge to prominence was yet to come.

---

33 *Spirit of 'Seventy-Six*, 113–14.   34 Ramsay, *History*, 1:235.
35 Ward, *War of the Revolution*, 2:849.
36 Joseph J. Ellis, *American Sphinx: The Character of Thomas Jefferson* (New York: Alfred A. Knopf, 1997), 44–45, 38.

32

<hr/>

COMBAT: THE WESTERN THEATER, I

> The very integrity of the young Republic depended on the contest of the specu-
> lators. Consequently, a study of land speculation does not present an altogether
> flattering picture of the "Fathers" of the Revolutionary period.
>
>   Thomas Perkins Abernethy, *Western Lands and the American Revolution*

In the years just preceding the outbreak of the war for independence, the
frontier regions between British colonists and tribal Indians rocked in
turmoil. Theoretically, the crown had laid down a line between the peoples
by the Royal Proclamation of 1763 and the treaties to implement it, but no
authority existed to enforce the Proclamation line. Garrisons stationed in
western forts were withdrawn to control eastern urban rebels, and squatters
known as "settlers" rushed to occupy lands for which they had only the
most tenuous pretensions of right, when they had any at all. Deputy Superintendent George Croghan declared that in 1769 "there were between four
and five thousand, and all this spring and summer the roads have been lined
with wagons moving to the Ohio."[1]

This fever infected both sides in the Revolutionary conflict. Though the
crown made an effort to preserve "crown lands" for the Indians, it was
unable to prevent some of its own officials from the common rapacity. We
have seen how Governor Lord Dunmore launched war against the Shawnees
in 1773 to open their territory to immigrants from Virginia who would have
to buy from him. Mostly, however, crown officials acquired rights quietly
that they hoped to cash in when times became quieter. Thus, Superintendent Sir William Johnson and General Thomas Gage picked up nominal
large tracts of land but delayed "settling" them. The Revolutionaries,
however, were in a hurry.

In 1775, Daniel Boone founded Boonesboro (near Lexington) in Kentucky and disposed of more than a million acres in a few weeks.[2] Boone acted

---

1 Calloway, *American Revolution in Indian Country*, 22.   2 Ibid.

as advisor to North Carolina's Judge Richard Henderson in the infamous treaty of Sycamore Shoals (Elizabethtown, Tenn.), which was denounced by Supt. John Stuart and North Carolina's royal Governor Josiah Martin. In return for "a cabin full of trade goods," Henderson obtained paper right to twenty-seven thousand square miles. The Cherokees, whose land it was, charged fraud and forgery, and Chief Dragging Canoe stormed out of the meeting threatening retaliation. Colin G. Calloway observes that the transaction was "in defiance of royal proclamation and tribal law."[3]

Supt. Stuart was in a bind. He emphatically ordered the Cherokees to refrain from "indiscriminate attack upon the Provinces," demanding that they use force only to assist regular troops and Loyalists. But no regular troops were about, and Loyalists were not ready to march as an organized force. And if Stuart were to preserve any credit among the Cherokees, he had to provide them with ammunition. He tried to ride two horses going in different directions. He provided the Cherokees with twenty-one packhorse loads of munitions, and he sent an order to the invaders at Watauga, Nolichucky, and Holston to withdraw. They were amused. They fabricated the pretense of a copy of his order in which they made him seem to threaten tribal war, and they sent it to the Committee of Virginia's Fincastle County, which relayed it to the congress in Philadelphia.

Meantime, events were brewing elsewhere. In May 1776, a party of Shawnee, Delaware, and Mohawk Northerners came to urge general tribal defense of territory, to which end the Cherokees should start fighting. Impetuously, some Cherokee warriors launched raids in early summer, but without much effect. The invaders had anticipated them by erecting stockades within which they took refuge so casualties were small. As also anticipated, Congress organized war against the Cherokees. Instructions were given to Virginia, North Carolina, South Carolina, and Georgia to coordinate attacks on the Cherokees with two thousand men each.[4]

Repeated blows followed the standard pattern of destruction of tribal towns and farms. Decentralization of Cherokee government disabled defense despite delivery of munitions by Supt. Stuart. As James H. O'Donnell sums up, "Each village unit had to struggle for its own survival."[5] He adds:

> However one views Indian affairs in the south in 1776, the conflict with the Cherokee dominates. The results of the war were to break the power of a major Southern tribe . . . to discourage other tribes in the region from similar behavior . . . to discredit the British Indian officials in the eyes of both their charges and their superiors, and to hearten the Patriots trying to defend their cause on several fronts.

3 Ibid., 189–90; O'Donnell III, *The Cherokees of North Carolina*, 9.
4 Ibid., 18. 5 Ibid., 23.

There was another result. The efforts of Supt. Stuart to control Indian warriors as auxiliaries to regular troops gave way to encouragement of just the "indiscriminate" attacks he had tried to forestall. In October 1777, the Secretary at War, Lord George Germain, "instructed Stuart to send his charges against the settlements" and at Detroit, "Lt. Col. Hamilton was instructed to send the Shawnee against Pennsylvania and northwestern Virginia."[6]

6 James H. O'Donnell III, *Southern Indians in the American Revolution* (Knoxville: University of Tennessee Press, 1973), 61.

33

———— • ————

COMBAT: THE NORTHERN THEATER, I

The British crown's empire spread over worldwide territories that required constant administration even while North American continental colonies were in rebellion. Ministers preoccupied with other responsibilities gave the primary task of suppressing the rebellion to the American Secretary, Lord George Germain. In the loosely coordinated government, Germain "came closer than any other official to being the director of the American war."[1] Always remembering that "the King necessarily played an active and crucial role in Parliamentary affairs . . . the ministers who fashioned the controversial laws and policies from 1763 to 1776 were really *his* ministers. The King favored, even urged, the use of force against his American subjects after 1773."[2]

As historian Don Higginbotham comments, "Germain and company made their greatest effort in 1776: raising and sending to America the most imposing military expedition in English history, a feat never again equaled in the war."[3] Some time was required to assemble the pieces for this massive project. One might be pardoned for thinking that its target was New England since that was the region most strongly flouting imperial unity under royal and Parliamentary direction, but that assumption would be erroneous. After the expulsion of British troops from Boston, the region of New England became a backwater of armed combat. The crown's strategy was to cut it off from the other rebels, to which end campaigning was directed at the "middle" states – those of New York, New Jersey, and Pennsylvania – and it was there where ministers and their generals learned some complex facts of American life.

Germain's first target was New York.

New York's struggles during the Revolution were probably more complex than those of any other state. It contained the most Loyalists, the most

---

1 Higginbotham, *War of American Independence*, 142–43.   2 Ibid., 118.   3 Ibid., 149.

blacks (slave and free) of all the northern states, the most clashes of rich and poor, the heaviest participation of Indian tribes; and it was the scene of the most extensive and intensive armed combat. Its irregularly shaped geography was populated by varied ethnicities distributed regionally. It contained one of the Revolution's major cities as well as widespread lands cultivated by both freeholders and manorial tenants. Manifestly, such intricacies can be dealt with here only in the most general way.

New York had several traditions unique to itself. Its "warpath of nations" from Albany through Lakes George and Champlain had seen armies heading both ways for more than a century, and in the Seven Years War Albany had been chosen as the staging area for Britain's conquest of French Canada just as Congress used it to try to conquer British Quebec.

From early colonial times, Massachusetts's aggressive Puritans had plotted to invade the Hudson Valley and had been rebuffed by New Netherlands and New York. The defenders had clandestinely co-opted Indians; on another occasion, New York's allied Mohawks trounced the "Praying Indians" who had been launched against them by Massachusetts. First the Dutch and then New York's English governors had made allies of the Iroquois League and had expanded the alliance into the Covenant Chain. Governor Thomas Dongan tried to wrest the Indian trade of Great Lakes tribes away from French Canada and the trade of the Susquehanna and Delaware tribes from William Penn.

When the Hamptons communities of Long Island tried to affiliate to Connecticut in the seventeenth century, New York's Governor Edmund Andros took a troop of cavalry to convince them otherwise. When Andros tried to expand his jurisdiction to the Connecticut River, the Puritan trainbands of Connecticut reduced *his* valor to discretion. Not content with this much tumult, Yorkers engaged in the bitter civil war of Jacob Eisler's Rebellion which was ended only by royal intervention and a rope for Eisler. New York also became the birthplace of the Revolutionary Sons of Liberty.

In brief, New York was a cockpit of political and military struggle. Internally it saw uprisings (and suppressions) of tenant farmers against their manor lords. Black slaves tried to burn the city and were punished by the government's atrociously burning *them*. Very plainly, this province was an empire in embryo.[4]

At the onset of the Revolution, New York contended in the courts with New Hampshire for jurisdiction over a large territory where the inhabitants rejected both. These intervening Green Mountain Boys seized royal Fort Ticonderoga in the first military triumph of the Revolution. They dragged its cannon over winter ice to drive the British out of Boston, and Congress sent General Montgomery to conquer Montreal by way of Ticonderoga.

4 Cf. Edward Countryman, *A People in Revolution: The American Revolution and Political Society in New York, 1760–1790* (Baltimore, Md.: Johns Hopkins University Press, 1981) Part 1.

We have seen how Congress invaded Quebec and how its troops were defeated and driven back. That was not the end of the matter. Bolstered by reinforcements from Britain, Governor and General Guy Carleton launched a counterattack along the same waterways that had brought Montgomery to Montreal. Suddenly an issue arose that had not been foreseen by the Americans: Carleton might close off their retreat so as to trap thousands of men.

A new American commander, General John Sullivan, misunderstood the situation so badly that he led two thousand more Americans into an impossibly vulnerable position. He advanced against Carleton's staging area and numerically superior forces at Trois Rivières on the St. Lawrence north bank. Regardless of alibis, he was beaten with heavy loss and escaped entrapment only by Carleton's slowness in following up.[5] Sullivan's men, like the remnants of Benedict Arnold's expedition, could retreat only through the neck of the bottle, south from Montreal through the Richelieu River, Lake Champlain, and Lake George. (Arnold's troops were not going to try to retreat through Maine by the wilderness route of their advance – not after losing nearly half their force there before ever seeing the enemy.)

"Sea power" became critical. If Carleton could get unchallenged control of the waterways, he could spring his trap and the way would be open for attacks on the American forts at Crown Point and Ticonderoga. Carleton and Benedict Arnold both strove to create small navies. Arnold's four small ships based at Crown Point were described by his superior Major General Horatio Gates as unarmed "Floating Wagons." Arnold and Gates worked feverishly to build and arm more ships while Carleton delayed in order to dismantle a major warship on the St. Lawrence and reassemble it on the Richelieu River. When ready, his fleet started southward.

General Gates warned Arnold against taking "unnecessary risk." If Carleton's fleet proved to be superior, Arnold was to withdraw toward the protection of Ticonderoga's guns. As always, Arnold ignored orders in order to grasp at glory. He challenged Carleton's stronger vessels at Valcour Island, took a bad beating in which he lost most of his own boats, and barely escaped with a whole skin.[6] But he convinced a number of susceptible military historians (always overwhelmed by *audacity*) that he had somehow "saved" Ticonderoga by sacrificing his fleet. There is no end to the mastery by which generals win battles on paper.[7]

The winter of 1776 approached, and Carleton retreated to quarters in Canada after taking and abandoning Crown Point. He seems to have withheld decisive blows against the Americans on several occasions. Paul David

5 Paul David Nelson, "Guy Carleton Versus Benedict Arnold: The Campaign of 1776 in Canada and on Lake Champlain," *New York History* 57 (1976), 339–366; reprinted in *Patriots, Redcoats, and Loyalists*, ed. Onuf, 227–366; pp. 343–44(orig)/231–32(reprint).
6 Ibid., 359–60(orig.)/247–48(reprint).   7 Ibid., 356/244.

Nelson comments that Carleton seemed torn "between a policy of conciliation toward his enemies and harassing them mercilessly."[8] As we shall see, other British generals also suffered from this sort of ambivalence. They performed professionally, but lacked desire to crush the Americans. Their goal was to reunite the empire if at all possible.

Secretary Germain had other objectives. While Carleton turned aside the American invasion of Canada, Germain laid plans to suppress the rebels entirely.

Edward Countryman notes that "between 1775 and 1782 the claimants to power in New York were many. Besides politicians in office and voters out of it, these were militant royalists, Vermont separatists, and armed Indians, as well as the armies of three powers."[9]

In New York, as elsewhere, voluntary committees were at the heart of the Revolution, and these had a long tradition in New York. One had taken over government under Jacob Leisler in 1689, and in 1766 the Sons of Liberty became active. Conservatives had learned how to "roll with the punch" by invoking the need for unity as excuse for themselves joining the committees and influencing them toward moderation.

The fighting at Lexington and Concord multiplied committees and their members and stimulated them to assume new powers. Whereas in Pennsylvania the old provincial assembly had authorized armed Associations that became its own undoing, in New York the committees assumed policing responsibilities without formal authorization and went on to take over the militia. Linking up with the Continental Congress, the committees became a government parallel to the existing one, establishing, in Professor Coutryman's phrase, "a situation of dual power."[10]

Gentlemen accustomed to holding power observed watchfully. Until these outbreaks, Yorkers had been governed by competition between two great families and their supporters – the Livingstons and the DeLanceys. It is significant, I think, that the Revolutionary Livingstons were Presbyterians while the royalist DeLanceys were Anglicans. But great lords may join popular movements without succumbing to them. New York had no greater lord than Robert R. Livingston who believed in "the propriety of swimming with a Stream which it is impossible to stem." To direct the course of the torrent, he thought, conservatives should "yield" to it with "well timed delays, indefatigable industry, and a minute attention to every favourable circumstance."[11]

Their careful trimming enabled the Livingstons and other conservatives to withstand the worst ravages of the Revolution and even to maintain their

---

8 Ibid., 365/253.   9 Countryman, *People in Revolution*, 135.   10 Ibid., 146.   11 Ibid., 166.

great estates. When manorial tenants of Livingston in the upper Hudson Valley broke into revolt in the spring of 1777, they were suppressed and punished by Revolutionary militias![12]

There was a wild card in this game. New York and New Hampshire contended for jurisdiction over a strip of mountainous territory inhabited mostly by very energetic, very aggressive Green Mountain Boys. The crown had awarded their territory to New York, and speculating Yorkers had thrown property claims over vast areas; but most of the settlers had come from New Hampshire under original authority – the New Hampshire Grants – from that province. The men on the scene, no matter where they originated, were determined to have freehold farms in contrast to leases as tenants of the great Hudson Valley lords, and they had formed action committees as early as 1769.[13]

These very rugged individualists captured Ticonderoga in May 1775, upon which they were accepted in the militia of New York's provincial congress, but conflicting land titles strained that marriage of convenience, and it soon broke up. Vermonters declared their own independence at Windsor in January 1777. Under pressure from New York, the Continental Congress refused to admit Vermont as a fourteenth state, so its vigorous citizens adopted a constitution in July. They reasoned that since America had separated from Britain, "the Arbitrary Acts of the Crown are null and void," including New York's jurisdiction, so the people were free to set up whatever government they pleased.[14]

So was born the State of Vermont – a very prickly polity from that day to this.

As we shall see, New York was soon surrounded on all sides by rivals and enemies. For a brief time politics had to give way to more urgent concerns.

While still in Boston, General William Howe devised a strategy for "strangling" the rebellion in New England by cutting that region off from support elsewhere. This called for British advances from Canada and New York City meeting somewhere near Albany, after which Massachusetts could be invaded from the west while the navy supported another pincer action from Boston.[15] Forced to evacuate Boston, Howe had to adapt his plan, but the scheme to cut off New England survived with the help of General John Burgoyne who supplanted Carleton at the northern end.[16] General Howe and his admiral brother, Lord Richard Howe, undertook the capture of New

12 Countryman, *People in Revolution*, 151.   13 Ibid., 55.   14 Ibid., 157.
15 Ira D. Gruber, "Lord Howe and Lord George Germain: British Politics and the Winning of American Independence," *William and Mary Quarterly* 3d ser., 22:2(1965), 225–243; reprinted in *Patriots, Redcoats, and Loyalists*, ed. Onuf, 189–207; pp. 232(orig)/196(reprint).
16 Nelson, "Guy Carleton Versus Benedict Arnold," 364/252.

York City. Washington anticipated the move and set up brave but doomed defenses.

The British began to arrive, 25 June 1776, and were joined by ships and troops from Halifax and Britain, and even a small contingent that had failed to capture Charleston, South Carolina. Altogether the forces amounted to 325 ships and ten thousand seamen carrying thirty-two thousand "trained, disciplined, professional soldiers, completely armed, fully equipped, abundantly supplied." Against them the Americans had "19,000 largely untrained, undisciplined, untried amateur soldiers, poorly armed, meagerly equipped and supplied, led by an amateur commander in chief, who was supported by amateur officers. They were backed by not a single warship nor a single transport, and their war chest was in large part a printing press in Philadelphia emitting issues of paper dollars."[17]

The Howe brothers landed and set up camp on Staten Island from which they invited the Continental Congress to send commissioners to negotiate with royal counterparts about reconciling with crown and Parliament. Benjamin Franklin, John Adams, and Edward Rutledge took time off from their multitude of tasks in order to go through the motions of politely rejecting unacceptable proposals.[18] This done, the Howes set about taking New York, starting with Long Island. Whereupon they found that the odds were even heavier in their favor than they had thought because Washington trusted General John Sullivan to stop them. Acting true to form, Sullivan "guarded" Jamaica Road with five mounted militiamen. Howe marched ten thousand soldiers along that road, who appeared suddenly and disastrously behind Sullivan's position.[19]

Washington still tried to salvage some sort of defense on Long Island, but finally decided on necessary retreat across the East River to Manhattan. Without bogging down in details, we may note that the Americans had some assets not itemized in statistics. This was their own country. Despite the British navy's immensity, it could not do whatever it pleased because of American resources along river shores. Cannon onshore kept the British ships at a wary distance. Oared "galleys" with a cannon on each buzzed about like dangerous mosquitoes. Most serious hazard for the British was posed by the fireships ordered by Washington to be launched among the warships. While these distractions worried the British captains, Washington's agents collected all the rowing boats along the rivers, and in the dark of night he removed his entire, supposedly trapped army across to Manhattan.[20]

17 Christopher Ward, *War of the Revolution*, 1:209.
18 Higginbotham, *War of American Independence*, 159; *Spirit of 'Seventy-Six*, ed. Commager and Morris, 448–56.
19 Ward, *War of the Revolution*, 1:215; Chap. 17.
20 See William L. Calderhead, "British Naval Failure at Long Island," *New York History* 57(1976), 321–338; reprinted in *Patriots, Redcoats, and Loyalists*, ed. Onuf, 209–26.

One student comments that Washington "had snatched a beaten army from the very jaws of a victorious force, and practically under the nose of the greatest armada ever seen in American waters."[21] But it was an upside down sort of triumph, and many of the men so saved from capture were immediately lost to desertion. Of eight thousand Connecticut militiamen, six thousand went home. Yet, after consulting Congress, Washington tried to save the city.

To shorten the story, he failed in a series of battles, and the beaten, demoralized remnants of his troops soon were on the march across New Jersey. It was then that they demonstrated military assets that cannot be quantified except indirectly. "The Revolution," according to Robert Middlekauff, "killed a higher percentage of those who served on the American side than any war in our history, always excepting the Civil War."[22] Given such apparent odds, why did the men fight on?

Many of them did keep their places in line despite heavy casualties, desertions, and imploding morale. Their situation never became worse than during the long, weary retreat of the fragments across New Jersey. "These are the times that try men's souls," wrote Tom Paine on his laptop drum desk, and no one cared to dispute him. "It is the business of little minds to shrink; but he, whose heart is firm, and whose conscience approves his conduct, will pursue his principles unto death."[23]

Paine himself was one of the reasons men kept on fighting. He marched with the men and understood them. He gave voice to their stubborn determination never to give up. He told them what they were thinking but lacked words to say. "Say not that thousands are gone: turn out your tens of thousands."[24] He made a victory out of the retreat:

> It is great credit to us that, with a handful of men, we sustained an orderly retreat for near an hundred miles, brought off our ammunition, all our field pieces, the greatest part of our stores, and had four rivers to pass. . . . Our new army, at both ends of the continent, is recruiting fast; and we shall be able to open the next campaign with sixty thousand men, well armed and clothed.[25]

In his own person, Paine was worth a regiment to Washington.

This was possible only because of the fundamental difference between Britain's professional troops and the American citizen armies. The mercenary professionals were motivated by *esprit de corps*; the Americans by love of homeland. The difference is so indisputably plain that to note it seems

21 Ward, *War of the Revolution*, 1:238.
22 Robert Middlekauff, "Why Men Fought in the American Revolution, "*Huntington Library Quarterly* 43:2(1980), 135–48; reprinted in *Patriots, Redcoats, and Loyalists*, ed. Onuf, 1–16; pp. 135/1.
23 Paine, *Rights of Man*, ed. Mark Philp, 69.   24 Ibid.   25 Ibid., 70–71.

embarrassingly trite, but in that difference was generated the power that made independence a fact as well as a declaration.[26]

The Americans had another unquantifiable asset in the difference between the generals. Britain's General Howe held off from crushing the Americans when they were beaten. Besides advancing slowly on land, he ordered the navy to refrain from bombarding coastal towns which it could have done at will. Seemingly he still hoped that the rebels might be reconciled with the empire.

General Washington, however, fought "for keeps." When forced out of New York, he was ready to burn the town to prevent its becoming a British asset, but Congress ordered its preservation. No matter how Washington's troops might be harassed and punished, he intended to win the last battle. Even after the debacle of New York and New Jersey, he turned about in the dead hours of 26 December, knowing that Britain's hired Hessians had celebrated a German Christmas, and struck them at daybreak at Trenton, New Jersey. Between surprise and hangovers, the Hessians put up small resistance and surrendered 918 men. Four hundred more escaped past General Sullivan.[27]

General Cornwallis rushed with reinforcements, but Washington eluded him by retreating back across the Delaware River, swollen with ice. Then, contrary to expectations, he recrossed again to liberate New Jersey. Eluding Cornwallis, Washington struck at Princeton to inflict three hundred British casualties, with few losses of his own, and once more he escaped pursuers. The embarrassed and angry British fell back on New Brunswick to await better weather.

In terms of logistics and morale, Trenton and Princeton demonstrated greater victories than would appear from the numbers of men involved. British soldiers *cost* more than Americans. Those Hessians had been brought four thousand miles to Trenton. Replacing them would not be easy, and it would certainly be expensive. Washington's men came from their own homes in regions close by. Trenton demonstrated the fallacy of thinking that Britain's greater population and financial resources guaranteed victory over less numerous Americans. Decisions would be made by soldiers delivered to the arena. For Britain, reinforcements required immense effort and cost before they could be brought to the action. Washington, on the other hand, found "that an army of sorts could be assembled and concentrated with considerable speed . . . [and] could be used effectively before it melted away."[28]

---

26 A careful analysis is in Charles Royster, *A Revolutionary People at War: The Continental Army and American Character, 1775–1783* (Chapel Hill: University of North Carolina Press, 1979), Chap. 2.

27 Higginbotham, *War of American Independence*, 168.   28 Ibid., 166.

Although Washington yearned for opportunity and resources to defeat the British in showdown battle, a student may conceive the function of the Continental Army in a somewhat different manner that requires its own approach to statistics. In this alternative conception, the Continentals had to keep British forces busy while American militias enforced the powers and programs of independence by policing the countryside. British Regulars greatly outnumbered the Continentals but measured only a fraction of American militiamen. As long as the British had to give their attention to the Continentals, they could not hinder the Revolution's continuance anywhere except in spaces they actually occupied. And America was vast.[29]

At Trenton, Washington showed that he could face up to the empire's most massive military effort, could take a beating from it and still strike back. Congress responded by giving him temporary dictatorial powers to rebuild his army.[30]

29 Cf. Royster, *Revolutionary People at War*, Chap. 2.
30 Ward, *War of the Revolution*, 1:305.

34

=========== • ===========

COMBAT: THE NORTHERN THEATER, II

In the north, tribal Indians had lived for many decades in the middle of imperial competition and had been forced to come to terms somehow with the belligerent great powers. Ever since "King Philip's War," Puritan New England had made a specialty of alienating Indians. This seemed obliging to French officials in Canada whose counterspecialty became alliance with those Indians. Nonsensical "Frontier" theory has disregarded these plain facts with an imaginary "line between civilization and savagery." In reality, however, even if the propaganda terms are accepted in place of historical fact, the Indians of the northeast were caught *between* two civilizations, and the elimination of New France did not change the situation. It substituted the British crown and its Quebec Act for the French empire, whereupon Britain's rebellious colonies invaded Quebec. All of which made life precarious, to say the least, for intervening Indians.

As usual, the contending great powers demanded help from Indians and refused to allow neutrality; Indians who declined active alliance were regarded and treated as probable enemies.

In the territory roughly occupied by the modern states of Vermont and New Hampshire lived a number of loosely related Abenakis who "at all times shared the goal of preserving their community and keeping the war at arm's length. All they disagreed on was the means to that end." Abenakis primarily were hunters accustomed to moving about, and the kinship band structure of their society permitted dispersing in response to local danger with reconstitution at other localities. The British Indian Department tried to pin them down, not very successfully, at the mission town of Odanak (St. Francis) on the south bank of the St. Lawrence River, and New England colonials shoved northward as relentlessly as North Carolinians pushed westward. Abenakis could cope more flexibly than the more sedentary southern Indians, but perpetual reduction of living space imposed limitations on flexibility; and when General Montgomery campaigned northward through Abenaki territory, options dwindled. Some reluctant warriors joined him while others chose Canada's Governor Carleton. As we have seen, Montgomery was killed and Benedict Arnold was chased back southward. Abenaki options grew fewer yet.

Abenakis had to live from day to day in the midst of all the marching and countermarching, and marching men could not hunt. Apart from the woe caused by casualties, merely making a living grew harder and harder. Soon General John Burgoyne recruited Indians for his counterinvasion of the "Americans," but this must be reserved for a future chapter.[1]

Before the conquest of New France, French officials had exerted tremendous, omnipresent influence among Indians by way of Catholic missions and far-ranging traders. Through their own agents, officials dealt directly with every tribe, indeed, every village. This was not the British way. British officials sought to simplify their task by anointing one tribal agency as responsible spokesman for a wide range of clients called "tributaries." In 1677 an alliance system called the Covenant Chain had been forged with a core partnership of the Iroquois Five Nations and the province of New York.

Both systems of imperial management of Indian affairs were shaken up at the very beginning of the American Revolution. We have seen, above, that the governor of British Canada tried to control the Abenaki bands by concentrating them at Odanak (St. Francis), but that place had been operated as a Jesuit mission, and it lost much allure when British Protestants took it over without evident interest in religion. The Abenakis could remember, also, how Rogers's Rangers had attacked and desolated the place during the Seven Years War.[2] The Abenakis felt wary about allying to Britain even though they saw New England squatters seizing their territory farther south.

More important than the Abenakis, because affecting more people over a wider expanse of territory, was the shake up among the Iroquois. Their much cherished Covenant Chain had begun as an alliance with the governor of New York. In 1755 it was anchored directly to the British crown in the person of Superintendent of Indian Affairs William Johnson, soon to become Sir William. At the onset of the Revolution, Sir William's successor demanded their allegiance, but Protestant missionary and rebel Samuel Kirkland had gained a following among the Oneidas and Tuscaroras. The League of Iroquois nations was riven by dispute.

Lexington and Concord precipitated a crisis. The battles took place in

---

1 Calloway, *American Revolution in Indian Country*, 65, Chap. 2. For Abenaki social and cultural systems see Colin G. Calloway, *The Western Abenaki of Vermont, 1600–1800: War, Migration, and the Survival of an Indian People* (Norman: University of Oklahoma Press, 1990).
2 Jennings, *Empire of Fortune*, 199–200 and notes.

April 1775. Supt. Guy Johnson convoked a great congress of Indian nations in May (prudently at Fort Ontario in Canada). In June the Continental Congress organized an Indian department, and in July it appointed Indian commissioners for the northern department, among whom Major General Philip Schuyler assumed seniority. The Iroquois, like other Indians, really wanted to stay out of the war, for their long experience taught that they would lose, no matter which side won. Historian Barbara Graymont observes:

> Never at any time prior to 1777 would a whole tribe of the Iroquois Confederacy make a full commitment to join in the war. The lack of control of the Grand Council over the constituent members of the Confederacy, which had frequently plagued the Six Nations since the coming of the white man, would in these trying days prove to be one of the greatest impediments to the continued unity and welfare of the once-mighty League. The Iroquois Confederacy was to suffer the penalties both of too much democracy and too much dependence on the white man.[3]

Aware of American plans to invade Canada, Governor Carleton and Supt. Johnson summoned sixteen hundred Indian allies to Montreal to prepare for defense. Guy Johnson wanted to launch them in what today is called a "pre-emptive" strike, but Carleton demurred that "the innocent might have suffered with the guilty," and he insisted on holding the Indians back for defensive purposes only.[4]

This worry about Indians fighting their own kind of war had never bothered the French who saw Indian guerilla warfare as one of their major assets; but we have seen how Supt. Stuart in North Carolina tried to control Indian war as Carleton did in defense of Canada. The same concern animated the other side for the time being. Congress was explicit in a treaty message at Albany in August: "This is a family quarrel between us and Old England. You Indians are not concerned in it. We don't wish you to take up the hatchet against the King's troops. We desire you to remain at home, and not join on either side."[5]

It all sounds very gentlemanly until one realizes it was rather one-sided. When English colonials warred against Indians, plenty of evidence shows that they committed unspeakable atrocities certainly on a par with the war of the "savages." Only when the issue became Indians attacking Englishmen was the desire expressed to make war as humane as possible.

Notably, in terms of politics, Congress's admonition was delivered to Iroquois persons at *Albany* where the Covenant Chain underwent alteration once again as the ancient council fire that had moved to Supt. Johnson's

---

3 Barbara Graymont, *The Iroquois in the American Revolution* (Syracuse, N.Y.: Syracuse University Press, 1972), 66.
4 Ibid., 67.   5 Ibid., 72.

house in 1755 now was rekindled at Albany in 1775. But only for some Iroquois.

It is enough for present purposes to note that loyalties to opposite sides in the War of the Revolution pulled Iroquois nations and persons apart in dissent so sharp that their centuries-old League closed down. In January 1777, the great League council fire at Onondaga was "covered." The disaster was blamed on a devastating pestilence, but the League had survived earlier epidemics. Samuel Kirkland suspected a ruse to open the way for some Iroquois to join the British troops at Niagara. For whatever reasons, the Onondagas' announcement was unmistakably explicit: "There is no longer a Council Fire at the Capitol of Six Nations . . . the Central Council fire is extinguished."[6]

Thus, united action by the Iroquois nations ceased, and each tribe thereafter made its own decisions. Thus, also, the Covenant Chain of confederated allies perished, never to be revived except as a name. Officers of both the Congress and the British crown were forced, willy-nilly, to adopt the former French policy of direct negotiation with all tribes individually.

Never again would the Iroquois League be accepted as a great power in the contests between empires.

With the motive of aggressive expansion, the American rebels were as willing to seize land from each other as from Indians. The tradition was as old as the colonies. A government or an organized body of determined men attacked Indians allied to a different government claiming jurisdiction over the Indians' land. The attackers then assumed jurisdictional right to themselves by "rights of conquest" or simply took over the place by swordright without bothering about other legalities.

In an earlier book, *The Invasion of America*, I have shown how the Puritans of Massachusetts Bay and Connecticut tried to grab territory from Rhode Islanders as well as the Narragansett Indians. Maryland's Lord Baltimore went after the Indians on Delaware Bay to take that land away from New York.[7] As early as 1750, Virginians laid plans to seize the region that was to become Pennsylvania's Pittsburgh. A Connecticut partnership called the Susquehannah Company sent an agent to the 1754 Albany Congress to get phoney Indian "deeds" to the Wyoming Valley of Pennsylvania (the Susquehanna "North" or "East" Branch). Having acquired some pieces of paper for appearance's sake, the Susquehannah Company teamed up with the infamous Paxton Boys who had massacred helpless Conestoga Indians lower down the river.[8] The Company sent "settlers" from Connecticut who

---

6 Ibid., 113.   7 Jennings, *Ambiguous Iroquois Empire*, 136–38.
8 Anne M. Ousterhout, "Frontier Vengeance: Connecticut Yankees vs. Pennamites in the Wyoming Valley," *Pennsylvania History* 62 (Summer 1995), 343.

assassinated Delaware Chief Teedyuscung and drove away his people in order to clear the site for "settlement."

Teedyuscung and his people had first been driven from their home in the Delaware Valley by the Proprietary Penns' "walking purchase"; had briefly warred against Pennsylvania and New Jersey during the Seven Years War; had made peace when presented with the Wyoming Valley for residence, by the province and their "uncles" the Iroquois; and had made their homes in cabins built for them by Philadelphia Quakers. The Connecticut invaders were stout Revolutionaries who named their town Wilkes-Barré in tribute to resistance leaders in the British Parliament. They armed for battle against Pennsylvania in the "Pennamite Wars."[9]

9 For Teedyuscung, see A. F. C. Wallace, *King of the Delawares: Teedyuscung, 1700–1763*; Paul A. W. Wallace, Indians in Pennsylvania (Harrisburg: Pennsylvania Historical and Museum Commission, 1961; Jennings, *Empire of Fortune*, passim. The Susquehannah Company is treated briefly in Jack M. Sosin, *Revolutionary Frontier*, 54–55; documentation is in *The Susque-hannah Company Papers*, 11 vols., ed. Julian Parks Boyd and Robert J. Taylor. Teedyuscung's village location is on Map 9, in *Atlas of Great Lakes Indian History*, ed. Helen Hornbeck Tanner et al. (Norman: University of Oklahoma Press, 1987). Robert Middlekauff notices that Connecticut's Sons of Liberty were "eager to maintain the claims of the Susquehannah Company," *Glorious Cause*, 141; and Gordon S. Wood, *Radicalism of the American Revolution*, 127, remarks that in 1774, Connecticut tried to annex Wyoming to one of its counties. Neither mentions Indians.)

35

SARATOGA

The year 1777 was dominated by two major British campaigns. British generals and Secretary Germain picked up Howe's old scheme of isolating New England by a march from Canada southward along the "warpath of nations," but with significant alterations. "Gentleman Johnny" Burgoyne was to command instead of Canada's Governor Carleton, and Burgoyne was to do it without help from Howe in New York City. Howe's original plan to go up the Hudson River to join forces with Burgoyne was dropped.[1] Indeed, Howe took on a quite different task – to take the rebel capital at Philadelphia. The two campaigns proceeded at the same time; however, for the sake of clarity, let us take them in order, Howe first.

Having been hurt by Washington in 1776, Howe petitioned for reinforcements from Britain. They were denied because the financial shoe was already beginning to pinch. Worried about resistance in New Jersey, Howe changed strategy to take advantage of his brother's great fleet. Transporting eleven thousand troops from New York via Cape Charles, he sailed to the head of Chesapeake Bay. From there, Howe and General Cornwallis marched to Brandywine Creek, engaged Washington's defenders, and had the good fortune to encounter General John Sullivan. Just as on Long Island, Sullivan deployed against the enemy where they were not and was surprised by them where they were. Again there was disaster.[2] Washington demonstrated once more his skill at keeping his army intact after defeat.

Howe outmaneuvered Washington and got between him and Philadelphia. Congress fled to Lancaster, and General Cornwallis marched into the city, 26 September 1777. Washington challenged with an attack on the British camp at Germantown (now part of Philadelphia) but fog caused his troops to fire on each other, and Washington had to retreat again. Don

---

1 Higginbotham, *War of American Independence*, 176–79.
2 Ward, *War of the Revolution*, 1:344–51.

Higginbotham takes cold comfort: "If the Continentals still had not worsted the enemy in formal combat, they made his victories highly expensive."[3]

After that, the best Washington could do was to cut off supplies from the countryside to Philadelphia so that food and gear had to be brought up the Delaware to the occupying troops. But in their winter quarters they enjoyed the comforts and amusements of the empire's second city, the first in America. Washington and his men wintered twenty-five miles off in cheerless Valley Forge where their "comforts" were provided by themselves and their chief amusement was close order drill under a Prussian master.[4]

General Burgoyne persuaded George III in personal argument that the thrust south from Canada would be advantageous, so Secretary Germain gave orders to Governor Carleton to provide troops. Carleton was to reserve thirty-seven hundred men for defense of Canada and to put Burgoyne at the head of seven thousand more. Lt. Col. Barry St. Leger was to bring an auxiliary force from the west, consisting of Indians (besides those with Burgoyne himself), Canadians, and American Loyalists. As Burgoyne pushed south, St. Leger's force was to march eastward through the Mohawk Valley from Oswego with the intention of joining Burgoyne at or near Albany. Complications set in at once, especially concerning the Indians.

Secretary Germain understood that management of Indian warriors required a specialist. In 1776, three men with proper backgrounds were in London: Guy Johnson, who had succeeded his uncle as superintendent of Indian affairs; Mohawk chief Joseph Brant who was Sir William Johnson's brother-in-law; and Daniel Claus who had been Indian agent in the Province of Quebec for fifteen years. These three servants of the crown were unsurpassed in expertise but not wholly harmonious among themselves.

Johnson and Brant returned to New York early in 1776 with a mission to win tribal support. Ordinarily they could have gained all the Iroquois Six Nations by a treaty at Onondaga's central council fire, but they discovered that the Iroquois League's fire had been "covered." The Onondagas blamed a devastating epidemic. "The Council Fire is extinguished," they informed, "and can no longer burn."[5] Events were to suggest that irreconcilable differences among the Iroquois tribal nations had been at least part of the reasons for the council fire's extinction.

Thus, when Burgoyne and St. Leger set off on their expeditions, they needed to recruit tribes individually. Burgoyne could get them from Canada, but St. Leger would have to approach the Iroquois and their associated

3 Higginbotham, *War of American Independence*, 187.
4 Donald Barr Chidsey, *Valley Forge* (New York: Crown Publishers, 1959).
5 Graymont, *Iroquois in the American Revolution*, 113.

Covenant Chain tribes, and both the Iroquois League and its Chain were dispersed. Nor was there any avid enthusiasm by Indians to get into this "white man's war." Indians generally, like Quakers, wanted to be neutral in a war that was certain to be ruinous for themselves no matter which side won. The crown's agents resorted to subterfuge. Warriors from distant Detroit were told only to come to a council, then were flooded with rum. By whatever means, warriors were recruited and started off against American Fort Stanwix, 26 July 1777.[6] Against seven hundred Americans in the fortress, St. Leger's attackers added up to fourteen hundred all told, of whom three hundred were British and Hessian soldiers, six to eight hundred Indians, and five hundred Loyalists.

An American relief party of a thousand militiamen under General Nicholas Herkimer was ambushed at Oriskany dreadfully with five hundred casualties. A foray from Fort Stanwix alarmed the British so that they retreated from the field. Both sides claimed victory, but casualties made the American claim seem hollow. Nevertheless, defenders of the fort held on to it, and besiegers continued to attack.

What is just as important about the battle of Oriskany was the fighting of Iroquois Senecas on the British side against Iroquois Oneidas with the Americans. The Oneidas and some Tuscaroras had been converted to Christianity by Presbyterian minister Samuel Kirkland who was strong for independence.[7] Against them, Mohawk Christians had Anglican John Stuart as their missionary.[8] Later, Oneidas and Mohawks revenged themselves by burning each other's homes and crops.[9]

Toward the end of August, General Benedict Arnold lifted the siege by a ruse. He sent agents into St. Leger's camp with lurid accounts of his huge (and imaginary) relief expedition on its way. The besiegers panicked and fled so precipitately that "rowdy Indians . . . turned against the straggling white soldiers they came across in the woods, beating and stabbing them, so that meeting with their Indian allies became a more threatening prospect for the retreating British army than encountering the enemy they were fleeing."[10]

So St. Leger's expedition never joined Burgoyne, whose main body, consisting of about seven thousand men, could ill afford loss of St. Leger's approximately fourteen hundred reinforcements.

Probably the campaign suffered even more from its commander's vanity. Burgoyne issued a proclamation intended to frighten the rebel Americans. About this, historian Christopher Ward was aghast at "Burgoyne the dramatist at his worst, at his almost unbelievable worst. It is difficult for one

6 Ibid., 126.   7 Calloway, *American Revolution in Indian Country*, 115.
8 Graymont, *Iroquois in the American Revolution*, 148–49.
9 Calloway, *American Revolution in Indian Country*, 34.
10 Graymont, *Iroquois in the American Revolution*, 144–45.

reading it now to realize it is not a parody of some less bombastic manifesto."[11]

While it seems likely that most generals have delusions of grandeur, reality is apt to catch up with more or less serious effect, depending to some extent on luck. For Burgoyne, luck was busy elsewhere.

He set off in mid-June from St. John's on the Richelieu River with his conglomerate army of Britons, Hessians, Canadians, Loyalists, and four hundred Indians, arriving impressively at Ticonderoga on the twenty-sixth. They certainly made an impression on defending General Arthur St. Clair, who made only the briefest effort at resistance before evacuating the fort secretly at night. Three of his regiments marched overland toward Skenesboro but were caught en route and bloodily defeated, losing half their men to death and capture. Those who fled by boat fared no better. Burgoyne's boats pursued and routed them at Skenesboro.[12]

The auspicious ease of these victories was highly deceptive. Quite apart from combat, three weeks of hard labor lay ahead of Burgoyne's men before they could reach Fort Edward at the head of the Hudson River. It was only twenty-three miles off, but they were not ordinary miles. American General Philip Schuyler set thousands of men felling trees across traces of path hardly passable in their natural state. Both sides fought the forests, Schuyler bringing the trees down, Burgoyne clearing them out of his way. In effect, the forest fought back; it cost Burgoyne time, but it also cost Schuyler men as troops demoralized by the easy surrender of Ticonderoga took to their heels. Desertion, as Christopher Ward remarks, "became an epidemic." Of Schuyler's four thousand men remaining on duty, "fully a third were Negroes, boys, or old men."[13]

Burgoyne worried about the delay as it consumed his provisions. He knew from a letter that General Howe would not be coming to join him, and he began to realize that St. Leger's reinforcements also would not appear. Badgered by Hessian Baron von Riedesel to find horses for his dismounted dragoons, and needing replenishments of food, Burgoyne launched a requisitioning party eastward into Vermont, which had just declared itself an independent state. To Vermont's appeal for help, New Hampshire responded with fifteen hundred volunteers and the veteran campaigner John Stark. While Burgoyne's men marched east into Vermont, Stark's marched west. There were complications.

Was there ever an uncomplicated episode in the entire American Revolution? Cantankerous Stark had specified he would not serve under the patrician General Schuyler, so when Schuyler sent orders to bring the New Hampshire brigade to his command, Stark's rejection was short and sharp.

11 Ward, *War of the Revolution*, 1:404.   12 Ibid., 1: Chap. 36.   13 Ibid., 1:421.

On the other side, Burgoyne's commander, Frederick Baum, had trouble because his Indians' looting and destruction scared Vermonters into running off with the livestock that Baum wanted to plunder for himself. Complications and all, the forces converged in Bennington.

The odds changed. Vermont militiamen and Stockbridge Indians joined Stark as well as a party from western Massachusetts. With a total of two thousand men, Stark faced Baum's eight hundred (which included ninety Loyalists). They battled in the rain that made many guns impossible to fire. In heavy, confusing fighting, Baum's men ran out of ammunition, he was killed, and his troops fled. Burgoyne rushed reinforcements that arrived tardily next day, and more Vermonters arrived against them. Though fighting was fierce, the end of it was unambiguous. Two hundred seven Germans died, and about seven hundred were taken prisoner. American casualties were thirty killed and forty wounded.

Congress voted thanks to Stark and appointed him a brigadier general in the Continental army. Philip Schuyler was not going to lord it over him.[14]

Bennington reduced Burgoyne's troops to about six thousand. The worst was yet to come.

Two new events sealed Burgoyne's doom. One concerned the command of Americans. Don Higginbotham observes that both General Philip Schuyler and General Horatio Gates "were politically oriented, and lobbied with Congress with as much enthusiasm as they ever devoted to stopping the enemy."[15] Schuyler was pompous and overbearing and disliked by New Englanders; Gates was no Napoleon, but New England liked him. Congress put Gates in command after Schuyler's retreats lost his political support.

A different sort of event aroused the countryside in fury, and never was history more ironic. Burgoyne's Indians killed young Jane McCrea who had come toward his army in order to meet her Loyalist lover among the troops. In customary fashion, the Indians took her scalp with its long tresses to show off in Burgoyne's camp. He was sick and outraged, but he could not punish the killers without losing all his Indians. He lost them anyway because he admonished them and tried to restrict them to fight less atrociously. But they were fighting for scalps, not for the glory of King George. They counseled and went home. Burgoyne was left with only eighty of his original five hundred.[16]

General Gates saw opportunity in the episode. "The miserable fate of Miss McCrea" he wrote to Burgoyne (and circulated his letter far and wide), "was partly aggravated by her being dressed to receive her promised husband; but met her murderers employed by you."[17] Miss McCrea was

---

14 Ibid., 1: Chap. 37.   15 Higginbotham, *War of American Independence*, 189.
16 Ward, *War of the Revolution*, 2:501.   17 Ibid., 2:496–97.

celebrated as a martyr, and the militias boiled up "with such wrath as had not filled their bosoms since the day when all New England had rushed to besiege the enemy in Boston."[18]

With all deference to the spirit of aroused chivalry, Gates's army had assets more effective than tribute to martyred Jane McCrea. He had arms, ammunition, even cannon that were delivered by courtesy of commissioner Benjamin Franklin in France, working by subterfuge with playwright Caron de Beaumarchais as secret agent for the French court. Through the false front of Hortalez et Compagnie, "the arms and ammunition that stopped Burgoyne at Saratoga originally came from French arsenals."[19] Washington's enemies overlooked this small matter as they contrasted his defeats to Gates's great victory. They failed to balance French supplies in the north against Washington's desperate, repeated pleas for arms, food, even shoes for his men. Nor could John Adams, consumed with spiteful envy, permit himself more than carping at Franklin.

Armchair generalship is not my intention. Details have been given so far in order to demonstrate the complexity and confusion inseparable from Burgoyne's advance and American resistance. This done, we may omit further detail and skip to the grand climax. Burgoyne struggled down the Hudson to Saratoga – he never reached Albany – and he surrendered his entire army on 17 October. The soldiers were kept as prisoners of war until war's end.[20] Some of the Hessians stayed permanently. They decided to be their own men in America rather than the duke's pawns in Germany; and, because their origin was European and their skin color acceptable, these enemy soldiers faced a happier future in a higher social caste than native American Indians or natives whose origin was Africa. In real history, as distinguished from fairy tales, there is no end of irony.

The capture of so many soldiers was the least part of American victory at Saratoga. Benjamin Franklin, who had been playing on French desires for revenge of their losses in the Seven Years War, had obtained secret subsidies from the crown and had shipped quantities of uniforms and munitions to the American armies. More than 90 percent of much-needed American gunpowder came from France.[21] Saratoga persuaded the French that Britain could be beaten, and France declared war in 1778. Suddenly the Americans would have a great navy on their side and the promise of regiments of highly

---

18 Ibid., 2:498.
19 Richard N. Rosenfeld, writer and compiler, *American Aurora: A Democratic-Republican Returns* (New York: St. Martin's Press, 1997), 338.
20 Higginbotham, *War of American Independence*, 179.
21 Orlando W. Stephenson, "The Supply of Gunpowder in 1776," *American Historical Review* 30 (1924–25), 277–81.

trained professional soldiers. George Washington would know what to do with such assets.

At the moment, however, they seemed like castles in the air.

There are romantic writers who attribute victory at Saratoga to the spectacular heroics on the field of Benedict Arnold. This notion overlooks much. Allowing full credit to Arnold for personal bravery and improvisation under fire, both of these were much in evidence earlier during his siege of Quebec (which he lost). At Saratoga, however, the Americans outnumbered the British more than two to one and were well armed, courtesy of France. One must spare some recognition also for the Oneida warriors whose gallantry at Oriskany prevented St. Leger from bringing reinforcements to Burgoyne. These facts far outweigh Arnold's theatrics.

Perhaps one might also consider General Burgoyne's pursuit of personal glory, which led him to so many wrong decisoins. In battle as in chess, the game depends on bad moves by one's opponents.

Burgoyne's surrender cheered Washington's troops, who had lost their country's capital and had to winter in bleak Valley Forge. The beautifully kept park there now must be supplemented by the eye of memory to give a picture of the hardships that included scanty and irregular rations because the British army had previously foraged through the rich surrounding countryside. An oral tradition of the Oneida Indians claims that they brought supplies of corn to the hungry soldiers. I have tried, without success, to track it to some written source, but can only say that Oneidas fighting for the Americans at Oriskany entitles them to some benefit of doubt.

Maundering about Washington sharing the hardships of his troops deserves nothing better than contempt. In reality, he lived in a solid Pennsylvania stone farmhouse (still standing) with all the comforts of the day, and his wife moved in with him.[22] His men built huts for themselves with what wood they could salvage, such as fence rails. Replicas still on show (and likely greatly improved over the haphazard originals) make it clear that those huts had no insulation against the bitter cold and were barely big enough for occupants to stand up and turn around. Washington and his officers rode their horses through snow and mud; the men slogged through on foot, not always shod. It is perfectly proper to recognize that Washington could not have performed his leadership functions if he had been subject to the same handicaps as his men, but let us please avoid slop. Those marvelously enduring men deserve tribute in their own right.

They learned the technical side of soldiering from "Baron" von Steuben who was a liar and poseur of the first order, but also a first-class teacher.

---

22 Chidsey, *Valley Forge*, 108.

(Who ever said that "those who can't, teach"?) It was a treat for the men just to hear him swear in French and German with an occasional *goddam* thrown in. They understood *his* meaning if not the dictionary's, and they watched carefully as he demonstrated the right way to handle a musket. With Washington's backing, Steuben made the officers drill the men in person instead of contemptuously shuffling the task onto noncoms. And we may note that he cut down – though he could not eliminate completely – the number of "batmen" servants – private soldiers required to do menial chores for officers of all grades. Steuben was outraged by men skipping drill in order to polish officers' boots.

As a democratic army, it lacked something, but even Steuben wrote to a friend, "You say to your soldier, 'Do this' and he doeth it; but I am obliged to say 'This is the reason why you ought to do that'; and then he does it." It is one of the more inspiring messages of the Revolution, but a cynic may wonder how many officers gave reasons for batmen to black their boots.[23]

For those who survived that awful winter, the spring months of 1778 brought three uplifting changes. The shad came up the Delaware and Schuylkill Rivers in their millions, and the men gorged on them. (That would be impossible in today's polluted waters that reduce shad to a rare delicacy.) The dogwood trees burst suddenly and sublimely into bloom. (Even today, Frenchmen cannot comprehend American tourists leaving the delights of Paris when dogwoods have come into bloom. Try driving the Colonial Parkway between Williamsburg and Yorktown during the season's enchantment.) And news arrived that France had joined the war, openly and officially. New hope was in the air.[24]

23 Ibid., Chap. 25; quote on 116; 122–24.   24 Ibid., Chap. 30.

36

COMBAT: THE WESTERN THEATER, II

General Howe and the British army enjoyed themselves in Philadelphia as empire-loving Loyalists became sociable. (I distinguish this kind from Quakers and pietists who were loyal to religious principles.) The rich Allen family, Old-Light Presbyterians and longtime supporters of the Proprietary Penns, emerged as overt enemies of the Revolution; and Anglican Joseph Galloway policed civilians for the occupying British besides organizing spying operations.[1] When General Howe was recalled to England, his officers gave an elaborate farewell ball for him, the Mischianza, in which they had full cooperation from plenty of attractive young Philadelphians fluttered by fancy uniforms. Congress, as aforementioned, decamped to Lancaster and disgruntlement.

But the affair at Saratoga outweighed the Mischianza, so Philadelphia had to be abandoned as General Clinton led his troops back across New Jersey to concentrate the forces in New York. Washington harried but was unable to disable them.

Again there is reason to notice that this was eighteenth-century war, as polite as war can get, for Clinton left Philadelphia intact instead of burning the city in the total-war fashion of other eras. (Maybe the belles of the ball softened military hearts?) Even so, British historian Hugh Edward Egerton remarked, "The excesses and depredations of the British and Hessian troops disgusted men of all parties."[2]

Many Loyalists doubted how comfortable the city would be for them without protectors, so they boarded British ships for New York, some to go on beyond to Halifax or London. Galloway went to London where he cursed Franklin as the fomenter of Revolution and collected five hundred pounds per year from the crown.[3]

---

1 *The Royal Commission on . . . American Loyalists, 1783 to 1785*, 85.
2 "Introduction," ibid., xxi.   3 Ibid., 86; Newcomb, *Franklin and Galloway*, 289.

While Howe marched to Philadelphia and Burgoyne lunged toward Saratoga, Secretary Germain planned a third offensive in the West. To call it *British* is stretching language a bit, as its executors were intended to be Indian warriors directed out of Detroit by Lt. Col. Henry Hamilton, known notoriously to Americans as "the hair buyer."[4]

In some respects, the situation was a repetition of the Seven Years War, with British officers replacing Frenchmen engaged in the same strategy that the French had called *beaucoup de ravages*; but the former Fort Duquesne under French control had become Fort Pitt in American hands. Indians were ready to take sides against those Americans because tribal territories were at stake and the Detroit British supported Indian defense of their homelands.

It speaks much about Revolutionary rhetoric that the same forces fighting to govern themselves in their own lands intended to seize Indian lands by armed force and to force freeborn Indians into subjection or exile. That fact had been driven home by Daniel Boone and the "settlers" of "Transylvania," Kentucky, and even more brutally by the massacre of the family of Logan the Mingo – a *friendly* Indian until that moment. "Then I thought I must kill too; and I have been three times to war since." This "friend of white men" was left with "not a drop of my blood in the veins of any living creature."[5]

As Fort Pitt had been Virginia's base under Lord Dunmore for depredations into Indian country, it became the Continental Congress's base of operations against Detroit. Virginians played a notable role in what happened there. Virginia's commissioners, Andrew and Thomas Lewis, recommended an expedition against Detroit, and Congress approved it, 2 May 1778.[6] Their logic was clear and simple: strike down the British organizing center and Indian hostilities would fall apart. However, the resources for this strategy were not as clear as the logic. The Virginians had recommended four regiments; Congress settled for two regiments of militiamen.

A political problem obtruded also. Though Virginians under Lord Dunmore had seized Fort Pitt, the place was claimed under charter right by Pennsylvania. To rise above this domestic issue, Congress decreed that its two regiments should consist of Virginians *and* Pennsylvanians, thus to eliminate "rights of conquest." Less innocently, the scales were weighted by the Virginia commander in chief who had immense claims to property where the expedition was to march. The generals of the Revolution were all up to their necks in politics, so it does not surprise that George

---

4 Ward, *War of the Revolution*, 2:256.
5 Jefferson, *Notes on the State of Virginia*, 232, 63. See Jennings, "Logan, James (c. 1725–1780), Mingo Indian," in *American National Biography* (New York: Oxford University Press, 1998).
6 Harvey H. Jackson, *Lachlan McIntosh and the Politics of Revolutionary Georgia* (Athens: University of Georgia Press, 1979), 74.

Washington chose Georgian Lachlan McIntosh to command, and McIntosh kept true to form.

McIntosh immediately reversed Fort Pitt's policy in Indian affairs. Pennsylvania's agent George Morgan (not a *commissioner*) had striven with the Delaware Indians to keep them neutral. They were the single large tribe still maintaining friendship with the United States, and as tribal "grandfathers" they were paid ceremonial deference. Virginia's commissioners recommended entangling them in military alliance, and McIntosh summoned Delaware chiefs to a treaty on 17 September.

Pennsylvania's George Morgan, the man most experienced in Indian affairs, was not there, and he denounced the treaty later: "There never was a Conference with the Indians so improperly or villainously conducted." Historian Randolph C. Downes judged the comment "quite correct."[7] The Indians were headed by White Eyes, The Pipe, and John Killbuck who signed the treaty as did Virginia's commissioners Andrew and Thomas Lewis. No Pennsylvanian signed even as an observer, raising a question about the circumstances under which this treaty was held.

According to historian Downes, "The Indians had no understanding of the fact that the treaty was one of alliance . . . the articles were misrepresented to the tribesmen . . . they did not know that in signing it they were 'accepting the war belt' as they termed it." Four months later, Chief John Kill Buck commented that the treaty articles "are wrote down false."[8]

There was special bait in Article VI, a vaguely worded pretense at a promise: "Should it for the future be found conducive for the mutual interest of both parties to invite any other tribes who have been friends to the interest of the United States, to join the present confederation, *and to form a state whereof the Delaware nation shall be the head, and have a representation in Congress.*" Even this nonpromise was contingent on "the approbation of Congress."[9] General McIntosh's apologetic biographer noted that the consent of Congress was never obtained; "it is possible that neither McIntosh nor the American delegation [read "Virginians"] believed that it would be."[10]

In this situation, there is an interesting sidelight on the importance of the Delaware people. They have been underestimated because of a maneuver in 1742 by which Onondaga Chief Canasatego invented an Iroquois conquest over the Delawares and so "made women" of them. This fabrication has delighted many anthropologists, starting with Lewis Henry Morgan, because it seems so very *Indian* in culture. But Canasatego invented it

7 Randolph C. Downes, *Council Fires on the Upper Ohio: A Narrative of Indian Affairs in the Upper Ohio Valley Until 1795* (Pittsburgh, Pa.: University of Pittsburgh Press, 1940), 216.
8 Ibid., 216–17.
9 *Indian Affairs, Laws and Treaties*, ed. and comp., Charles J. Kappler. 2 vols. (1904); Vol. 2 reprinted as *Indian Treaties, 1778–1883* (New York: Interland Publishing, 1975), 1st doc. (italics added). 10 Jackson, *Lachlan McIntosh*, 79–80.

in behalf of Pennsylvania which put its power behind him. *That* was the Iroquois conquest.[11]

It is gradually becoming clear that the "grandfather" Delawares had been revered as mediators among the tribes (thus "women"). A Cayuga tradition is explicit that they functioned to make peace between Iroquoians and Algonquians.[12] A new, fiercely documented essay by Jon William Parmenter portrays the Delawares as independent and influential leaders among the western tribes during Pontiac's War preceding the American Revolution. It seems therefore that the proposal by Lachlan McIntosh to recommend an Indian state under Delaware leadership was a shrewd device to play on their self-conception of eminence.[13]

It quickly became evident that McIntosh's ragtag army could not even stagger as far as half way to Detroit, let alone capture the place. Congress changed his orders to "invade the Indian territory and destroy their towns."[14] The militiamen, all good frontier democrats, decided to start the destruction with the Indian closest to them. They murdered White Eyes who had been guiding them, "under circumstances that made it possible for him to be buried secretly" and blamed smallpox. "Thus was lost," wrote Mr. Downes, "one of the most trusting Indian friends the American people ever had."[15]

When McIntosh's half-starved, nearly naked troops reached Delaware headquarters on the Tuscarawas River, he delivered a pompous oration to the gathered Indians to assure them of his great power and immovable intention to punish any Indians who deviated from his orders. At which something happened that I have never seen reported in any other meeting of Indians and soldiers: The Delawares *laughed* at this bombastic ass![16]

Finding conquest not likely in the immediate future, McIntosh returned to get to the prizes of politics. The sorry garrison he left at his Delaware fort (Fort Laurens) was attacked by the "white Indian" Simon Girty, but Girty withdrew on news that another Virginia expedition, under George Rogers Clark, had taken the Anglo-French outpost at Vincennes in the Illinois country.

The original strategy for McIntosh's expedition, before reality dawned, had been to build a chain of stations through Indian country toward Detroit. McIntosh's utter military incompetence forced rethinking about trying to set up stations without resources to sustain them. Randolph C. Downes summarizes: "From this time until the end of the Revolution, the *United*

11 Jennings, *Ambiguous Iroquois Empire*, 343–45. 12 Ibid., 23–24.

13 Jon William Parmenter, "Pontiac's War: Forging New Links in the Anglo-Iroquois Covenant Chain, 1758–1766," *Ethnohistory* 44:4 (Fall 1977), 617–54; *Indian Affairs*, ed. Kappler, treaty dated 17 September 1778, 1, 1st doc., par. VI.

14 Jackson, *Lachlan McIntosh*, 80. 15 Downes, *Council Fires*, 216–17.

16 Calloway, *American Revolution in Indian Country*, 38.

States had to let the northwestern frontier take care of itself."[17] But this decision did not come until General McIntosh had let the political cat out of his bag. He told Pennsylvania's Vice-President George Bryan "that if the west were conquered by *Virginia* troops, Pennsylvania's claims in that area would be greatly weakened."[18]

In politics, McIntosh knew what he was about. His strong bias toward Virginia reflected his strong interests as a plantation slave owner. Those interests seemed threatened by persons advocating abolition of slavery. "Let us therefore," he wrote privately, "keep the proper time for it in our own power while we have it."[19] Not surprisingly, General Washington supported him staunchly against all critics. Against that combination, Pennsylvania's interests in conflict with Virginia's were invisible.

Christopher Ward's comment is apt: "Although there was no fighting in the old settled parts of Virginia after the departure of Lord Dunmore and his bobtail forces until the closing period of the war, there was much and bitter fighting upon lands west of the Appalachians owned, or at least claimed, by the Old Dominion."[20] We have seen how George Washington aimed the McIntosh gambit toward lands claimed by Washington. There were many other claims by Virginia gentry. The Old Dominion contained what was probably the country's greatest concentration of large-scale land speculators. As aggressive British noblemen had once schemed and lobbied for charters to colonies across the Atlantic, Virginians long aimed at vast properties across the Appalachians. They had triggered the Seven Years War with their activity in the West.[21] The Revolution opened the region to rights of conquest for their own state regardless of the interests of the United States, provided that Virginia made its own conquest. This was going to be expensive, and only a minority of Virginians were big dealers in land, so when Thomas Jefferson, George Mason, and Richard Henry Lee took Governor Patrick Henry into their plan, they had to persuade the assembly to authorize a campaign by a bit of double-talk. In public, they were sending George Rogers Clark to defend communities already made by the "Transylvania" invaders of Shawnee lands whom they newly legitimized as Virginia's Kentucky County.[22] Secretly, Clark was ordered to attack the British base at Kaskaskia on the Mississippi River and to go on to Detroit if feasible.[23]

Clark was a better choice than McIntosh had been. Though frontier response to his recruiting was minimal, and it diminished further when he

---

17 Downes, *Council Fires*, 227.   18 Jackson, *Lachlan McIntosh*, 90 (emphasis added).
19 Ibid., 146.   20 Ward, *War of the Revolution*, 2:850.
21 Jennings, *Empire of Fortune*, Chaps. 2–4.   22 Alden, *South in the Revolution*, 282.
23 Ward, *War of the Revolution*, 2:853–54.

told the truth about his objective, he took off down the Ohio from its Falls (today's Louisville) with 175 men. They left the river shortly beyond the mouth of its Tennessee River tributary and marched overland to avoid alarming the Kaskaskians. It had been a harrowing march, but Clark's men found the place undefended and took it without firing a shot.

From that base, Clark headed toward Vincennes on the Wabash River where complications developed. Detroit's Governor Hamilton marched there also and got there first. Resourceful Clark invented ruses to frighten off Hamilton's Indians and the French inhabitants of Vincennes, and he forced Hamilton and his Regular troops to capitulate. It was embarrassing! What was Clark to do with all those prisoners? Apparently he sent off a number on parole.

Yet, notwithstanding his victories, Clark was never able to muster resources to advance upon Detroit. But he had accomplished the land speculators' purpose.[24] Virginia now had its own claim to the transmontane West, distinct from those of the confederated American states.

Among some writers a racist notion seems to prevail that Indians were empty vessels waiting to have their heads filled with friendship or hostility by whatever Europeans had access to them. This is part of the description of Indians as subhuman "savages" unable to think for themselves. In this conception, British agents at Detroit and Niagara filled western Indians with hatred for the Revolution's *white* people. (It escapes notice that the British were also "whites.") With this sort of management the "savages" were launched to perpetrate their horrors in the backwoods.

This outlook is war propaganda written by victors. Indians were at least as rational, and much more reasonable, than other persons of their era. They acquired fierce hostility because the Americans were invading their homelands and evicting the occupants. When Shawnees attacked Kentuckians, the "settlers" had taken Shawnee homes and driven the Indians out. Western Delawares and Mingoes tried to hold the invaders east of the mountain rampart after having been forced west of it themselves. The British had no need to create hatred; the Americans were very busy themselves at that task. British agents needed only to provide arms and ammunition and a little advice about strategy. Indeed, remnants of evidence suggest strongly that British professional soldiers followed rules then current among military men for harming only male combatants while withholding severe punishment from women, children, and noncombatant old men. It is an odd reversal of positions in which the British adopted customs formerly held among eastern Indians.

24 Ibid., 855–62.

Frontier Revolutionaries, on the other hand, practiced total war against Indians. Their aim was not merely to win but to extirpate the Indians, to which end they used methods that had originated under Oliver Cromwell in Ireland and had been continued by the duke of Cumberland in Scotland's Highlands. Kill, burn, destroy. Take no prisoners. Leave no property intact, for "the only good Indian is a dead Indian." And the only acceptable land is land "free to be taken."

Writings about western fighting always stress the personal sadism of Indian warriors, but attribute frontiersmen's acts to rational strategy. Thus destruction of an Indian village and extermination of all its inhabitants is *necessary* elimination of a nest of savagery rather than the satisfaction of bloodlust. But both sides took scalps, both sides burnt cabins and crops, and both sides slaughtered whatever victims were unfortunate enough to be within reach. Frontiersmen's sadism is as much in evidence as the warriors'. *And*, it must never be forgotten, even for an instant, the frontiersmen were *invaders*, not merely "pioneers." The Indians had been the pioneers in this land. When all this is realized, one can begin to understand the fury of Indian resistance to the invaders, and why it continued not only for the duration of the American Revolution but well into open warfare against armies of the victorious new United States.

Kentucky and Ohio had been Shawnee country. Colin G. Calloway comments:

> For many Shawnees, the outbreak of the Revolution simply meant that one war merged into another and that the struggle against Virginian aggression would continue. . . . Cornstalk, Nimwha, Kishanosity, and other chiefs told the Virginians, "We are often inclined to believe there is no resting place for us and that your intentions were to deprive us entirely of our whole Country."[25]

As if to prove him right, militiamen later broke into a cabin where Cornstalk and three others were being held hostage, and murdered them all.[26] Not only the rabble had such attitudes. Calloway reports that "Thomas Jefferson wanted to see the Ohio Shawnees exterminated or driven from their lands."[27] The attitude was consistent with all of Jefferson's dealings with Indians.[28]

Among the other Indians in Ohio were towns of Delaware converts to the Moravian church who accepted pacifism as an essential part of their religion. These Christians had been persecuted ever since their conversion in the vicinity of Bethlehem, Pennsylvania. Contemptuous Delaware warriors killed some during the Seven Years War. Surrounding European immigrants

25 Calloway, *American Revolution in Indian Country*, 162–63.   26 Ibid., 167.
27 Ibid., 172.   28 Joseph J. Ellis, *American Sphinx*, 200–02.

conflated them with hostile warriors and threatened so fiercely that the provincial government evacuated them to Philadelphia – which is to say that they lost their lands. The ill-famed Paxton Boys rode into the city to massacre these Christian pacifists and incidentally to overthrow the provincial assembly. Missionary John Heckewelder has observed, "it soon became evident that they [the Paxton Boys] aimed at nothing short of overturning the whole form of government . . . and then to take the reins of government into their own hands."[29] It is an interesting disclosure of a substance behind the phrase *frontier democracy*.

The city mobilized in numbers intimidating to those Paxtonites. For the Delawares, however, their defense was far from glorious because they had been housed in the city's "pest house" where fifty-six died of smallpox.[30] More died of exposure and exhaustion as they wearily trudged toward hoped-for refuge in a roundabout trek to the west.[31] After years of marching and recuperating at temporary stops along the way, they arrived at the Tuscarawas River in Ohio where the countryside seemed heartbreakingly like the land of their rearing in Pennsylvania. Their Moravian missionaries accompanied them and shared their hardships.

One might think that these devout and exemplary Christians had suffered enough, but worse was to come. They built new communities at Gnadenhütten, Lichtenau, and Schönbrunn where for a brief interlude life became idyllic though "the frontier people of Virginia, living on the Ohio below Wheeling [where they had massacred Mingo James Logan's family] had . . . been in the habit of stealing the Indians' horses."[32]

Once again, the Christian Indians found themselves caught between enemies. British-allied warriors tried to capture the missionaries who upheld the Christians' determination to stay peaceful. But American militiamen decided that pacifism was just a mask for hidden support of hostile warriors. To be brief, a militia company came to Gnadenhütten, was hospitably received, then massacred ninety-six absolute, unresisting pacifists, making sure to pilfer their goods.

Upon hearing of the atrocity, warriors mobilized to retaliate. Upon learning this, "The Militia having in those parts no further Opportunity of murdering innocent People, and no Stomach to engage with Warriors set off home with their Horses and Plunder they had taken, and afterwards falling upon the Peaceable Indians on the North Side of the Allegheny River opposite Pittsburgh killed several of those."[33]

One might anticipate expressions of outrage from great leaders of the Revolution, but when George Washington heard of the Christians' martyr-

29 [John Heckewelder], *The Travels of John Heckewelder in Frontier America*, ed. Paul A. W. Wallace, reprint of *Thirty Thousand Miles with John Heckewelder* (1958) (Pittsburgh, Pa.: University of Pittsburgh Press, 1985), 80.
30 Ibid., 81. 31 Ibid., Chap. 6. 32 Ibid., 157. 33 Ibid., 197.

dom, he ordered only that no soldier "was to allow himself to be taken alive."[34] It must be conceded that Washington understood what to expect. A band of militiamen intending to plunder Upper Sandusky met warriors under Delaware Captain Pipe. The warriors won the battle and captured Colonel William Crawford who "made atonement."[35]

There is more detail in another source. Crawford was scalped alive, hot ashes put on his head, and then he was slowly roasted alive. British officers who had been trying to restrain their Indians were revolted but understood the atrocity's cause. General H. Watson Powell explained that the Delawares "were so closely connected with the Moravians that they must have taken this severe revenge in order to retaliate that massacre, as the conduct of the Indians upon the Ohio last year was so very different."[36]

In the summer of 1776, Virginians at Fort Pitt sent a request to New Orleans for help. Governor Luis de Unzaga y Amézaga responded cautiously so as to avoid protest from Britain. Through the merchant Oliver Pollock, Unzaga sent gunpowder from the king's stores. It was shipped up the Mississippi and Ohio Rivers, "just in time to save those posts [of Ft. Pitt and Wheeling] from falling into the hands of the British and Indians."[37]

When Ft. Pitt asked for more a year later, the new Acting Governor of Louisiana, Bernardo de Gálvez sent arms, ammunition, and *provisions!* In his first year as Acting Governor, Gálvez sent seventy thousand dollars worth. The supplies from New Orleans were essential to Virginia's western forays. They came back via Ft. Pitt to George Rogers Clark, whose exploits we have seen. Besides these, Gálvez's agent at St. Louis (San Luis) reported accepting and storing shipments of goods until George Rogers Clark should ask for them. Historian Katherine Wagner Seineke remarks that without the credit and goods from New Orleans, "Clark would have had a hard time to sustain his garrisons in the west."[38]

---

34 Ibid., 199.   35 Ibid.

36 Graymont, *Iroquois in the American Revolution*, 253. N.B. In this account, I have followed the report of a missionary who was denounced by that prince of liars, Francis Parkman. After sweating over Parkman's corrupt volumes of misinformation for about thirty years, and after making something like history out of his dime novels, I feel no need to condescend to his much-inflated and quite false reputation. I have documented his falsehoods in two articles berated but unanswered: "A Vanishing Indian: Francis Parkman Versus His Sources," *Pa. Mag. of Hist. and Biog.* 87:3 (1963), 306–23; and "Francis Parkman: A Brahmin Among Untouchables," *William and Mary Quarterly*, 3d ser., 42:3 (July 1985), 305–23. The honest reports of missionary John Heckewelder, trusted by experts of the American Philosophical Society, are confirmed from various other sources cited by Barbara Graymont and Colin G. Calloway (and myself). Parkman's idolators need to examine their consciences and their creed.

37 John Walton Caughey, *Bernardo de Gálvez in Louisiana, 1776–1783* (Berkeley: University of California Press, 1934), 86–87.

38 Ibid., 91–92; Katherine Wagner Seineke, *The George Rogers Clark Adventure in the Illinois, and Selected Documents*, with Introduction by Robert M. Sutton (New Orleans, La.: Polyanthos, 1981), 241, 96.

Indeed, Clark lost several small garrisons to counterattacks by British agents and Indians, especially those under the charismatic frontiersman Simon Girty. Clark's fortified major posts held out, but his only new advances were sweeps into Shawnee country to lay it waste.

In February 1778, a Philadelphia adventurer named James Willing started down the Ohio from Ft. Pitt with thirty men and picked up a hundred more eager for plunder. They attacked and looted British posts at Natchez and Manchac, and seized the brig *Neptune*. Continuing downstream to New Orleans, this irresponsible and uncontrollable gang became a headache for Gov. Gálvez. On 6 May 1778, Gálvez wrote to Virginia's Gov. Patrick Henry about the support he was giving "with money" to Willing's raiders, "although I am ignorant whether I will have the approval of my Court." Regardless of royal favor, "I shall not spare any effort or trouble that may redound to the benefit of those colonies because of the special affection that I have for them."[39]

Willing and his gang made problems, both because of their dissolute and expensive behavior and because of British protest.[40] Willing was not a lovable hero. His demands and depredations caused the bankruptcy of the real hero, merchant Oliver Pollock.[41]

Finally in the summer of 1779, Spain declared war and Gálvez was formally appointed Governor. He immediately took the offensive with a new campaign upriver against British posts along the lower Mississippi and captured them all, along with 550 regular soldiers, plus sailors and armed Negroes. A remarkable component of Gálvez's force was formed by militiamen who had been deported by Britain from their homeland of Acadia (Nova Scotia) in 1755. Historian Caughey said they "behaved splendidly" for Gálvez.[42] One can sense the satisfaction of these "Cajuns" at the new turn of events.

Confusion literally became thrice confounded. Charles Mouet de Langlade, a métis of mixed French-Ottawa parentage, had reconciled to British conquest of Canada and had taken office under the British.[43] In 1780 he led a force of French and Indians against Spanish St. Louis where the population was French. As Charles Balesi remarks, "In yet another instance, French were going to fight French under foreign flags."[44]

Menominee and Winnebago Indians were repelled by the defenders' cannon at St. Louis, and George Rogers Clark rushed to aid the militia at

39 Ibid., 241.   40 Caughey, *Bernardo de Gálvez*, Chap. 7.
41 Ibid., 133–34.   42 Ibid., 161, 163.
43 Paul Trap, "Mouet de Langlade, Charles-Michel" in *Dictionary of Canadian Biography*, 4:563–64.
44 Charles J. Balesi, *The Time of the French in the Heart of North America, 1673–1818* (Chicago: Alliance Française Chicago, 1992), 302.

Cahokia across the Mississippi. Balesi's understatement is more than justi-fied: "The whole region [was] in an extraordinary state of flux."[45]

In December 1780, Frenchmen from Cahokia raided British-controlled (but French-populated) Fort St. Joseph in Michigan and were beaten off by the French Lieutenant Dagneau de Quindre. Whereupon the Spanish com-mander at St. Louis sent a new expedition back to Fort St. Joseph in January 1781. This was led by French Captain Eugenio Pourré who commanded the St. Louis militia. The fort was captured and held for a day, but Spanish Gálvez emulated Virginian Clark with claims of conquest over the St. Joseph and Illinois Rivers.[46]

Only one thing is certain in this microcosmic welter of imperialisms. Whichever empire would come out victorious, the Indians would lose. Everybody, it seems, could claim Indian lands except the native people who lived on them.

Gálvez had his eye on bigger game. Striking quickly, he made British Mobile surrender on 14 March 1780.[47] A hurricane disrupted further plans, but he reorganized and took Pensacola, the capital of West Florida, 10 May 1781. His royal master gloated that the British thereby were expelled from all the coasts of the Gulf of Mexico.[48] Gálvez wanted to attack Jamaica also, but developments elsewhere eliminated his chance.

One might think that such a valuable ally would have rejoiced the Ameri-can rebels, but realism forbids such sentimentality. By rights of conquest, Clark and Gálvez claimed the Illinois River, and Virginia designated the region as its County of Illinois.[49] South Carolina was not content with Spanish conquest of Florida. Carolinians thought that Florida belonged to them.

As though such happenings lacked sufficient interest, still more com-plexity involved the Chickasaw and Choctaw nations of the lower Missis-sippi Valley. The incessant labors of Britain's southern superintendent of Indian affairs, John Stuart, had allied these two large tribes to patrol the river in opposition to "the King's Enemies."[50] Stuart died in 1779, and the Chick-asaws announced a policy on their own account. Having observed coopera-tion between Spanish officials and French colonists, they threatened retaliation. "We know what quarter to take Satisfaction in, for it is no new thing to us for We allways knew that the french bought our Hair till lately."[51]

They were very tough, these Chickasaws. When Virginia challenged

---

45 Ibid., 303.   46 Ward, *War of the Revolution*, 2:862.
47 Caughey, *Bernardo de Gálvez*, 182.   48 Ibid., 210–13.
49 Balesi, *Time of the French*, 300. (I owe special thanks to Helen Hornbeck Tanner for her coun-seling to investigate Spanish participation in the Revolution.)
50 Calloway, *American Revolution in Indian Country*, 225.   51 Ibid., Chap. 8; 225.

them to peace or destruction, the chiefs responded, "We are a Nation that fears or Values no Nation as long as our Great Father King George stands by us for you may depend as long as life lasts with us we will hold him fast by the Hand."[52] Thomas Jefferson dealt with that attitude. However sphinxlike he might be in other respects, his behavior toward Indians was always clear and consistent. He wanted to get rid of them. He ordered the building of Fort Jefferson below the junction of the Ohio with the Mississippi, and he tried to turn the Kickapoos against those obstinate Chickasaws. When Bernardo de Gálvez attacked Pensacola, Choctaws and Chickasaws rallied to its defense, but got little help there from their British allies. When the town capitulated to Gálvez in May 1781, the Indians – nearly eight hundred of them – returned home. Necessarily they began to rethink their alliance with Britain, and thought harder when the 1783 Peace of Paris resulted in British withdrawal from Chickasaw territory. What to do? Colin Calloway comments, "The Americans represented one source of trade and protection, but only one, and the advantages offered by American allegiance were always tempered by American land hunger."[53] Every American proposal included a demand for cession of territory that the Chickasaws refused to consider.

The Spaniards who had fought, like the Americans, against Britain had not thereby adopted American goals, and they offered alternative and competitive alliance to the Chickasaws. So long as Spain kept an active presence in the Mississippi Valley, the Chickasaws could play the familiar tribal game of pitting the empires against each other, but Spain's gradual retreat downstream after 1795 backed the tribe up against an American wall. In this new situation, American agents stopped the traditional diplomatic practice of seeking favor by gifts. Instead, they encouraged Chickasaws to run up debts at government trading posts (the old "company store" technique). "They will always cede lands," wrote Jefferson, "to rid themselves of debts." So they did, and as Calloway summarizes, "The United States proceeded to strip the Chickasaws of their ancient domain."[54]

No matter how loyally a tribe fulfilled the obligations of alliance, no matter how sturdily it stood to its arms, the great tide of Europe's landless peoples swept all before it. And the imperialists who prided themselves on their virtue behaved toward weaker indigenous peoples as brutally callously as expanding Europeans had during the Middle Ages.

52 Ibid., 226.   53 Ibid., 234.   54 Ibid., 242.

37

"WEST" IN THE MIDDLE

The North Branch of the Susquehanna River flows through the rich and beautiful Wyoming Valley that became the home of Chief Teedyuscung and his eastern band of Delawares as part of the peace settlement after the Seven Years War. Unhappily for those Indians, the valley was claimed by Connecticut as well as Pennsylvania and the Iroquois Six Nations. A "Susquehannah Company" was formed in Connecticut and drove out Pennsylvania's settlers in fighting that evolved into the "Pennamite Wars." In April 1763, arsonists fired all the Delaware cabins and murdered Chief Teedyuscung who lived there as an Iroquois guest. The other Indians fled to refuge in Canada, and the Susquehannah Company sent settlers to take over the valley. Paul A. W. Wallace remarks, "The evidence is persuasive that friends of the Susquehannah Company were at the bottom of this. Certainly it seemed so to Teedyuscung's son, John, who, with a band of Delaware warriors, swept to his revenge in that valley and killed or captured every white man found in it."[1]

Connecticut sent more settlers who built several communities that throve until they became targets during the American Revolution for the British Indian Department and its allied Iroquois Indians who claimed prior right to the valley. Led by Major John Butler and Seneca Chief Sayenqueraghta, an expeditionary force of 464 Iroquois and 110 British Rangers descended the Susquehanna in June 1778. They found that 800 able-bodied men defended the place from eight forts. Wintermoot's and Jenkins's forts were challenged and surrendered on terms that were honored, but Forty Fort chose to fight. In the subsequent battle, more than 300 Connecticut men died (Butler said 376). Other forts then surrendered on terms.

An unspecified number of persons were plundered of clothing and goods, and a thousand houses were burned besides the eight forts. The shocking event became known as the Wyoming Massacre with much

1 [Heckewelder], *Travels*, ed. Wallace, 446, 70; Jennings, *Empire of Fortune*, 434–37.

embroidery of imagination. Stripped of the war propaganda, it was not much different from what might have been expected in European warfare. Major Butler reported "with sincerest satisfaction . . . that I can with great truth assure you that in the destruction of this settlement not a single person has been hurt of the inhabitants, but such as were in arms, to those indeed the Indians gave no Quarter."[2] Obviously that last clause offends the modern sense of decency, but it was by no means exclusive to Indians. Indeed, American frontiersmen do not appear in the records to have confined their killing of Indians to men in arms. (And, sorry to say, modern bombs dropped from aircraft rarely distinguish noncombatants.)

Perhaps the devastation reconciled Connecticut to interstate peace-making when Congress adjudicated in 1782 by awarding Wyoming to Pennsylvania, with compensation to Connecticut of the Western Reserve in Ohio.[3]

The ruination of Wyoming Valley aroused much anger among Revolutionary leaders. Beyond the event itself, the threat of Indian raids against farming communities required releasing men to do militia duty who were needed for cultivation. (The same problem faced the Indians who were constantly on the edge of famine.) General Washington determined to strike at the organizing base of such frontier war, but he tempered attack with awareness of feasibility. Farther west, the campaign against Detroit had been revised to destruction of Indian towns. (None, by the way, was first challenged to surrender on terms.) Now the obviously desirable assault on British Niagara was adjusted to a more practicable campaign against Iroquois communities and fields.

For this purpose, Washington chose New Hampshire's Major General John Sullivan. Sullivan had marched the wrong way in Canada and had botched tactics on Long Island and at Brandywine. When sent against Newport, Rhode Island, he had so offended his co-commanding French admiral that the latter sailed off and the siege had to be abandoned. But Sullivan had to be caressed because of his strong influence among the politicians of New England. We may not forget how he and John Adams, with an assist from John Hancock, had rigged a forgery to attack Philadelphia's Quakers.[4] Washington was a Virginian who needed New England's support in the Revolution's very political armed forces.

Curiously, Pennsylvanians opposed this expedition. They had long depended on alliance with the Iroquois, and undoubtedly they expected to return to that tie after the war, but such readjustment would become diffi-

---

2 Graymont, *Iroquois in the American Revolution*, 168–72.
3 "Westmoreland 1774–1682," *Atlas of Early American History*, ed. Cappon et al., 92.
4 See Chap. 28, above.

cult after an attack on the Iroquois by way of Pennsylvania. (And, anyway, the raid on Connecticut's people at Wyoming had worked in Pennsylvania's interest.)

"Sullivan's demand for troops and supplies was insatiable."[5] Though he took charge, 28 March 1779, he was still at Easton, Pa., at the end of May.[6] Meantime Col. Goose Van Schaick marched in April from Ft. Stanwix with five hundred men. He laid waste the town of Onondaga in classic style of war against Indians, killed twelve and took thirty-three prisoners; all while Sullivan continued to demand more of everything before starting off. Onondagas took refuge with Senecas where they planted new corn but depended on British Major John Butler for food until their new crops could mature. The experience solidified their alliance with the British.

Sullivan kept true to form. He left Easton, 18 June, and reached Wyoming on the twenty-third. "There he squatted," writes Dr. Graymont, "until the end of July, waiting for the remainder of his supplies and expected troops to catch up to him."[7] He benefited strangely from the incredulity of senior British commanders who could not believe that so huge an expedition would be devoted to what they considered a minor objective. The Indians, of course, thought otherwise.

Mohawk chief Thayandanegea, who was also Captain Joseph Brant, led warriors to outflank Sullivan by attacking communities in the upper Delaware Valley. (Another oddity occurred in this strangely unpredictable style of war. Capt. John Wood was taken prisoner by Brant's force. By coincidence he gave Brant's hand the Master Mason's grip. As Brant had become a Mason while visiting England, he mistakenly identified Wood as a lodge brother and ordered his men to spare this prisoner. He was quite vexed when he later learned the truth, but Capt. Wood's reaction was to apply for membership in the Masonic lodge. It seems like a hard way to recruit.)[8]

Sullivan crawled along. On 22 August, his force was joined at Tioga by more men under Brigadier James Clinton to bring the total fit for duty to 4,469.[9]

The gods of war have their own plans. Although "it was a mystery to many why Washington had chosen John Sullivan . . . it was most fortunate . . . that Sullivan had delayed so long." British generals mistakenly thought he would aim for Detroit, and the crops he was about to destroy could not be replanted until another season.[10] The British error may have been due to secret information from Benedict Arnold who demanded ten thousand pounds for his treachery.[11]

5 Graymont, *Iroquois in the American Revolution*, 194.   6 Ibid., 196.   7 Ibid., 197.
8 Ibid., 301–02.   9 Ibid., 206.   10 Ibid., 208.   11 Van Doren, *Secret History*, 210.

At Newtown, against the advice of British officers, some Indian warriors insisted on defending against Sullivan though outnumbered eight to one and facing cannon. A blast of artillery fire routed them, and thereafter Sullivan's campaign became little more than a parade through Iroquoia.[12] Except for the destruction. "In all, forty villages, numerous isolated houses, at least one hundred sixty thousand bushels of corn, and an uncounted quantity of other vegetables had been destroyed on the expedition" which cost fewer than forty soldiers.[13] The entire region was laid waste, but this region was intended to be a prize of war, so no sympathy was expressed by Revolutionary leaders. Oddly, some of the soldiers engaged in the ravaging wrote letters expressing qualms at what they were doing. They were astonished by the prosperity they so busily ruined. The crops and orchards and well-built homes contrasted favorably with surrounding communities of "white" farmers and fitted badly into the soldiers' conceptions of Indian savagery.

Evacuated Iroquois families retired among the British at Niagara where provisions had been short before they came. Within a couple of months half of them relieved the strain on supplies by refuging elsewhere. Sullivan's campaign failed to defeat Indian warriors who stayed on the warpath more angrily than ever, until and after peace between Americans and British. But the destruction created something close to a human vacuum in the Finger Lakes region of "upstate New York." After the war, when two thousand Iroquois fled into Canada, General Haldimand bought a large territory for them from the Mississaugas which became the Six Nations Reserve, somewhat whittled down in size.[14] New Englanders poured into the former Iroquois homeland to make the ethnic dichotomy that subsequently appeared in New York's politics and culture.

This section relies on the work of Dr. Barbara Graymont which is comprehensive, accurate, and highly detailed. If there can be definitive histories, her book is one of them.

In this complex war with its multiplicity of issues and parties, it was inevitable for betrayals to occur at some points. One can be astonished only by their infrequency. Political test oaths and other repressive actions designed to guarantee loyalty punished only the principled opponents of independence. *Un*principled persons masked their feelings, met requirements for overt conformity, and betrayed secretly.

In 1776, the anchor point in Manhattan for American positions was Fort Washington. The British took it easily and captured twenty-seven hundred soldiers with large quantities of scarce arms; and the otherwise baffling ease

---

12 Graymont, *Iroquois in the American Revolution*, 208–212. 13 Ibid., 218.
14 Ibid., 263–64, 293–94.

of their victory is now explained by the exact knowledge they had acquired of the fort's situation and structure. These were delivered by Adjutant William Demont of the 5th Pennsylvania regiment who sneaked over to Earl Percy with the fort's detailed plans. British-born Demont professed that he had changed sides because of loyalty to the crown, and he got little personal compensation.[15]

In Massachusetts, the price of treachery was simply money, paid quarterly by General Gage to Dr. Benjamin Church, a member of the provincial congress and its committee of safety, who had the confidence of John Hancock and the Adamses. Church blundered and got caught, but was saved from the hangman by the timely disposition of his papers by a confederate. He served some time in jail, and eventually boarded a schooner that was lost. The crown pensioned his widow £150 per year after the war.[16]

The case of the Rev. Jacob Duché is almost hilarious. Rector of Christ Church and St. Peter's in Philadelphia (where Benjamin Franklin had a pew), Duché was made chaplain of the Continental Congress and he preached up a storm for the Revolution. Until Howe took Philadelphia. Then Duché prayed for the royal family. He seems to have thought that Revolutionaries should not have to mix with common people.

He wrote to persuade Washington to leave the "illiberal and violent men" of the Revolution – men "whose minds can never mingle with your own." Among them, some Pennsylvanians were "so obscure that their very names have never met my ears before," and among the New Englanders "can you find one that, as a gentleman you could wish to associate with?" Therefore, Washington should return to the fold. (I wish I could have seen John Adams's face when he read that.)

It seems funny now but in 1777 Washington knew better than to keep this gem secret. He sent it to Congress, and Duché took ship for England.[17]

Other, more serious cases occurred, not all of which came to light until long after the war. Historian Carl Van Doren drew information in *Secret History of the American Revolution* from the manuscript papers of Generals Clinton and Gage, among others. Of them all, the most famous and the most misunderstood until those papers became available was the secret treachery (botched and exposed) of Major General Benedict Arnold, which could have spelled disaster for the Revolution. Mr. Van Doren summarizes Arnold's character. "Traditional guesses about Arnold, either that he was a villain out of melodrama or that he was a disillusioned hero honestly converted to the enemy, give way to facts which show him to have been bold, crafty, unscrupulous, unrepentant: the Iago of traitors."[18] (Since when, I wonder, has Iago not been considered a villain?)

15 Van Doren, *Secret History*, 17.   16 Ibid., 19–23.   17 Ibid., 39–43.   18 Ibid., v.

Clare Brandt has written more recently that "Arnold's tactical acuity and flair for battle put him in a class by himself; he was one of the best, if not *the* best fighting general at Washington's disposal."[19] The key word in this judgment is *tactical*. Arnold's contemporary, Aaron Burr, elucidated his strengths and limitations. "Arnold is a perfect madman in the excitement of battle, and is ready for any deeds of valor; but he has not a particle of moral courage. [This, from Burr!] He is utterly unprincipled and has neither love of country or self-respect to guide him. Nor is he to be trusted except under the watchful eye of a superior."[20]

Like many prominent Revolutionaries, Arnold's primary object of glorification was himself. We have seen (in Chapter 31) how he thrust himself on the Green Mountain Boys to seize credit for the capture of Ticonderoga. Also how he took an army to capture Quebec and avoided having to serve under General Montgomery (Arnold was then a colonel) by forcing his army through such wilderness that he lost nearly half his men before even seeing an enemy soldier. Admirers have praised this tremendous feat of endurance without noticing its wrongheadedness.

Arnold's flamboyance became glamorous. It must be said for him that he was always in the thick of fighting, and this sort of front line leadership gained him favor among enlisted men. It also gained him wounds and considerably less favor among officer peers who regarded him correctly as very pushy.

He commanded Philadelphia after Howe's withdrawal, and there he courted and married Peggy Shippen whose social standing and wealth offset her Loyalist sympathies. Arnold clambered up the ranks to become major general, and he solicited and was given command of the fortifications at West Point on the Hudson River. He did not get West Point until August, but he was already angling to sell it in May. He very deliberately opened negotiations with General Clinton on his own initiative. The negotiations, with Arnold's stipulated demands, are printed as an appendix in Van Doren's *Secret History*. Arnold even gave information about General Washington's movements that almost allowed Clinton to capture Washington.

Arnold had profited greatly, but rather stupidly, from graft while he commanded in Philadelphia.[21] In his arrogance, he drew the wrath of the dominant powerful politicians, Timothy Matlack and Joseph Reed, who brought charges that prompted Arnold to demand a court-martial for clearance.[22]

19 Clare Brandt, *The Man in the Mirror: A Life of Benedict Arnold* (New York: Random House, 1994), 168.

20 Edward Dean Sullivan, *Benedict Arnold, Military Racketeer* (New York: Vanguard Press, 1932), xi.

21 Ibid., 244–46, 251–52.　22 Brandt, *Man in the Mirror*, Chap. 14.

Before the court could be held, angry Arnold communicated secretly to the British command his willingness to be useful for a whopping big price. General Clinton evaded commitment to such precise pay off until he could understand just what was being sold. In August, Arnold gained command of West Point and aroused greater interest from Clinton.

Clare Brandt believes that Arnold took his bride into his schemes on their honeymoon and that she established the necessary connections by writing to Major John André who had wooed her during the British occupation of Philadelphia.[23] Van Doren and Brandt have described the details of the plots minutely; they do not matter here. In brief, Major John André became the go-between to arrange Arnold's betrayal of West Point, but he got caught when trying to get back to the British lines. Ironically, his captors seem to have been intent on robbery rather than military security. They searched André and found damning papers. A reporting mix-up through the wrong channels permitted Arnold to escape by rowing out to a British ship in the Hudson. André suffered execution by hanging.

Arnold then claimed rank in the British army and led a raid on New London, Connecticut (his boyhood home), where he captured a dozen American privateers, burned the town, and presided over a massacre of eighty American prisoners within Fort Griswold after the fort's surrender.[24] Though he obtained grants of money from the crown, which hoped to use him to gain other converts from the rebels, he had not created the role of outraged hero required for that purpose; he botched his later business dealings and went steadily downhill, socially and financially. His life became an object lesson in retribution for treachery.

Arnold was sent on the New London raid when General Clinton became suddenly aware that Washington had outfoxed him and was unstoppably marching south to engage General Cornwallis at Yorktown. That affair requires discussion in the context of events in the southern theater of operations.

23 Ibid., 184, 194, 201, Sullivan, *Benedict Arnold*, 290.   24 Brandt, *Man in the Mirror*, 249–52.

38

———— • ————

COMBAT: THE SOUTHERN THEATER

In terms of men killed or captured, and despite much typically American braggadocio, the British score in plain numbers seems to have been higher than their opponents', even after Saratoga; but numbers out of context can be misleading. All of Washington's recognized losses, and those of the Canadian fiasco, had resulted in men lost as casualties and captives in distressing quantities. Indisputably, the carefully trained professional soldiers of Britain were superior to the Americans' amateur and ill-disciplined militiamen in man-to-man combat. American sharpshooters with Pennsylvania rifles were serious foes, but they could not withstand determined bayonet charges.

Offsetting that advantage, the Revolutionaries could afford more losses than the British. An American casualty was replaced from a manpower pool near at hand. In contrast, the loss of a royal regular required substitution from Britain or Germany at cost of much time, training, and money. Even when American Loyalists joined the royal forces, they had all the faults of the Patriot militia; and their record shows little value on the battlefield.

Saratoga was important to French statesmen, not because it showed Americans winning – it did not so long as Washington was still in Valley Forge – but rather because the victory demonstrated Americans as potentially valuable allies against Britain in France's long feud. When France declared war, it did not engage to help Americans – such a concept reverses reality – rather, France launched war all over the world wherever there were British targets, *and France aimed to win French objectives*. In this scheme, the American Revolutionaries presented a sideshow valuable for diverting British resources. It is quite relevant that just as French arms were critical for the victory at Saratoga, so the decisive final victory in America (when that time came) was won at Yorktown by French forces that outnumbered the Americans on land as well as at sea. (And the Americans wore French-donated uniforms.) True, the command was George Washington's, but he could not even have dreamed of it with only his own resources. More of that later.

On their own, the Americans could fight only defensively with the hope of wearing out the patience of royal forces. British generals had to cope with the sheer size of the country. They could and did take targeted cities – Quebec, Montreal, Boston, New York, Philadelphia, Newport, Norfolk, Charleston – but to what end? They could not begin to spread occupying troops over that vast land; Massachusetts proved that.

The generals understood this. So did Members of Parliament, including the first minister Lord North, whose dearest wish was to resign and let someone else cope with the impossibility. But King George whipped him back into his halter. Adamant George would hear no talk of recognizing the independence of his "provinces."[1]

Loss at Saratoga and war with France compelled rethinking of objectives. The northern arena had to be abandoned as hopeless, but perhaps conquest of the south might detach that great territory from the rebels and keep it still for the empire. Coastal regions could be mastered without real difficulty; lots of Loyalists could be counted, especially in western counties; Indians had no love for the conquering Americans; and vast numbers of slaves needed only the opportunity to escape to freedom. It looked promising. The strategists turned south.

Taking advantage of naval supremacy, General Clinton started to roll up the rebels from their extreme state (i.e., from Georgia) on the assumption that it was too distant for hurried reinforcements to be sent by land from the north. This was correct. Savannah fell easily in January 1779 and was converted to a British base for a march against Charleston in South Carolina. Complications set in when the French fleet under Comte d'Estaing sailed in from the West Indies and nearly recaptured Savannah, but poor coordination between American and French forces, assisted by the timely threat of a hurricane, sent d'Estaing away empty-handed. Thus the possession of Georgia's tidewater region became an asset for General Clinton in 1780 when he sailed south to attack Charleston with eighty-five hundred men.

Defending General Benjamin Lincoln was trapped in Charleston without hope of help. On 12 May 1780 he surrendered the city and fifty-five hundred men, a number almost as large as Burgoyne had been compelled to give up at Saratoga.[2] For the Americans the loss was not so traumatic because there were more where those men had come from. Nevertheless, the loss of Charleston was genuine, and the city became a British base in the South comparable to New York City in the North. Had it been used optimally, the plantation South might have been detached as desired from the United

---

1 Peter D. G. Thomas, *Lord North* (London: Allen Lane, 1976), 109–10, 113–14.
2 Higginbotham, *War of American Independence*, 357.

States. The base was exploited swiftly and energetically by deep thrusts into rebel territory as far as supply lines permitted. Bodies of auxiliary Loyalist troops were organized, and slaves of rebel masters were confiscated. (This was not always the same as "freeing" them. They might be freed from old masters only to be transported to the West Indies and sold to new ones.) So South Carolina "lost approximately 25,000 slaves during the war, representing about one-quarter of its immediate pre-Revolutionary population."[3]

With all this activity, British commanders in the South made two mistakes consistently. As itemized by Don Higginbotham, "they failed to digest their acquisitions before gulping down more territory, and they neglected to give the tories adequate protection."[4] Perhaps they had no real choice. To "digest" that enormous territory would have required occupying it with troops in every county, and so would the task of protecting the Loyalists. The British simply did not have that many troops, and could not get them, especially not after war with France required troops all around the world. Loyalist recruits looked good as statistics, but they had a habit of running away in combat and thus exposing their part of the front. Some seemed to ignore discipline in order to fatten on plunder. That sort of conduct made no friends among masses of undecided persons.

The "Tories" (Loyalists) were supposed to be waiting in numbers among the former western Regulators who had earlier fought against tidewater aristocrats. That hatred of the low-country patriots – so British thinking went – would translate into love of the crown. So it did with some of the westerners, but the formula failed for others who rallied to the Revolution and defeated the Loyalists most notably in a pitched battle at Kings Mountain, 7 October 1780.[5] (May I speculate that Germans who had recently migrated south from Pennsylvania were among those unexpected Patriots? The American Germans of that era feared and hated all sorts of royalty.)

However that may have been, the British under General Cornwallis and his cavalry cohort Banastre Tarleton made spotty progress rampaging through the South. Their victory at Charleston had eliminated nearly all the Patriots' military force in the eastern South. General Horatio Gates, the victor of Saratoga, scrabbled together a defending army in upper South Carolina, only to be routed completely at Camden, 16 August 1780, after which Camden became Cornwallis's biggest inland base. Gates showed lead-

3 Philip D. Morgan, "Black Society in the Lowcountry,' in *Slavery and Freedom in the Age of the American Revolution*, ed. Ira Berlin and Ronald Hoffman (Charlottesville: University Press of Virginia, 1983), 110–11.
4 Higginbotham, *War of American Independence*, 355.
5 Don Higginbotham in *Blackwell Encyclopedia of the American Revolution*, 311–12.

ership there by beating all his men in flight.[6] After that he was no longer mentioned as a rival to Washington.

With Gates out of the way, Washington was freed of political pressure. He appointed the very able Nathaniel Greene to command what was left in the South. Here again was an odd twist of circumstance. Gates was a trained and experienced military man who lost; Greene was a former Quaker from Rhode Island who showed how to exhaust the British victors until *they* ran to refuge. He adopted guerilla tactics of a kind that seem very "modern"; avoiding direct confrontation, he haunted Cornwallis's flanks, never letting the British settle down to enjoy ground taken. He chose able associates. He cooperated with "swamp fox" Francis Marion who disrupted enemy supply lines, struck at British forces, and "terrorized Loyalists." His methods do not bear close examination.[7] Greene sent General Daniel Morgan against Cornwallis's vicious cavalry leader, Lt. Col. Banastre Tarleton who had "the reputation of a ruthless killer who refused quarter to beaten opponents."[8] (His portrait shows the very model of a dashing dragoon.) Tarleton met more than his match in Daniel Morgan at the Cowpens on 17 January 1781. His Tory Legion lost more than nine hundred men as compared to Morgan's seventy-two.[9]

Justice to Tarleton requires uncomfortable notice that his methods were general in the South on both sides of the conflict. We can be sure that Francis Marion's terrorizing was not gentle. Nowhere else was the Revolution's character as a civil war more evident. General Greene's aide William Pierce was horrified by "such scenes of desolation, bloodshed and deliberate murder." He tried feebly to salvage some American virtue: "The people, by copying the manners of the British, have become perfectly savage." Greene himself did not blame the British: "The Whigs and Tories persecute each other, with little less than savage fury. There is nothing but murders and devastations in every quarter."[10] Their use of the term *savage* is especially notable; ordinarily that word was reserved for Indians.

Greene hovered constantly around Cornwallis's main force. He picked up more soldiers (apparently from Virginia) until his force outnumbered Cornwallis's, and then he dared battle at Guilford Courthouse, 15 March 1781. (He had to use those short-term militiamen before they went home.) In one respect, Cornwallis won this fight by forcing Greene to withdraw, but Cornwallis lost 500 men to Greene's 250, rather remarkably in the circumstances. On those terms, Greene won the battle. Don Hig-

---

6 Ibid., 310.   7 J. Mark Thompson in *Blackwell Encyclopedia*, 754.
8 *Blackwell Encyclopedia*, 784; cf. Ward, *War of the Revolution* 2:705–6.
9 Higginbotham in *Blackwell Encyclopedia*, 312.
10 Charles Royster, *Revolutionary People at War*, 277–78.

ginbotham remarks that Cornwallis's army was "no longer an effective fighting machine after Kings Mountain, Cowpens, and Guilford Courthouse."[11]
He "found himself almost completely destitute of supplies" in a hostile
countryside.[12] He limped for rest and replenishment to Wilmington on the
coast of North Carolina.

Greene instantly took advantage of Cornwallis's withdrawal by marching to drive other British troops from their bases in South Carolina. The
pattern of Guilford Courthouse was repeated when Greene lost an attack
on Camden where a competent commander turned him back, but Greene
made the position so untenable that it had to be evacuated. This situation
became almost routine throughout the South as able British commanders
withdrew in good order from positions that Greene's pressure made impossible to hold.

To make these advances into South Carolina, Greene left Virginia wide
open. A British raid into the Chesapeake region had met no opposition in
mid-1779 and had successfully destroyed and looted stored supplies. Benedict Arnold followed through in 1780, again without serious resistance.
Cornwallis took note and came north from Wilmington in April 1781 to try
to get Virginia under control. The ease of these British campaigns is remarkable. Thomas Jefferson was governor and Virginia was the largest and
richest of the American states, but Jefferson did little or nothing practical
to stop the marauders.[13] George Washington sent a small contingent under
Lafayette all the way from Peekskill on the Hudson, but it was so heavily
outnumbered that Lafayette could do no more than dance around the British
fringes. It looked as though Cornwallis would get his wish; he could go and
come and loot and ruin at will.

I have noticed in earlier pages how the British high command abstained
from total destruction of coastal cities that they might easily have per-
petrated even in Boston by naval bombardment, and elsewhere by arson.
It seems, however, that as the war progressed attitudes hardened. A new,
unpublished paper by Allen Kulikoff recites pilferage, plunder, and
ravaging of property as well as violence to noncombatants in efforts to win
the war by breaking the Revolutionaries' spirits. Details must wait until
this is published, but attacks on one kind of property can be noticed because
they were proclaimed ever since Lord Dunmore had confiscated slaves
in 1773. Such plunder could even be justified on high moral grounds since
Lord Chief Justice Mansfield had effectually freed the slaves in Britain in
1772.

British commanders in the South tried to crush the rebels' system of

---

11 Higginbotham, *War of American Independence*, 312.
12 Ward, *War of the Revolution*, 2:795.   13 Ibid., 2:869.

agricultural production by seizing its labor force. Richard S. Dunn has studied the "severe dislocations" of Cornwallis's invasion of Virginia. In 1781, he reports, the tidewater counties lost so much black population that "these eleven counties had 12,000 fewer Blacks than they had listed in 1755."[14]

14 Richard S. Dunn, "Black Society in the Chesapeake, 1776–1810," in *Slavery and Freedom in the Age of the American Revolution*, ed. Berlin and Hoffman, 58.

39

YORKTOWN

Washington despaired. Far from being able to launch a counteroffensive, his resources were so depleted that he had to *impress* food for his men in camp, and this policy had made no friends for the Revolution. In May 1781 he wrote (very privately, in his journal), "Instead of having the prospect of a glorious offensive campaign before us, we have a bewildered and gloomy defensive one, *unless we receive a powerful aid of ships, land troops and money from our generous ally.*"[1]

There came another instance of great reward for bread cast upon the waters. In this case it was Washington's welcome and friendship for the enthusiastic volunteer, the Marquis de Lafayette. After campaigning a while with Washington, this young nobleman returned to France to lobby ardently with minister Vergennes for strong help to the Americans. He consorted with Benjamin Franklin, then the American minister to France, and their appeals prevailed.[2]

Troops and a fleet ordered from France settled in at Newport, Rhode Island, which had been evacuated by the British when General Clinton consolidated his forces at New York. From Newport, Lt. Gen. Rochambeau introduced himself and put himself under Washington's command, along with fifty-five hundred professional French soldiers and a small fleet of naval ships of the line. A cordial correspondence opened up.[3]

It was not preordained. As noticed earlier, much friction had occurred at Newport in August 1778 between Admiral d'Estaing and General Sullivan, and plenty of anti-French feeling still hung on in America from the Seven Years War. To guard against reviving it, Rochambeau was instructed from Paris to announce his subordination to Washington. This could not have been easy for him. He was the older man and a veteran of much combat in

---

1 Ward, *War of the Revolution*, 2:880 (emphasis added).
2 Van Doren, *Benjamin Franklin*, 616.   3 Higginbotham, *War of American Independence*, 379.

Europe, and his military resources were greater than Washington's. He had more troops that were better trained and better equipped, and he had a navy. Nevertheless he obeyed orders dutifully.

Washington rejoiced that he would now be able to attack Clinton in New York. Obsessed with that project, he told Rochambeau, 4 June 1781, "I know of no measure, which will be so likely to afford relief to the southern states, in so short a time, as a serious menace against New York." Rochambeau kept his disapproval private.[4]

This must be noticed because of much historical comment to the effect that Washington brilliantly feinted against New York just to delude Clinton, then switched cleverly to campaign southward. There is small basis for that opinion. Washington hinted at it after the war when Noah Webster asked him for a statement, but a series of documents shows that the Yorktown campaign was French in inception, in resources, and in the climactic siege being conducted "by the book" – the military bible of engineer Vauban.[5] We may forgive Washington for wanting credit for winning a great, decisive battle after his long string of losses in the field, but his fame was well earned by keeping the war going with amateurs and funny money. Not many professionals could have matched that.

Then, what did happen? Between 21 and 24 July, Washington and Rochambeau conducted serious reconnaissance of Clinton's lines at New York. Even with France's contribution, their combined forces for attack were far fewer than Clinton's fortified veterans. This was impossible. As Christopher Ward comments, "The wonder is that an attack should have been seriously considered."[6]

The two generals had known hopefully since June that a new and much larger French fleet under Admiral de Grasse was on its way, but it could not reach the North American coast until 15 July at earliest.[7] Rochambeau recommended to de Grasse that he enter Chesapeake Bay on his way, then continue to help attack New York, and in his postwar memoirs, he stated his "private opinion" that an enterprise on the Chesapeake should be conducted.[8]

Washington dithered irresolutely, but de Grasse settled the matter with a letter to Rochambeau, "a clear, concise, and definite letter that cleared the air, resolved all doubts, and determined the course of the war."[9] He announced that he would sail *to the Chesapeake* between August and mid-

4 *Diplomatic Correspondence of the American Revolution*, ed. Jared Sparks. 12 vols. (Boston, 1829–30), 8:66, 77.
5 Higginbotham, *War of American Independence*, 382.
6 Ward, *War of the Revolution*, 2:881.   7 *Diplomatic Correspondence*, ed. Sparks, 8:75.
8 Ibid., 8:76n, 77n.   9 Ward, *War of the Revolution*, 2:882.

October, after which he would have to return to the West Indies because of a commitment to Spaniards there. This was not consultation; it was more in the nature of an ultimatum.

De Grasse told what he could deliver and where; Washington could take it or leave it. The admiral promised three thousand troops, much artillery, and twenty-five or more warships. "Washington was equal to the occasion, although his hand was in some degree forced by Grasse."[10]

Washington did not stand and sputter on his rank. He had sense enough to reach out for de Grasse's manna on de Grasse's terms, so that in effect the admiral determined the coming strategy. This does not quite accord with the fulsome praise given to Washington for the plan, but he acted instantly and correctly to take advantage of de Grasse's plan. He received de Grasse's letter on 14 August. On the twenty-first, his two thousand men and Rochambeau's more numerous French troops started southward.[11] Washington's troops protested about remaining unpaid for a long time, so Finance Minister Robert Morris borrowed twenty thousand dollars – in real money (not worthless paper) – from Rochambeau. For just long enough, Clinton failed to catch on to the new expedition; until 2 September he still thought Washington's goal was New York City.

They passed through Philadelphia to the head of Chesapeake Bay, arriving 6 September. De Grasse's transports picked them up, and they went ashore near Williamsburg on the twenty-sixth. De Grasse was punctual, and he was joined by eight more ships of the line under Admiral de Barras from Newport. When a smaller British fleet challenged, it was beaten off.

Cornwallis was trapped at Yorktown with about 6,000 defenders. The besiegers included 7,800 professional French soldiers, and 8,845 Americans, of whom more than half seem to have been amateur militiamen and Virginia state troops. Washington had the honor of command, but from inception to victory, this battle was a French party. Cornwallis capitulated on 19 October, surrendering about 8,000 soldiers and seamen. It was all neatly timed. Clinton's rescue expedition from New York appeared off the Chesapeake capes on the twenty-fourth, after it was all over. It seems somehow apt that this dramatic end to Britain's rule in Virginia should have come within a day's march of its beginning at Jamestown.

Britain still held coastal posts along the Atlantic: at New York, Wilmington, Charleston, and Savannah; and de Grasse sailed off after Yorktown fell. But Parliament now understood the impossibility of denying the late provinces their independence. Though George III remained adamant, he lost control of Parliament. Enough had to be enough. On 4 March 1782,

10 Ibid., 2:883.　　11 Ibid., 2:882.

the House of Commons demanded peace, declaring that "it would consider as enemies to his Majesty and the Country all those who should advise or by any means attempt the further prosecution of offensive war on the Continent of North America, for the purpose of reducing the revolted Colonies to obedience by force."[12]

Franklin had foreseen that America was too big to be forced into obedience. Again, it seems aesthetically right that this shrewd old practitioner of realpolitik, who had done so much to start the war, and so much toward winning it by achieving French alliance, should now become the major commissioner to negotiate the peace.

Since 1066, Frenchmen and Englishmen had fought perpetually until France was driven out of North America in the Seven Years War. At Yorktown, France had the satisfaction of paying off an ancient grudge.

But at what a cost!

French finances were far from overflowing. The new war brought on by alliance with the United States (and lost elsewhere than at Yorktown) pushed France's absolute monarchy to the edge of bankruptcy and its own overthrow. When Benjamin Franklin cozened minister Vergennes into extravagant expenditures, he parlayed the American Revolution into Act One of the French Revolution. Whatever the lesson may be about aristocrats siding with self-governing commoners, it is clear as to keeping militarism within affordable limits.

12 Ibid., 2:895–96.

Part IV

THE CLONE ESTABLISHES ITS FORM

40

———— • ————

WHAT NEXT?

Yorktown guaranteed that Britain would have to give formal recognition to the fact of American independence. Thus far, it represented victory for the Revolutionaries. Other issues, however, remained to be sorted out and dealt with, none in isolation. Each required adjustment in relation to all the others.

What was the nature of the United States of America? Was it to be a confederation of highly independent states sovereign in their own right and merely cooperating with each other? Or was it to become the *empire* dreamed of by so many leaders?

Who would have power to govern? *Who* would have citizenship?

How would the "rights of Englishmen" be maintained and enlarged in liberty?

Where would the new entity's boundaries lie?

The winning of accepted independence answered none of these questions. They were recognized as essential, but proposed answers varied widely and sometimes discordantly.

To unify the struggle against Britain, Congress had considered a practical, makeshift confederation already in 1776. It ran into the rocks of three major obstacles: voting by states or by population; apportionment of common expenses to be calculated according to free populations only or to whole populations including slaves; and disposition of western lands by Congress or by claiming states. (At the very beginning of the struggle, the West loomed as the great prize of victory – but whose was it?)[1]

Setting possibly divisive issues aside, Congress sought unity by concentration on winning the war. The state bosses in Congress implemented its "recommendations" to their states almost as if they were laws. But they were not really laws, as became quickly evident when recommendations were made to apportion state quotas to finance Congress. States became very

1 Jack N. Rakove, in *Blackwell Encyclopedia*, 290–91.

remiss in complying with such requests, and Congress had no power to tax, so Congress resorted to printing what was presented as money. This stuff fooled nobody; it found few takers among businessmen and farmers as it inflated to a sixtieth and less of its pretended value. Rich speculators bought much of it from soldiers disgusted with their trashy pay. Some soldiers protested in demonstrations that authoritarian gentlemen denounced as "mutinies." Righteous authoritarians saw nothing wrong in demanding that soldiers fight in the good cause at their own expense. Nevertheless, it became certain that any postwar government would have to create a stable currency or go under.

Congress stalled by borrowing abroad, especially from Holland. This was made easier for emissary John Adams by Dutch knowledge of land values. These were no secret. Even before the Declaration of Independence, Tom Paine had written, "It is by the sale of those [western] lands that the debt may be sunk . . . and the quit-rent reserved thereon will always lessen, and in time, will wholly support the yearly expence of government."[2] Statesmen regarded the western lands figuratively as "money in the bank," but they had to clarify its ownership.

Congress made shift by various devices based on great expectations, but even such methods required some agreed understandings on sharing the expected fruits of victory; and the deplorable, frequently expressed truth was that these high-minded gentlemen united in the grand cause of liberty did not trust each other. If they did not, why should historians?

What follows is a brief analysis directed to what the Revolutionaries did and accomplished with regard to Land, Power, and People, with a final summing up of the entire book.

2 Paine, *Common Sense*, Appendix.

41

———— • ————

LAND

Long before Yorktown, Members of Congress anticipated the problems of dividing up the western spoil. The committee appointed to draft Articles of Confederation reported in August 1778 that Congress should decide all interstate disputes concerning boundaries, jurisdiction, "or any other cause whatever." Further, that Congress should regulate trade and manage "all affairs with the Indians." But this deliberately euphonious terminology added a reservation: "provided that the legislative right of any state within its own limits be not infringed or violated."[1]

Through this barn door, Virginia marched with George Rogers Clark and the establishment of Virginia's Illinois County north of the Ohio River and west to the Mississippi. True, the Articles of Confederation had not yet been confirmed by the states, and would not be until 1781, but Virginia's delegates had signed the Articles in August 1778, and with full knowledge of their provisions both houses of Virginia's legislature set up Illinois County in December.[2] Clearly this was a deliberate effort to get the western territory within Virginia's limits before Congress could assume control. In Virginia the land grabbers were far ahead of the libertarian patriots, when they were not the same men.

Other states also had chartered claims to western territory, and they were not amused by Virginia's attempted coup. If Virginia had made good on its claims, Illinois, Indiana, Ohio, and the headwaters of the Ohio River around Pittsburgh would all today be part of Virginia; but the region lay under counterclaims by Massachusetts, Connecticut, New York, and Pennsylvania. Negotiations began quietly. Finally, the Virginians were persuaded to "cede" their claims north of the Ohio River. The mere terminology is loaded in their favor by elevating a quitclaim to the level of a territorial cession. But Virginia imposed a condition. It would "cede"

1 Article IX in *Documents, of American History*, ed. Commager, 1:111–16.
2 Balesi, *Time of the French*, 300.

territorial sovereignty only if Congress would guarantee previously created legal rights of *property*, and these "rights" covered vast areas.

From Seven Years War days, Virginia had granted bonus western lands to the province/state's soldiers and their gentry/officers who aimed at acquiring much of those grants. This is a rarely mentioned, all-engrossing feature of George Washington's life. In 1767, Washington told his agent William Crawford to "evade" Pennsylvania's law by registering an illicitly large tract of land in small parcels, this to be done with the connivance of "an Acquaintance of mine" in the land office. He "infringed" Virginia law, according to Bernhard Knollenberg, by seizing lands to which he was not entitled, surveying them illicitly through a man unqualified by law who laid them out in violation of legal stipulations as to size and location, and all to the detriment of Washington's Virginia comrades-in-arms for whom these lands had been intended. "The more he got of the allotted 200,000 acres, the less was available for the enlisted men to whom it was promised."[3]

In 1769, Washington tried again to get larger shares of the bounty lands by arguing with Governor Botetourt that only men who had served under Washington (as well as Washington himself) were entitled to bounty lands under Dinwiddie's earlier proclamation, thus excluding Virginians who had served under other officers at other times.[4]

Dinwiddie's earlier proclamation of bounty lands, 19 February 1754, had granted lands "For encouraging Men to *enlist*." That term excluded officers who were *commissioned*. Washington's partner George Mercer forged this to say, "For Encouraging Persons to *Enter* into His Majesty's Service," thus making officers eligible for the grants originally intended only for enlisted men. Mercer also made the proclamation say that lands would be proportioned according to recommendations of "their superior officers," which meant Washington above all. Washington won official approval of the forgery, which he certainly understood, in 1769, and lands were parceled out in 1773. Washington's own "proportion" was 20,147 acres, 10 percent of the 200,000 acres available, and Mercer picked up 13,532 acres additional.[5]

Let us return to the hard bargaining between Virginia and Congress concerning Congress's demand for a quitclaim of Virginia's interests in the western lands. Washington's earlier example shows quite clearly that the Virginia gentry would hold stubbornly to their property claims, and

---

3 Washington to William Crawford, 21 Sept. 1767, in *Writings*, ed. Fitzpatrick, 2:468; Knollenberg, *George Washington*, 92–100, quote at 99.
4 Washington, *Writings*, ed. Fitzpatrick, 2:528–32.
5 *The Virginia Soldiers' Claim to Western Lands Adjacent to Fort Pitt*, ed. Willis Van Devanter (New York: privately printed at Spiral Press, 1966, short, unpaged).

Virginia was not alone in that respect. But Congress needed to seize and sell those western lands to pay its own expenses and to control expansion.

As Peter S. Onuf remarks, "the western problem dominated Congressional politics . . . absorbing more energy – to less apparent effect – than anything other than the conduct of the war itself."[6] In order to have any western policy at all, Congress had to get cession of state claims; indeed, the states' approval of the Articles of Confederation in their entirety hinged upon such cessions. Maryland led a group of small states that refused approval of the Articles until cession should be made. To placate them, Congress requested the states with territorial claims to cede. This plea of 6 September 1780 was followed by a resolution, 10 October, promising development of the west for the common benefit of the whole United States.

Virginia responded with an unacceptable act of cession. Besides its insistence on confirmation of Virginia's land titles in the claimed regions (and rejection of grants made by other states), Virginia withheld cession of the Kentucky county lands south of the Ohio River. The small states refused to go along.

New York proposed a possible alternative to circumvent Virginia's conditions. New York had claims to an enormous sweep of territory including the same lands claimed by Virginia, but New York's claims had no charter basis. Yorkers claimed by virtue of "rights" supposed to be held by their Iroquois "dependents." The Indians of this region supposedly had been conquered by the Iroquois who (again, supposedly) were dependents of New York. This claim had been given diplomatic weight during the Seven Years War by British diplomats and their maps. It was nonsense, but useful in diplomacy, and the Yorkers now took virtue to themselves by ceding their claim unconditionally to Congress. Virginians were not impressed.[7]

Yorkers hoped to get Congress's support for New York's effort in a different direction to reclaim the communities that had set themselves up as independent Vermont. This hopeful quid pro quo never completed. Though Congress happily accepted the unconditional cession of New York's western claims, it avoided tangling with very tough Vermonters who played coyly with possible return to the arms of King George, and Virginia simply ignored the precedent of New York's western cession. *Nothing* was simple in these maneuvers.[8]

---

6 Peter S. Onuf, in *Blackwell Encyclopedia*, 346.
7 Ibid., Section 35. New Yorkers claimed through their alliance with the Indians of the Covenant Chain. For the Chain's genesis and evolution under Iroquois leadership, see Jennings, *Ambiguous Iroquois Empire*, esp. Chap. 2.
8 Onuf, in *Blackwell Emcyclopedia*, Section 35.

Then Britain signed the Treaty of Paris, 3 September 1783, ceding territory all the way to the Mississippi River, and the disposition of those lands lacking confirmed jurisdictions could no longer be put off. Oddly, the deadlock was broken by New York State. Something had to be done about the Iroquois homelands that General Sullivan had devastated and left invitingly open to squatters. Massachusetts claimed that territory by virtue of its sea-to-sea colonial charter, and Yorkers were highly conscious of Massachusetts's many efforts to fulfill its charter "grant." Yorkers moved prudently to guarantee their own jurisdiction.

The traditional way of preempting competitive territorial claims was to acquire a quitclaim/cession from Indians asserted to be aboriginal owner-occupiers of the territory.[9] In 1783, when Congress moved to confirm peace with Britain by a treaty of peace with the Iroquois, Yorkers scented danger to themselves; and when Congress planned to demand compensatory Indian deeds, Yorkers forestalled that hazard by moving to get their own deed first. Governor George Clinton invited the unpacified Iroquois tribes to a treaty at Fort Stanwix, 5 September 1784. Barbara Graymont observes, "The primary object, in the view of the state, was not only to conclude a peace but to obtain a land cession."[10] But the wary Indians, though they approved peace and friendship, shied away from ceding lands. A few weeks later, 2 October, Congress's commissioners met with an odd lot of delegates from the Iroquois, and worried Yorkers hung around "to Counteract and frustrate" anything proposed by Congress "that may Eventually prove Detrimental to the State."[11] By order of the commissioners, the Yorkers were shoved aside from observing or hearing the conference transactions.[12]

Congress's commissioners came to the treaty conference with strongly held and very definite ideas. They had been urged to end the tradition of treating with the Indians as peers from other nations. Congress's committee chairman insisted that they should be treated as dependents of the state of New York.[13] This did not mean that New York should dictate terms of surrender. Iroquois lands must be ceded *to the United States* in a four-mile strip from Niagara to Buffalo Creek, and this was not negotiable because the Iroquois had become "a subdued people." Commissioner Arthur Lee hectored them, "you have been overcome in a war which you entered into with us, not only without provocation, but in violation of most sacred obligations."[14]

Congress's committee had also instructed the commissioners to divide

---

9 For the origin of this device, see Jennings, *Invasion of America*, 131–33.

10 Graymont, *Iroquois in the American Revolution*, 267.

11 Ibid., 272.   12 Ibid., 279.

13 Calloway, *American Revolution, in Indian Country*, 282.

14 Graymont, *Iroquois in the American Revolution*, 281–82.

the Indians by treating with them separately, and the commissioners obeyed by refusing to let the Iroquois act as spokesmen for Indians west of New York State.[15] Thus was broken the century-old Covenant Chain that had elevated the Iroquois to highest status among their confederated tribes. Under such heavy pressure, the Iroquois delegates divided. Mohawk Captain Aaron Hill professed to speak "not only on the part of the Six Nations [of Iroquois] but also on that of the Ottawa, Chippewa, Hurons, Potawatamas, Messasaugas, Delawares, Cherokees, Shawnees, Chickasaws, Choctaws, and Creeks," but Seneca Captain O'Bail (Cornplanter) disavowed Hill's position. "As to the territory westward," said O'Bail, "you must talk respecting it with the Western Nations toward the setting of the Sun – They must consult of what part they must cede to the United States."[16]

The commissioners' dictation certainly humiliated the Iroquois and struck out from beneath them the support they had acquired through sheer gall when professing to make policy for all those allied tribes who were by no means united in accepting such domination. Some of them, indeed, may have rejoiced at the removal of that domination. The Iroquois had evolved a smooth trick of protecting their own lands by selling off their allies' lands – whether or not rightfully.

Far from feeling defeated by the Treaty of Fort Stanwix, the western tribes rejected it entirely, along with any assumption that the Iroquois could determine their commitments or speak in their behalf. On that point, the westerners agreed with Congress, but that was the only point. War continued in the west.

Pennsylvania also had commissioners at Fort Stanwix, whose influence on events was greater than appeared on the surface. Pennsylvanians wanted assurance of their state's jurisdiction over all the territory specified in the colonial charter granted to William Penn by King Charles II. As we have seen, Virginia had seized control of part of that territory at the headwaters of the Ohio River, and Pennsylvania wanted it back. The simplest approach was to follow the example of William Penn, to recognize the Indian right and purchase it; then, with possession of the Indian right backing up Pennsylvania's own charter right, Pennsylvania would be one up on Virginia. But, unless Congress first made formal peace with the Indians, Pennsylvania would have to make its own peace with tribes who would then remain in a state of enmity with the other states. What, then, would be left of Congress's supposed monopoly of the conduct of Indian affairs?

On 12 September 1783, Pennsylvania did Congress the courtesy of

15 Ibid., 266.
16 Jennings, in *The History and Culture of Iroquois Diplomacy*, ed. Francis Jennings et al. (Syracuse, N.Y.: Syracuse University Press, 1985), 58.

requesting approval of its intended Indian purchase. Congress stalled, being still enmeshed in its difficulties with Virginia, so Pennsylvania decided to proceed anyway, regardless of Congress's approval. Congress faced the ridiculous possibility of losing any role in Indian affairs, for the other states would soon have followed Pennsylvania's precedent. In this dilemma, Congress capitulated to Virginia's demands for cession of its western claims on conditions; how else could Congress avoid the total loss of its own authority in the west?

On 23 February 1784, Pennsylvania appointed its commissioners to treat with the Indians. On 1 March 1784, Congress accepted Virginia's cession conditions, and the national domain came into being.[17] On 4 March, Congress appointed its own commissioners to treat with the Indians at Fort Stanwix, and they seized control of the treaty conference, as described above. Saving face in this manner, Congress's commissioners then allotted time to Pennsylvania's commissioners for the specific purpose of purchasing property within what were now Pennsylvania's unchallenged bounds.

And Virginia quietly pocketed its gains elsewhere. Other states also had western claims. Massachusetts and Connecticut demanded compensation for their sea-to-sea charter provisions and negotiated privileges in the west. North Carolina did not cede its western land claims to Congress until 1789, Georgia not until 1802.[18] But Virginia's cession of territory north of the Ohio River cleared the way for Congress to enact Northwest Ordinances from 1784 to 1787. These were among the most innovative laws ever passed in the history of empires, and the most far-reaching. Here we must note that the treaties of Fort Stanwix were rejected by western Indians who remained at war with the United States for another eleven years.

In 1784, free at last from Virginia's and Britain's encumbrances, Congress passed the first Northwest Ordinance to establish official jurisdiction north of the Ohio River. Squatters swarmed into the territory to frustrate Congress's plans for an income from land sales. Jurisdiction meant nothing until administration should be established. After some experimenting, Congress responded to pressure from land speculators by enacting the final Northwest Ordinance, 13 July 1787.[19] With this law, the United States took their place in imperial British tradition, but with a difference.

Legally, the territory was formed in the image of colonies to be governed by officers sent by Congress, with assemblies enacting laws submitted to Congress for approval. (Shades of the Privy Council's supervision!) But

17 Jennings, "The Indians' Revolution," in *The American Revolution*, ed. Young, 341–42 and n62, 348.
18 Calloway, *American Revolution in Indian Country*, 284.
19 *Documents of American History*, ed. Commager, 128.

Congressmen remembered also how they had fought free of the British empire, and they worried much about the settlers expected to populate these new western colonies called territories. Would the westerners be loyal to the states that had spawned them? The question could be answered with another: Had the states stayed loyal to the empire that had spawned *them*? The mountains barred law enforcement from Philadelphia or New York, much as they had foiled Britain's power, and the Mississippi River beckoned to the westerners' trade more attractively than struggling past those same mountains to eastern ports. Not for one minute did Congress trust those westerners to be grateful for the East's benevolence, and Spaniards and Frenchmen lurked at the edge of the western colonies, ready to seduce them away. (This suspicion was well grounded in the discovery of real conspiracies.)

A *new* species of empire was required and was invented. The western colonies were to be nurtured until they reached maturity, defined as "sixty thousand free inhabitants thereof," whereupon they should be admitted "into the Congress of the United States, *on an equal footing with the original States in all respects whatever.*"[20] Thus the Congress guaranteed that liberty-loving westerners should "forever remain a part of this Confederacy of the United States of America."[21] On these terms, the original thirteen states thrust forth their empire, by sharing it, eventually across the North American continent to the Pacific coast and beyond to the Hawaiian islands. They have become fifty states, with no end in sight. Not since the ancient Roman empire had anything of the sort been tried.

In due course, five new states were indeed created from the northwest territory/colony, and they became decisive for northern victory when the empire tore itself apart in the immense Civil War between northern and southern states. Indeed it may be said with much conviction that another provision of the Northwest Ordinance guaranteed that victory when Article 6 decreed, "There shall be neither slavery nor involuntary servitude in the said territory." As we shall see, struggles to enforce this provision foreshadowed the Civil War.

Considering the whole human population of the region, one sees a fault line in the Northwest Ordinance and in the intentions of its enacters. It was another variant of the Declaration of Independence's semantics expressed as "all men are created equal." Notoriously, that utterance included no blacks among *men*. So also, in the Ordinance, no Indians were included among the legal *persons* or *inhabitants* of the law. French and Canadian persons who had settled before American jurisdiction in Kaskaskia, St.

---

20 Ibid., Article 5, emphasis added. 21 Ibid., Article 4.

Vincent's, and neighboring villages, and who professed themselves citizens of Virginia, were guaranteed continuation of "their laws and customs now in force among them, relative to the descent and conveyance, of property." No such sanction was given to Indians who had settled rather earlier than the French and who also had customs regarding property.

Regardless of rhetoric, Indians were not welcome. How high-mindedly they were assured that "their lands and property shall never be taken from them without their consent," but this was eyewash. There were ways of convincing Indians to give consent. Though "they shall never be invaded or disturbed, unless in just and lawful wars authorized by Congress," such authorization was not hard to obtain, and in itself it produced wars satisfactorily just and lawful.

Indians protested strongly against the 1784 Treaty of Fort Stanwix. Shamefaced Governor Haldimand of Canada tried to recompense Britain's abandoned Iroquois allies by purchasing a large tract at Grand River and turning it over to them.[22] Some Iroquois settled there to become the Six Nations Reserve. Others, however, insisted on returning to their homelands in New York, reproaching the United States for breaking its own promises.[23]

Western tribes flatly rejected the assumption of the commissioners at Fort Stanwix – who had asserted that the Indians had been "subdued" during the Revolutionary War. The westerners confederated and took the warpath. After enactment of the United States Constitution in 1787, the new federal government dispatched armies in "just wars authorized by Congress," but the Indians disagreed about their justice, and proved beyond argument that they had not been subdued. In October 1790, they defeated General Joseph Harmar in two battles near modern Fort Wayne, Indiana. In November 1791, they routed Northwest Territory Governor Arthur St. Clair at modern Fort Recovery.

President George Washington and Secretary of War Timothy Pickering sent a third expedition under Washington's old colleague General Anthony Wayne, who took more care than his predecessors. The Indians attacked Wayne at Fallen Timbers in 1794, but he drove them off and held his position. Neither they nor he wanted to continue the war, so they joined each other in treaty at Greenville in 1795. As the U.S. government had political and diplomatic problems in the east, it wanted to stabilize its western region. Secretary Pickering instructed General Wayne to make all necessary concessions for the sake of obtaining "such a peace as shall let the Indians go

---

22 Graymont, *Iroquois in the American Revolution*, 263–64.
23 Thomas S. Abler, *Chainbreaker: The Revolutionary War Memoirs of Governor Blacksnake* (Lincoln: University of Nebraska Press, 1989), Appendix 3.

away *with their minds at ease.*" Otherwise, he thought, "it may be but the era of renewed hostility."[24]

Putting the Indians' minds at ease required going back to the kind of treaty negotiations familiar to them – the kind that had evolved under the British empire – and Pickering told General Wayne to revert to that. He rejected the conquest assumption of the Fort Stanwix treaty with explicit guidelines to General Wayne for his forthcoming Treaty of Greenville.

> The unfortunate construction put by the first Commissioners on our treaty of peace with Great Britain and thence continued by General St. Clair in 1789 . . . a construction as unfounded in itself as it was unintelligible and mysterious to the Indians – a construction which, with the use made of it by the British Advisors of those Indians, has probably been the main spring of the distressing war on our frontiers . . . cannot be too explicitly renounced.

Pickering knew the price of peace: "The land is theirs (and this we acknowledge)."[25]

Pickering's candid statement cannot be reconciled with the invention frequently intoned by apologists for expansion – the assertion that the land was "free to be taken." Indisputably, as time went on, the land *was* taken, but always thereafter under sanction of legalistic pretensions. I like the justification quoted from a southern Congressman – sometime in the 1950s as I remember – "We stole the land fair and square."

The Greenville treaty reestablished a formally agreed boundary between the United States and the tribes, thus renewing Britain's policy in that regard. From the former claims of absolute sovereignty, it salvaged only a right of preemption for the United States, requiring only that when the tribes wished to cede lands the United States should be the only recipient. To this the tribes agreed.[26]

The Northwest Ordinance and the 1795 Treaty of Greenville stimulated record numbers of immigrants west of the mountains. Within fifteen years after Greenville, some 230,000 newcomers settled in Ohio.[27] Such numbers were not to be resisted by the scattered Indians who could only stall and delay thereafter in treaty after treaty; but their struggles were not wasted. The tribes who fought for freedom kept it for their own generation. Even

---

24 The process by which the Treaty of Greenville came into being was long and tortuous. Source materials trace it in *The New American State Papers: Indian Affairs*, 4, ed. Thomas C. Cochran (Wilmington, Del.: Scholarly Resources, 1972), 13–177. The treaty terms are in ibid., 4:150–52, followed by the minutes of the treaty conference. Quotation from *Anthony Wayne, A Name in Arms*, ed. Richard C. Knopf (Pittsburgh, Pa.: University of Pittsburgh Press, 1960), 403.

25 *Anthony Wayne*, ed. Knopf, 403.

26 *New American State Papers*, ed. Cochran, 4:150–52.

27 John Long in *The Settling of North America: The Atlas of the Great Migrations into North America from the Ice Age to the Present*, ed. Helen Hornbeck Tanner et al. (New York: Macmillan, 1995), 72.

today, though tribal independence is long gone, their descendants reap financial benefits from the legal principles established then.

Thus the United States demonstrated its continuation of British imperialism. Dorothy V. Jones states the principle in the very title of her fine book, *License for Empire: Colonialism by Treaty in Early America.* "In the brief period 1763–74," Dr. Jones notes, "North American Indians were signatories to thirty treaties, or 39 percent of the total" in the world treaty system, "and Asian Indians to thirty-one treaties, or 40 percent of the total." North America and its European colonials were integral to the worldwide system, and the dominant European descendants continued the pattern after they gained independence for themselves.[28]

A historian of ideas has found "no evidence that the word 'race' was used at all in the Americas to differentiate Europeans and Africans until after 1776."[29] The American historian Reginald Horsman comments that "while blacks, of course, were central to the general development of American thought on race . . . in dealing with the Indians the United States began to formulate a rationale of expansion which was readily adaptable to the needs of an advance over other peoples and to a world role."[30]

Alfred F. Young draws attention to a kind of radicalism responding to rising expectations widespread during the Revolution that became frustrated in its outcome. Americans who were neither black nor Indian, having overthrown British rule, became aware of "a national ruling class." This rising consciousness generated "impulses to radicalism" that appeared, among other ways, in enthusiasm for the French Revolution.[31]

George Washington, John Adams, and their Federalists worried much about ideological contagion from the French Revolution. The United States Constitution's Bill of Rights, after hard struggle, was conceded to the "mob" primarily to protect the status and property of unpopular aristocrats.

One must refine the concept of radicalism. It is not and never was identical with democracy. The radical John Hancock and the Adamses aimed at changing the social order only by substituting their own power for the British crown's. Mutinous soldiers of the Pennsylvania and New Jersey Lines wanted their earned pay; they were not striving to overthrow their

---

28 Dorothy V. Jones, *License for Empire: Colonialism by Treaty in Early America* (Chicago, Ill.: University of Chicago Press, 1982), 4, 16.
29 Stephen Small, "Racist Ideologies," in *Transatlantic Slavery Against Human Dignity*, ed. Tibbles, 112.
30 Reginald Horsman, *Race and Manifest Destiny: The Origins of American Racial Anglo-Saxonism* (Cambridge, Mass.: Harvard University Press, 1981), 100.
31 "Afterword" in *Beyond the American Revolution: Explorations in the History of American Radicalism*, ed. Alfred F. Young (DeKalb: Northern Illinois University Press, 1993), 328.

governments. The farmers of Shays's Rebellion and the Whiskey Rebellion were not so much intent on tearing something down as on simply bettering their own conditions. Resentment against the perceived ruling class deflected into aggression against Indians. Instead of conflict with the ruling class, seizure of Indian lands could be effected with its complicity. Thus, perpetual conquest diverted rebellious sentiment into the satisfaction of demands for personal advancement at the expense of Indians instead of the wealthy. It needed only tacit redefinition of Indian property into land free to be taken, regardless of legalities, and the ruling class would put the standing army at service to the takers.

Defeat of Indians promoted parallelism and convergence of the interests of other Americans. Richard W. Van Alstyne makes the point with different phrasing: "When the United States started on its career as an independent state, its growth pattern was fully established and visible to its imaginative and far-seeing leaders, who regarded its 'proper dominion' as bounded only by the shores of the continent."[32] Later generations expressed their own conception of themselves as a conquering Chosen People by their belief in a Manifest Destiny.

By identifying democracy with easy conquest, a stamp was put on the American empire that must be given grave thought in modern times. Vietnam proved that future conquest will not be so easy.

32 Van Alstyne, *The Rising American Empire*, 195.

42

PEOPLE

Immigration south of the Ohio River came from the slave states and duplicated their reliance on the economic system of slavery. In 1792, Kentucky was admitted to the union as the first new slave state. North of the Ohio, however, settlers rushed in from a wide range of eastern regions. Many had stopped briefly in the east after originating abroad. Despite the appearance of chaos, migration into the Old Northwest occurred on patterned flows. Overall, it did not sprawl aimlessly. Rather, the river served to carry settlers from adjacent Kentucky and Virginia, but others from New England pushed west below the Great Lakes; and the two channels of migrants locked in political struggle over the issue of slavery.

Although immigration accounted for only about 15 percent of the strong increase of population, it strongly influenced the direction of slavery's expansion. John H. Long remarks that immigrants were attracted "chiefly by economic opportunity" and "most immigrants avoided the South, where they could not compete with the system of slavery."[1] In the long run these newcomers preserved the Old Northwest as free land.

To be sure, the Northwest Ordinance decreed no slavery, apparently in response to the wishes of large-scale investors from Massachusetts; but the Ordinance held some ambiguities. Of these, the most serious concerned slaves and their masters already resident in the Northwest when the Ordinance was enacted. The Ordinance could not take effect against them ex post facto, and newcomers had little difficulty affirming that they had been on the scene before enactment. No agency enforced the Act against immigrants from the South bringing their slaves along or falsely classing them as "indentured servants." In the North, however, no enforcement was necessary because immigrants along that channel neither wanted nor tolerated slaves.[2]

1 *Settling of North America*, ed. Tanner et al., 80.
2 Finkelman, *Slavery and the Founders*, Chap. 3.

Of all the cultural distinctions between northern and southern states, slavery aroused greatest stress because it became an issue of morality as well as economics. During a brief period of the Revolution, some Virginians conceded that treating human persons as property could not be justified on moral grounds.[3] George Washington would bequeath freedom to his many chattels, and Thomas Jefferson wrote to oppose the institution though Jefferson never could quite relinquish the income from it by which he satisfied his very expensive tastes. These two Virginians, though formally Anglican in religion, comforted their moral impulses, like other masters, with a vague Deism allowing latitude for personal behavior.

Not so the New Englanders whose Puritan traditions dictated stern conceptions of morality enforced by intolerant bigotry. (How strange are the paths of Progress!) By the time of the American Revolution, the Puritans' descendants had concluded that slavery was sinful and should not be tolerated. Vermont's state constitution banned it, which was easy for the mountaineers to do where blacks were nonexistent and plantations impractical. In Pennsylvania, where nearly seven thousand slaves did exist and respect ran high for all species of property, the assembly began in 1780 to move for gradual emancipation.[4] Under that act, slaves born earlier remained enslaved, but children born thereafter to slave mothers became free at age twenty-eight.[5]

Massachusetts's Chief Justice William Cushing determined in 1783 that the law must be consistent with the Declaration of Independence's inspiring phrase that had been incorporated in the state's constitution to reaffirm that all men were born free and equal. Such grand phrases, wrote Justice Cushing, were "totally repugnant to the idea of being born slaves," and by the scratching of his pen he abolished "perpetual servitude of a rational creature."[6]

A year later, Connecticut and Rhode Island enacted gradual emancipation laws.[7] Congress, however, bowed to the slave states, so it rejected Thomas Jefferson's proposal in 1784 to exclude slavery from western territories; but in 1787 the Northwest Ordinance included such a ban, seemingly in response to investors from Massachusetts. Laggard New York (which included more slaves than any other northern state) waited until 1799 to enact gradual emancipation, and New Jersey hung behind until 1804. But they did finally join the movement.

3 *Spirit of 'Seventy-Six*, ed. Commager and Morris, 402.
4 Ibid., 405–06.   5 Nash and Soderlund, *Freedom by Degrees*, 3, 5.
6 *Spirit of 'Seventy-Six*, 406–07; "Cushing, William," in *Dictionary of American Biography*. Cushing's ruling discloses that Massachusetts, like England, had never authorized slavery by law.
7 David Brion Davis, *The Problem of Slavery in the Age of Revolution, 1770–1823* (Ithaca, N.Y.: Cornell University Press, 1975). The sequence of state actions against slavery is listed in a calendar, 23–36.

Thus the great movement that had started in England even before the outbreak of Revolutionary independence made gradual headway in America and the Revolution's rhetoric about liberty began to have substance for some persons formerly held in thrall. Semantics must be attended to. These were human persons by biological definition, but (like Indians) had been excluded from *legal* society. Even after transformation from animal property to humanity, they were still condemned to a social *caste* barred by perceived *race* from full intermingling with members of the conquest caste. Americans, for a long time, called the offspring of mixed racial parentage "half breeds." Englishmen have called them more accurately "half castes."

Americans, writes Reginald Horsman, "never lost the belief that they were a special, chosen people, a people destined to change the world for the better."[8] This notion came into conflict with the existence and expansion of chattel slavery. The intellectual dilemma required an acceptable rationalization. "If slavery was to continue then it became essential to demonstrate that the fault lay with the blacks, not with the whites."[9] On that assumption, the chosen people could maintain their complacent self-conception.

Blacks did not agree. "For black people, Western nations achieved their industrial growth and economic prosperity on the backs of blacks; [they finally] abolished slavery primarily for economic reasons, have discriminated against black people ever since, and are unrepentant about any of it."[10]

Much history, still in progress, was required for evolving blacks and whites into acceptance of each other as peers after their contradictory conditions and conceptions in the era of the American Revolution.

The progress of that evolution began in the North. In effect, the issue of slavery divided the United States geographically into two empires, and as they expanded westward they kept parallel courses. A wave of free-soil emigrants brought Ohio into the Union as a free state in full accord with the Northwest Ordinance, but Indiana and Illinois became political battlegrounds in the North while Kentucky and other states south of the Ohio River installed slavery without dispute. Until 1850, *all* new slave states admitted to the Union were located south of the Ohio River; free states were north of it.[11]

John Hope Franklin observes that more than geography separated "the two worlds of race." Though new Englanders might concede that blacks had "as good a right to freedom as we have," freedom was conceived within limits. "Even where the sentiment favoring emancipation was pronounced,

8 Horsman, *Race and Manifest Destiny*, 82.   9 Ibid., 101.
10 Small, "Racist Ideologies," in *Transatlantic Slavery*, 123.
11 Finkelman, *Slavery and the Founders*, 187n52.

it was seldom accompanied by a view that Negroes were the equals of whites and should become a part of one family of Americans."[12]

For present purposes, it is enough to notice that the northern and southern American empires grew ever more disparate as they grew in size, but they managed to compromise politically until 1860 by means of a shared government in which the slave states dominated. This was possible because of a shared ideology of racial conceptions. James Madison recognized that the great division of *interests* in the United States "did not lie between the large and small states: it lay between Northern and Southern" and this difference occurred "principally from their having or not having slaves."[13] This conflict of material interests could be overcome by mutual acceptance of race assumptions so that North and South could, and did, cooperate to dispossess and exile Indians from their homelands all the way across the continent; and they warred against the Mexicans who were conceived to be inferior because of race mixture.[14]

One must somehow contrive to keep a straight face when contemplating the Americans' assumptions of purity of "blood"; much historical mingling of peoples in Europe as well as America must be blanked out of consciousness. But the race-proud conquerors did so delude themselves and did manage to share power on these assumptions until finally the clash of their material interests threw the slave-plantation southern expansionists against the money power of the Northerners.

Opinion polls had not yet come into vogue, so it is impossible to say definitely how large a fraction of the whole population was constituted by the aggressive, conquering Revolutionaries. Even among self-consciously "white" Euro-Americans, a number maintained loyalty to the British crown in more or less active ways. Some Loyalists actively joined auxiliaries to British armed forces.[15] Others simply refused to endorse Revolutionary associations and militias. A special case included Quakers and sectarian Germans in Pennsylvania who rejected the use of arms by either side in the war and tended therefore to hold conservatively to the pre-Revolutionary status quo. All of these dissidents were repressed and persecuted by the Revolutionaries. To call their treatment democratic is to mangle language.

The Religious Society of Friends (Quakers) went through transformation that revealed interior fault lines. As in other religions, many "birthright" Friends accepted variously the creed of the religious culture in

---

12 John Hope Franklin, *Race and History: Selected Essays, 1938–1988* (Baton Rouge: Louisiana State University Press, 1989), 132–33.
13 Quoted in Finkelman, *Slavery and the Founders*, 11 (italics added).
14 Horsman, *Race and Manifest Destiny*, Chap. 12.
15 *Atlas of Early American History*, ed. Cappon et al., 126.

which they had grown up. Revolutionary excitement aroused many young Quakers to reject pacifism and either to leave the Society voluntarily or to be "disowned" by it.[16] In the tumultuous period embracing the Seven Years War and the Revolution, orthodox Quakers reaffirmed traditional religious tenets by rejecting office in governments based on compulsion, and their religious opponents strengthened that movement by test oaths that excluded Quakers from the electoral franchise as well as public office. But because the Friends' religion required members to do good – to work for the general welfare – its pacifism did not imply being passive in the midst of sin and evil.

Banished from power, the revivalist movement turned to help the peoples oppressed under the Revolution: the Indians and blacks, especially those held in slavery. Led by the Pemberton brothers – Israel Jr., John, and James – Quakers formed the Friendly Association for Regaining and Preserving Peace with the Indians by Pacific Measures, which negotiated Delaware Indians off the warpath of the Seven Years War.[17] Following this, the Quakers founded a committee on Indian affairs that sent missions to Senecas and Shawnees and has continued to function to the present day.

Individual Friends had opposed slavery in general, and some had manumitted their own holdings as early as 1712, but they had encountered much opposition within their own Society. Not until 1754 was the Philadelphia Yearly Meeting able to announce its abhorrence of slaveholding; and "the Quaker leadership embraced abolitionism as part of the crusade for moral revitalization."[18]

This marked a change of direction. During Quaker domination, Pennsylvania's government had enacted a harsh slave code. After the change, however, as David Brion Davis remarks, "It would be difficult to exaggerate the central role Quakers played in initiating and sustaining the first antislavery movements."[19]

This role was performed on both sides of the Atlantic as Pennsylvania Quakers communicated constantly with their religious brethren in England. Along the way to showdown, Pennsylvania's Quakers worked more and more insistently toward the great goal of freedom for slaves, beginning with their own members. With the support of the Yearly Meeting, John Woolman and Anthony Benezet personally visited every local Meeting and every Friend known to own at least one slave, and both journeyed to England.

16 In 1761, the London Yearly Meeting authorized disownment of slave traders. Many American Quakers were involved in the trade until the Philadelphia Yearly Meeting threatened disownment (*in 1774*) Davis, *Problem of Slavery*, calendar.
17 Jennings, *Empire of Fortune*, Chaps. 15, 17.
18 Nash and Soderlund, *Freedom by Degrees*, 53–54; Hugh Thomas, *The Slave Trade: The Story of the Atlantic Slave Trade, 1440–1870* (New York: Simon and Schuster, 1997), 460.
19 Davis, *Problem of Slavery*, 213, 215.

In Pennsylvania, other churches kept silent about the subject although some individuals, like Benjamin Rush and Thomas Paine, spoke out.[20] In England the Quakers were aided by Methodist John Wesley's *Thoughts Upon Slavery*, which quoted extensively from Anthony Benezet. Other Englishmen took strong stands. Dr. Samuel Johnson toasted, "Here's to the next insurrection of the negroes in the West Indies." Even the House of Commons, under Quaker prompting, appointed a commission to look into the slave trade.[21]

In 1776 there came a climax that at this distance in time seems heart rending. The colonies roared for liberty through Independence; in the same year, the Philadelphia Yearly Meeting decreed disownment for Friends who refused to "clear" themselves of the sin of slaveholding. Then, when political and religious opponents of Quakers seized power in Pennsylvania, they soon punished the Friends with disenfranchisement, test oaths, and harsh fines. The Presbyterians who had long feuded with Quakers organized themselves as Constitutionalists "and under such leaders as Joseph Reed and George Bryan, lashed out at their opponents."[22]

But the Quakers would not shut up, and their antislavery propaganda so shamed the anti-Quaker Constitutionalist proclaimers of "liberty" that Pennsylvania in 1780 enacted the first law to "abolish" slavery. Like the Constitution enacted by the same party, the rhetoric of this law far outran its performance. It was so hedged and qualified that not a single slave was freed, nor could be for at least twenty-eight years.[23]

Suffering under oppression, Quakers nevertheless continued their campaign to forward emancipation by private and individual actions. They founded an organization for that purpose in 1784 but apparently were handicapped by their political situation during the Revolution; in 1787 they reorganized it as the Pennsylvania Society for the Abolition of Slavery and recruited like-minded non-Quakers. Besides its constant propaganda, this society took advantage of fine print qualifications in the law and went to court in behalf of slaves in special situations. They "restored to liberty upwards of one hundred persons" between 1784 and 1787. After 1787, the society "began to function as the nation's first freedmen's bureau," in the phrase of Gary B. Nash and Jean R. Soderlund. "It intervened in the job market to secure positions for former slaves, created schools and promoted education, offered moral advice in broadsides and home visitations, and tendered legal assistance to those in need."[24]

Interestingly, the abolitionist society won the support of Benjamin Franklin who consented to act as its president. Surprisingly, his first vice-

20 Nash and Soderlund, *Freedom by Degrees*, 98.   21 Thomas, *Slave Trade*, 477, 478.
22 O. S. Ireland, "The Crux of Politics," 472/390.   23 Thomas, *Slave Trade*, 482.
24 Nash and Soderlund, *Freedom by Degrees*, 123, 128.

president was Quaker James Pemberton.[25] Their reconciliation marked Pennsylvania's postwar reversion from Revolutionary "liberty" to prewar toleration.

I have attended at length to the Quakers because of the dishonest viciousness visited upon them by some historical writers. They will appear once more in the next chapter concerning power.

The Revolutionaries were keenly conscious that many Americans did not share their passion for Independence – and were just as keenly determined to prevail against all such dissidents, of whom the Quakers were only one type. The new American states all adopted measures of repression, legal and extralegal. "Tarring and feathering," according to Hugh Edward Egerton, "were a rough-and-ready method of dealing with offenders whose cases were not deemed worthy of more serious treatment," but to undergo that humiliation did not necessarily immunize a victim against the "more serious" affliction of loss of property.[26]

We have seen in Chapter 16 how the Boston mobs destroyed homes of officials loyal to the crown. By the end of the war, Loyalists made claims upon the crown amounting to £10,358,413 for property destroyed or confiscated by the Revolutionaries.[27] Not all such claimants deserve pity. In this complex conflict, one British observer thought that the interest of certain loyal officials prompted them "to promote the continuance of the war, such as quartermasters and their deputies, *ad infinitum*; barrack-masters and their deputies, *ad infinitum*, commissaries and their deputies, *ad infinitum*, all of which make princely fortunes."[28] Profiteering from war is nothing new. Nevertheless, the record shows that many other victims "lost their all through loyalty to the British connexion."

Permanent exile was the severe punishment of such victims, and they were many. Ultimately, between forty and fifty thousand Loyalists settled in Canada, creating a major boost in general population and a significant increase of speakers of English.[29] About half were from New York, and large numbers from Virginia, New Jersey, Connecticut, Pennsylvania, and Massachusetts. About sixteen thousand Loyalists migrated from the Carolinas and Georgia to Caribbean and Atlantic islands, many of whom had first fled to one of the Floridas.[30]

A superb atlas of America's great migrations allots pages to the Loyalists and a detailed map of their movements. It estimates about 15 to 20 percent of Loyalists were "permanently uprooted or dispersed." About a thousand New Englanders joined General Thomas Gage when he sailed

25 Ibid., 124–25.   26 Egerton, "Introduction," *Royal Commission*, xxiv.
27 Ibid., xl.   28 Ibid., l.
29 *Atlas of Early American History*, ed. Cappon et al., 127, map 59.   30 Ibid., 127–28.

from Boston for Halifax in 1776. The greatest number left New York when the British evacuated at the end of the war, but many of them had gravitated to that city during its occupation. About nine thousand persons found their ways to England.[31]

So great was the growth of Nova Scotia that a new province of New Brunswick was split off from it. For the like reason, Quebec was divided to make Upper and Lower Canada. A startling consequence of the moving about was the British decision in 1792 to pick up 1,196 African American refugees and send them to help establish Sierra Leone in Africa. We have already noticed, in Chapter 41, the provision made to settle Iroquois Indian Loyalists in Canada.

The editors of *The Settling of North America* remark that "The American Revolution dislocated a greater number of people in North America than any other event on the continent up to that time."[32] This extraordinary atlas fills a gap that has long cried out for substance; its masses of data cover "the great migrations into North America from the ice age to the present" and do so in attractive, easily digestible form deserving highest praise.

In Britain, in contrast with the American Revolutionaries' repression of opposition, discussion of the conflict remained open and free throughout. Members of Parliament, including Edmund Burke and John Wilkes, spoke in behalf of the Americans' cause, and the City of London's Common Council rejected proposals to give voluntary financial support to the armed forces. The press spoke out freely.[33]

In uncoordinated actions, advocates of governmental reform associated their proposals with sympathy for the Americans. When news arrived in London of Cornwallis's surrender at Yorktown, it became the signal for demands to discontinue military action in America and to dismiss the ministry. The movement floundered in confusion until the House of Commons adopted a motion on 27 February 1782 condemning further prosecution of hostilities in North America. On 15 March, Commons began deliberating a motion of no confidence in the ministry, and within five days the ministers resigned collectively.[34]

John Sainsbury argues that the pro-Americans justified their assertion "that the American War of Independence was in fact a civil war; and in so doing they helped to establish a vibrant tradition of domestic dissent over British foreign policy that has survived until the present century." Stubbornly, "through their sympathetic response to events in America, the pro-Americans helped to effect a transformation in the movement for political reform in Britain."[35]

31 *Settling of North America*, ed. Tanner et al., 70, 71.   32 Ibid.   33 See Chap. 18, above.
34 Sainsbury, *Disaffected Patriots*, Chap. 6.   35 Ibid., 163, 164.

Apart from long-standard issues of reform, a new movement grew in Britain. Peace with the United States had started to restore commerce, especially in its most profitable department, the slave trade; and "among some in England, after the loss of the American colonies, antislavery became a 'means to redeem the nation, a patriotic act.' "[36] In 1787, a group of Quakers in London took the lead in founding a Committee for Effecting the Abolition of the Slave Trade; and this committee, according to Hugh Thomas, "marked the transition of what had hitherto been the Quaker cause of abolition into a national, even an international, movement."[37]

To follow further that movement here would stray from this book's scope. It is enough to note the launching of the movement in the wake of the American Revolution while, most regrettably, as our next chapter will show, slavery and the slave trade increased in America following the Revolution.

The West lay most attractively before the new empire, but it had to be made accessible. Though Indians were pacified, and legal procedures were formalized for adding new states to the Union, natural obstacles abounded. Capitalistic land speculators built rough wagon roads and prevailed on the federal government to build more. The Ohio River and Great Lakes carried heavy traffic westward, soon to be supplemented by canals and railroads.[38]

The land invited, and the frontier became visibly the frontier of Europe. Even before the Revolution, Thomas Paine had proclaimed that "Europe, and not England, is the parent country of America." He added, "Not one third of the inhabitants, even of this province [of Pennsylvania] are of English descent."[39]

A special effort must be made to recall the pre-Revolutionary mixture of peoples. After that war, natural increase accounted for most of the general growth of population, but foreign-born persons made up 15 percent, and their offspring became part of the "natural" increase. The polyglot mixture hides under governmental institutions of English tradition so that one must look for cultural enclaves such as Frenchmen along the Mississippi, Spaniards in the Floridas, and Germans in Pennsylvania and North Carolina. (In the 1990s, the U.S. Census determined that more Americans descended from German ancestry than from any other European nationality.)

Not a single American state has grown with a wholly homogeneous population, even if only Europeans are counted, though the governments of all

36 Thomas, *Slave Trade*, 487–88.   37 Ibid., 493.
38 *Settling of North America*, ed. Tanner et al., 72.   39 Paine, *Common Sense*, 22–23.

descend from English institutions. By the great power of racial conceptions, varied Europeans are merged as "whites" to share in what has been called *herrenvolk democracy*, and it was in this form that governmental power spread across the continent as legal institutions.

This was the liberty attracting immigrants from Europe along with the availability of *land* for peasants who could hope to get none in their native lands except through successful revolution. The combination of land and political representation did constitute greater real democracy for "white" immigrants than they could enjoy anywhere else in the world. Englishmen preserved some civil liberties appearing uncertainly in America, but American farmers and working people averaged more income and personal property than their English counterparts. "The American Revolution left an enduring impression on British reform. . . . English libertarian values had helped shape the ideological perspective of colonial radicals; now the American adaptation of these values in the crucible of revolutionary change was, in turn, nourishing and reviving the domestic reform tradition." Thus, John Sainsbury.[40]

Influence was reciprocal. The cloned empires expanded parallel to each other and acted constantly upon each other though, like twins, they developed as individuals. The *herrenvolk democracy* of America extended liberty to persons in white skins. The libertarian democracy of Britain maintained itself on gradations of social class. If Britain learned from America to make political representation actual instead of virtual, America long resisted making it color-blind.

Britain led the way on that path during and after the American Revolution.

The human persons of America's western regions have been presented by "mainstream" historians in terms set by what is called Frontier Theory. This reflects the race biases of conquest policies that stereotype "whites" as *civilized*, Indians as *savage*, and persons of African origin as *subhuman*. In an empirical study of actual people, Daniel H. Usner Jr. has concluded that, "For too long, 'frontier' has connoted an interracial boundary, across which advanced societies penetrated primitive ones." In reality, frontiers were "networks of cross-cultural interaction through which native and colonial groups circulated goods and service."[41]

Such "frontier exchange" economies involved "the diverse and dynamic participation of Indians, [Euro-American] settlers, and slaves" until "tougher laws controlling interaction . . . heightened ethnic tensions and

---

40 Sainsbury, *Disaffected Patriots*, 165.
41 Daniel H. Usner Jr., *Indians, Settlers, and Slaves*, 6.

accelerated the buildup of interracial barriers." In the locale of the lower Mississippi Valley of Mr. Usner's study, "the plantation economy began to replace the frontier exchange economy as the main framework of cross-cultural relations."[42] What had been a cooperative strategy for mutual subsistence transformed gradually, as an export-directed economy supplanted the frontier exchange economy and "colonial officials intensified measures to control interaction among settlers, slaves, and Indians."[43] The preceding fluid intermixture simply vanished from historical attention.

Probably it would be too wishful to conclude that people of the frontier west needed only to be left alone in order to get along peacefully with each other. One must not forget that the "settlers" had come in the first place in order to acquire the Indians' lands, nor that exploitation was the very purpose of slavery. Yet it seems clear that tensions and interethnic hostilities heightened in response to policies of conquest by the institutions of "civilization."

More empirical studies are needed. For students to understand the peoples of the frontiers, it is necessary to study *them* rather than abstractions invented to justify conquest. "Civilization" overpowered the liberties of frontiersmen as surely as it overmastered indigenous peoples.

The Revolutionaries understood this. They admitted new western states to their Union as peers of the founders because the founders feared that westerners would rise to fight for independence even as the founders had. Frontier liberties had to be brought under control by a central power.

42 Ibid., 7–9.   43 Ibid., 282.

43

POWER

Complaints are everywhere heard from our most considerate and virtuous citizens, equally the friends of public and private faith, and of public and personal liberty; that our governments are too unstable; that the public good is disregarded in the conflicts of rival parties; and that measures are too often decided, not according to the rules of justice and the rights of the minor party; but by the superior force of an interested and over-bearing majority. However anxiously we may wish that these complaints had no foundation, the evidence of known facts will not permit us to deny that they are in some degree true.

"Publius," The Federalist X [James Madison] 22 November 1787

Elections, my dear Sir, Elections to Offices which are great objects of Ambition, I look at with terror.

John Adams to Thomas Jefferson, 6 December 1787

The siege of Yorktown effectively ended the war for American independence, but it left many social and political issues unsettled. The war united the former colonies for victory; it did not homogenize their very diverse material interests nor their ideological traditions.

The United States of America constituted their federation as a sovereignty among modern nations unique by being bound together under terms of a written constitution. Taken at face value, this document seems clear, but ever-suspicious politicians found much ambiguity in its terms and they demanded amendments before ratifying it. As lawyers, they understood how words and phrases can contort meanings as fun-house mirrors reflect images. In due course, a sage came to believe that "the Constitution is what the judges say it is," and a genial cynic remarked that those judges "follow the election returns."

An enormous literature has been made, much of it reveredly famous, to analyze the motives and meanings of the Constitution Founding Fathers. The texts have required concentrated attention from scholars throughout entire careers. I do not have years available to follow their example; and, besides, all these assertions, contradictions, and hairsplittings give me a headache. I must approach the subject along a different path. Explicitly, I think of the Constitution as an assemblage of constantly changing rationalizations. Their meanings for the Constitution makers are evident from what the Founders did more reliably than from what they said.

Power concerned them greatly. How was power to be divided between the states and their jointly shared government? How was it to be apportioned between large and small states? As between the citizens and their officers of government, could officers wiser than the rabble be entrusted with enough power to rule? Wisdom did not guarantee virtue. Could the common people be kept under controls to prevent licentiousness? How could property be guaranteed? How could the southern slave states protect their special interests against northern free states? How could the profits of northern commerce be stabilized against southern assaults on prices? Most immediately urgent, how could the transmontane West be prevented from hiving off to independence for itself in imitation of the example already set by the East?

Such matters weighed heavily on the mind of the great land speculator George Washington. (He owned rights to sixty-three thousand acres of western lands.) "I can forsee no evil greater than disunion," he wrote to James McHenry.[1] Washington knew well that easy transportation was the key to pulling East and West together and making his land rights salable to immigrants. As a private, though famous, person, he participated in a company to create a canal on the upper Potomac River, but ran into the obstacle of counterclaims by Virginia and Maryland to authority over navigation on the river (with more claims to be expected when the canal should get to Pennsylvania). Under Washington's patronage, commissioners from the states met at his Mount Vernon home, 25 March 1785, and arranged coordination of policies. Their success led Virginia's legislature to invite all the states to a new conference in September 1786 at Annapolis, Maryland, to broaden interstate cooperation.

The response was ho-hum. Only five states actually sent commissioners. State political bosses had no desire to set up an authority higher than themselves, so the Annapolis conference could do no more than recommend the holding of still another conference in May 1787. A cool Congress delayed acting on this recommendation until 21 February 1787 and then warily limited it "for the sole and express purpose of revising the Articles of Confederation."[2]

But a shocking event made men of influence and power revise their

---

1 Thomas P. Slaughter, *The Whiskey Rebellion: Frontier Epilogue to the American Revolution* (New York: Oxford: University Press, 1986), 87.
2 Mark D. Kaplanoff, in *Blackwell Encyclopedia*, 453–54.

beliefs about centralized power. In September 1786, the same month as the Annapolis conference, the Revolutionary War veteran Daniel Shays led a farmers' revolt in western Massachusetts.

Thomas P. Slaughter comments acidly on the background of Shays's Revolt. "Nothing like the mythical classless frontier society ever existed in the western country." Instead of accumulating land, property owners were losing ground to big speculators; in this society of extreme social and economic turmoil, "most settlers were living at a bare subsistence level and conditions were getting worse."[3] Yet population grew in spurts as land-hungry people deludedly launched themselves to invade Indian lands and complain loudly about Indian resistance. As often as not the resistance expressed itself in horrible atrocities that frequently were reciprocated. The frontier people demanded protection from government for their persons and invasions. In their simple assumptions, Indian savages had no right to the lands properly awaiting occupation by "whites." Hated almost equally with Indians were the great land speculators whose legal devices stood in the way of ownership by squatters – and who typically were Easterners.

If government could not protect them, the frontier people would seek protection from other governments. Their delegations approached colonial authorities of Spain and even of the Britain that was so recently the enemy. As early as 1783, a delegation from Vermont – still unaffiliated to the United States – visited Quebec's Governor Haldimand to suggest that their independent state be annexed to Britain.[4] Vermont was not accepted as the fourteenth state of the Union until 1791.

Other quarrels over sovereignty broke out in the District of Kentucky, where Virginia's rule was resisted, and in North Carolina where three western counties temporarily constituted themselves as the State of Franklin.

The Revolution enabled former colonials to shake off the British crown's power. It left intact their own power over blacks and Indians. It left in confusion the issue of power by each of the new states against the others.

The followers of Revolutionary veteran Daniel Shays demanded redress of grievances against the political leaders who had transformed the colony of Massachusetts into a Commonwealth, had done so with the indispensable support of the Westerners, and had seized state power in order to tax and exploit those same Westerners. Captain Shays's role was remarkably symbolic because of his background. He had been among the minutemen who rushed to Lexington in April 1775. He had served in the battle of Bunker Hill, again at the crucial capture of Ticonderoga, and had capped his service

---

3 Slaughter, *Whiskey Rebellion*, 65.   4 Ibid., 43.

by helping to defeat the British army under General Burgoyne at Saratoga. He was a model of the citizen soldier without whom the Revolution could not have succeeded.[5]

But Shays and other veterans suffered from postwar policies in victorious Massachusetts by losing property through foreclosures for debt and taxes. Captain Shays came forward to lead protesters who stopped the foreclosures by blockading courthouses.

At this point, leading Revolutionaries showed a previously undisclosed aspect of their zeal. While Shays had rushed *to* Lexington Green in 1775, greatly famed Samuel Adams and John Hancock had rushed *from* it. When Shays protested against the exploitation of an administration led by Adams and Hancock, Adams denounced the Shaysites with fury, and Governor Hancock mobilized state troops and marched them against the insurgent Westerners.

The uprising collapsed, and "about a dozen" of its leaders were condemned to death by the Supreme Court though later pardoned. Shays escaped to Vermont and ended his days in New York State. There is no end to irony. In old age, Shays was awarded a pension from the federal government for his soldiering against Britain.[6]

Boston's new rulers stamped out protest as fiercely as George III had done, but not until the Shaysites had alarmed political leaders, former Revolutionaries, throughout all the Confederation. When Washington's Virginia tried again to convene delegates to contrive greater central power, fearful state leaders had become ready to cooperate.[7]

The delegates met in sweltering Philadelphia during the summer of 1787. Commentators have noticed that the delegates were upper-class types and have concluded that they were hostile to the Revolutionaries' great goal of liberty for the masses. This logic assumes such a goal for the earlier Congress that wrote the Declaration of Independence. We have seen the untruth of that assumption. The findings of this book point to the Constitution of 1787 as the Revolution's *culmination*, consistent with its launching and proceedings. The delegates' social classes were similar in profile to the background of the delegates to the Revolution's Congress.

Two overriding issues concerned the delegates to the Constitutional convention. Voting rights were all-important. The delegates were too sophisticated to believe in politicians' altruism. Some sort of sharing of power would be necessary. The adopted solution was a bicameral Congress, with an upper house Senate in which states had equal votes, two senators per

5 *Encyclopaedia Britannica*, 15th ed. (1993), 10:711.   6 Ibid.
7 James Madison, *Notes of Debates in the Federal Convention of 1787* (1840), intro. by Adrienne Koch (New York: W. W. Norton, 1987), 13.

state. This provided fair treatment for small states that might otherwise be overwhelmed by the large ones. To guard against the contrary possibility of small states combining to exploit the larger ones, voting was to be done according to population in Congress's lower house. When states' interests conflicted, the two houses would balance each other.[8]

Well and good, but defining population set up a snag. Slaves were not recognized as people in law though everyone knew that failing to count them as part of a state's population would shrink giant Virginia considerably below New England. Much more complex than just big and little, the issue set southern states (with slaves) against those of the North that were in the process of ending slavery. Fearful of having their property taken away, southern delegates gave an ultimatum: They must have protection for slavery "or they would oppose the Constitution."[9]

They got protection and something more than that. As South Carolina's Charles Cotesworth Pinckney told his state's legislature, "We have made the best terms for the security of this species of property it was in our power to make. We would have made better if we could; but on the whole, I do not think them bad."[10] He had good reason to feel complacent. Though the word *slaves* does not appear in the Constitution reported out by the convention, slaves appear in disguise as *other persons* than *citizens* or *free inhabitants*. This word magic was used because northern delegates, perhaps fearful of anger from their constituents, were ashamed to say *slaves* plainly. The device for counting slaves without naming them appears in Article I, Section 2, as the "three-fifths rule": "Representatives and direct Taxes shall be apportioned among the several States . . . according to their respective Numbers which shall be determined by adding to the whole Number of free Persons, including those bound to Service for a Term of Years, and excluding Indians not taxed, three fifths of all other Persons."[11]

Massachusetts's Elbridge Gerry interpreted this to imply that four southern voters would have more political power than ten northern voters.[12] That discrimination was guaranteed in the election of a president by the creation of an electoral college embracing the total of electors equal to the total number of each state's representatives and senators. As the three-fifths rule determined the number of representatives, southern free white citizens acquired greater political weight, man for man, than northern free white citizens. The process contributed in some degree to the Presidential elec-

---

8 The issues are presented readably in Catherine Drinker Bowen, *Miracle at Philadelphia* (Boston: Little, Brown and Co., 1966).
9 Finkelman, *Slavery and the Founders*, 14.   10 Ibid., 7.
11 *The Debate on the Constitution*, ed. Bernard Bailyn, 2 vols. (New York: The Library of America, 1993), 1:968.
12 Finkelman, *Slavery and the Founders*, 9.

tions of the "Virginia Dynasty" of Jefferson, Madison, Monroe, and William Henry Harrison.

Although southern slave owners gained more from the Constitution than their fair share of protection for their distinctive species of property, northern merchants demanded and got favor for their kind also. Northerners wanted a federal government that would control commerce between states and levy taxes to support the government. The impasse was circumvented by a "dirty compromise" concisely described by Paul Finkelman: "The South Carolina delegation would support the commerce clause if New England would support a prohibition on export taxes and protection for the slave trade."[13]

Delegate Luther Martin reported that "the eastern States [New England], notwithstanding their aversion to slavery, were very willing to indulge the southern States, at least with a temporary liberty to prosecute the slave trade, provided the southern States would in their turn gratify them, by laying no restriction on navigation acts."[14] It may be that their own heavy involvement in the very lucrative slave trade softened northern merchants from banning it. *Everything* connected to slavery was dirty.

The Revolution's violence had reduced the number of slaves in the plantations, and masters were determined to restore their losses by importing more. They must have their way or they would walk out of the Union. To gratify them, the slave trade was to be permitted long enough to make up the masters' losses, then possibly to be banned. 1808 was fixed upon as the date to decide – but only to decide *whether* to make the trade illegal, not to mandate that decision. Paul Finkelman comments that "at no time did the Convention consider a clause flatly prohibiting the trade" and "the slave trade clause is a specific exception to the general rule giving Congress complete power to regulate all commerce *but* slave importation."[15]

The Constitution also provided a Fugitive Slave clause, which provided a right for masters "to recover our slaves in whatever part of America they may take refuge, which is a right we had not before." This on the authority of General Charles Cotesworth Pinckney.[16] So early was the need foreshadowed for an Underground Railroad.

One may note with interest another provision of the Constitution that contradicted specifically the instrument used by the Revolutionaries to seize power in Pennsylvania and elsewhere. Article VI declares that officers of the states and the United States were to be bound "by Oath or Affirmation to support this Constitution; *but no religious Test shall ever be required* as a

13 Ibid., 22.   14 Ibid., 28.   15 Ibid., 29.
16 Ibid., 31. The Fugitive Slave clause at issue is the Constitution's Article IV, Section 2, par. 3.

Qualification to any Office or public Trust under the United States (italics added). Had that been in effect in 1776, it would have disabled Pennsylvania's Revolutionaries from gaining control by persecuting Quakers as they did. The consequences can only be guessed at.

The issue was well understood at the time the United States Constitution came up for ratification. It was seen in Pennsylvania as negation of the state's never-ratified constitution – never permitted, indeed, to be voted upon by the citizens. Quakers solicited support for the new federal basic law.[17] The managers of the repressive state constitution opposed the federal one. James Wilson signed both the Declaration of Independence and the federal Constitution, and he led in the overthrow of the state constitution. They knew what they were doing.

What shall we think then of frequently found opinions that the state constitution was highly democratic and that the federal Constitution was reactionarily conservative? One must distinguish. Certainly the federal law sustained and promoted the institution of slavery, but Article VI was included by framers who knew how the state law had been used and were determined to prevent that for the future. Terms such as *radical* and *conservative* have meaning only according to usage and experience, regardless of rhetoric. Article VI is a bastion of democracy.

But once again the issue of race rises. Slaves were *black*; the test laws banned by Article VI had reference only to *whites*.

17 Benjamin Rush, in *The Debate on the Constitution*, ed. Bailyn, 2:256.

Part V

MORE CONQUESTS

44

• ═══════════════

CLIMAX

All statesmen were overwhelmed by the sheer size of the territory they had gained by their peace treaty with Britain. They expected sectionalism to strain their structure of government and were happily astonished by the agreements of the Constitutional convention. As it turned out, the most dangerous sectional issues for the time being were West versus East instead of the expected North versus South. The slavery issue dividing North from South was eased for that generation at the expense of the slaves by giving the big southern planters what they wanted. Easterners were willing enough to give land to the Westerners at the expense of the Indian tribes, but other issues arose. *Little* planters of the West lacked the power of the Southerners, and they were unable to dictate terms to the wealthier and more populous East.

They defied the newly established federal government by refusing to pay taxes that Congress had been authorized by the Constitution to levy. Thomas P. Slaughter observes that "the taxing authority of the proposed national government would be no less, and was certainly designed to be even greater than anything attempted by the British government during the 1760s and 1770s." A major cause of the American Revolution had been traditional English hatred of excise taxes, and "one of the earliest fiscal measures of the new Congress was the whiskey excise of 1791."[1] Westerners' reaction to American excises copied the colonials' reactions to British excises.

Besides taxes, the federal government needed income from sale of western lands that dwindled from the effects of Indian raids scaring off purchasers. Eastern large-scale land speculators feared the loss of their investments unless the Westerners and the Indians were reduced to reliable obedience. President George Washington himself was one of the largest speculators.

President Washington tried to eliminate tribal opposition by sending

1 Slaughter, *Whiskey Rebellion*, 23, 27.

armies to beat it down. The Indians defeated two armies until strategy and policy were changed. At Fort Stanwix in 1784, commissioners had maintained that Britain's loss to the Revolutionaries implied the defeat of Britain's tribal allies. The Indians disagreed, and their defeat of American armies suggested need for change of American policy. General Anthony Wayne undertook the task. After winning the battle of Fallen Timbers in 1794, he reverted to negotiations as had been practiced by the colonies under the crown. In the Treaty of Greenville in 1795, Wayne recognized tribal territories and agreed to a boundary line between them and the United States.[2] Whereupon the situation swept out of control.

Thousands of immigrants poured over the boundary line. Thus one of the obstacles to U.S. sovereignty became inoperable, practically though not honorably. Western "settlers" intended to take the land regardless of treaties. In their outlook, the Indians were invaders rather than defenders of homelands. The real invaders, called settlers, assumed that the lands were "free to be taken," and this phrase has been imposed on the books of nationalist historians.

With the removal of Indian resistance came its replacement by increased "settler" resistance to constitutional authority. Within fifteen years after the Greenville treaty, 230,000 newcomers lived in the state of Ohio.[3]

Opposition to the excise grew throughout the West. Regions east of the mountains paid the tax, but nobody did in the frontier regions. In 1792, political rallies and mob violence broke out in western Pennsylvania. "The frontier of every state south of New York experienced unrest. In the degree and kind of protest there was little to mark western Pennsylvania as unique."[4] Tax collectors were tarred and feathered, and their homes ravaged. Resistance to the American government took much the same forms as had resistance against the British crown, and repression also followed as in the Revolution's course.

Under the Constitution's authority, the government of the United States was more powerful in the West than Britain's had been. To suppress the antitax "treason," the government mobilized and marched an army to the most visible seat of disturbance in the vicinity of Pittsburgh. This army was larger than either Burgoyne's at Saratoga or Cornwallis's at Yorktown, and it frightened western rebels into flight without necessity for battle.[5]

More than taxes were at issue. Ratification of the Constitution by nine required states had been achieved only after sometimes bitter debate. At the same time that the federal government solidified its power, a contrary political force reached out from the French Revolution to win widespread

2 *Anthony Wayne*, ed. Knopf, 397–98.   3 *Settling of North America*, ed. Tanner et al., 72.
4 Slaughter, *Whiskey Rebellion*, 117.   5 Ibid., Chap. 13.

following in the states. President Washington warned against "self-created [democratic] societies" that if not "discountenanced . . . will destroy the government of this country."[6] Thus Washington signaled that his Federalist supporters should not allow the political Revolution divorcing the states from Britain to decline into a social revolution propagating democracy.

The Father of his Country was certainly the father of the Constitution, and the uses he made of it in suppressing the Whiskey Rebellion demonstrated why opponents had struggled against its ratification. They feared and opposed excise taxes because of the power given to tax collectors to invade privacy while searching for taxable goods. They dreaded the power of a standing army capable of overriding local authorities. George Washington had fought against such powers when they were exerted by the British government, but when they came into his own hands he used them without hesitation.

A party formed behind Washington's program, notably extending beyond geographic sections. This new Federalist party encountered opposition even within Washington's Virginia. His Virginia neighbor, George Mason, had been a delegate to the Constitutional convention, but refused to sign its document. Considering Mason's eminence and Revolutionary experience, his refusal is puzzling until one examines his stated reasons. "There is no declaration of rights," objected Mason, "and the laws of the general government being paramount to the laws and constitutions of the several States, the declarations of rights in the separate States are no security."[7] Among Mason's other objections, he faulted "no declaration of any kind for preserving the liberty of the press, the trial by jury in civil causes; nor against the danger of standing armies in time of peace."[8]

Opponents in Pennsylvania agreed with Mason about the omission of a Bill of Rights and listed propositions for such a Bill. Other states also became arenas for struggle over personal rights until finally a list was accepted as the Constitution's first ten Amendments without which the Constitution would not be ratified. A student must notice, however, that these protections have often been violated and still are. An example will be noticed below.

A detailed argument favoring a Bill of Rights is "The Dissent of the Minority of the Pennsylvania Convention," which is gruesomely amusing when its high-flown rhetoric is compared to the track record of its signers. These were men who had imposed the wartime state constitution on Pennsylvania by legal trickery posing as the progress of democracy. They had never permitted it to come to review by the state's citizens, and they had presented it as the epitome of democracy when what it did in fact was to

6 Ibid., 221.   7 *Debate on the Constitution*, ed. Bailyn, 1:346.   8 Ibid., 1:348.

establish the power of a small clique over the majority. Armed with that power, and with firearms, they had persecuted and disfranchised the pacifist religions of Quakers and Mennonites and had blocked the postwar restoration of rights to these minorities.[9]

"The right of conscience shall be held inviolable" declared the clique in its attack on the majority's effort to restore citizenship rights to pacifists. Rarely has demagogy been more blatantly propounded. This time, however, it failed of its purpose. (How confusing these issues become when studied only from the parties' rhetoric!) Untangling fact, it appears that the majority of the state assembly had been prevented by the minority's devices from calling a new convention to revise the wartime trickery that disfranchised Pennsylvania's founding Quakers. The procedure for ratifying the new federal Constitution suggested a way out of the legal difficulty. Let the minority tell the rest in its own way.

> On the 28th of September last [1787] a resolution was proposed to the assembly by a member of the house who had been also a member of the federal convention, for calling a state convention, to be elected within *ten* days for the purpose of examining and adopting the proposed constitution of the United States. . . . [In such a convention, though summoned for its stated purpose, the majority could continue its business to revise the state constitution.] This attempt was opposed by a minority, who after offering every argument in their power to prevent the precipitate measure without effect, absented themselves from the house as the only alternative left them, to prevent the measure taking place . . . some of the members were seized the next day by a mob collected for the purpose, and forcibly dragged to the house, and there detained by force whilst the quorum of the legislature, *so formed*, compleated their resolution."[10]

In short, the majority won its way and "the bells of Christ Church rang." The outcomes of this struggle were ratification of the United States Constitution, enactment of a new state constitution, and submission of it to an approving electorate. Thus the Pennsylvania franchise rose once more to its prewar levels. The political weathervane Dr. Benjamin Rush was a triumphal Federalist in this struggle. But the special conditions of Pennsylvania had transformed the power relations of Federalism that soon were to become as clear there as elsewhere, and Dr. Rush would change again.

John Adams succeeded Washington as President and shared his views about authority, especially his own authority. On the opposite side, Thomas Jefferson viewed the radicalism of the French Revolution favorably. Jefferson withdrew from Washington's authoritarian party and stood forward as a

9 See. Chap. 28, above.
10 *Debate on the Constitution*, ed. Bailyn, 1:529; Ireland, *Religion, Ethnicity, and Politics*, 22–27.

champion of civil liberties.[11] A collision was bound to occur. It was fought out most clearly in Pennsylvania where terminology unfortunately obfuscates. The anti-Federalist party in Pennsylvania was known as Constitutionalist because its members strove to maintain their power under the wartime *state* constitution. Their opponents supported the U.S. Constitution, but in that state they were called Republicans.

The state constitution had a facade of personal rights masking the substance of their violation. State Republicans strove to destroy the facade in order to replace it with substance of civil liberties. It all makes sense when one distinguishes identifiable facts from windy rhetoric.

The advent of the U.S. Constitution startled the state Constitutionalists into realizing they had lost control. Knowing how they had contorted the language of law into power above law, they worried that their own devices might be turned against them by the new victors, and they became ardent proponents of a Bill of Rights in the federal Constitution overmatching the facade of rights in their state document. It is almost like strobe lighting playing on the state's politics. Happily, widespread public demonstrations convinced Federalists that their Constitution would die unratified until they adopted the first Ten Amendments protecting citizens against arbitrary government. Stress *citizens*. Nearly a century and a great civil war would go by before more Amendments would extend protection beyond racial limits.

The first of the Bill of Rights Amendments has become accepted so unarguably for its practical value that its tremendous significance as a cultural advance is often overlooked. "Congress shall make no law respecting an establishment of religion, or prohibiting the free exercise thereof" becomes world-shaking in context. It contradicted directly the various faiths of its enacters who generally subscribed to the biblical Old Testament's Ten Commandments. The first of these commanded; "I am the Lord thy God . . . *Thou shalt have no other gods before me.*" This is not reconcilable with religious tolerance. As the Founding Fathers knew that an attempt to establish any church would raise up its competitors in arms, they chose rationality and harmony instead.

The entire history of Christianity up to that moment had been invariably partnership between state and church – a particular church in every instance – to enforce the church's creed and institutions upon persons subject to the state. In 1787 proponents of hostile faiths adopted tolerance to be able to cooperate in a common government.

Tolerance was truly revolutionary. It had been the hallmark of the Quaker

11 Ellis, *American Sphinx*, 166–68.

utopia in Pennsylvania, and it had been suspended by devices concocted to overthrow not only Quaker domination but even Quaker participation in politics and government. Tolerance was restored in Pennsylvania under the new postwar constitution, and it was confirmed by the federal Constitution's Bill of Rights.

It is really rather breathtaking to have happened at all, and even more so when one considers how this First Amendment has endured even through the rupture of the Civil War down to the present day. Its limits must be observed. It applied only to *citizens* of the United States – Indians and slaves remained subject to predation and control – but avoidance of conflict with each other enabled the herrenvolk democracy to share the management of a giant territory.

At least in this one respect, the United States Constitution, as amended, deserves its reputation as a pillar of human liberty. Every subsequent effort at international cooperation rests at bottom on the principle of religious tolerance; the United Nations proclaims it. Quaker sufferings in the Revolution had not been wasted.

Pennsylvania had still another role to play in the interplay of federal power with the states. President John Adams determined to suppress the radical party sympathizing with the French Revolution. Adams's Federalists enacted the Alien and Sedition Acts that put powers in his hands greater than those of King George III and plainly violated the Bill of Rights amendments to the U.S. Constitution.[12]

The Alien Act of 1798 empowered President Adams to deport from the United States "all such aliens as he shall judge dangerous" or such as he suspects of treasonable machinations. The Sedition Act punished with fine and imprisonment "any false, scandalous and malicious writing or writings against the government of the United States . . . with intent to defame the said government." It was a republican government's version of lèse majesté, and Adams used it to jail editors opposed to himself.

The partnership of northern merchants and southern planters broke up as Thomas Jefferson went into Adams's opposition; Jefferson fell back upon states' rights as a feasible means of combating Federalist domineering. In 1798 the Supreme Court had not yet gained power to declare laws unconstitutional, so it is possible for Henry Steele Commager to comment, "it was not unreasonable for those who feared the centralizing tendencies of the federal government to assert that the States were the proper parties to decide this question." With this assumption, Jefferson prevailed on the legislature of Kentucky to invoke the Constitution's First Amendment with a

---

12 The laws are in *Documents of American History*, ed. Commager, 1:175–78.

declaration that the Sedition Act "which does abridge the freedom of the press, is not law, but is altogether void and of no effect"; and James Madison wrote a resolution for the General Assembly of Virginia that the Alien and Sedition Acts "are unconstitutional."[13]

Adams had the armed forces – the standing army he had so often assailed – and he ignored the protests until an incident occurred that threw the issue into the next presidential elections. This was the so-called Fries's Rebellion – a 1798 protest in *eastern* Pennsylvania against excise taxes. An auctioneer named John Fries declaimed against the taxes. A collector encountered violence in the form of "hot water" poured upon him by a woman from a second-story window. If tradition was followed, this hot water would have been poured from a chamber pot.[14]

John Adams would not tolerate such treasonable challenges to righteous authority and the majesty of law. He marched an army into the "Pennsylvania Dutch" counties. It inflicted much genuine violence on the inhabitants and the *Reading Eagle* newspaper, and it disenchanted the Germans from Federalism. John Fries wondered what the fuss was all about. When seized by Adams's Troops he was astounded to learn he was charged with treason. Even more astoundingly, he was convicted and sentenced to death. But an aroused public protested so vehemently that Adams pardoned the heinous crime.[15] (Remembering Adams's frame-up of Quakers – see Chapter 28, above – I wonder how many such contrivances should be charged to him.)

The episode of "Fries's Rebellion" generally escapes notice in standard histories so it seems important to draw attention to the barbarities of the army that paraded through Pennsylvania under full sanction from President John Adams. "Civil" gangs as well as the military acted like storm troopers without restraint, except that imposed by gatherings of indignant armed civilians.

The military commander ordered Jacob Schnyder, editor of the *Reading Eagle*, to be stripped and lashed, and this was done without any sort of process except the officer's order. In Philadelphia a gang of thugs dragged the *Aurora*'s editor William Duane out of his office, knocked him down, circled his prostrate body, and kicked and beat him into unconsciousness. The victims' offenses consisted of having opposed the programs of the Federalist party with President John Adams at its head.

---

13 Ibid., 178–84. John Adams thought that he and Jefferson "were in agreement concerning the Constitution and forms of government in general; they differed on measures of administration and other details." *The Adams-Jefferson Letters*, ed. Lester J. Cappon (Chapel Hill: University of North Carolina Press, 1959), 286. Could he really have believed that the Alien and Sedition Acts were merely details of administration?

14 Rosenfeld, *American Aurora*, 608–9.   15 Ibid., 611, 777, 780, 797.

Political opposition was stretched and contorted to *treason* as demonstrated by Justice Samuel Chase's charge to the jury trying John Fries.

> The court are of the opinion that any insurrection or rising to resist . . . the execution of any stature of the United States for levying or collecting taxes . . . under any pretence, as that the statute was unjust, burthensome, oppressive or unconstitutional is a levying of war against the United States . . . military weapons . . . are not necessary to make such an insurrection or rising amount to a levying of war.

Not surprisingly, this charge led the jury to find John Fries guilty.[16]

The outcome of the "Fries's Rebellion" was outrage among the Pennsylvania Germans who turned strongly against Federalism in the elections of 1800. Whereas George Washington had preserved support for Federalism when he suppressed the Whiskey Rebellion in western Pennsylvania, Adams outraged former Federalists – Dr. Benjamin Rush among others – and the state's Electors voted decisively for Thomas Jefferson as President.

Thus Adams, Massachusetts, and Federalism went into decline. The Alien and Sedition Acts were allowed to expire, and democracy actually made headway in the United States – for white males. In the twisting ways of history it became identified with states' rights and Virginia's slaveholding gentry. That, too, would change.

I do not agree with John Adams's idolators who included himself at their head. Strictly as a politician of the wheeler-dealer variety, Adams labored incessantly in the Continental Congress to win delegates for independence. His outpourings of self-praise inflate his image out of all proportion to reality. His dedication to liberty cannot withstand examination of his role in the frame-up of Quakers, and at the end he exposed his much-touted conceptions of statesmanship with the Alien and Sedition Acts. This was a hollow hero.

16 Justice Chase's charge is at *American Aurora*, 780. The organized Federalist violence against opponents is in the same book in the interstices of references to the John Fries episode, n. 15 above.

45

———————————— • ————————————

IN SUM

It's the race issue – everything from cross burnings to affirmative-action debates
– that is the central political dynamic of our time.
        John McCarron, *Chicago Tribune*, 15 November 1999, p. 19

This chapter discusses one historically dominant theme: the intertwined behavior of conquest and its invented justification by the concept of race.

As a federal republic, the United States was formed by partnership of thirteen colonies cloned from the British empire. All of them had been founded as enterprises to conquer the peoples previously occupying North American land, and all were intended to seize and repopulate the land. Part of the new population was brought in duress as slaves from Africa.

At a given point in growth, the most powerful colonials chafed against ultimate rule from Britain and determined to break free from the British empire in order to establish their own empire. They proclaimed much war propaganda about resisting slavery and demanding liberty, but the issue was power – whether ultimate power should rest in Britain or among the ruling classes in the colonies. Definitely, this was not an uprising of the whole people except possibly in New England but doubtfully even there. John Adams estimated off the cuff that a third of "the people" wanted independence, a third opposed it, and a third were indifferent. Adams's remark requires more analysis than it has received.

In the first place, "the people" for Adams did not include all persons of the human species – only those recognized as legal entities. Indians and slaves were not people. Clearly they also were not among persons wanting independence. Indians took arms against the Revolution, and slaves fled from it when given opportunity. Even among the fully legal persons, more than seventy thousand Loyalists fled to Halifax, Ontario, the West Indies, and Britain. How many stayed in place regardless of harassment cannot be estimated. In Pennsylvania, Loyalist sympathies were so strong that Adams organized suppression of them by armed force. Blow away all the rhetoric and what is left is a minority determined to establish its own power by force, not only as against Britain, but also as against opponents in America.

The Continental Congress conducted the Revolutionary War with no liberty for opponents of any kind. Basic objectives included conquest of Indians (not "conquest of the wilderness") and seizure of their lands on any pretext or none. Southerners – slave-owning Southerners – insisted on confirmation of their peculiar institution and got this at the same time that Britain was in the process of ending slavery.

The Revolutionaries wanted to reduce Indians and slaves permanently below human status. The means for this was to classify them together as nonwhite. This racist classification served all purposes of social caste as well as legal disfranchisement. It has survived in less intense but still genuine form through Civil War, Reconstruction, Indian reservations, massive immigration, industrial revolution, and urbanization.

In this book *race* refers to a socially accepted concept; it has long been discredited as a biological fact.[1]

A good friend chides me for giving too little notice to historical persons who really did struggle and sacrifice for liberty for all. I am uncomfortable with that criticism, especially because of my own youthful experience as one of the strugglers. Yet I have written no more than what the evidence seemed to indicate, and I will not cover up; there has been much too much of that.

Human animals are capable of behavior demonic as well as angelic, and sometimes both from the same creature. The western squatters who strove genuinely for liberty and property against eastern speculators in land were also the persons – the same persons – who stole Indians' property and massacred Indian persons without compunction. John Hancock and the Adams cousins who fought so valiantly for freedom from British rule were also the persons who thundered against Shaysites and sent troops to suppress them. Thomas Jefferson, who wrote so eloquently of human rights, never extended those rights to persons of color. The Pennsylvanians who concocted the "most democratic" state constitution used it to drive Quakers out of political society while satisfying an old grudge, and never permitted even the rest of society to vote on that constitution.

It seems to me that the best service to be performed in behalf of strugglers for liberty is to talk straight – to show the complexity and ambiguities of their struggle, and to recognize humanity even where the strugglers did not. All men *are* brothers, and all women *are* sisters.

---

1 See Ashley Montague, *Man's Most Dangerous Myth: The Fallacy of Race*, 4th ed. (Cleveland, Ohio: World Publishing, 1964); John Hope Franklin, "The Two Worlds of Race: A Historical View," (1965), reprinted in Franklin, *Race and History*, 132–52; Gary B. Nash, *Race, Class, and Politics: Essays on American Colonial and Revolutionary Society* (Urbana: University of Illinois Press, 1986).

A question arises: If membership in the British empire was so lethal to liberty, how did Canada manage to grow into the prosperous, independent country it so plainly is? Pursuing heresy further, if the American Revolution had never occurred, or had failed, would the horrors and bloodshed of the Civil War have been avoided? This is to court punishment for sacrilege, yet it seems legitimate and perhaps useful as speculation.

Despite the grasping of powerful and conscienceless men, even racially disadvantaged persons have gained from the spillover of wealth made available by the repopulation of the continent. Although America has often been called "a white man's country," gradual elimination of some legal barriers to mixing has eased movement between castes. Some members of the undercastes have risen to share rights and privilege formerly barred. More importantly, the undercastes have learned how to exert political power.

Despite much turbulence and violence, the Statue of Liberty's torch casts a long beam today. Some "liberated" persons in other countries – Idi Amin, for example – have taught that under certain circumstances imperialism may be easier to live under than its alternatives.

Nevertheless, it all seems pretty bad, and one cannot palliate the evils done to people of color. The cult of mastery has even spread so far as to warrant the late twentieth-century creation of concentration camps in the United States, not only for citizens of Japanese ancestry (we have become ashamed of that), but enacted during the cold war for all dissidents, without restriction of ethnicity. (Senator Hubert H. Humphrey initiated this, which we have suppressed from memory, and President Richard Nixon had the sour satisfaction of finally closing the camps.) They were genuine concentration camps with high fences and guards, and our sole consolation must be that they were never actually used.

That last is not a slight matter in an age of death camps and gulags. Something in Anglo-American history has preserved most of us from the ultimately worst governmental cruelty to persons. The rhetoric of liberty has behind it centuries of struggle by common people and elite sympathizers who detest the denial of life and dignity to other persons. Tom Paine recognized those struggles and added his own life work to them. *These* were the sources of our liberties today, in Britain as well as America, not just the change from one set of masters to another.

The Revolution seems to have developed new assumptions about the nature of the state. As it seems to me, royal masters of state formerly regarded themselves as above their people, and responsible only to the presumed divinity that had so elevated them. The battling rise of Parliament began a historical process of raising the people to become *part* of the state instead of merely being *under* it. This much is fairly clear.

It seems to me that the process was accelerated by the American Revolution's overthrowing the existing state and replacing it by governments explicitly responsible to the people, but this process was equivocal. It simultaneously freed the people from requirement to obey a ruler above themselves and endowed the people as *chosen* by divinity to wield all the powers and enjoy the privileges formerly reserved to the ruler.

The people's perceived definition of themselves as a white race became immensely important as a means of organizing power and equally as a source of delusion. It inspired and energized conquest, but sooner or later the offspring of Europe must encounter the multitudinous offspring of Asia, and those vastly numerous Asians will not tolerate presumptions of white superiority. Hong Kong's return to China marks a great political divide.

It would be best all around to discard the delusions of race and to accept the need to share power and cooperate. That will require a new and greater revolution.

Perhaps it may seem to some critics that I have written to sensationalize the subject. If so, I respectfully disagree. This book is not at all what I intended except in its effort to include all the people involved in the Revolution. *That* was what sensationalized the book, rather to my discomfort.

Given the options of reporting my sources straightforwardly or producing what John Mack Faragher has called (in another connection) "an exclusionist reading of the past,"[2] I had no real choice.

My book undoubtedly contains error; it is certainly not definitive. Yet I hope this inclusionist reading will inspire new understandings and initiate new explorations by readers as it did for me.

2 In *Contact Points: American Frontiers from the Mohawk Valley to the Mississippi, 1750–1830*, ed. Andrew R. L. Cayton and Fredrika J. Teute (Chapel Hill: University of North Carolina Press, 1998), 324.

BIBLIOGRAPHY

Abernethy, Thomas Perkins. *Western Lands and the American Revolution.* New York: D. Appleton-Century, 1937.

Alden, John Richard. *The South in the Revolution, 1763–1789.* A History of the South III. Baton Rouge: Louisiana State University Press and Littlefield Fund of University of Texas, 1957.

Aldrich, James Mott. "The Revolutionary Legislature in Pennsylvania: A Roll Call Analysis." Ph.D. diss., University of Maine, 1969.

American Archives. Comp. Peter Force. 5th series, 2 vols. Washington, D.C.: M. St. Clair and Peter Force, 1851.

American Aurora: A Democratic-Republican Returns. Ed. Richard N. Rosenfeld. New York: St. Martin's Press, 1997.

American Political Writing During the Founding Era, 1760–1805. Ed. Charles S. Hyneman and Donald S. Lutz. 2 vols. Indianapolis: Liberty Fund, 1983.

The American Revolution: Explorations in the History of Radicalism. Ed. Alfred F. Young. DeKalb: Northern Illinois University Press, 1976.

The American War of Independence, 1775–83. London: British Library Publications, 1975.

Anderson, James Donald. "Thomas Wharton, Exile in Virginia, 1777–1778. "*Virginia Magazine of History and Biography* 89 (1981), 425–447. Pp. 379–447 in *Patriots, Redcoats, and Loyalists,* q.v.

Andrews, Charles M. "The American Revolution: An Interpretation." *American Historical Review* 31 (Jan. 1926), 219–232.

———. *The Colonial Period of American History.* 4 vols. New Haven: Yale University Press, 1934–1938.

Anthony Wayne, A Name in Arme. Ed. Richard C. Knopf. Pittsburgh, Pa.: University of Pittsburgh Press, 1960.

Aptheker, Herbert P. *American Negro Slave Revolts.* Studies in History, Economics, and Public Law 501. New York: Columbia University Press, 1943.

Atlas of Early American History: The Revolutionary Era, 1760–1790. Ed. Lester J. Cappon et al. Princeton, N.J.: Princeton University Press, 1976.

Atlas of Great Lakes Indian History. Ed. Helen Hornbeck Tanner et al. Norman: University of Oklahoma Press, 1987.

Bailyn, Bernard. *The Ideological Origins of the American Revolution.* Cambridge, Mass.: Harvard University Press, 1967.

Bailyn, Bernard. *The Ordeal of Thomas Hutchinson.* Cambridge, Mass.: Harvard University Press, 1974.
———. *The Peopling of British North America: An Introduction.* New York: Alfred A. Knopf, 1987.
Balesi, Charles J. *The Time of the French in the Heart of North America, 1673–1818.* Chicago: Alliance Française Chicago, 1992.
The Blackwell Encyclopedia of the American Revolution. Ed. Jack P. Greene and J. R. Pole. Cambridge, Mass.: Blackwell Publishers, 1991.
Bleackley, Horace. *Life of John Wilkes.* New York: John Lane Co., 1917.
Bockelman, Wayne L., and Owen S. Ireland. "The Internal Revolution in Pennsylvania: An Ethnic-Religious Interpretation." *Pennsylvania History 41* (1974), 125–159.
Brandt, Clare. *The Man in the Mirror: A Life of Benedict Arnold.* New York: Random House, 1994.
Breen, T. H., "Ideology and Nationalism on the Eve of the American Revolution: Revisions *Once More* in Need of Revising." *Journal of American History* 84:1 (June 1997), 13–39.
Brewer, Holly. "Entailing Aristocracy in Colonial Virginia: 'Ancient Feudal Restraints' and Revolutionary Reform." *William and Mary Quarterly*, 3d ser., 54:2 (April 1997), 307–346.
Bridenbaugh, Carl. *Mitre and Sceptre: Transatlantic Faiths, Ideas, Personalities, and Politics.* New York: Oxford University Press, 1962.
Brown, Wallace. "The Loyalists in the West Indies, 1783–1834." Pp. 73–96 in *Red, White and True Blue*, ed. Esmond Wright, q.v.
Brunhouse, Robert L. *The Counter-Revolution in Pennsylvania, 1776–1790.* Harrisburg: Pennsylvania Historical Commission, 1942.
Burke, Edmund. *On the American Revolution: Selected Speeches and Letters.* Ed. Elliott Robert Barkan. New York: Harper and Row, 1966.
Buxbaum, Melvin H. *Benjamin Franklin and the Zealous Presbyterians.* University Park: Pennsylvania State University Press, 1975.
Calloway, Colin G. *The American Revolution in Indian Country.* Cambridge: Cambridge University Press, 1995.
Cassirer, Ernst. *Language and Myth* (1924). Tr. Susanne K. Langer. Reprinted. New York: Dover Publications, 1946.
Caughey, John Walton. *Bernardo de Gálvez in Louisiana, 1776–1783.* Berkeley: University of California Press, 1934.
Chainbreaker: The Revolutionary War Memoirs of Governor Blacksnake. Ed. Thomas S. Abler. Lincoln: University of Nebraska Press, 1989.
Chidsey, Donald Barr. *Valley Forge.* New York: Crown Publishers, 1959.
Christie, Ian R. "The Imperial Dimension: British Ministerial Perspectives During the American Revolutionary Crisis, 1763–1776." Pp. 149–166 in *Red, White and True Blue*, ed. Wright, q.v.
———. *Wilkes, Wyvill and Reform: The Parliamentary Reform Movement in British Politics, 1760–1785.* London: Macmillan, 1962.
Churchill, Winston S. *A History of the English-Speaking Peoples*, 4 vols.; III: *The Age of Revolution.* New York: Dodd, Mead and Co., 1957.
Colonial British America: Essays in the New History of the Early Modern Era. Ed. Jack P. Greene and J. R. Pole. Baltimore: Johns Hopkins University Press, 1984.
Condon, Ann Gorman. "Marching to a Different Drummer – The Political Philosophy

of the American Loyalists." Pp. 1–18 in *Red, White and True Blue*, ed. Wright, q.v.

Congress at Princeton: Being the Letters of Charles Thomson to Hannah Thomson, June–October 1783. Ed. Eugene R. Sheridan and John M. Murrin. Princeton, N.J.: Princeton University Library, 1985.

Countryman, Edward. *A People in Revolution: The American Revolution and Political Society in New York, 1760–1790*. Baltimore, Md.: Johns Hopkins University Press, 1981.

Crane, Verner W. *Benjamin Franklin and a Rising People*. Boston: Little, Brown and Co., 1954.

Davies, K. G. "The Restoration of Civil Government by the British in the War of Independence." Pp. 111–133 in *Red, White and True Blue*, ed. Wright, q.v.

The Debate on the Constitution. Ed. Bernard Bailyn, 2 vols. New York: Library of America, 1993.

De Vorsey, Louis, Jr. *The Indian Boundary in the Southern Colonies, 1763–1775*. Chapel Hill: University of North Carolina Press, 1966.

Dictionary of Canadian Biography (DNB). Toronto: University of Toronto Press, 1966– .

Documents of American History. Ed. Henry Steele Commager, 2 vols., 7th ed. New York: Appleton-Century-Crofts, 1963.

Downes, Randolph C. *Council Fires on the Upper Ohio: A Narrative of Indian Affairs in the Upper Ohio Valley Until 1795*. Pittsburgh, Pa.: University of Pittsburgh Press, 1940.

Draper, Theodore. *A Struggle for Power: The American Revolution*. New York: Times Books, 1996.

Dunn, Richard S. "Black Society in the Chesapeake, 1776–1810." Pp. 49–82 in *Slavery and Freedom in the Age of the American Revolution*, ed. Ira Berlin and Ronald Hoffman, q.v.

———. *Sugar and Slaves: The Rise of the Planter Class in the English West Indies, 1624–1713*. Chapel Hill: University of North Carolina Press, 1972.

Egerton, Hugh Edward. "Introduction," pp. xiii–lii, to *The Royal Commission on . . . American Loyalists, 1783 to 1785*, q.v.

Ellis, Joseph J. *American Sphinx: The Character of Thomas Jefferson*. New York: Alfred A. Knopf, 1997.

English Historical Documents. Gen. ed. David C. Douglas. Vol. X: *1714–1783*, ed. D. B. Horn and Mary Ransome. London: Eyre and Spottiswoode, 1957.

Exiles in Virginia: with Observations on the Conduct of the Society of Friends during the Revolutionary War . . . Comp. Thomas Gilpin. Philadelphia: Published for Subscribers.

Finkelman, Paul. *Slavery and the Founders: Race and Liberty in the Age of Jefferson*. Armonk, N.Y.: M. E. Sharpe, 1996.

Fischer, David Hackett, *Albion's Seed: Four British Folkways in America*. New York: Oxford University Press, 1989.

———. *Paul Revere's Ride*. New York: Oxford University Press, 1994.

Fisher, Sydney George. *The True History of the American Revolution*. Philadelphia, Pa.: J. B. Lippincott Co., 1902.

Foner, Eric. *Tom Paine and Revolutionary America*. New York: Oxford University Press, 1976.

[Francis, Philip]. *The Letters of Junius* (1783). London: printed by G. Woodfall for F. C. and J. Rivington, 1812. 2d ed., 1814. My edition published by Routledge, London, n.d., ed. George Woodfall.

Franklin, John Hope. *Race and History: Selected Essays, 1938–1988.* Baton Rouge: Louisiana State University Press, 1989.

Gipson, Lawrence Henry. *The Coming of the Revolution, 1763–1775.* New York: Harper and Brothers, 1954.

Graymont, Barbara. *The Iroquois in the American Revolution.* Syracuse, N.Y.: Syracuse University Press, 1972.

Greene, Jack P. "The Origins of the New Colonial Policy, 1748–1763." Pp. 95–106 in *Blackwell Encyclopedia,* q.v.

———. *The Quest for Power: The Lower Houses of Assembly in the Southern Royal Colonies, 1689–1776.* Chapel Hill: University of North Carolina Press, 1963.

———. *Understanding the American Revolution: Issues and Actors.* Charlottesville: University Press of Virginia, 1995.

Greene, Jack P., comp. and ed. *The Nature of Colony Constitutions,* q.v.

Gruber, Ira D. "Campbell, John [4th Earl of Loudoun]" P. 710 in *Blackwell Encyclopedia,* q.v.

———. "Lord Howe and Lord George Germain: British Politics and the Winning of American Independence." *William and Mary Quarterly,* 3d ser., 22 (1965), 225–243. Reprinted, pp. 189–207, in *Patriots, Redcoats, and Loyalists,* ed. Onuf, q.v.

Hackluyt, Richarde. *A Particuler Discourse . . . Known as Discourse of Western Planting* (1584). Ed. David B. Quinn and Alison M. Quinn. London: Hakluyt Society, 1993.

Hann, John H. *Apalachee: The Land Between the Rivers.* Gainesville: University of Florida Press/Florida State Museum, 1988.

Harlow, Ralph Volney. *Samuel Adams: Promoter of the American Revolution: A Study in Psychology and Politics.* New York: Henry Holt and Co., 1923.

Hawke, David Freeman. *Benjamin Rush, Revolutionary Gadfly.* Indianapolis: Bobbs-Merrill Co., 1971.

[Heckewelder, John]. *The Travels of John Heckewelder in Frontier America.* Ed. Paul A. W. Wallace. Reprint of *Thirty Thousand Miles with John Heckewelder* (1958). Pittsburgh, Pa.: University of Pittsburgh Press, 1985.

Heward, Edmund. *Lord Mansfield.* Chichester, West Sussex, England: Barry Rose (Publishers), 1979.

Higginbotham, Don. *The War of American Independence: Military Attitudes, Policies, and Practice, 1763–1789.* Boston, Mass.: Northeastern University Press, 1983.

Horsman, Reginald. *Race and Manifest Destiny: The Origins of American Racial Anglo-Saxonism.* Cambridge, Mass.: Harvard University Press, 1981.

Indian Affairs, Laws and Treaties. Ed. and comp. Charles J. Kappler, 2 vols., 1904. vol. 2 reprinted as *Indian Treaties, 1778–1883.* New York: Interland Publishing, 1975.

Ireland, Owen S. "The Crux of Politics: Religion and Party in Pennsylvania, 1778–1789." *William and Mary Quarterly,* 3d ser., 42 (Oct. 1985), 453–475; reprinted in *The Revolution in the States,* ed. Peter S. Onuf, q.v.

———. "The Ethnic-Religious Dimension of Pennsylvania Politics, 1778–1779." *William and Mary Quarterly,* 3d ser., 30 (1973), 423–448.

————. "The People's Triumph: The Federalist Majority in Pennsylvania, 1787–1788. *Pennsylvania History* 56:2 (April 1989), 93–113.

————. *Religion, Ethnicity, and Politics: Ratifying the Constitution in Pennsylvania.* University Park: Pennsylvania State University Press, 1995.

Jackson, Harvey H. *Lachlan McIntosh and the Politics of Revolutionary Georgia.* Athens: University of Georgia Press, 1979.

Jefferson, Thomas. *Notes on the State of Virginia* (1787), ed. William Peden. Chapel Hill; University of North Carolina Press, 1954, reprinted 1982.

Jennings, Francis. *The Ambiguous Iroquois Empire.* New York: W. W. Norton, 1984.

————. *Benjamin Franklin, Politician* (New York: W. W. Norton, 1996).

————. *The Empire of Fortune.* New York: W. W. Norton, 1988.

————. *The Invasion of America.* Chapel Hill: University of North Carolina Press, 1975.

————. "Logan, James (c. 1725–1780)." In *American National Biography.* New York: Oxford University Press, 1998.

————. "Tribal Loyalty and Tribal Independence." Pp. 19–31 in *Red, White and True Blue,* ed. Wright, q.v.

Jensen, Merrill. *The New Nation: A History of the United States During the Confederation, 1781–1789.* New York: Alfred A. Knopf, 1950.

Jones, Dorothy V. *License for Empire: Colonialism by Treaty in Early America.* Chicago, Ill.: University of Chicago Press, 1982.

Jordan, Winthrop D. *White Over Black: American Attitudes Toward the Negro, 1550–1812* (1968). Reprinted Baltimore, Md.: Penguin Books, 1969.

"Junius." See Francis, Philip.

Kay, Marvin L. Michael. "The North Carolina Regulation, 1766–1776: A Class Conflict." Pp. 71–123 in *The American Revolution,* ed. Alfred F. Young, q.v.

Knollenberg, Bernhard. *George Washington: The Virginia Period, 1732–1775.* Durham, N.C., 1964.

————. *Origin of the American Revolution, 1759–1766.* New revised edition. New York: Collier Books, 1961.

Kruman, Marc W. *Between Authority and Liberty: State Constitution Making in Revolutionary America.* Chapel Hill: University of North Carolina Press, 1997.

Lee, Arthur. See *Nature of Colony Constitutions,* ed. Greene.

Leigh, Sir Egerton. See *Nature of Colony Constitutions,* ed. Greene.

Lemay, J. A. Leo. *The American Dream of Captain John Smith.* Charlottesville: University Press of Virginia, 1991.

The letters of Junius (1783). See Francis, Philip.

Lincoln, Charles H. "The Revolutionary Movement in Pennsylvania, 1760–1776." Ph.D. diss. Philadelphia: University of Pennsylvania, 1901.

Marshall, Peter. "First Americans and Last Loyalists: An Indian Dilemma in War and Peace." Pp. 33–53 in *Red, White and True Blue,* ed. Wright, q.v.

————. "The Incorporation of Quebec in the British Empire, 1763–1774." In *Of Mother, Country and Plantation,* Proceedings of the Twenty-Seventh Conference in Early American History, ed. Virginia Bever Platt and David Curtis Skaggs. Bowling Green, Ohio: Bowling Green State University Press, 1971.

McCrum, Robert, William Cran, and Robert Macneil. *The Story of English.* New York: Viking, 1986.

Menard, Russell R. "Financing the Lowcountry Export Boom: Capital and Growth in Early South Carolina." *William and Mary Quarterly*, 3d ser., 51:4 (Oct. 1994), 659–676.

Middlekauff, Robert. *Benjamin Franklin and His Enemies*. Berkeley: University of California Press, 1996.

———. *The Glorious Cause: The American Revolution," 1763–1789*. New York: Oxford University Press, 1982.

———."Why Men Fought in the American Revolution," *Huntington Library Quarterly* 43 (1980), 135–148. Reprinted, pp. 1–16, in *Patriots, Redcoats, and Loyalists*, ed. Onuf, q.v.

Milanich, Jerald T. "Franciscan Missions and Native Peoples in Spanish Florida." Unpublished MS. University of Florida, Gainesville.

Miller, John C. *Origins of the American Revolution*. Boston: Little, Brown and Co., 1943.

Montross, Lynn. *The Reluctant Rebels: The Story of the Continental Congress, 1774–1789*. New York: Harper and Brothers, 1950.

Morgan, Philip D. "Black Society in the Lowcountry, 1760–1810." In *Slavery and Freedom in the Age of the American Revolution*, ed. Berlin and Hoffman, q.v.

Morris, Richard B. *Seven Who Shaped Our Destiny: The Founding Fathers as Revolutionaries*. New York: Harper and Row, 1973.

Nash, Gary B., and Jean R. Soderlund. *Freedom by Degrees: Emancipation in Pennsylvania and Its Aftermath*. New York: Oxford University Press, 1991.

The Nature of Colony Constitutions: Two Pamphlets on the Wilkes Fund Controversy in South Carolina by Sir Egerton Leigh and Arthur Lee. Ed. and comp. Jack P. Greene. Columbia: University of South Carolina Press, 1970.

Nelson, Paul David. "Guy Carleton Versus Benedict Arnold: The Campaign of 1776 in Canada and on Lake Champlain." *New York History* 57 (1976), 339–366. Reprinted, pp. 227–254, in *Patriots, Redcoats, and Loyalists*, ed. Onuf, q.v.

New American State Papers: Indian Affairs. Ed. Thomas C. Cochran. Wilmington, Del.: Scholarly Resources, 1972.

Newcomb, Benjamin H. *Franklin and Galloway: A Political Partnership*. New Haven, Conn.: Yale University Press, 1972.

Nobbe, George. *The North Briton: A Study in Political Propaganda*. New York: Columbia University Press, 1939.

O'Donnell, James H., III. *The Cherokees of North Carolina in the American Revolution*. Raleigh, N.C.: Dept. of Cultural Resources, 1976.

———. *Southern Indians in the American Revolution*. Knoxville: University of Tennessee Press, 1973.

Olson, Alison G. "The Changing Socio-economic and Strategic Importance of the Colonies to the Empire." Pp. 17–27 in *Blackwell Encyclopedia*, ed. Greene and Pole, q.v.

Onuf, Peter S. "State-Making in Revolutionary America: Independent Vermont as a Case Study." *Journal of American History* 67 (1981), 797–815. Reprinted, pp. 37–55, in *The Revolution in the States*, ed. Onuf, q.v.

———. "The West: Territory, States, and Confederation." Pp. 346–355 in *Blackwell Encyclopedia*, ed. Greene and Pole, q.v.

Ousterhout, Anne M. "Controlling the Opposition in Pennsylvania During the American Revolution." *Pennsylvania Magazine of History and Biography* 105:1 (Jan. 1981), 3–34.

————. "Frontier Vengeance: Connecticut Yankees vs. Pennamites in the Wyoming Valley." *Pennsylvania History* 62 (Summer 1995), 331–363.

Paine, Thomas. *Rights of Man, Common Sense (1776), and Other Political Writings*. Ed. Mark Philp. Worlds Classics reprint. New York: Oxford University Press, 1995.

The Papers of Benjamin Franklin. Ed. Leonard W. Labaree et al. (New Haven, Conn.: Yale University Press, 1959–).

Parmenter, Jon William. "Pontiac's War: Forging New Links in the Anglo-Iroquois Covenant Chain, 1758–1766." *Ethnohistory* 44 (Fall 1997), 617–654.

Patriots, Redcoats, and Loyalists. Ed. Peter S. Onuf. New York: Garland Publishing, 1991.

Postgate, Raymond. *"That Devil Wilkes"*. Rev. ed. London: Dennis Dobson, 1956.

Price, Jacob M. "The Great Quaker Business Families of Eighteenth-Century London." Chapter 20 in *The World of William Penn*, ed. R. and M. Dunn, q.v.

Quarles, Benjamin. *The Negro in the American Revolution* (1961). Reprint. Chapel Hill: University of North Carolina Press, 1996.

————. "The Revolutionary War as a Black Declaration of Independence." Pp. 283–301 in *Slavery and Freedom in the Age of the American Revolution*, ed. Berlin and Hoffman, q.v.

Rawlyk, G. A. "The Reverend John Stuart: Mohawk Missionary and Reluctant Loyalist." Pp. 55–71 in *Red, White and True Blue*, ed. Wright, q.v.

Ramsay, David. *The History of the American Revolution*. Ed. Lester H. Cohen. 2 vols. Indianapolis: Liberty Fund, 1990.

Red, White and True Blue: The Loyalists in the Revolution. Ed. Esmond Wright. New York: AMS Press, 1976.

The Revolution in the States, 1775–1820. Ed. Peter S. Onuf. New York: Garland Publishing, 1991.

Rosenfeld, Richard N. *American Aurora: A Democratic-Republican Returns*. New York: St. Martin's Press, 1997.

The Royal Commission on the Losses and Services of American Loyalists, 1783 to 1785 (1915). Ed. Hugh Edward Egerton. Reprinted New York: Burt Franklin, 1971.

Royster, Charles. "'The Nature of Treason': Revolutionary Virtue and American Reactions to Benedict Arnold." *William and Mary Quarterly*, 3d ser. 36 (1979), 163–193. Reprinted, pp. 319–349, in *Patriots, Redcoats, and Loyalists*, ed. Onuf, q.v.

————. *A Revolutionary People at War: The Continental Army and American Character, 1775–1783*. Chapel Hill: University of North Carolina Press, 1979.

Rudé, George. *Wilkes and Liberty: A Social Study of 1763 to 1774*. Oxford: Oxford University Press, 1962.

[Rush, Benjamin]. "An Address to the Inhabitants of the British Settlements in America Upon Slave-Keeping" (1773). In Vol. 1, pp. 217–231, of *American Political Writing*, ed. Hyneman and Lutz, q.v.

[————]. *Letters of Benjamin Rush*. Ed. L. H. Butterfield, 2 vols. Princeton, N.J.: Princeton University Press, 1951.

[————]. *Observations Upon the Present Government of Pennsylvania, in Four Letters to the People of Pennsylvania*. Philadelphia: Styner and Cist, 1777. (Photostat at Newberry Library.)

Rutland, Robert Allen. *The Birth of the Bill of Rights, 1776–1791*. Reprinted. New York: Collier Books, 1962.

Ryerson, Richard Alan. *The Revolution Is Now Begun: The Radical Committees of Philadelphia, 1765–1776*. Philadelphia: University of Pennsylvania Press, 1978.

Sainsbury, John. *Disaffected Patriots: London Supporters of Revolutionary America, 1769–1782*. Kingston, Ont.: McGill-Queen's University Press, 1987.

Schlenther, Boyd Stanley. *Charles Thomson: A Patriot's Pursuit*. Newark: University of Delaware Press, 1990.

Seineke, Katherine Wagner. *The George Rogers Clark Adventure in the Illinois, and Selected Documents*. New Orleans, La.: Polyanthos, 1981.

Selsam, J. Paul. *The Pennsylvania Constitution of 1776: A Study in Revolutionary Democracy*. Philadelphia: University of Pennsylvania Press, 1936.

The Settling of North America: The Atlas of the Great Migrations into North America from the Ice Age to the Present. Ed. Helen Hornbeck Tanner et al. New York: Macmillan, 1995.

Shy, John. *Toward Lexington: The Role of the British Army in the Coming of the American Revolution*. Princeton, N.J.: Princeton University Press, 1965.

Slaughter, Thomas P. *The Whiskey Rebellion: Frontier Epilogue to the American Revolution*. New York: Oxford University Press, 1986.

Slavery and Freedom in the Age of the American Revolution. Ed. Ira Berlin and Ronald Hoffman. Charlottesville: University Press of Virginia, 1983.

Society, Freedom, and Conscience: The American Revolution in Virginia, Massachusetts, and New York. Ed. Richard M. Jellison. New York: W. W. Norton, 1976.

Sosin, Jack M. "The British Indian Department and Dunmore's War. "*Virginia Magazine of History and Biography* 74 (Jan. 1966), 34–50.

———. *The Revolutionary Frontier, 1763–1783*. New York: Holt, Rinehart and Winston, 1967.

Speck, W. A. "The International and Imperial Context." Pp. 384–407 in *Colonial British America*, ed. Greene and Pole, q.v.

The Spirit of Seventy-Six: The Story of the American Revolution as Told by Participants. Ed. Henry Steele Commager and Richard B. Morris. New York: Harper & Row, 1967.

Stuart, Reginald C. *United States Expansion and British North America, 1775–1871*. Chapel Hill: University of North Carolina Press, 1988.

Sullivan, Edward Dean. *Benedict Arnold, Military Racketeer*. New York: Vanguard Press, 1932.

Sutherland, Stuart R. J. "Montgomery, Richard." In Vol. 4, pp. 545–550, of *Dictionary of Canadian Biography*, q.v.

Swagerty, William Royce, Jr. Beyond Bimini: Indian Responses to European Incursions in the Spanish Borderlands, 1513–1600, Ph.D. diss., University of California, Santa Barbara, 1981.

Sydnor, Charles S. *American Revolutionaries in the Making: Political Practices in Washington's Virginia* (1952). New York: Free Press, 1966.

Thomas, Hugh. *The Slave Trade: The Story of the Atlantic Slave Trade, 1440–1870*. New York: Simon Schuster, 1997.

[Thomson, Charles]. "The Papers of Charles Thomson." In *Collections of the New-York Historical Society for the Year 1878*. Publication Fund Series. New York, 1879.

Tousignant, Pierre. "The Integration of the province of Quebec into the British empire, 1763–91; Part I: From the Royal Proclamation to the Quebec Act." In Vol. 4, pp. xxxii–xlix, of *Dictionary of Canadian Biography*, q.v.

Transatlantic Slavery: Against Human Dignity. Ed. Anthony Tibbles. Liverpool: National Museums and Galleries on Merseyside, 1994.

The Trial of John Almon, Bookseller . . . For Selling JUNIUS's Letter to the K——. London: J Miller, 1770.

Usner, Daniel H., Jr. *Indians, Settlers, and Slaves in a Frontier Exchange Economy: The Lower Mississippi Valley Before 1783*. Chapel Hill: University of North Carolina Press, 1992.

Van Alstyne, Richard W. *The Rising American Empire* (1960). Reprinted. Chicago: Quadrangle Paperbacks, 1965.

Van Doren, Carl. *Benjamin Franklin* (1938). Reprinted. New York: Garden City Publishing Co., 1941.

——. *Secret History of the American Revolution*. New York: Viking Press, 1941.

Ward, Christopher. *The War of the Revolution*, 2 vols. Ed. John Richard Alden. New York: Macmillan, 1952.

Warren, Mercy Otis. *History of the Rise, Progress, and Termination of the American Revolution* (1805). Reprint ed., Lester H. Cohen, 2 vols. Indianapolis: Liberty Fund, 1989.

Washington, George. *Writings*. Ed. John C. Fitzpatrick, 39 vols. Washington, D.C., 1931–1944.

Watson, J. Steven. *The Reign of George III, 1760–1815*. Oxford: Oxford University Press, 1960.

Wells, Robert V. "Population and Family in Early America." Pp. 39–52 in *Blackwell Encyclopedia*, ed. Greene and Pole, q.v.

Williams, Basil. *The Whig Supremacy, 1714–1760*. 2d ed. rev. by C. H. Stuart. Oxford: Oxford University Press, 1962.

Wood, Gordon S. *The Creation of the American Republic, 1776–1787* Chapel Hill: University of North Carolina Press, 1969.

——. *The Radicalism of the American Revolution*. New York: Alfred A. Knopf, 1992.

Wood, Peter H. *Black Majority: Negroes in Colonial South Carolina From 1670 Through the Stono Rebellion*. New York: Alfred A. Knopf, 1974.

The World of William Penn. Ed. Richard S. Dunn and Mary Maples Dunn. Philadelphia: University of Pennsylvania Press, 1986.

Wright, Esmond. "Bermuda in 1776: Loyalist – or Just Neutral?" Pp. 99–108 in *Red, White and True Blue*, ed. Wright, q.v.

Wright, J. Leitch, Jr. *Anglo-Spanish Rivalry in North America*. Athens: University of Georgia Press, 1971.

Young, Henry J. "Treason and Its Punishment in Revolutionary Pennsylvania." *Pennsylvania Magazine of History and Biography* 90 (1966), 287–313. Pp. 351–377 in *Patriots, Redcoats, and Loyalists*, ed. Onuf, q.v.

Zimmerman, John J. "The Sam Adams of Philadelphia," *Mississippi Valley Historical Review* 45 (1958), 464–480.

INDEX